Ex   Libris

Ann Oram

THOMAS CLARKSON: A BIOGRAPHY

Thomas Clarkson:
A Biography

Ellen Gibson Wilson

MACMILLAN

First published 1989

Published by
THE MACMILLAN PRESS LTD
Houndmills, Basingstoke, Hampshire RG21 2XS
and London
Companies and representatives
throughout the world

Printed in Great Britain by WBC Print, Bristol

British Library Cataloguing in Publication Data
Wilson, Ellen Gibson
Thomas Clarkson: a biography
1. Slavery. British abolitionist movements.
Clarkson, Thomas, 1760–1846
I. Title
322.4'4'0924
ISBN 0–333–47270–5

Every true man is a cause, a country and an age; requires infinite spaces and numbers and time fully to accomplish his design; – and posterity seem to follow his steps as a train of clients. A man Caesar is born, and for ages after we have a Roman Empire. Christ is born, and millions of minds so grow and cleave to his genius, that he is confounded with virtue and the possible of man. An institution is the lengthened shadow of one man, as, Monachism, of the Hermit Antony; the Reformation, of Luther; Quakerism of Fox; Methodism of Wesley; Abolition of Clarkson. Scipio, Milton called 'the height of Rome;' and all history resolves itself very easily into the biography of a few stout and earnest persons.

Ralph Waldo Emerson

Contents

List of Plates

The author and publishers wish to thank the sources (see above) for illustrative material.

Preface

Thomas Clarkson (1760–1846) was almost too good to be true – courageous, visionary, disciplined, self-sacrificing – a man who gave a long life almost entirely to the service of people he never met in lands he never saw. He had his faults as well. He was often guileless, tactless, obsessive, impetuous, humourless and pointlessly punctual and, worst of all, he threw out most of his papers. He did not dream that anyone would ever write his life-story.

Naturally, not many have tried. The last biography of Clarkson was published more than fifty years ago. His historic achievement as the originator and chief propagandist of the British campaign to abolish the slave trade has been obscured when not altogether forgotten, even though slavery and antislavery, as subjects, were never more popular than they are today.

With some new-found material, and a closer look at old sources, it is now possible to see Clarkson's genius in a fresh light and to draw a more accurate and rounded portrait of this appealing yet heroic figure.

Clarkson discovered the inhumanity of the African slave trade when he was a student at Cambridge and his outrage endured until his death at the age of 86, while he was engrossed in the antislavery movement in America. The abolitionists were a heterogeneous band who transcended barriers of religion and politics to reach their common goal and Clarkson symbolises their daring and their perseverance. He believed unfalteringly in liberty and compassion in times unfriendly to both. He was a private citizen throughout his life and yet he changed the way that his generation looked at the world. He taught that slavery was a crime.

He was also the husband of one of the wittiest women of her day, the close friend of Wordsworth and Coleridge, a gentleman farmer, a classical scholar and a devout Christian, distinguished by quakerish simplicity. It was Coleridge who likened him to a moral steam engine, a 'Giant with one idea', with that mixture of irritation and reverence his devotion to one cause provoked in those who loved him.

In writing this overdue biography, I happily acknowledge first the important advice and help of my husband, Henry S. Wilson. Mr Richard M. Clarkson, a constant source of stimulation and encouragement, and his sister Mrs A. M. Wray, collateral descendants of Clarkson, have given me the same kind of cooperation that their parents Mr and Mrs Augustus Clarkson extended to Professor Griggs in his earlier biography. I am also grateful to Dr R. G. M. Keeling and Mr Peter Keeling, descendants of John Clarkson, for their interest and help and to Mr and Mrs Richard Innes for allowing me to see Playford Hall where Clarkson spent his last thirty years.

The sources for Clarkson's life are far-flung and I am grateful especially to libraries in the United States which have so readily made material available to a distant scholar. None has been more generous than the Huntington Library, San Marino, California, the richest repository of Clarkson papers outside Britain, and my thanks go to Mary L. Robertson, curator, for unfailing responsiveness. I am also much indebted to the staffs of the Trevor Arnett Library, Atlanta University, Atlanta, Georgia; Boston Public Library; Olin Library of Cornell University, Ithaca, New York; William R. Perkins Library, Duke University, Durham, North Carolina; Moorland-Spingarn Research Center, Howard University, Washington DC; New Bedford Free Public Library, Massachusetts; New York Historical Society; Schlesinger Library at Radcliffe College; and the George Arents Library, Syracuse University.

In Britain, I am particularly obliged to the Shropshire Record Office at Shrewsbury for helping me to compile a transcript of the Diary of Katherine Plymley. I also thank the owner of that document, Mr Charles E. Corbett, for his kind permission to quote it. I am deeply indebted to Dr Williams's Library, London, for access to the invaluable Henry Crabb Robinson papers.

It brings back happy memories to acknowledge the friendly cooperation of staff at other places in Britain, including (in London, unless otherwise indicated) Allen and Hanbury Limited, Bodleian and Rhodes House Libraries of Oxford University; British Library and Manuscripts Department; Cambridge University Library; Cumbria County Library, Carlisle; Humberside Record Office, Beverley; Ipswich Borough Libraries; Keele University Library and the Trustees of the Wedgwood Museum who allowed me to see the Wedgwood archive there; Lambeth Palace Library; Library of the Religious Society of Friends; Liverpool City Libraries Record Office; John Rylands University Library of Manchester; National Library of Wales, Aberystwyth; National Portrait Gallery; North Yorkshire County Libraries, especially at York and Malton, and the access provided to the Inter-Library Loan services; Public Record Office, St John's College Library, Cambridge; St Paul's School, Barnes; Suffolk Record Offices at Bury St Edmunds and Ipswich; University College; Wilberforce House, Hull; Wisbech and Fenland Museum; Wordsworth Library, Grasmere; and the J. B. Morrell Library and the Borthwick Institute of Historical Research of the University of York.

Two manuscript collections have moved since I consulted them. The Granville Sharp papers were seen at Hardwicke Court by kind permission of the late Miss Olive Lloyd-Baker and now are deposited at Gloucestershire Record Office, and the late Mr C. E. Wrangham graciously allowed me to see his collection of Wilberforce papers, now at the Bodleian Library.

Ellen Wilson
Bulmer
York

Chronology

1760	Clarkson born at Wisbech, Cambridgeshire, 28 March.
1783	Quaker committee formed to seek abolition of slave trade.
1786	Prize essay published.
1787	Nonsectarian committee launches national campaign.
1788	Privy Council inquires into slave trade; Pitt introduces subject in Commons; Dolben regulating act passed.
1789	Privy Council reports; Commons decides on new hearings; Clarkson seeks French abolition in Paris, following Revolution.
1791	Wilberforce motion to abolish slave trade loses 163–88; Sierra Leone Company chartered.
1792	519 petitions to Parliament; Dundas amendment for gradual abolition passes Commons; Lords start new inquiry; 300 000 boycott sugar.
1793	Louis XVI guillotined; French declare war; Clarkson suffers nervous exhaustion.
1794–1795	Foreign slave trade bill passes Commons; public campaign fades.
1796–1803	Clarkson marries Catherine Buck; makes home in Lake District; son is born; friendships with poets begin.
1804	Abolition campaign revives; a bill passes Commons.
1806	Pitt dies; Grenville forms administration; ban on slave trade to captured colonies passes both houses; Fox dies.
1807	Parliament bans slave trade.
1808	Clarkson's *History of the . . . Abolition* published.
1814	755 000 sign against peace treaty article reviving French slave trade; society formed to trade with Sierra Leone; Clarkson to Paris to influence French opinion.
1815	First audience with Russian emperor, in Paris; correspondence with Haiti begins.
1818	Second interview with Emperor Alexander, at Aix-la-Chapelle.
1823/4	Start of antislavery campaign.
1833	Wilberforce dies; Emancipation Act passed.
1837	Son killed in accident.
1838	Apprenticeships ended in West Indies; Clarkson attacked by Wilberforce sons; replies.

1840   Presides at world's antislavery convention in London; writing now aimed at American emancipation.
1846   Dies at Playford Hall, Suffolk, 26 September.

1

The Man and the Cause

Of the two great Englishmen who led the glorious crusade to abolish the British slave trade, one – Thomas Clarkson – has suffered an unkind eclipse. In their day the names of Wilberforce and Clarkson were readily twinned in the public mind but, 200 years on, only Wilberforce, the parliamentary champion of the cause, might be called a household name.

Yet Clarkson conceived the campaign and mobilised the national voice behind it until, at the end, it was politically irresistible. He was an agitator far ahead of his time, fact-finding, pamphleteering and organising the inhabitants of towns throughout the kingdom. He believed in the power of an informed people and, as the 'apostle of Africa'[1] persuaded them to support radical legislation affecting property and prosperity. He was the architect and later the historian of the first national campaign for human rights that Britain had known. Hundreds share credit for the final victory but his contemporaries looked to Clarkson as the mastermind, the link 'by which it is all managed',[2] as they worked to destroy the traffic in black Africans which had been sanctioned by government for centuries and on which a significant part of the British imperial economy depended. Late in his life, Clarkson symbolised the cause throughout the western world.[3]

It is conceivable that another advocate could have been found in Parliament.[4] It may even be speculated that abolition legislation might have passed sooner in more adept political hands than Wilberforce's. But another Clarkson is unimaginable. His whole life was focused upon the slave question; indeed he was the only man in the movement who made it his career.

His obsessive behaviour impressed and amused his friends. 'He has never more than one thought in his brain at a time, let it be great or small', wrote the poet Coleridge. 'I have called him the moral steam-engine, or the Giant with one idea.'[5] 'As soon as he is satisfied that any measure *ought* to succeed, it is not possible to convince him that it *cannot*', said another close observer.[6]

1

Wilberforce and Clarkson formed an inspired partnership, but were almost comically unalike. Clarkson in his prime was a handsome – some said majestic – figure, more than six feet tall with bold features and large, very blue and candid eyes.[7] When he entered public life he wore a modish short and curled powdered wig, later his own thick and tousled hair which changed from red to white just as his face developed the furrows of care and conflict. He dressed habitually in black. In society, he made some people uncomfortable for he had little small talk and frequently withdrew into his own dark thoughts. He was methodical, rigorously punctual but painfully sensitive and passionate to a fault. His quiet voice was more suited to a committee than a hall.

Wilberforce was little over five feet tall, a frail and elfin figure who in his later years weighed well under 100 pounds.[8] His charm was legendary, his conversation delightful, his oratory impressive. He dressed in the colourful finery of the day and adorned any salon with his amiable manner. Yet his object in life – no less than the transformation of a corrupt society through serious religion – was solemn. The abolition of the slave trade was to become the major political expression of his religious belief, at least the one of most interest to historians, but many other causes ate into his time. His own view was that the introduction of Christian missionaries into India was the 'greatest of all causes, for I really place it before the Abolition'. In the more than forty years he was involved with slavery, there was 'no month, very likely no week, when he was not engaged in other Evangelical matters'.[9] Nor should it be forgotten that he sat for England's largest county, Yorkshire, for 28 years and was well versed in the state of the wool trade, the effects of a tax on imported pig iron and the harsh necessities of unreformed elections.[10]

Because he did not like to hurt or disappoint anyone, Wilberforce was prey to a thousand distractions. Regularity and method were strangers to him. 'When I look into my own mind', he once confessed endearingly, 'I find it a perfect chaos.'[11]

Clarkson and Wilberforce also differed in politics, for Wilberforce, although he rejected a party label, was deeply conservative and a loyal supporter of the government led by his friend William Pitt, while Clarkson, also not a 'party man', was a Whiggish 'friend to liberty' who harboured grave doubts about unrepresentative governing institutions and sympathetic hopes for the early French Revolution.

In spite of all disparities, Wilberforce and Clarkson were stead-fast collaborators. Each understood the great value of the other to their joint endeavour. Each accepted the other's eccentricities. Religion barred the way to closer friendship. Wilberforce was on the whole only intimate with persons of his own evangelical persuasion. Clarkson, an orthodox Anglican but no respecter of form, found much to admire and emulate in the Society of Friends, or Quakers, among whom he was most at ease.

Clarkson expressed their interdependence well when he de-scribed the Abolition Committee as a human body made up of separate members each with a function to perform and each essential.

> For what, for example, could I myself have done if I had not derived so much assistance from the committee? What could Mr Wilberforce have done in parliament, if I . . . had not collected that great body of evidence, to which there was such a constant appeal? And what could the committee have done without the parliamentary aid of Mr Wilberforce?[12]

Leaders who could cross class, regional and religious barriers, (Clarkson found this easier than most men of his period or station), were essential to ignite interest in the cause. In the 1780s Britain was the greatest slave-trader in the world. Its rich West Indian islands were cultivated under an entrenched system of black slavery which was fully accepted as a necessary element in the commercial life of the nation. Only a few questioned its morality or validity. If pressed, the average citizen might have defended slavery on the ground that it was a necessary evil, and as old as history.

The slave trade was profitable; in its public image, unusually so. There was no shortage of men and women ready to invest their savings in a Liverpool slaver. They were not wholly wrong. In one recent study of the Liverpool slave trade the profits in 74 voyages averaged $10\frac{1}{2}$ per cent at a time when yields on consols (consoli-dated stocks) were 3 per cent. It was a risky business, and returns fluctuated wildly but enough voyages realised 20 to 50 per cent to dazzle the investing public.[13]

It is now believed that the slave trade would not have been killed by economic forces in due course if the abolitionists had never existed. White European indifference was a good friend to black slavery. Africa, where slaves were bought or seized by force, was a long way off – the stuff of exotic travel books. The West Indian plantations were 4000 miles away, well out of sight, and they fed the sweet addiction to sugar. The absentee plantation-owners were ornaments in British society. They bought seats in Parliament and built magnificent country palaces. Government collected welcome revenue. The factories of Manchester and Birmingham hummed as they turned out trade goods for the African slavers.

It was in such a climate that Thomas Clarkson's vocation was revealed to him when he was still at university. For the next 61 years, slavery dominated his mind. Why? We look to his early years for clues to his obsession and the sources of the strength he needed to pursue it. Clues are, indeed, all we can hope to find. Although few childhoods are much documented, Clarkson's formative period is more shadowy than most, thanks to his own passion for tidying up.

'I have destroyed *almost* all my Papers', he boasted to his executor, mentioning among the remnant that escaped the fire his writings on religious matters and letters from a few 'great Men'. 'I have burnt every *other Paper* ... which does not relate to the Executorship in order that your valuable time may not be broken in upon by reading them.'[14]

And his surviving relatives continued such purges from time to time. A great-grandniece recalled in 1932 how her own aunt threw out 'packets and packets' of old letters in the certainty that no one would have time or inclination to read them. She often remarked how interesting they were. Among them were letters to and from Thomas's beloved Catherine Buck.[15] Catherine could confirm that her husband approved this ruthless cull of family archives. 'My Husband is a great destroyer', she told a friend, '& especially of papers containing any thing complimentary to himself.'[16] He did nothing to encourage and did not expect a full-scale biography, and none was published for 90 years after he died.[17]

He was born on 28 March (baptised 26 May) 1760, the year George III ascended the throne, at the Free Grammar School in Wisbech, capital of the Cambridgeshire fens and a thriving inland port on the River Nene.[18] His father was headmaster of the school in Ship Lane (now Hill Street) and the family lived in the ample house behind the 16th-century school.[19]

Being 'learned in the Latin and Greek languages, and imbued with virtuous morals', Thomas's father was paid £12 a year to run the institution where fifty boys were introduced to 'grammatical knowledge and polite learning'. Some £90 to £100 came from pupils' fees, and with other income from school properties Clarkson provided comfortably for his family. He was appointed by the town burgesses in 1749 after serving as a curate at Royston in Hertfordshire. He was also afternoon lecturer for the Wisbech parish church and curate of neighbouring Walsoken.

John Clarkson was a model of devotion to duty and although he died when Thomas was very young, his example must surely have been held before his two sons and daughter as they grew up.[20] He had been born in Thirsk in the old North Riding of Yorkshire and baptised on 20 December 1710, the eldest of seven children born to Thomas and Ann Sadler Clarkson. His father was a weaver and later a merchant in the coarse linen trade that occupied so many of the local inhabitants then. The town at the edge of the Hambleton Hills served as a market centre for an area stretching from Whitby on the North Sea to the textile town of Leeds.[21]

Clarkson was and is a common surname in Thirsk but church records for this branch can be traced with reasonable certainty to 1610 and reveal a solid line of respectable tradesmen and artisans.[22] Seeking wider horizons for his first born, Thomas Clarkson (the weaver) entered John in the grammar school then conducted in the crypt of St Mary's Church. From there the youth was sent to a school in Shipton run by the scholarly Reverend John Clarke. As a young man, probably an assistant teacher, John Clarkson moved with Clarke to the Beverley Grammar School in 1735. Clarke must have been an exemplary figure in his pupil's life as a man who had risen from humble origins to become a famed classicist and an accomplished and affectionate teacher.[23]

At the advanced age of 31, John Clarkson was admitted to St John's College, Cambridge, probably assisted by one of the school's fellowships for those intended to be ordained. At Cambridge he earned his bachelor of arts degree in 1746. He was ordained in London two years later.[24]

His first appointment was as curate of Royston where the vicar was Dr Edward Banyer, member of a prominent Wisbech family of Huguenot descent.[25] Banyer's sister, Anne, was married to a somewhat dissolute Royston physician, Alpe Ward, who came from a landed Norfolk family. Their only child, a daughter also named Anne, was 13 when Clarkson first saw her. She was remarkably pretty when she made her debut in London at the age of 15, and, according to family lore, received a proposal from the young Irish lawyer Edmund Burke.

Mr Clarkson's prestigious appointment to Wisbech Grammar School doubtless owed as much to the Banyer influence as to his own good qualities, for another sister of Dr Banyer was married to the Wisbech vicar, Dr Henry Bull. Two years after Clarkson had settled in, Mrs Ward lost both her husband and her brother and moved with her daughter to Wisbech. There Anne Ward and John Clarkson were married on 29 December 1755. She was 20 and he 45. Their first son John was born in 1756 but died in infancy. A daughter Anne, Thomas and another John, born in 1764, completed the family.[26]

Thomas was barely 6 when the headmaster died suddenly on 31 March 1766, aged 55. The story of his last days was often recounted:

> He filled [all his situations] with so much energy & devotedness and usefulness at the same time that he gained the respect & love of the inhabitants. . . . He ever regarded it as one of his most important duties to visit the poor of his Parish [Walsoken] especially in seasons of sickness not only for the purpose of relieving their temporal wants which he did to a great extent, but also to administer to them the soothing and welcome consolations of religion. The duties of the grammar school engaged nearly the whole of the day & left little more than the hours of evening for these visits of mercy & he often did not return into the Town till after midnight, but he allowed neither darkness, nor the coldness of the night nor the tempestuousness of the bitterest winter weather to frustrate his design. He used always to walk on foot with his Lanthorn in his Hand on these occasions. . . . It was on one of these visits to the sick poor of his parish, that he caught a fever which deprived him of his life. The news of his death caused an universal burst of sorrow as soon as it was known in those parts.[27]

Small Thomas did remember the weeping crowd that attended the funeral. The church's passing bell tolled across the shuttered town as the body was lowered into a grave opened inside the altar railings of the Church of St Peter and St Paul. The heavy old lantern that lighted those merciful errands was treasured in Thomas's home all his life.[28]

In spite of the distance between Yorkshire and Cambridgeshire Mr Clarkson had kept in touch with his northern family and he had preached at Thirsk at least twice after ordination. But his children necessarily grew up without close contact with the North. Their grandmother Clarkson died in 1747 before any of them were born and their grandfather a year after their father. In his later travels, Thomas was to renew the Yorkshire ties. This stable and provincial ancestry can be counted one of the sources of the characteristics Thomas and his brother John shared: forthright manner, simple tastes, scorn of pomp and preferment and ease with persons of all faiths and classes. For them there was always an important world outside London.

Any attempt to trace the reasons for Clarkson's choice of mission must include his religious heritage. In his saintly father he had a perfect model of self-sacrifice for higher duty. The Anglican faith he learned as a child stayed with him to the end. He believed that the abolition movement began with the earliest teachers of Christianity and saw himself in that great chain. The impulse that 'forced [me] into the great work', he was convinced, came from God.[29]

His childhood was spent in the genteel world of his mother's family. Widowed after only 11 years of married life, she moved with the children from the school to what is now 8 York Row, a gabled town-house off the Wisbech High Street which was part of an estate left to her cousin Lawrence Banyer and in which she had a life tenancy. She must have been a woman of great energy and strong character, able to surmount early widowhood, rear three small children alone and overcome the handicap of rheumatism which crippled her most of her life.[30]

Each year Mrs Clarkson took her children for visits of several months to other cousins, the Samuel Gibbs family, at Horkesley Park in Essex. The boys attended the grammar school in Wisbech until in 1775 Thomas, now 15, and expected to follow his father's career in the church, entered St Paul's School in London. His brother John left home in 1777, aged 13, to join *HMS Monarch* at Portsmouth as a midshipman under the patronage of Captain (later Sir) Joshua Rowley, a distant relation and neighbour at Horkesley Park.[31]

For 15 years Clarkson's life had passed in small town and rural scenes and these, too, formed part of his inheritance. With its 4000 inhabitants Wisbech was second only to Cambridge in county importance. The family lived near the bustling cobblestoned marketplace and not far from the quay where vessels loaded their cargoes of foodstuffs for London and the Continent. Outside the town stretched the level fenland crisscrossed by drainage ditches and dikes and dotted with gaunt windmills. It was fertile land that gave prosperity to the region but it had an eerie, solitary look. Defoe spoke of its 'base unwholesome air' and Pepys called it 'most sad'. But Cobbett, who likened the fens to a sea in a dead calm admired the beautiful grass and plump sheep.[32] It is still perhaps the least enchanting of British countrysides, except in spring when the bulb fields blossom. Almost as familiar to the Clarkson children, however, was the gently rolling landscape surrounding Horkesley Park overlooking the winding Stour on the Suffolk–Essex border where ancient hedged fields, woods and mellow mansions blended romantically.

At school Thomas was plunged into the great City of London. St Paul's in his day was housed in a seventeenth-century building facing the east end of the cathedral churchyard. The school's academic character was established after 1505 when John Colet, spiritual adviser to Sir Thomas More, was appointed dean of the cathedral. The school accommodated 153 boys and by Colet's will was administered by the Mercers Company.[33]

Although like most public schools, St Paul's had been started to provide free education to poor boys, it had always served the rich as well. The Clarkson links with the City through the wealthy Gibbs family may have led to the choice of this school for him. The pupils paid fees and supplied their own books. Carrying their wax candles they swarmed into the high hall each day at 7 a.m. and took their seats on the benches which rose in three tiers along the walls. It was always freezing cold; no fires were allowed at any time.

The high master during Clarkson's schooldays was the totally undistinguished Dr Richard Roberts, famous only for the blows he lavished upon his provoking charges. Stolid by nature, he only came to life, they said, when he was 'plying the cane'. He would slouch into the hall at 7.30, his rusty black clothes awry, his nose blue with cold, blinking himself awake as he sat down at a desk in the centre of the cavernous hall. The boys were called before him to recite. It was a favourite prank for an unprepared youth to engage a fellow conspirator to blow out the master's taper at a crucial moment, whereupon Roberts' would 'cut away right and left in the dark'. If he could not catch the wrongdoer, he took his rage out on the head boy of each class. As the school's historian noted, the boys' uniforms of short jackets and knee breeches 'lent themselves admirably to corporal punishment'.[34] Clarkson developed a thorough dislike of public school education.

Some of the philosophy of an earlier high master, George Thicknesse, who believed that boys were sensible creatures capable of being governed by reason, may have survived to his time, however. At any rate, Thomas did well at St Paul's. When he was admitted in 1779 to St John's at Cambridge, he trailed honours and prizes. He had won a Gower exhibition of £20 a year, offered for sons of deceased clergymen, and he was awarded a Pauline exhibition worth £40 a year.[35] So he joined his father's college with a comfortable difference in his resources. He was able to keep a hunter and follow the pursuits of the 'young gay men' of the time,[36] although not on the scale of the rich and often idle youths who joined as fellow commoners.

The college curriculum, unusually, required mathematics for an honours degree. Two of Clarkson's later friends, Wilberforce who entered before him and Wordsworth who followed in 1787, avoided maths and left without honours as the majority of undergraduates did. Clarkson and Wilberforce did not meet at Cambridge. The wealthy youth from a Hull mercantile family was admitted in 1776 at age 17 and left college the year that Clarkson came up. While Clarkson pursued academic distinction, Wilberforce entered public life, taking a seat in Parliament for Hull in 1780 and for Yorkshire in 1784.

Clarkson was a brilliant scholar and his disciplined mind was further honed by his classical studies. He was granted his bachelor's degree in 1783 with a first in mathematics and on 23 June ordained deacon at Winchester. In 1784 he won the Latin essay prize for middle bachelors.[37] No one yet had taken two essay prizes at Cambridge and Clarkson determined to do so.[38] While reading towards his master of arts degree Thomas took the fateful step of entering the competition for senior bachelors on a question set by the vice-chancellor Dr Peter Peckard: *Anne liceat invitos in servitutem dare?* 'Is it lawful to make slaves of others against their will?'

Dr Peckard was known as an advocate of civil and religious liberty. In a university sermon at St Mary's Church he denounced the activities of the British 'Man-Merchants' and warned that the crime of the slave trade 'being both of individuals and the nation, must sometime draw down upon us the heaviest judgment of Almighty God who made of one blood all the sons of men, and who gave to all equally a natural right to liberty'. When Clarkson undertook to root out the crime, Dr Peckard was one of the first persons he drew into the movement.[39]

Like some other prominent persons Dr Peckard had been inflamed by reports in 1783 of the slave ship *Zong* whose captain, in a scheme to collect insurance for what seemed the inevitable loss of a sickly cargo of slaves, had 132 of them thrown overboard alive. Granville Sharp, the eccentric genius whose solitary legal battles to prevent West Indian owners from taking their slaves out of England by force, had, since 1772, effectively made slaveholding illegal in England, lost his attempt to have the captain prosecuted for murder.[40]

Clarkson saw the essay contest mainly as an intellectual challenge. He had only two months to overcome his profound ignorance of the subject.[41] His primary sources were the papers of a dead (unnamed) friend who had worked in the slave trade and the eyewitness accounts of slavery from officers who had served in the West Indies during the American War, including his brother, now a naval lieutenant retired on half pay.

According to intimates, Clarkson's was not a quick mind but he excelled by diligence and now he immersed himself in the harrowing world of slavery. The slowly growing body of literature on the subject was unknown to him until he chanced upon a new edition of Anthony Benezet's *Some Historical Account of Guinea ... with an Inquiry Into the Rise and Progress of the Slave Trade*, published by a recently formed Quaker committee devoted to exposing the evils of the trade. With unscholarly candour, Clarkson later wrote, 'In this precious book I found almost all I wanted.'[42] The Philadelphia Quaker whose writings had made such a profound impact on John Wesley and Granville Sharp now claimed another disciple in Clarkson.

Never in his dry studies so far had Clarkson encountered such a heart-sickening topic and he lived with it day and night, leaving a candle lit when he went to bed so that he could jot down his thoughts as they rose to his mind. When he came to write, he had 'expected pleasure from the invention of the arguments from the arrangement of them, from the putting of them together, and from the thought ... that I was engaged in an innocent contest for literary honour.'

But the facts overwhelmed him: 'It was but one gloomy subject from morning to night. In the daytime I was uneasy. In the night I had little rest. I sometimes never closed my eye-lids for grief. It became now not so much a trial for academical reputation, as for the production of a work, which might be useful to injured Africa.'

When he had finished, he left Cambridge for London and in June 1785 he was summoned back as the winner of first place to read his essay to generous applause in the Senate House.[43]

'Through him', Dr Peckard later wrote, 'I took upon myself as in some degree a Promoter of the glorious attempt to set the slave at liberty.'[44]

When Clarkson first revolted at human bondage it was the prevailing form of labour in most of the world. Just over a century later chattel slavery had been abolished in the Americas and was disappearing in Africa in the wake of the 'most successful human rights movement' in modern history.[45] In fewer than fifty years and in Clarkson's lifetime, slavery was outlawed in British possessions.

But that was the future. Now, as Clarkson rode back to London, he was still absorbed by his grisly subject. In his agitation, he would dismount and walk a while, then climb back into the saddle. Above Wadesmill in Hertfordshire, 'I sat down disconsolate on the turf by the roadside and held my horse. . . . If the contents of the Essay were true, it was time some person should see these calamities to the end. Agitated in this manner I reached home.'[46]

For the next few months he searched his heart. 'I walked frequently into the woods, that I might think on the subject in solitude, and find relief to my mind there. But there the question still recurred, "Are these things true?" Still the answer followed as instantaneously "They are". – Still the result accompanied it, "Then surely some person should interfere".'[47] He did not fully recognise himself as that person for nearly a year.

As he went down from Cambridge with his master of arts degree, Clarkson was an impressive figure with the security of a happy childhood and singularly successful school and university career behind him. He looked forward to a brilliant future in the church; a schoolmaster had seen him as a future bishop.[48] His fortune was small,[49] but enough. A gravity unusual for one of 25 years had settled over him and soon it would become impossible for him to set the question of slavery to one side. He lived in its shadow. It was said that he was 'naturally gloomy and depressed' but it was not from nature that he developed that air. He had the unhappy talent for 'making all his public anxieties personal griefs'.[50]

Those close to him came to understand that he could only survive the emotions which swept over him by holding them sternly in check. The intensity of his commitment eventually left no room for superficial graces. Yet, although he became a legend in his lifetime, friends spoke of the 'sweetness' of his character.[51] One who met him in 1825 when he had been forty years in antislavery, observed that Clarkson never acted the 'great man' to whom 'one quarter of the world would pay homage as its deliverer'.

'Clarkson seemed . . . truly great, for he could come down a little. He took you by the hand with a fatherly smile; and he heard your questions and observations as if he were learning somewhat from you.' He was never too hurried for the confidences he easily drew from others, and women especially found him easy to talk with. He was particularly fond of children and never too busy or tired to respond seriously to their questions, holding their small hands in his large one or stroking their hair as he talked. Panton Corbett was so eager to please him that he read Clarkson's first essay at the tender age of 6 and was moved to tears, while his sister Josepha made sweet bags of lavender to tuck into his saddlebags. Clarkson marvelled that the child should think so kindly of him.[52]

The following pages do not attempt to trace the history of British abolition which has been studied many times and with ever increasing insights, but only to tell of the life and labour of one good man who contributed so significantly to the outcome.

2

The Originator

Innocently thinking that he was almost alone in his discoveries and anxious to do something for 'injured Africa', Clarkson gave the summer and autumn of 1785 to translating and expanding his Latin prize essay for the general public.[1] Working in Wisbech, he had the energetic aid of his brother John, Thomas's first convert to the cause. Although four years apart in age and of markedly different temperaments, for John was genial where Thomas was grave, the brothers were the closest of friends.[2]

By January 1786, Thomas was in London to find a printer for the half-finished work. The well-known Thomas Cadell assured him that a Cambridge prize essay would certainly have a 'respectable circulation among persons of taste'. Clarkson, however, already thought of a movement: he longed to attract 'useful people . . . such as would think and act with me'.[3] By chance (or his 'finger of Providence') he encountered Joseph Hancock, a Quaker from Wisbech, who, learning what brought Clarkson to town, promptly took him to James Phillips, the printer and bookseller in George Yard, Lombard Street, who had issued most of the British and American antislavery tracts which had so far appeared in London. In Phillips, Clarkson acquired a perceptive editor whose judgement and skill helped Clarkson to polish and complete his essay.[4]

Clarkson was overjoyed to fall amongst the Quaker activists of whose efforts he had been curiously unaware in his Cambridge cloister. William Dillwyn, a pupil and assistant to Anthony Benezet and now a merchant in Britain, was a central figure.[5] At his home in Walthamstow he tutored Clarkson in the development of antislavery thought on both sides of the Atlantic. Clarkson learned of Granville Sharp's persistent attempt to establish the rights of slaves in Britain and of the Reverend James Ramsay's writings on West Indian slavery which had provoked the first public controversy on the subject. He was told of the committee named in 1783 by the London Yearly Meeting for Sufferings to promote total abolition of the slave trade and gradual emancipation. A subcommittee of six, including Dillwyn, was engaged in spreading their views. The Quakers had petitioned Parliament, placed articles in London and provincial papers, issued a book by Joseph Woods and an important sermon by the Anglican Bishop Porteus. Some 11 000 copies of Benezet's *Case of our Fellow Creatures, the Oppressed Africans* were sent to influential people.[6]

The Friends, Clarkson discovered, had 50 000 members in the land communicating through a network of 150 correspondents on whom Clarkson eventually would build his broader movement. Yet all their efforts so far had been so quietly managed as to pass almost unnoticed, as his own experience testified.[7]

Outside the Quaker circle, Clarkson and Granville Sharp formed an immediate bond when they discovered an apparent kinship through a Bradford branch of the Clarksons.[8] Ramsay came to London to meet the new recruit. 'The day star of African liberty was rising', Clarkson's heightened senses told him.[9] But he was conscious that no plan united the separate strands and that the question was still not before Parliament.[10]

Of James Phillips's many services to Clarkson, none was more important than his introduction to a cousin, Richard Phillips, a Welsh-born solicitor about to join the Society of Friends. He became Clarkson's 'active and indefatigable coadjutor', both an intelligent partner and a warm friend. 'In him I found much sympathy, and a willingness to cooperate with me', Clarkson wrote later. 'When dull and disconsolate he encouraged me. When in spirits, he stimulated me further.'[11]

If Clarkson has been neglected in latter-day history, Phillips has been utterly forgotten, although Clarkson's history of the abolition makes abundantly clear how significant he was. From their first meeting, the two young men worked as a team, with Phillips freely offering the advice and expertise that Clarkson required for his grand schemes. Phillips knew politicians and officials and the way things were done in London. They had the same probing minds, the same persistence and the same methodical discipline in research. Together they worked out the strategy that eventually led to the formation of a national and nonsectarian movement in the spring of 1787.[12]

Clarkson's *Essay on the Slavery and Commerce of the Human Species, Particularly the African* was published in London in June 1786 (and almost simultaneously in the United States).[13] A substantial book (256 pages), it traced the history of slavery to its decline in Europe and revival in Africa, made a powerful indictment of the slave system as it operated in the West Indian colonies and attacked the slave trade supporting it. In reading it, one is struck by its raw emotion as much as by its strong reasoning. Clarkson conjures scenes of blood and desolation in Africa, destroys the arguments of racial inferiority and defends Christianity against claims that it sanctioned slavery. He contends that there cannot be 'any *property* whatever in the *human species*' since Christianity bound all men (meaning here and elsewhere in this book humankind) to account for their actions hereafter, and only the free could be accountable. Christianity's first doctrine was brotherly love, removing distinctions between Jew and Gentile, Greek and barbarian, bond and free that existed before the gospel came.

After he has described the awful toll in the capture, transportation and 'seasoning' of Africans in the Caribbean, which meant that thousands perished before one useful labourer was obtained, Clarkson exclaims, 'Gracious God! how wicked, how beyond all example impious, must be that servitude, which cannot be carried on without the continual murder of so many and innocent persons!'

He concludes, 'For if liberty is only an adventitious right; if men are by no means superior to brutes; if every social duty is a curse; if cruelty is highly to be esteemed; if murder is strictly honourable, and Christianity is a lye; then it is evident, that the *African* slavery may be pursued, without either the remorse of conscience, or the imputation of a crime. But if the contrary of this is true . . . it is evident that no custom established among men was ever more impious; since it is contrary to reason, justice, nature, the principles of law and government, the whole doctrine, in short, of natural religion, and the revealed voice of God.'[14]

Public response was gratifying: Clarkson became a minor celebrity. In the sober estimate of William Smith MP, one of the earliest supporters, Clarkson's first book justified all past and stimulated all future attempts at abolition 'unanswerably, & I should have thought, irresistibly'.[15] It marked a turning point for British abolition and in hindsight, Clarkson, with that lack of false modesty others took for vanity, said so. He endorsed one copy with the bald assertion that the essay 'may be said to have been the cause of all that had been done on that subject [i.e. the abolition of slavery] throughout the whole world'.[16]

Encouraged by his new friends, Clarkson set out to make

committed supporters of all the well-connected people he knew to expand the Quakers' 'little intercourse with the world'.[17] Most of the names that meant so much to him mean little to us now. Who among us knows of Bennet Langton, Dr John Baker or Lord and Lady Scarsdale? But Langton, a Lincolnshire landowner, classical scholar and particular friend of the late Dr Johnson, was known at court and to members of both Houses of Parliament. Dr Baker's Mayfair chapel numbered many rich and important people in its congregation. The Scarsdales, at the risk of offending relatives with West Indian interests, were moved by religious convictions to offer their help. Clarkson's *Essay* made a deep impression on all of them.[18]

That summer of 1786 Ramsay invited the zealous young clergyman to spend a month at his vicarage at Teston in Kent. With the publication two years before of his seminal *Essay on the Treatment and Conversion of the African Slaves in the British Sugar Colonies* and his *Inquiry into the Effects of Putting a Stop to the African Slave Trade and Granting Liberty to the Slaves* Ramsay had aroused the fury of the West Indian planters and their friends. He had lived 19 years on St Christopher and his exposures of cruelty and hardship were treated as treachery. He had been warned of 'merciless revenge'.[19] Around Ramsay raged the 'first controversy ever entered into on this subject, during which, as is the case in most controversies, the cause of truth was spread', Clarkson said.[20]

Ramsay, 27 years Clarkson's senior, rejoiced at the younger man's interest and approved the first steps he had taken. In character they were not unlike, singleminded to a fault, convinced of their own rightness, 'impatient, impetuous, enthusiastic and sometimes tactless'.[21]

At Teston Hall lived Sir Charles and Lady Middleton who, with Bishop Beilby Porteus had persuaded Ramsay, on his return from St Kitts, to publish his views. Middleton (later Lord Barham) was comptroller of the navy and MP for Rochester. At dinner at the Hall one day, elated by this congenial and high-minded company, Clarkson declared that he was ready to give his life to the cause.[22]

His second thoughts, in the cool of a morning walk, were the same. In his eightieth year, and in his last public appearance, Clarkson took no personal credit for the decision.

I was literally forced into it, I was thinking of . . . the multiplied injuries, which the unhappy people, who are now the object of your sympathy were made to undergo in Africa – on their passage and in the Colonies. All the tragical scenes . . . passed in horrible review before me; and my compassion for their sufferings was *at that moment* so great, so intense, so overwhelming, as to have overpowered me and compelled me to form the resolution, which I dared not resist, it was at my peril to resist, of attempting their deliverance. *Thus I was forced into* the great work. . . . I have often indulged in the belief that this feeling might have come from God. To him therefore, and not to such a Creature as myself, you are to attribute all the honour and all the glory.[23]

It was not an impetuous decision. It was a year since Wadesmill. He had met most of those still living who had acted before him and he had enlisted valuable new supporters. He estimated that perhaps £1000 – a small fortune – would have to be raised[24] and many more allies enlisted to confront the well-entrenched slave trade. 'A little labour now and then' would not suffice: one person must make it the 'business of his life'.[25] Every other possible candidate had professional, mercantile or family responsibilities. Clarkson alone, unmarried and not yet embarked on his church career, fitted the role. His family would be disappointed and the thought of sacrificing his own good prospects staggered even him.

'I had ambition', he admitted. 'I had a thirst after worldly interest and honours, and I could not extinguish it at once.' Yet as he turned over possible objections in his mind 'my enthusiasm instantly, like a flash of lightning, consumed them'.[26]

'Never was any cause, which had been taken up by man in any country, or in any age, so great and important . . . never was there one, in which so much good could be done; never one, in which the duty of Christian charity would be so extensively exercised; never one, more worthy of the devotion of a whole life towards it.'[27]

Clarkson's vision was of one unified plan of action engaging widespread participation and directed towards destroying the legal basis of a centuries-old commercial enterprise. To his part as catalyst he brought unbounded energy, utter conviction, powers of concentration and above all, his time.

There was no simple title for him then and there is none now. He speaks in his own record of preparing himself to be a 'manager in the cause' and again writes, 'I began to qualify myself for the management of this great cause.'[28] His unique, undefined, wide-ranging contribution creates problems for historians, who have given him a variety of labels, often tending to belittle or suggest that he was some sort of hired hand – an unforgiveable insult to an eighteenth-century gentleman. It is time to know him as he was known to his contemporaries as the 'originator' of the Committee for the Abolition of the Slave Trade[29] and the architect of the ensuing campaign.

Suffused with 'sublime and happy feelings', Clarkson left Teston with several introductions from Middleton and an offer of access to naval records relating to the slave trade on the African coast and in the port of London. In London he reported his decision to William Dillwyn and Granville Sharp and at James Phillips's house he met two more members of the Quaker abolition committee, Samuel Hoare, Jr, the merchant and banker, and Joseph Gurney Bevan, a leading chemist.[30] His determination pleased them all. That night he took lodgings at the Baptist Head Coffee House in Chancery Lane to be near Richard Phillips, whose chambers were in Lincoln's Inn.[31]

Their first discussions were over how Clarkson should now spend his time. It was 'our opinion' that the first goal would be a parliamentary inquiry to bring the subject to public notice. To get it they would lobby, distributing copies of Clarkson's *Essay* among MPs and discussing it with them, and in order to make best use of the opportunity when it came, expand Clarkson's knowledge of the slave trade so that he could argue on hard fact. Phillips would arrange letters of introduction and assist in research in his free time. This programme absorbed Clarkson through the winter of 1786–7.

Regular meetings were held at which the pair reported to the Quaker subcommittee. At the first one, and at the insistence of Bevan and Hoare, the committee decided to defray expenses by buying up the rest of the edition of the *Essay* at cost though Clarkson and Phillips were not members but acting on their own independent plan. Eminent volunteers offered to help hand books around, including Langton, Dr Baker, Bishop Porteus, the Scarsdales and Middletons, Sir Herbert Mackworth, Lord Newhaven and Lord Balgonie (later Leven).[32]

Clarkson began his fieldwork at the port of London, an easy walk from his lodgings, before tackling the greater slaving centres of Bristol and Liverpool. London was still the financial and commercial heart of the plantation economy. Here the interests of West Indian planters mingled with those of the merchants who gave them credit, shipped supplies and marketed their sugar, rum and molasses. Together they made a powerful West Indian lobby, penetrating the highest levels of government, Parliament and commerce. Behind the leading figures were ranks of small investors: tradesmen, clergy and modestly fixed widows who bought shares in slave ships.[33] The triangular trade was too familiar to attract much thought. The ships carried British manufactures – cloth, guns, ironware, drink – to barter on the African coast for slaves. Densely packed with human cargo the ships then made the brutal Middle Passage to Jamaica or Barbados or another colony where the survivors were auctioned before the ship was reloaded with plantation produce for the voyage home. Clarkson was to denounce the trade as a hydra-headed monster nursed by the worldly interests of many bodies of men. 'Hence the merchant – the planter – the mortgagee – the manufacturer – the politician – the cabinet minister – lifted up their voices against the annihilation. To protection in this manner by his hundred interests it was owing that the monster stalked in security for so long a time.'[34]

His friend Bennet Langton, a man of worldly sense as well as social grace, warned Clarkson not to be too optimistic, for many thousands had a stake in the trade.[35]

Clarkson would never forget the first African trader he boarded. The *Lively*, not a slave ship, anchored with an exotic cargo of ivory, beeswax, palm oil and the pungent melegueta pepper known as grains of paradise. Clarkson bought samples of everything and when the ship's mate showed him beautifully woven and dyed cloth Clarkson's heart was stricken by the thought that the skilled craftsmen who had created it might 'be made slaves, and reduced to a level with the brute creation'. His purchases were the start of a collection with which Clarkson eventually filled the compartments of a small trunk. He carried this with him for years, opening it like some eager travelling salesman before anyone who pictured Africa as a dark uncivilised place or doubted the humanity and ingenuity of Africans. Here were legitimate riches for British markets.[36]

When Clarkson first stepped on the deck of a slave ship, the *Fly*, a bare glimpse of the dark hold, protected by gratings, where the slaves had been packed and of the barricado on deck where they had been herded filled him with such horror, sadness and finally anger that he had to leave abruptly.[37]

Clarkson interviewed as many men as he could find who had followed the trade or observed it as army or navy officers on the coast, and among his informants was the Reverend John Newton whose useful life as a cleric followed an astonishing career in the slave trade.[38]

Almost nightly Clarkson called on Richard Phillips and they 'unfolded' their thoughts to one another. When Clarkson gained access to customs house records at London through Middleton's good offices and received Liverpool muster rolls from William Rathbone, a leading Quaker timber merchant there, the pair of them began an analysis which exposed a shocking toll among British seamen on slave ships. Half never came back and a fifth perished. The findings, augmented by later research, became one of the abolition's most successful arguments against the trade.[39] Clarkson and Phillips would start work at 9 p.m. and seldom finish before 1 a.m. the next morning when, weary and red-eyed, they would walk in the silent precincts of the inns of court talking over their findings and pondering how to make use of them.

Phillips also obtained, mainly from planters themselves, records of West Indian estates which seemed to show that well-treated slaves reproduced so successfully that their owners no longer had to depend upon the slave trade for new labourers.[40]

The small committee of Quakers was kept abreast of it all and after a few months Clarkson and Phillips openly proposed that they join forces. To face a parliamentary inquiry would require great strength. It would also take money and the Quaker business-men were well positioned to raise and manage it. Clarkson now judged that 2000 guineas would scarcely be enough to see an abolition bill through Parliament. William Dillwyn responded that from the time they first heard of his *Essay* they had hoped to make use of Clarkson.[41]

By now Clarkson was a familiar figure in Quaker circles, which was not a common thing for an Anglican clergyman to be. The sect then was set apart by dress and many rules and customs peculiar to its members. Clarkson saw only that they reasoned as he did, that liberty was a natural right and that since Christ had died for mankind, all men were fundamentally equal. The Quakers were disciplined and serious. Dogma, ritual and hierarchy seemed of small consequence among them.[42] Friends visiting London for the Yearly Meeting were not surprised to meet Clarkson at their hosts' tables. 'He was very free in Conversation', one wrote after such an encounter, '& is much devoted to serve this oppressed people, having declined some advantageous offers of promotion in the church that he may properly attend to this Business.' He added, 'He is a plain sort of man and seems very agreeable in the company of Friends.'[43]

Clarkson was decisively influenced by the relationships. 'The gravity, great earnestness, and quakerish simplicity of his appearance ... made his presence a sort of phenomenon among great men, and men of the world. He was at home only among the quakers and other sectaries', wrote a family friend.[44]

Clarkson's authority for the arguments advanced in his *Essay* grew steadily, and nowhere was this more valuable than in lobbying Members of Parliament. Clarkson's historic meeting with Wilberforce (apparently in early 1787) was a particularly testing experience since Wilberforce indicated that he was already interested and he had searching questions to ask.[45] It seems likely that Middletons had mentioned the two men to one another. Wilberforce was invited to Teston a few weeks after Clarkson had been there. The Middletons, too, believed that a parliamentary inquiry would advance the cause and had been casting about for a suitable MP to introduce it. Middleton did not feel himself equal to the task.[46] But Clarkson introduced himself to Wilberforce by leaving a copy of the *Essay* at the house in Old Palace Yard.

Since his spiritual conversion a year earlier, Wilberforce had been seeking a serious cause to justify his staying in Parliament. Clarkson was encouraged by Wilberforce's readiness to look deeply into the subject and Wilberforce admired Clarkson's decision to make abolition his life's work. They agreed to meet often.[47]

Wilberforce did not tell Clarkson that he had privately agreed (at the Middletons') to introduce the issue if no better spokesman could be found, so when Clarkson reported their conversation to Richard Phillips they concluded that Clarkson should continue to call upon other Members of Parliament, 'but with this difference, that I should never lose sight of Mr Wilberforce'.[48]

Wilberforce's biographers have been reluctant to give Clarkson credit for influencing Wilberforce's final decision, stressing instead the advice of William Pitt, Wilberforce's intimate since university days; the inspirational conversation at Teston Hall; the counsel of his spiritual adviser John Newton; the impact of Ramsay's essays; and the knowledge he had gained from a friend who went to

Antigua.[49] Abolition sentiment was rising in many still-separate quarters. Certainly Clarkson turned up at a propitious time and Wilberforce from then on made good use of Clarkson's expert knowledge. Clarkson, unlike all others, had a plan and a nucleus of supporters.[50] Thus, if Wilberforce decided to pursue abolition in Parliament, helping hands were ready. Even at 27, Wilberforce may have known himself well enough to realise he needed them. Sir George Stephen, his nephew and admirer, perceived Wilberforce's basic fault as 'busy indolence'. 'He worked out nothing for himself; he was destitute of system, and desultory in his habits; he depended on others for information, and he required an intellectual walking stick.'[51]

As a friend of the prime minister, however, with access to everyone in government; as an accomplished speaker and a popular figure now becoming known for his piety, Wilberforce represented almost everything the abolitionists sought in a parliamentary leader. In addition, the controversy bound to develop would not erode his political base – the immense county of Yorkshire – since its chief port, Hull, was the only important seaport in Britain with no African or West Indian trade.

Clarkson found Wilberforce 'daily becoming more interested in the fate of Africa'. Clarkson suggested evening meetings at Wilberforce's house with other MPs and some of the abolitionists already active, such as Sharp, Ramsay and Dr George Gregory.[52] At the first of these gatherings Clarkson read a preliminary version of what was to become his second major publication and one of his most influential ones, *An Essay on the Impolicy of the African Slave Trade*. He meant to prove that the slave trade was not only inhuman and unjust but a graveyard for seamen and an impractical way of providing plantation labour. 'Providence', wrote Clarkson, 'in ordaining laws relative to the agency of man had never made that to be wise which was immoral.'[53]

The lobbying of Wilberforce was followed attentively by the Quaker committee in the City. As the likelihood increased that he might agree to become their parliamentary advocate, the members prepared to set up the broader organisation which Clarkson had proposed. They waited only for Wilberforce's signal.[54] Clarkson went to seek it but, surprisingly, quailed at the task. Where the cause was concerned, he had been bold. Only his profound sense of mission can explain this lapse. Too much was at stake. He had no obvious second choice and all his hopes for a united abolition campaign depended upon getting the issue before Parliament. Dejected, Clarkson 'actually went away without informing him of my errand'.[55]

One does wonder why Wilberforce did not put Clarkson out of his misery by telling him plainly that he intended to become the spokesman, for he is always portrayed as having been interested well before Clarkson turned up on his doorstep. He cannot have been ignorant of why Clarkson was so attentive, so generous in imparting his discoveries, so happy to answer the questions Wilberforce raised. Wilberforce knew all about lobbying and was constantly besieged by constituents with various axes to grind. His biographer sons tell us that his chief preoccupation in 1787 was obtaining a Royal Proclamation against vice and organising a society to enforce it.[56] He may have been indecisive to the last about committing himself to abolition.

But there is another possible explanation. Searching for ways to fulfil the 'awful sense of his duty as a Christian' (Clarkson's words), Wilberforce may have given the particular subject of the slave trade no more than cursory thought until the persistent Clarkson appeared.[57] How else can we account for the fact that he did not read Clarkson's talked-about *Essay* when it came out instead of after Clarkson left it at his house more than six months later? He recognised the book as decisive in turning his attention seriously to the subject.[58] How else to explain his failure to refer to his half-promise to the Middletons? Clarkson told the Quakers that Wilberforce 'had never yet dropped the least hint' that he would speak for them in Parliament.[59]

There might, of course, be political reasons for not taking Clarkson into his confidence about the talks he was having with Pitt and Grenville. Abolition was slipping into public debate and Pitt had warned Wilberforce, 'Do not lose time or the ground may be occupied by another.'[60]

In any case, after his ignoble visit, Clarkson sought help from his older and more socially sophisticated friend Bennet Langton and they agreed to approach Wilberforce in the pleasant atmosphere of a dinner party. The company chosen for the momentous event in May 1787 was typical of Langton's popular gatherings of men in politics and the arts. With Wilberforce and Clarkson he invited the MPs Sir Charles Middleton, Isaac Hawkins Browne and William Windham, along with Sir Joshua Reynolds and James Boswell, Dr Johnson's friend.[61] The conversation was duly steered to the slave trade. Clarkson expounded on the mortality of seamen in the trade and exhibited his African samples for their edification. Langton, probably suggesting that Wilberforce was the ideal person to plead the cause in Parliament (for some such 'delicate compliment' was dropped), drew from Wilberforce roughly the same answer he had given the Middletons: he would take it up when he was better prepared and if no more suitable person could be found. They had already made known that none could be. Clarkson took his words as a final avowal and obtained permission to tell his friends in the City.[62]

To Clarkson the day of Wilberforce's declaration at Langton's table was the 'happiest day I had then spent in my whole life'. He had 'good reason' (which he never shared) to know that Wilberforce would not have taken up the cause at that time without him. 'It was "the Hour & the Men".'[63]

3

At the Perilous Fountainhead

The morning after Langton's dinner party Clarkson appeared at James Phillips's printshop to ask him to summon the Quaker abolitionists to hear the news that Wilberforce had taken up the cause. The members were easily reached; it would be their fourth meeting that May of 1787.[1] In the brief interval of waiting, Clarkson sounded out by letter and in person Dr Peckard, Lord Scarsdale, Dr Baker and others about joining a society to work for the abolition of the slave trade. He had his answers in a day or two and all agreed that a society should be formed.

When Clarkson read his notes on Wilberforce's decision to the Quakers it was the signal to launch a national nonsectarian movement to back up parliamentary action.[2] From Clarkson's account, and his is the only surviving fairly detailed record, the novel plan which he had developed with such advisers as Dillwyn and Richard Phillips, called for an organisation country-wide led by a London-based committee. The membership of this executive committee was agreed in advance, another piece of meticulous spadework with the Clarkson hallmark, and it met for the first time on 22 May 1787.[3] The members were Granville Sharp, 'father of the cause in England'; William Dillwyn, Samuel Hoare, Jr, George Harrison, John Lloyd and Joseph Woods, five of the original Quaker subcommittee of six (Dr Thomas Knowles from his deathbed wished them well); four more from the Society of Friends: John Barton, Joseph Hooper, James Phillips and Richard Phillips, and two other Anglicans in addition to Sharp: Clarkson and Philip Sansom.[4]

In dwelling now, as I shall, on the way the abolitionists functioned I hope to be paying tribute to the audacity and skill shown in this first of all national campaigns to win public support. Also, because this is his story, I hope to clarify Clarkson's place in the Committee and the country. Arguably Clarkson's chief contribution to abolition was his conception of this new form of extra-parliamentary action, yet he has been portrayed in modern times as a functionary of the Committee, 'directed', 'authorised', 'summoned' or 'ordered' by it. Such commands do not appear in the official record. Clarkson, exactly like every other member, 'is desired' by or 'requested' by common resolution to write this letter, seek that interview or audit such and such an expense account. Even in this atmosphere of fraternity and equality, Clarkson dominates much of the business when in town, and his reports when travelling influence its direction. (The other most prominent figure on the record is the treasurer Samuel Hoare, but the diligence of Dillwyn, the Phillipses, Sansom, Harrison, Woods and the others is heroic.)[5]

Clarkson's writings are treated as the most important of the scores the Committee published and they are the most widely distributed. The idea that Wilberforce directed the Committee from its inception, as his sons claimed after his death, is, frankly, rubbish.[6] It was indeed his 'valuable ally' and its work was coordinated with his political moves. Wilberforce never identified himself closely with the Abolition Committee, speaking of it in a detached way as a City group 'set on foot by a few Quakers' and one of several signs of a growing interest in abolition. He doubtless met individual members informally but his first official contact was a request in October 1787 for information, and a subcommittee of Sharp, Hoare and Sansom (Clarkson was in Liverpool) was named to confer with him from time to time.[7] Wilberforce and the Committee worked in independent but interconnecting ways.

Hoare was the only officer named at the outset. Clarkson served as 'secretary' until mid-June, after which members took monthly turns keeping the minutes and calling the meetings. All shared the letter-writing. The absence of officers and a chain of command was quakerish. The Society of Friends governed itself without a head and reached decisions by consensus, without recorded votes. In Clarkson's eyes the twelve committeemen represented all the strands in the history of abolition, united at last in a 'regular system'. He employed the metaphor of a great river fed by tributaries to show how each contributor swelled the torrent that ultimately swept away the slave trade.[8]

In addition to Christian piety, the committeemen brought worldly experience of varied occupations and benevolent enterprises. With the exception of Sharp and Clarkson, they were rich. The

Quakers in particular, without access to universities and therefore most professions, and denied public offices and titles, were conspicuously successful in trade and commerce.[9] 'I believe no committee was ever made up of persons, whose varied talents were better adapted to the work before them', Clarkson wrote.[10]

They were a faithful, hardworking band, usually meeting at least weekly at half past five or seven o'clock in the evening. They used James Phillips's premises until July when they moved into a first-floor room at 18 Old Jewry where the rent of £25 a year included the servant who lit the fire and candles for them before they arrived from their offices or dinner tables. After six months, under pressure of work, they employed John Frederick Garling to keep the minutes and send out notices, but the mounting correspondence was still dealt with by the individual members.

On 4 September 1787, the Committee formally designated Sharp as chairman although it seems to have been accepted from the start that he would hold the office. Hoare, however, signed and received all the correspondence till then, even when Sharp was present.[11] He was chosen as a tribute to his early work and also because he was not a Quaker. He accepted the title but never took the chair. Clarkson, who eventually attended more than 700 meetings with him, said that Sharp 'always seated himself at the lowest end of the room, choosing rather to serve the glorious cause in humility ... than in the character of a distinguished individual.'[12]

'Much business has *been done in my name*', Sharp was to tell his brother. Over his signature the Committee could write 'in the *ordinary stile*', abandoning 'every peculiarity which might seem to belong to a particular Sect; for they hoped to have the Society consist of all denominations of Christians ... this is a great concession! but a *very sensible* one.'[13]

Quaker forms of address still aroused anger and ridicule in some other religionists. Friends used 'thou' instead of 'you'. They banned all forms that tended to 'puff people up', as with Sir, Madam, even Mr, implying Master. They refused to say 'Your Excellency' or 'Your Honour' or 'My Lord'. They addressed everyone as 'Friend' or by the given and surnames. They would not say, in signing, 'your humble and obedient servant'. They did not use the names of days or months for days were called after heathen rituals (as Sunday for sacrifice to the sun) and months named for Roman gods or some meaningless antique plan. Their 'plain' language might bring a hostile response.[14]

In searching for a title, the Committee was forced to define its aims. Did members seek to abolish only the traffic in slaves or slavery itself? It was soon decided that abolition of both evils was too monumental a task and by aiming too high 'we might lose all'. Either object, once achieved, they reasoned, perhaps naively, would bring about the other. Furthermore, abolition of the trade was a clearly legitimate goal since government had a right to regulate or abolish any branch of commerce. Emancipation, on the other hand, could be seen as meddling with property rights, a murky role for government. It would also be interfering with the internal affairs of the colonies while the slave trade was entirely in the hands of the imperial power. Again, emancipation might provoke disorder, or be seen to hand liberty to people unfit for it as yet. The name finally chosen was the Society for Effecting the Abolition of the Slave Trade.[15]

Granville Sharp was the only one of the 10 present on 7 June 1787 to plead for an assault on slavery itself. '[W]ith a loud voice . . . and both hands uplifted to Heaven' he warned that the Committee would stand 'guilty before God, for shutting . . . slaves all the world over, out of the pale.' So long as slavery existed there would be a slave trade.[16] That he remained the figurehead leader was a clear sign of the importance he attached to the new body.

The issue never died. Few of their contemporaries ever believed that the sole target was the slave trade. Their radical supporters were often restive over the official pragmatism. John Cartwright was not the only one to send a donation towards the 'emancipation of Negroes'[17] and the Committee periodically had to reiterate that its object was not emancipation 'as charged'. On his travels, Clarkson insisted that emancipation 'was no part of our plan'.[18]

The Committee began its work in an atmosphere of high enthusiasm and optimism. At the second meeting on 24 May 1787 Hoare reported subscriptions of £136[19] and Clarkson was ready with a propaganda piece, a short tract distilled from his *Essay* which he believed, rightly, was too long for popular consumption. Two thousand copies of this *Summary View of the Slave-Trade, and of the Probable Consequences of Its Abolition* were ordered for immediate use.[20] In this pamphlet, Clarkson announced a forthcoming work which would explain the impolicy of the slave trade, as well as its inhumanity. It was to collect material necessary to complete this book and to locate evidence for a future parliamentary hearing that

Clarkson proposed a journey to Bristol and Liverpool 'before the passions of men had . . . been heated by any public agitation'. His colleagues approved and told him to draw on the treasurer for expenses. He was asked to submit an account of his disbursements to date and came up with a modest bill for £67.[21]

With the start of the travels, which were to take him 35 000 miles in the next seven years, Clarkson began to make himself better known outside London. The Bishop of Bangor, Dr John Warren, a vicar at Wisbech when Clarkson was a boy and a friend whom Clarkson had consulted about attitudes in the House of Lords, warned him bluntly not to make himself so conspicuous in a controversial cause, for it would fatally damage his prospects in the church.[22] Since he had abandoned all thought of career for as long as it took to outlaw the slave trade, the fatherly advice went unheeded.

The series of investigative journeys he proposed, planned and carried out[23] were, again, an innovation. Clarkson wished to go to the 'fountain head', the major slaving ports of Bristol and Liverpool, to acquire a comprehensive understanding of this trade. Roger Anstey believed that Clarkson's journeys were comparable in importance to his writings because 'probably only by such means could the abolitionists have learned the weaknesses of the institution they had set out to destroy'.[24]

He travelled almost entirely on horseback, for riding was the most efficient way to go in all weathers and all roads and he thought the exercise was good for him. He could be flexible in his route and in the solitude of the saddle he could think and read.[25] More than any other single individual, he made abolition a national movement, for wherever he went he personified the Society and its ruling Committee. He inspired and informed supporters where they had come forward, and recruited new subscribers and correspondents. He addressed small groups brought together in an inn or private drawing room with contagious enthusiasm. 'I would follow you 500 mile to enjoy your conversation', said a Shropshire gentleman after he had met Clarkson.[26] He was listened to with breathless attention and reminded at least one man of St Paul preaching at Athens.[27] He personally wrote regularly to 400 people for the next seven years to help knit these pockets of local interest into the grand design.

The journeys were dangerous, exhausting and exhilarating, but the youthful Clarkson lived in hope 'that every day's labour would furnish me with that knowledge which would bring this evil nearer to its end'.[28] He followed a punishing schedule of inquiry by day and writing up his findings well into the small hours of night.

When he rode out of London on 25 June 1787 on the first of these field-trips his spirits were low, for he had paid a farewell call on Wilberforce and found him ill in bed. The MP had given Clarkson his hand and his best wishes, but Clarkson feared that 'it would be in this case, as it is often in that of other earthly things, that we scarcely possess what we repute a treasure, when it is taken from us'.[29]

But, a countryman at heart, he was cheered by a grand view of Windsor Castle and the pleasant landscape around Reading, and the 118-mile journey passed in relaxed enjoyment in spite of steady rain.[30]

From a mile away, Bristol looked intimidatingly large, lying in a haze and bathed in the melancholy sound of church bells. 'I began now to tremble', Clarkson wrote, 'at the arduous task I had undertaken, of attempting to subvert one of the branches of the commerce of the great place which was then before me'.[31]

The ships that plied the triangular route crowded into the very heart of the town 'as far as you can see, hundreds of ships, their masts as thick as they can stand by one another'[32] along the quays of the River Avon, which faced streets of houses. No wonder, as Clarkson found, everyone talked so freely of the trade. Slaving represented only 12 per cent of Bristol's overseas commerce but since the merchants believed their West Indian cargoes depended upon a continuous supply of slaves, they were stout supporters of the traffic.[33]

Clarkson carried introductions to Quakers along his route and in Bristol his contact was Harry Gandy, a conveyancer who as a youth had sailed on two slaving voyages to Sierra Leone before he joined the Society of Friends. The Men's Monthly Meeting here was actively distributing antislavery tracts. Gandy introduced Clarkson to seven other Quaker families and for some time these were his sole informants.[34] As he mentions no other lodgings, they were probably his hosts as well.

He was a meticulous investigator who traced each rumour to its source and accepted no tale he could not corroborate with other testimony. But even by his severe tests he collected a thick catalogue of horrors, involving cruelty to slaves and, as his earlier research had promised, to British seamen in the brutalising trade.

Clarkson unfortunately was not capable of cynicism or a cool detachment towards his research subject. Even words on a page had haunted him at Cambridge. At Bristol he walked amongst the perpetrators. He worked to the point of exhaustion, became thinner, sallow, rheumatic, but the physical toll could have been repaired, in time; the mental torment stayed. 'My feelings became now almost insupportable. I was agonized to think that this trade should last another day. I was in a state of agitation from morning till night'.[35]

Information was easy enough to come by, especially at first. Clarkson boarded two little sloops being fitted out for sale as private yachts in the West Indies and measured the space for the 100 slaves they would carry from Africa. It came to three square feet for each adult.[36] A surgeon's mate, James Arnold, told of savage beatings given slaves as his ship lay off the coast. When two victims rebelled one was shot and the other fatally scalded with hot fat.[37] Arnold promised to keep a journal for Clarkson on his next voyage. But why sail again? 'Cruel necessity' was his answer.[38] A seaman so mercilessly punished that he repeatedly tried to jump overboard had been chained to the deck for the duration of his voyage and Clarkson found him in his lodgings, heavily bandaged, delirious and near death.[39]

Clarkson's outraged reaction in such cases was to take the ship's officers to court. The deputy town clerk advised against it since an investigation would take months and his witnesses would either have to go back to sea or stay at home at Clarkson's expense. Nonetheless, he was so incensed by the fatal beating of William Lines that he took the witnesses before the magistrates to lodge a complaint of murder. At least four men connected with the slave trade sat on the bench and shot Clarkson 'savage looks' but a warrant was issued and the mate arrested. From then on Clarkson was publicly shunned by ship's officers 'as if I had been a wolf, or tiger, or some dangerous beast of prey. Such of them as saw me before hand, used to run up the cross streets or lanes ... to get away.'[40]

The William Lines case came to a bitter end. The trial was called unexpectedly early at the Old Bailey and, on a return visit to Bristol at the end of his tour, Clarkson risked his life crossing the Severn in a storm to find two of his witnesses who had gone to work in a Welsh coal mine. He saw them off to London before collapsing with sore throat and fever but by the time his party reached court the mate had appeared and the case had been dismissed for lack of evidence.[41]

Since ill-treatment was no secret and desertions were common in Bristol crews, Clarkson was curious as to how men were persuaded to sign on. The landlord of the Seven Stars guided him to the crimping houses along Marsh Street. They made nineteen tours, each from midnight to the small hours, and Clarkson saw the rowdy atmosphere of dancing, rioting and drunkenness in which young men, often deep in debt, fell easy prey to the promise of higher wages offered by the slave trade. Should they be reluctant, the ship's mates would stupefy them with drink and strike a deal for their inert forms with the landlords. Even the high wages were a fraud, for the men might be paid in the reduced currency of the West Indies.[42]

Only Harry Gandy among all the Bristol informants he met was willing to go to London to testify if needed, when Clarkson met Alexander Falconbridge, an 'athletic and resolute-looking man', who had made four voyages on slavers as a surgeon but who for two years now had been practising as a physician in Bristol. Rather hopelessly, Clarkson put the usual question to him and received an unequivocal 'yes'. 'Never were words more welcome to my ears', he remembered. 'The joy I felt rendered me quite useless . . . for the remainder of the day.'[43]

Falconbridge could supply many details that fleshed out Clarkson's picture of the trade with all its intrinsic violence. As he was to demonstrate in evidence to the parliamentary inquiry and in his tract, *An Account of the Slave Trade on the Coast of Africa*, written essentially by Richard Phillips and published by the Committee in 1788, Falconbridge was blunt, factual, sensitive to cruelty but not given to sermonising, and he carried great weight.[44]

Clarkson gained access to the customs house records with the friendly aid of the venerable Josiah Tucker, for years a rector in Bristol and now dean of Gloucester Cathedral, who was deeply interested in Clarkson's research. He kept the younger man company at Merchants Hall as he painstakingly copied the muster rolls to compare their figures with those he had collected for London and Liverpool.[45] Convinced that the time was near 'when the public voice should be raised against this enormous evil', Clarkson began to encourage petitions. Since the very first citizens' petition on abolition had gone to Parliament in 1783 from Bridgwater, Clarkson rode there to confer with the initiators, the Reverend

George White and John Chubb, a friend of Charles James Fox and head of the local parliamentary reform committee. Their petition, seeking both an end to slavery and the slave trade, was tabled and the local MPs told them there was not 'the least disposition to pay any further attention to it'. Clarkson gave them a report on the London Committee and his Bristol findings as well as copies of the *Summary View* and took away their promise to send a second petition when it might be needed.[46]

Forming local support groups, although not part of his original plan in making the fact-finding tour, followed logically. At Bristol the Quaker men's committee was already in place. Clarkson helped to form another which included Anglicans and Baptists as well as Friends. Joseph Harford, twice High Sheriff and local councillor, was first chairman. The committee inserted *Summary View* in the local press and was ready to petition Parliament on a signal from London.[47] Among what Clarkson dubbed the 'respectable' merchants were several trading in African products who were pleased to share their information and give him samples of woods, gums, cotton and rice for his growing collection.[48]

This is an imperfect account of the Bristol experience. The rich details lie in his history of the abolition as well as various parliamentary papers. Clarkson sent a series of letters reporting his progress to Hoare from 24 July to 9 October. In the first he proposed that the useful Dr Falconbridge join him at Liverpool and be given £10 to compensate for time lost in his practice. With the Committee's assent (if Falconbridge 'is really a man of good character') came a gentle caution, in the Quaker style, 'I hope the zeal and animation with which thou hast taken up the cause will be accompanied with temper and moderation.'[49] Clarkson's feelings must have shown.

Clarkson pressed on to Liverpool, then the slaving capital of the world, pausing at each major town along the way – Gloucester, Worcester, Chester – to contact mayors, clergymen and editors who gave him encouraging promises of cooperation. At Bath earlier, the editor had agreed to carry abolitionist articles, free of charge.[50]

Although as at Bristol the slave trade was only a part of the massive commerce that crowded Liverpool's six miles of docks, it set the tone and the 'horrible facts concerning it were in everybody's mouth'.[51] For the first time Clarkson saw tools of the trade displayed in a shop window and he bought iron handcuffs, leg shackles, a hideous thumb screw and a *speculum oris* such as was used to wrench open the mouth of a slave who refused to eat.[52]

'Every brick in your infernal town is cemented with an African's blood', George Frederick Cooke, the tragedian, drunk on stage as usual, taunted an audience which booed his performance. 'Almost every order of people is interested in a Guinea cargo!' claimed a contemporary writer and Clarkson later told friends, 'Even the ladies there make no scruple to drink for the first toast after dinner success to the slave trade.'[53]

Abolition sympathisers existed in Liverpool but they were less active and far less open than Clarkson's Bristol friends. Here Liverpool's interests came first, most had friendly business links with the slave trade, and while they disliked it in principle, they favoured a gradual reformist approach. Their writings on the subject were usually unsigned. At least eight Liverpudlians subscribed to the abolition society but no supporting committee was established and no petitions were sent.[54]

Except for William Rathbone, Clarkson saw little of them and his activities disturbed them. He called on another Quaker, Isaac Hadwen, whom he had met at the London Yearly Meeting, and he went to see the poet and writer Edward Rushton, once an officer on a slave ship who was saved from drowning by a slave and, befriending the slaves in return, had contracted ophthalmia and returned home blind. He had freely described the evils of the slave trade and boldly signed his work.[55]

Clarkson also visited William Roscoe, a wealthy self-made man of many talents who had recently offered the profits of his poem, *The Wrongs of Africa*, to the Abolition Committee. Clarkson thought it beautiful and quoted it at length in his history where it is a reminder of the romantic and unfocused emotions which thoughts of Africa and slavery then aroused.[56] Roscoe introduced Clarkson to Dr James Currie, the Scottish physician who wrote the anonymous preface to Roscoe's work. Dr Currie condemned the slave trade, but only in private.[57] There seemed to be no offer of hospitality and Clarkson took rooms at the King's Arms public house. If he noticed the coolness of his reception he never commented upon it. He could not know that his fellow committeeman, John Barton, had asked Roscoe to send him a confidential report on Falconbridge, who joined Clarkson at Liverpool, and had said of the traveller, 'His zeal and activity are wonderful but I am really afraid he will at times be deficient in caution and prudence, and lay himself open to imposition, as well as incur much expense, perhaps sometimes unnecessarily.'[58]

At the King's Arms, Clarkson and Falconbridge dined in the public room which, as the visitors became notorious for their prying, filled with hostile locals who tried to provoke Clarkson with loud remarks about madmen bent on the destruction of Liverpool and 'all its glory'. With immense effort, the hot-tempered and thin-skinned Clarkson responded with what he regarded as reasoned dignity. He had cause to be grateful for Falconbridge (who went armed, though Clarkson did not know it). When Clarkson was derided for never having seen the African coast, the doughty doctor would interject, 'But I have. I know all your proceedings there, and that his statements are true.' Clarkson judged that in this public debate he and Falconbridge 'beat our opponents out of the field'.[59]

Even among the hundreds who had abandoned the trade Clarkson found no one willing to testify, for it was feared that their houses would be pulled down in revenge. They came to him privately 'to tell me that I was right, and to exhort me to persevere'.[60] Clarkson searched shipping records, talked with any merchants and captains who would talk with him and enlarged his sample collection but concentrated chiefly on the effects of the trade on seamen because they flocked to him.[61] They hung about the door of the King's Arms, to the fury of other patrons, until, out of consideration for his patient landlord, Clarkson took rooms in Williamson Square to meet his informants. He also used the place to write his reports and sometimes he slept there.[62] His general conclusion that the slave trade was proved to be 'one barbarous system from the beginning to the end' because of its very nature drew sharp criticism from ostensible friends of the cause. After Clarkson had left the town, Dr Currie complained that he had tried to defame the traders, the great majority of whom were 'men of general fair character'. More than one showed 'uncommon integrity and kindness of heart', he declared in a letter to Wilberforce. They followed a trade sanctioned by long custom and law and should not be reproached for that. Currie asserted, without naming him, that Clarkson preferred the testimony of the 'lowest class of seamen' to that of these virtuous citizens. He accused Clarkson of going about 'in diguise' although Clarkson never adopted a false identity in his life and indeed was too well known for his own comfort.[63]

It is believed to be Dr Currie who, under the *nom de plume* of Gustavus, denounced Clarkson's methods in a letter which appeared in the *Gentleman's Magazine* in March 1788. While applauding Clarkson's motives, the writer urged that 'zeal be tempered by discretion ... and freed from personal and scurrilous invective'. He implied that Clarkson used the evidence of 'unprincipled common sailors and dock landladies' a theme picked up by Gilbert Francklyn from Jamaica when he assailed the 'Reverend Author ... who, in the different masks of an African sailor and pettifogging attorney is said to have visited the alehouses and brothels of Liverpool to find out witnesses to the enormities committed by the masters of Guinea ships'.[64]

At Liverpool Clarkson probed further into a case he had heard about first in Bristol, the killing of Peter Green while his ship lay in the Bonny River. Falconbridge was sure the notorious tale was true for when he visited the area later the Africans were still talking about it.[65] Clarkson spotted the Liverpool ship (the *Vulture*) in a wet dock and boarded it after scrambling across the decks of the ships between. The crew responded well to his questions until he asked about deaths in general and Peter Green's in particular. When Clarkson obtained the muster roll he read that 16 seamen had died on the year-long voyage which ended in June 1787, Green among them, and at a date which showed his death occurred in Africa.[66]

Clarkson was nearly ready to leave Liverpool when he met George Ormond who had sailed in Green's ship. As Ormond told it, Green, a steward, was wrongly accused of assault by a black woman interpreter who belonged to the owners when he refused to give her the key to the wine store in the captain's absence. In consequence, the captain, resting at intervals and spelled by two mates, flogged Green for two and a half hours, ripping his back open with the cat-of-nine-tails and beating his brains out with a knotted rope. He was still alive when cut down and they shackled him and lowered him into a boat alongside. He was found dead the next morning and buried on Bonny Point.[67]

Clarkson demanded corroboration and got it from a shipmate whom Ormond questioned while Clarkson listened concealed in an adjoining room. It was one of the men Clarkson had spoken to on board the vessel.[68]

Clarkson wanted to charge the three ship's officers with murder but was dissuaded by unnamed acquaintances who assured him the trio would be tipped off by the magistrates and escape arrest. They warned Clarkson further that he was now so hated that he would be torn to pieces and his lodgings burned down if he brought on a trial.[69] He desisted but sent Ormond to London, at his own expense, to 'keep him out of the way of corruption' till he could decide how to proceed. When he encountered another man from the same sorry crew he sent him to London, too.[70]

It must have been rumour of his interest in the hideous death of Peter Green that led to an attempt either to frighten or kill him. Clarkson was alone on the pierhead watching the small boats tossing in a heavy gale and when he turned to walk back he was confronted by eight or nine men who charged him, shoving him towards the end of the pier. Among his assailants was the 'murderer of Peter Green' and he recognised two others who had insulted him at the King's Arms. Clarkson believed at that moment they were determined to throw him into the sea and make it look an accident. He 'darted forward. One of them against whom I pushed myself, fell down. Their ranks were broken. And I escaped, not without blows, amidst their imprecations and abuse.'[71]

Clarkson's best source among 'respectable' citizens was Robert Norris, a retired slave captain, now a leading merchant, to whom he was introduced by Rathbone. Norris was an intelligent and polite man and they talked several times. He gave Clarkson the manuscript of a voyage to Africa which contained examples of cruelty in the trade. He even offered a draft of legislation which might curb and ultimately prohibit slaving.[72]

Liverpool had become increasingly dangerous, and further investigation seemed futile so after a brief look at muster rolls at Lancaster, Clarkson rode to Manchester[73] where an abolition committee, headed by Thomas Walker, a reform-minded merchant, welcomed him heartily. Shortly before Clarkson's arrival, these activists had launched a petition and an abolition sermon had been preached in the town.[74]

They insisted that Clarkson preach at the Collegiate Church the next day. The posters for the event were, in fact, already up.[75] On the Sunday the church was packed and some fifty black people were clustered around the pulpit when Clarkson entered, nervous and a bit embarrassed, and made his way up the aisle. The sermon he had composed during the night was built around a text from Exodus: 'Thou shalt not oppress a stranger, for ye know the heart of a stranger, seeing ye were strangers in the land of Egypt', Moses' advice to the Israelites to treat the aliens in their midst with compassion. This precept, said Clarkson, was one of universal obligation and it had been entrenched in Christianity 'that we should not do that to others, which we would be unwilling to have done unto ourselves'.[76] Today the African 'drinks the cup of sorrow, and . . . drinks it at our hands'. Torn from land, family and friends, the African was forced into degradation as the 'possession of a man to whom he never gave offence'. He enlarged on the humanity of Africans with anecdotes given him in his researches. How inconsistent, he declared, to pray for God's mercy on ourselves 'who have no mercy upon others'. He predicted, as Granville Sharp might have done, that the judgement which destroyed Tyre and Sidon, the Bristol and Liverpool of Biblical times, would fall upon Britain and for the same sin of the slave trade. He called on the congregation to join the cause of abolition so that 'the stain of the blood of Africa is not upon us'.

The stillness told Clarkson he had touched their hearts. They too, were strangers, for Manchester in 1787 was a city of uprooted people, migrants from the countryside to its booming factories and mills. They wove the cotton carried from the slave-labour plantations of the Caribbean and North America.

When Manchester's petition was sent to Parliament it had been signed by nearly 11 000 persons, more than a fifth of the total population, and with it the abolitionists sent 100 guineas to the London Committee.[77]

Elated by Manchester, Clarkson left for London. He had been away for more than five months and the Committee needed a second edition of his *Essay*, incorporating his fieldwork findings, and the new study of the impolicy of the slave trade as quickly as possible. He had collected the names of more than 20 000 seamen in the slave trade and he knew what had become of each one.[78]

4

People to Parliament

When Clarkson rejoined the Committee in November 1787, he was happily surprised to learn of the rapid growth of the movement. Working strenuously, the Committee was publishing tracts by the thousands of copies and attracting correspondents in almost every county. The members welcomed their peripatetic friend with cordial thanks for his 'unwearied assiduity & perseverance' at the slave ports.[1] Before he retreated to Wisbech to work uninterruptedly on the impolicy of the slave trade Clarkson revised his original essay for a new printing.

He also arranged for the witnesses to the murder of Peter Green to be questioned closely by Sir Sampson Wright, head of police, who thereupon applied to the Liverpool magistrates to arrest the accused ship's officers, but they had sailed.[2] Recklessly, Clarkson had hoped to start proceedings in nine instances of brutality to seamen uncovered on his tour. The threat of action encouraged the captain of Green's ship finally to offer some compensation to the witnesses for their personal injuries but Clarkson never got to trial in any case. The Committee, unprepared for this sort of expense, was reluctant to share the financial burden. When Sharp obtained a writ of habeas corpus against a captain who was holding two black sailors picked up from a Spanish shipwreck, however, the Committee did agree to indemnify him.[3]

Until now the slave trade had been attacked mainly on humanitarian grounds and a slave medallion from the Wedgwood factory became the movement's potent symbol. When Josiah Wedgwood, the potter, joined the Committee (it was enlarged to 30 in the first year) his offer of a seal design by William Hackwood was gratefully accepted. It depicted a kneeling African in chains, his hands lifted in poignant supplication, framed with the words 'Am I Not a Man and a Brother?', the title of Dr Peckard's influential sermon. Clarkson, for one, had the seal engraved on a large carnelian for his own use. Produced as a black-and-white cameo, the image was distributed in thousands. Clarkson alone gave out 500 on his travels. It was inlaid in gold on snuff-boxes and set into bracelets and hairpins. Women could wear it though they were barred from signing petitions. For once, Clarkson observed prissily, fashion promoted justice.[4]

Clarkson dwelt upon the heartless and irreligious nature of the slave trade in his first essay and he was quick to quote and circulate the poetry written by sympathisers, but he knew that appeals to emotion cut no ice with the vested slaving interests and the parliamentarians who spoke for them. It was necessary to demonstrate that there was a lucrative alternative for merchants trading to Africa and that slaving, because of the cost in British seamen's lives, was against the national interest. It was necessary to show planters that with new supplies of labour cut off, their debts would fall and their slaves increase in value. This was the task he undertook in his second major work, *Essay on the Impolicy of the African Slave Trade*, which he dedicated to his new colleague, William Wilberforce.[5]

His most telling revelation was that the slave trade, far from being a nursery for naval recruitment in time of war, was a grave. It destroyed more men in a year than all other branches of commerce in two, and more seamen than slaves perished in the voyages. The evidence he had collected at the slaving ports, plus 'ocular demonstration, as far as a sight of their mangled bodies will be admitted as a proof', together with the facts uncovered in his unsuccessful legal pursuits documented his case. For every statistic he could supply a name. When he said that of 5000 sailors on the triangular route in 1786, 2320 came home, 1130 died, 80 were discharged in Africa and unaccounted for and 1470 were discharged or deserted in the West Indies he could not be refuted.[6]

Visions of profits of the order of 30 per cent had always attracted investors and merchants. Clarkson challenged this dream; this was an enterprise only for gamblers, what with competition driving up slave prices on the African coast, a high death-rate on the Middle Passage and the likelihood of finding the West Indian market glutted on arrival. The full voyage occupied at least a year and bills of payment could be deferred for up to three years. Bankruptcies were common in Liverpool.[7]

Clarkson proposed an alternative trade. He put together an enticing picture of the fertility and mineral wealth of West Africa. Its products could replace dearer goods from South America or the Far East. He was convinced that Africans had a commercial spirit that would seize upon a trade opening like this.[8]

Before he had finished the book, he heard from Wilberforce that the privy council's committee for trade and plantations had agreed to look into African trade in general and the buying and selling of slaves in particular. The order setting the first slave-trade inquiry in motion was signed on 11 February 1788 and Clarkson reached London three days later. At a special Committee meeting on 16 February it was decided that Clarkson would prepare the evidence for the abolitionist side. Dillwyn, Hoare and Joseph Smith would assist and Richard Phillips as the Committee's solicitor would organise the presentation.[9]

Behind the parliamentary battle about to commence was waged the most comprehensive propaganda campaign yet seen and rarely if ever to be matched. A wave of sympathy for the cause would be generated throughout the country. The 500 circular letters announcing the organisation of the Society for Effecting the Abolition of the Slave Trade had produced not only the expected endorsement of the Society of Friends but pledges of support from the General Baptists[10] and many prominent Anglicans. Scattered individuals such as the Reverend John Toogood of Dorset, who had been writing to his local paper calling for abolition, discovered they had 'coadjutors'.[11] In Shropshire Archdeacon Joseph Plymley (later Corbett) volunteered to sponsor in his diocese of Lichfield and Coventry what became the first petition from established churchmen.[12]

Certain members of Parliament responded enthusiastically, among them William Smith who was to give the Committee more of his time in the next few years than any MP except Wilberforce. MPs William Morton Pitt and James Martin were added to the Committee.[13]

When the Committee pooled names of acquaintances to draw up a distribution list it was found that they had friends in 39 counties. Since Quakers still dominated the Committee, it was no surprise that nine-tenths of these were Quakers[14] but their ranks were steadily expanded by others, in ever-widening circles. Many responses were suitable for publication, such as one from Robert Boucher Nicholls, dean of Middleham, whose acquaintance with slavery in the United States and West Indies allowed him to argue for humane treatment of slaves as a means of avoiding the necessity of a slave trade.[15]

The aged Methodist leader John Wesley offered to reprint an

enlarged edition of his *Thoughts Upon Slavery* with a specific endorsement of the new Society which he commended to 'Him, who is able to carry you through all opposition'.[16]

Pamphlets and books streamed from the Phillips presses. Works by Clarkson and Benezet were reissued, Falconbridge's account of four slaving voyages was published and the Reverend John Newton wrote his painfully descriptive *Thoughts Upon the African Slave Trade*, filled with unforgettable images of slaves packed as close as 'books upon a shelf', at the mercy of drunken crews. Each new publication seemed to elicit others. The Reverend James Dore published a sermon based on Newton's exposé which urged churches to collect funds to help the abolitionists present their case to Parliament. Hardly an edition of a newspaper or monthly periodical appeared without a letter or an essay on the subject. Even the trial of Warren Hastings was overshadowed by the agitation for abolition in press and pulpit and among people of all parties. 'Odd tricks without number are every night lost at the whist table by talking of it.'[17]

As it opened a correspondence with men of like persuasion in the United States, Ireland, France, Germany and Sweden[18] the Committee in its first year issued 'not at random, but judiciously, and through respectable channels', as Clarkson put it, 51 432 pamphlets or books and 26 526 reports and other papers. It had also inspired 103 petitions to Parliament.[19]

Now persuasion through the printed word, aimed at the educated minority, was never controversial. Petitioning on a mass scale, however, had scarcely been tried before and it raised a spectre of popular commotions.[20] To Clarkson, who wanted the nation to implore Parliament with one voice to halt the slave trade, the appeals that piled up on the table of the House of Commons were joyful evidence that the nation had been stirred. The Committee shared this view. It not only received and publicised the petitions as they poured in but promoted one in the City, asked the Reverend Christopher Wyvill what he could do in Yorkshire and sent a circular letter to every mayor of a town not yet heard from. Wilberforce, who did not believe in popular agitation in general, also wrote to Wyvill, a good political ally, urging that the 'little kingdom' of Yorkshire not 'be backward in its endeavours to rescue our fellow-creatures from misery, and retrieve our national character from the foulest dishonour'.[21]

From February to May 1788 the prayers arrived almost daily at

Westminster. Some were signed by the sort of people Parliament was used to hearing from: the aldermen of the City of London, faculties of Oxford and Cambridge, the bailiffs of Bridport, the Edinburgh Chamber of Commerce, and individuals of rank and fortune. But most came from 'inhabitants' of such scattered places as Colchester and Falmouth, Worcester and Chesterfield, Nottingham and Carlisle, Grantham, Newcastle-upon-Tyne, Bedford, Lincoln, Leeds, Rotherham, Salisbury and Warrington.[22] Two thousand signed at Sheffield, 1800 in York and the monster petition with 10 639 names from Manchester had been left in 10 public places for signing. The committee Clarkson fathered in Bristol held its first public meeting in January, drew up a petition which was left in the Guildhall one week for signatures, opened a subscription and sent a hundred guineas to the Committee.[23]

Many petitions cited 'exact intelligence' such as Clarkson had fed into the abolition argument. 'Impolicy' as well as 'sin' became part of the abolition vocabulary. The petitions were couched in moderate language, urging Parliament in its wisdom to do what was right. Even Manchester prayed for regulation, not outright abolition.[24]

With popular enthusiasm at a high pitch, the privy council inquiry, where public opinion would have virtually no effect, seemed a diversion and Manchester leaders, among others, wondered what Wilberforce was playing at in agreeing with Pitt to hold it. Like Pitt, who couldn't carry his cabinet on the issue, Wilberforce foresaw formidable opposition and wanted to establish a solid factual base for an abolition act. Pitt hoped that the inquiry would be finished by May so that the Commons could debate the subject before the session ended.[25]

Fox sympathised with the Manchester men when they complained that their parliamentary spokesman was trying to lower the public voice. Fox wrote to Thomas Walker:

There are many reasons why I am glad [Wilberforce] has undertaken it rather than I, and I think as you do, that I can be very useful in preventing him from betraying the cause, if he should be so inclined, which I own I suspect. Nothing, I think but such a disposition, or a want of judgment scarcely credible, could induce him to throw cold water upon petitions. It is from them and other demonstrations of the opinion without doors that I look for success.[26]

Fears deepened when Wilberforce became seriously ill in January 1788. He tried to keep working from his sickbed but suffered a relapse of what seems to have been ulcerative colitis. One eminent doctor gave him less than a year to live, another a fortnight. It was opium, a commonly prescribed painkiller of that day, which saved him and he took a controlled dose of it daily for the rest of his life. At the beginning of April he was sent to Bath to take the waters with a promise from Pitt to introduce abolition in the House in his place.[27]

Before leaving London, Wilberforce arranged a conference between Clarkson and Pitt. Concealing his already serious interest, for whatever reasons, Pitt grilled Clarkson in two intense sessions, possibly to test him for future quizzing by the privy council. Clarkson armed himself with books, papers and his precious sample chest. Pitt seemed especially moved by more than 100 pages of muster rolls listing seamen's names and their fates. In the long struggle ahead there were those who expressed doubts about Pitt's commitment but Clarkson was never one of them. He spent many hours with the prime minister 'in his closet' and always found him 'hearty in the cause'.[28]

The privy council inquiry opened with evidence supporting the slave trade. Pitt assured Clarkson that any witness he might bring would be heard next. Unfortunately, Clarkson's list was short: James Ramsay, John Newton, the Dean of Middleham and his Bristol friends Harry Gandy and Falconbridge. He had high hopes of Robert Norris who had been so helpful in Liverpool but discovered to his chagrin that Norris had come up to London to speak for Liverpool's slaving interest. 'Though the Liberty of Negroes seems now to be the favorite Idea, the Liberty of Britons to pursue their lawful Occupations should not be forgotten', Norris was now saying. Pitt and Bishop Porteus undermined his credibility by letting it be known that he had furnished quite opposite information to Clarkson.[29]

But the procession of slave-trade witnesses had a devastating impact. '[I]n the higher circles . . . I had the mortification to hear of nothing but the Liverpool evidence, and of our own credulity', Clarkson recollected.[30]

The tide turned when the abolitionists began to appear with two star witnesses procured through George Harrison of the Committee, the eminent Swedes, Charles Berns Wadström and Dr Andrew

Spaarman, who had just returned from a scientific expedition to Senegal.[31]

Meanwhile the delay in bringing abolition to the floor of the Commons was worrying the Committee at the Old Jewry and dismaying the public which had petitioned so clamorously. Lord Hawkesbury, who led the inquiry, was painfully thorough, seeking evidence abroad as well as at home. Procrastination suited the slave trade interests. Two-thirds of the session had slipped by, an impatient delegation from Manchester (consisting of Thomas Walker and Thomas Cooper) was about to descend on the Committee and members knew nothing of Pitt's promise to Wilberforce.[32]

On 8 April, the Committee 'being of Opinion that a Motion should be made as soon as possible' resolved that Clarkson, Sansom and Woods should compose a letter to Wilberforce. When this reached Bath, Wilberforce was too ill to read it and his mother and friends sent word to Pitt to handle everything.[33] Pitt conferred with Granville Sharp on 21 April and the chairman brought unwelcome word to the Committee next day that abolition could not be introduced into the Commons so late in the session. However, Pitt would move a resolution binding the House to discuss the slave trade fully next year. The Committee which kept records on all members and their viewpoints immediately began lobbying MPs. Clarkson had the easy task of calling on Fox but all of them reported a 'very favourable reception'.[34]

When Pitt rose in the House on 9 May 1788 he characterised the slave trade as the most important subject ever raised there and he referred to the petitions expressing deep public concern. Mature deliberation, however, should await the privy council report, he said, and he moved a resolution binding the House to discuss the question early in the next session. Until then he would not express any opinion upon it and he hoped no one else would.[35]

This was too much for Fox, who promptly precipitated the first parliamentary debate on the issue.[36] Calling attention to the table loaded with petitions, Fox denounced the 'disgraceful traffic' which ought not to be regulated but destroyed. Edmund Burke chided the House for not responding earlier to the people's pleas and warned MPs not to let committees of the privy council do their work for them. He, like Fox, favoured abolition of the trade and he further asserted that slavery 'ought not to be suffered to exist'. Sir William Dolben, MP for Oxford University, who had made a horrified personal inspection of a slave ship in the Thames, dwelt on the 'crying evil' of the Middle Passage. He described shipboard horrors of slaves chained hand and foot, stowed like 'herrings in a barrel' and stricken with 'putrid and fatal disorders' which infected crews as well. Ten thousand lives, he warned, might be lost between this parliamentary session and the next unless steps were taken to restrict the numbers carried.[37]

The Liverpool members, Bamber Gascoyne and Lord Penrhyn, chairman of the Standing Committee of Planters and Merchants, along with other MPs advised study and postponement but no one opposed Pitt's resolution when the vote was put.

The exchange was spirited and it had fixed a stigma on the trade. 'Several rose up at once to give relief, as it were, to their feelings', Clarkson recalled. 'They who were heard spoke with peculiar energy, as if warmed in an extraordinary manner by the subject. There was an apparent enthusiasm on behalf of the injured Africans. It was supposed by some, that there was a moment, in which, if the Chancellor of the Exchequer had moved for an immediate abolition of the Trade, he would have carried it that night.'[38] The Committee distributed 10 000 copies of the debate.

Leadership of the cause was now seized by the independent member Sir William Dolben who moved on 21 May for leave to bring in a bill to regulate conditions on board slave ships.[39] He was seconded by Samuel Whitbread. Opposition was slight and the bill quickly passed to its second reading.

Liverpool MPs were willing to consider regulation but the lobby they spoke for demanded an inquiry. The House heard evidence for two weeks. The witnesses for the slave trade were virtually the same as those who had appeared before the privy council. The abolitionists produced no witnesses at all and instead, armed with Clarkson's data on mortality plus a voluminous report which Pitt had commissioned on the dimensions of Liverpool slave ships, drew damaging admissions from the trade's defenders. Sir Charles Middleton and Pitt, but especially William Smith and Henry Beaufoy, led the questioning. Robert Norris was notable for his efforts to show how delightful the slave ships were: '[The slaves] had sufficient room, sufficient air, and sufficient provisions. When upon deck, they made merry and amused themselves with dancing. As to the mortality . . . it was trifling. In short, the voyage from Africa to the West Indies was one of the happiest periods of a Negro's life.'

Examination disclosed that each slave had a commodious 5½ foot by 16 inch space to lie in, spent up to 16 hours of every 24 chained to his neighbour and the deck, and after a meagre meal of water, yams and beans was forced to jump in his irons (or 'dance') for exercise.

Traders pleaded that they would be ruined if they could not take two adult men or three smaller persons per ton, but their own figures showed profits from voyages carrying fewer slaves.

The bill fixed the number of slaves in proportion to the ship's tonnage at what was considered a tolerable level. Pitt threatened and cajoled and the bill passed by 56 to 5. It was badly drawn and two more versions were needed before it was acceptable to the Lords. Even then, to get it, Pitt had to warn his cabinet that he would resign if the measure failed. His opponents would not risk the fall of the government on this issue and the bill went through to receive royal assent on 11 July.[40]

Thus was adopted the only legislation affecting the slave trade until abolition itself in 1807. Ironically it was no part of the abolitionists' plan. 'It was the best bill which could be then obtained', Clarkson commented, but 'the survivors, however their sufferings might have been a little diminished, were reserved for slavery.'[41] Under the Dolben Act the slave trade set new records in the next 10 years.

The abolitionists counted gains in public understanding and political expertise and began looking forward to victory in 1789. Wilberforce's health was steadily improving[42] and it was probable that he would be able to attend the new session. If not, Pitt had promised to move the abolition.

Before the privy council adjourned its inquiry for the summer Clarkson was called to testify. Out came his specimen chest with its 'living evidence' as he spun his dream of a lucrative trade to replace slaving. Most of his testimony bore on the peculiarly heavy loss of British seamen. On his tour, 61 individual cases of cruelty had been brought to his attention by seamen from slave ships. 'I speak', he said, 'as a feeling Witness of their Sufferings.'

His statistical analysis of the mortality of seamen in the slave trade, compared to deaths in vessels sailing to the East Indies, Russia, Greenland or Newfoundland, proved that slaving destroyed more seamen in one year than all other trades in two. The slave trade 'cannot possibly rear any Seamen for the State', he asserted. Liverpool alone, despite curtailment of shipping during the American war, accounted for 15 165 seamen lost since 1771 in the 1101 ships that sailed from there to the coast of Africa.

'I assure your Lordships, that in undertaking to lay these Facts before you, I have undertaken a disagreeable Task.... I have no Pique or Prejudice against any Man concerned in this Trade.... I have no Interest or Emolument in Writing.... I shall never deceive you, unless I am deceived myself', he concluded.[43]

The potential of Africa fascinated Clarkson more and more. Both he and his brother John followed closely the establishment of the new settlement that Sharp called the Province of Freedom at Sierra Leone in 1787. Not only would it prove a haven for blacks stranded in Britain who wished to return but for whites who wanted to try their fortunes there. It would become a base for a legitimate Afro-British commerce which would drive out the slave trade.[44] Both Thomas and John Clarkson were among the whites who applied to go to Sierra Leone in 1788. Among others were the Swedish scientists and Falconbridge. In one of his regular letters to the 'Worthy Inhabitants' of the Province of Freedom, Sharp on 16 May 1788 asked them to reserve free lands for these enthusiasts. He recommended Thomas as an 'able, strenuous and successful advocate for the liberty and natural rights of the Negros'.[45] The campaign, thought Clarkson, would be over in 1789.

Clarkson's *Essay on the Impolicy of the African Slave Trade* was published in mid-1788. Perhaps for that reason he sat, about this time, for his first formal portrait at the Charlotte Street studio of Carl Frederik von Breda, another Swedish friend. He is posed with a quill pen, the trademark of this inveterate pamphleteer, and an open copy of *Impolicy*. He gazes gravely into the distance, confident, handsome under a neat powered wig. A friend who bought a print thought the portrait 'extremely like' and painted 'con amore'.[46]

Thwarted in its object of seeing abolition enacted on the strength of popular support, the Committee issued a year-end report to rally its supporters. It had been intended to present this accounting at a general meeting of subscribers in London, but the plan was abandoned on the advice of several members and Wilberforce, who warned against 'giving any possible occasion of offence to the Legislature by forced or unnecessary Associations'. The reports were posted to country supporters, 200 to such strongholds as Manchester, Birmingham and York, but 25 to Liverpool as well. The Committee reported subscriptions totalling £2760 2s 7d and expenditures of £2131 13s 0d. The largest items were printing (£1106 19s 9d) and 'Collecting Information & Evidence, Travelling Charges, subsistence of Evidence during Examination' (£618 10s 6d).[47]

In June Clarkson had presented a plan to blanket the country with county committees but as he looked into it with John Cartwright and Richard Phillips, the costs in time and money loomed too large, and they settled for encouraging letters to places likely to organise and search for evidence on their own while Clarkson toured the south coast. To help inexperienced supporters evaluate potential witnesses, Clarkson drew up a set of 145 questions to put to them, and these were duly printed in neat tables and sent out.[48]

He directed his own attention to the major naval bases where he could use Sir Charles Middleton's introductions and to the towns and villages where navy men lived or retired. Once again evidence was elusive.

'One would have thought, considering the great enthusiasm of the nation on this important subject, that they, who could have given satisfactory information upon it, would have rejoiced to do so', he grumbled.[49]

Little things deflected the timid. When Clarkson took out his pen and ink bottle, his informants became embarrassed or frightened. He was obliged to abandon notes, commit his 145 questions to memory and write down the answers as quickly as he could afterward. His usual blunt approaches sometimes caused them to deny everything and flee. He tried to train himself to an unfamiliar delicacy.[50]

He discovered that those in government service were fully aware of Pitt's deeply divided administration and unwilling, for their own security, to offend either side. After riding 1600 miles and talking with 47 men capable of helping him, Clarkson persuaded only nine to be examined.[51]

Clarkson founded three branch committees on this two-month circuit, at Poole, Exeter and Plymouth,[52] and at Plymouth acquired the prize of the tour, the plan and section of a loaded slave ship, from the local chairman William Ellford. With James Phillips and other Committee members, Clarkson reworked it in London, applying the idea to the *Brookes* of Liverpool. The resulting plan exhibited 482 tightly packed bodies. No space was allowed for 'necessary tubs'. The new regulating act would cut this cargo to

454. On a previous voyage the *Brookes* had carried 609.

Published in April 1789, the startling diagram was distributed far and wide and prints hung in every abolitionist home. Along with the Wedgwood cameo, it fixed the public image of the slave trade. This, Clarkson wrote, was the 'Elysium, which Mr Norris and others had invented for them during their transportation from their own country'.[53]

The privy council resumed its inquiry in November. Clarkson's small haul of witnesses was reinforced by a few from the Committee, others from Wilberforce and still others unearthed by correspondents armed with the 145 questions.[54] In February 1789, with 18 abolitionist witnesses yet unheard, he learned that the privy council was preparing its report. After his pleas, three more were allowed from the anti-slave-trade side. The last was still in the room when James Arnold, the Bristol surgeon's mate, made a dramatic entry. He had returned from Africa only days before with the journal he had promised Clarkson he would keep. Others had testified from memory or hearsay. Arnold had graphic on-the-spot notes. The council agreed to hear him.[55]

The privy council reported on 25 April in 850 dense pages which laid out the conflicting testimony but passed no judgement on it, and it was a monumental task for Wilberforce to master the bulky document before the Commons debate. Ramsay, Clarkson and Dr William Burgh of York toiled with him 'from dawn till long after candle light' over a period of nearly three weeks either in London or at the Middletons' home. Wilberforce got four copies from Pitt which the men divided, each taking a section to condense into notes which Wilberforce could refer to when he opened the debate. Clarkson specialised in the treatment of seamen and the prospects for trade in African goods and produce. Hannah More, visiting Teston Hall at the time, spoke of 'Mr Wilberforce and his myrmidons' closeted by the hour. 'I tell him I hope Teston will be the Runnymede of the negroes, and that the great charter of African liberty will be there completed.' One Sunday Clarkson preached at Ramsay's church.[56]

Defenders of the trade were not idle. Meetings were called, letters swamped the papers (so open to abolitionist propaganda before) and the Africa merchants from Liverpool and Bristol joined with the London Committee of Planters and Merchants to sponsor rallies, petitions and parliamentary lobbying. They portrayed the abolitionists as absurd, the planters as victims of slander and the

Africans as barbarians for whom slavery if not too good was good enough. Frightening estimates of compensation were bruited.[57]

Wilberforce rose to begin the debate in the Commons on 12 May 1789. 'I had not prepared my language, or even gone over all my matter, but being well acquainted with the whole subject I got on', he wrote diffidently afterward. His address lasted for three-and-a-half hours in this, his first appearance as the parliamentary leader of the cause. He was eloquent, and both lauded and supported by Pitt, Fox, Burke and others. The Committee was highly pleased and sent its thanks for his 'unparalleled assiduity & Perseverance'.

Wilberforce did not move for outright abolition of the slave trade but asked approval of 12 propositions summarising the privy council report which had been recommended by Pitt and Grenville. The slave trade's spokesmen were in no mood to yield ground on their implied criticisms and stepped in smartly with demands for a new inquiry by the House, which was finally agreed. Wilberforce said he need not introduce new testimony; the abolitionist case stood. Everyone thought the hearing would be brief, perhaps one sitting. Instead, the slaving interests prolonged it so skilfully that when the House adjourned on 23 June, their witnesses were still testifying. The whole question 'by the intrigue of our opponents' was put over until 1790.[58]

On 20 July Ramsay died, just five days short of his 56th birthday and a martyr to the cause. The last weeks had seen a vicious attack upon him in the national press and his friends were certain that the abuse hastened his passing. In a last letter he told Clarkson, 'Whether [the bill] goes through the House or not, the discussion attending it will have a most beneficial effect. The whole of this business I think now to be in such a train as to enable me to bid farewell to the present scene with the satisfaction of not having lived in vain.'[59]

The Abolition Committee wound up the year with a report declaring 'unanimously & firmly . . . that the evils with which this Traffick stands charged in the clearest Evidence . . . cannot be reached by any thing short of total abolition' as Clarkson had argued in another pamphlet hurried out during the session. The renewal of the Dolben regulating act seemed to prove the point. Obviously disturbed by the evidence of seamen, Parliament made small improvements for them – they would have better food and no longer have to sleep on the open deck or in the rigging. But nothing was done for the slaves.[60]

The unexpected parliamentary *débâcle* left Clarkson weary and inconsolable. Even the 'delay of an hour' in relieving the suffering of slaves struck him as criminal. He could not comprehend how any Englishman could put commercial gain ahead of humanity. Reading into the midnight hours he would weep, grow angry, and pace his room vowing 'perpetual warfare against this impious trade.'[61]

Then, laying aside grief as useless, he offered to travel once more to the north and east, to seek new evidence and encourage the local groups of disconsolate supporters. His journey had barely begun when he was called back to London. Wilberforce and the Committee wanted him to go to France.[62]

5

The Shock of Revolution

The visit by a leading British abolitionist to France in the turbulent winter of 1789 was intended to find out whether the ancient rivals might mutually agree to abolish the slave trade. A visit also would encourage the sister movement at work in Paris. The question often arose in the British debate: if Britain destroyed its trade would it not simply be taken over by France? Humanity would gain nothing, it was argued, while British commerce suffered and the French grew rich.[1]

The 'commotions' which had shaken France since May and the storming of the Bastille on 14 July were reported in the British papers and created widespread interest but very little alarm. It was generally believed that the French were trying nothing more radical than to transform a despotic regime into something more like the British constitutional monarchy.[2] Even the conservative Wilberforce wrote a French friend, 'I sympathize warmly in what is going forward in your country' and until mid-July of 1789 he had planned to go himself. He yielded, however, to the pressure of friends who worried about the safety of someone so close to government. An 'agent whose presence could excite no remark' would serve as well.[3]

Clarkson was perfectly willing to go. 'As I had no object in view but the good of the cause, it was immaterial to me where I went.'[4] After consulting Wilberforce and the Committee, he set out on 7 August 1789. He was to employ a secretary-interpreter in Paris and the cost of the expedition was to be jointly borne by himself, the Committee and Wilberforce.[5]

Clarkson's credentials were impeccable. He was not only the best-informed Englishman on the subject of the slave trade but also the one best known in France through his writing and contacts with men in the French abolition movement which had, in fact, been modelled on the London example. Brissot de Warville (sometimes called the 'Clarkson of France') had written the Committee at its inception[6] and passing through London on the way to the

United States in 1788 he had attended at least one committee meeting, at which he was given introductions to abolitionists in New York and Pennsylvania. The work of the Quakers attracted him during an earlier stay and now he met and was much influenced by Sharp and Clarkson. He was elected a corresponding member of this 'heavenly work' but the Committee decided not to accept his kind offer to raise funds in France.[7] Back in Paris he initiated the Societé des Amis des Noirs with Étienne Clavière as president and early members including the Marquis de Lafayette, Comte de Mirabeau, Duc de la Rochefoucauld, Marquis de Condorcet and M. Pétion de Villeneuve. Lafayette notified the London Committee when the new group was formed and the Committee replied with books.[8] Clarkson, now 29, was to meet the elegant nobleman who had served on General Washington's staff during the American Revolution and become his lifelong friend and correspondent.

As in London, the French abolition leaders devoted much of their time to education, initially publishing translations of English language works by Clarkson, Benezet and Wesley. Clarkson's *Impolicy*, with its argument that the slave trade was untenable, had caused a sensation.[9]

The French trade at the time of Clarkson's journey was at an all-time peak and with the start of organised abolition work, colonial interests were lobbying even more vigorously than usual. Most Frenchmen, however, were much more interested in their swift-moving politics at home than in their distant colonies.[10] This surprised Clarkson.

Clarkson landed at Calais on 7 August and immediately inquired of 'yᵉ Robbers so much talked of' for the British papers had carried news of robbery and murder since the fall of the Bastille. No one knew of any such incidents thereabouts and he went on, unmolested, to Boulogne to spend the night. He travelled on to Paris by the rapid post chaise, sleeping at Amiens and Chantilly before reaching Paris on the afternoon of 10 August.[11]

Calais had looked to him like an English country town at election time, for the citizens and soldiers alike were decked in cockades and he saw these jaunty ornaments all along his route, the only visible sign of the Revolution. The French poor, however, reminded him of the economic crisis at the root of the uprising. He was besieged by beggars everywhere.

If you alighted from your Carriage either at a Village or a Town, you was [*sic*] instantly attacked. Even on the Road ... you did not escape – on rising Ground where your Horses could not trot ... a Number of miserable Persons solicited your Charity.... This degrading sight, while it taught me, as an Englishman, to put a superior Value on the Institutions of my own Country ... taught me at the same Moment to abhor the despotism of the ancient Government of France & ... to feel a lively Interest in the Idea that it had been dissolved.

Strangely, however, the French poor looked much healthier than the poverty-stricken British and Clarkson found an explanation for this as well. He attributed it 'to their abstinence from spirituous Liquor. Everybody knows, who has been in France, it is a rare thing to see a Frenchman drunk.... I never saw any old people, or the description of yᵉ Country Poor, whose faces were so fine, so comely, or so venerable.'

The crucifixes and carved wooden shrines to the Virgin on the roadsides annoyed him deeply. The people he saw kneeling before them were in a 'state of Slavery'. He rejoiced that the Revolution might foretell the 'dawning of the Day when religion would be kept open to free Enquiry ... when all the superstitious shackles would finally drop to yᵉ Ground'.

At Chantilly Clarkson was diverted by a tour of the Prince of Condé's magnificent home; the stables alone – with 300 horses in them – were as large as George III's palace. The prince had fled abroad. The woods about, protected by the rigorous French law, were teeming with game. When Clarkson made the return journey six months later 'not a Hare, Pheasant or Partridge was discoverable.... The peasantry about had taken the liberty of destroying them either for their pleasure or their food.'

Dropped in Paris at the Hôtel de l'Europe, Clarkson drank a dish of coffee and joined the lively crowds on the boulevards. British accounts had spoken of gloom. He found nothing but gaiety. Fire-eaters, troupes of actors and dancing bears entertained a 'People whose Hearts appear'd light & happy beyond Description'. He found his way to the Bastille where crowds wandered freely through the grim prison. Workmen had started to tear down the battlements and the sightseers gleefully helped by wrenching out stones and hurling them into the ditch below. Clarkson found a Latin inscription scratched on a stone in the wall of a prisoner's

cell, readable but for the name of the captive: ' — — wrote this Line
in the anguish of his heart' and paid two workmen to prise it out of
the wall. He brought it home to England.

Except on the personal level, for Clarkson's political philosophy
was enriched by his first sight of France, his mission was a failure
since abolition of the slave trade did not even reach the floor of the
National Assembly, much less pass. In a sense, he felt, he had
wasted his time.[12]

He was welcomed warmly by the French abolitionists who were
at first glance a more distinguished body than their British counter-
parts but because there were such insatiable demands upon their
time – many were members of the National Assembly which
seemed to sit continuously at Versailles or involved in municipal
affairs at the Hôtel de Ville – committees were thinly attended. His
friends were certain that once the Revolution was secure, abolition
would follow as a natural consequence of an enlightened government. A Declaration of the Rights of Man had been adopted in
August 1789 asserting that all men were born and remained free
and equal.

Much of the time, Clarkson acted alone. Although the first
minister, Jacques Necker, was too busy to give more than a few
minutes to a deputation, he invited Clarkson to dine occasionally
and when Necker was away, Mme Necker spoke for him.

With great difficulty Clarkson arranged a meeting to discuss
strategy and after prolonged argument, the consensus was that
while the subject of abolition might properly be raised in the
National Assembly it would be better to leave a decision to the
legislature which would succeed it in March 1790. A controversial
measure rushed through in this heated atmosphere might jeopar-
dise the Revolution. Opponents would claim that French commercial interests were being sacrificed to Britain's. Everyone knew that
the House of Commons, after 18 months' consideration, had not
yet acted on abolition. Clarkson wanted to know whether it would
be harder to carry the motion in the new legislature. They thought
not; the Constitution was greatly admired and under it the slave
trade could not stand. However, pugnacious Mirabeau, who was
not present, decided to introduce a motion in the Assembly and he
had many questions to put to Clarkson.

For days Clarkson had been questioning Geoffroy de Villeneuve,
aide-de-camp to the Chevalier de Boufflers, Governor of Goree, who
accompanied Wadström and Dr Spaarman on their expedition up

the Senegal. He was a mine of new material on African society and on slaving. Combining his own knowledge with Villeneuve's, Clarkson inundated Mirabeau with a series of twelve letters, each 16 to 20 pages long, between November and January.[13] Mirabeau usually responded with lavish praise. But when Mirabeau sounded out other members of the Assembly, he was disappointed to find that every one had been canvassed by the planter-lobby so successfully that out of 1200 he had only 300 firmly on his side. Another 500 would support him if England also acted. He asked Clarkson to take a letter to Pitt explaining this dilemma. Clarkson doubted that Pitt would or could reply.

As at home, Clarkson found that in Paris he had to placate fears that abolitionists aimed to destroy the institution of slavery, not just the traffic in slaves, but in Paris he added that the Revolution 'can never be kept from the Negroes' and 'should they rise, the proprietors would lose their estates entirely and France its colonies'.

He pleaded that France should abolish the trade whether Britain did so or not. France's 'Honour and Her Reputation are at Stake'. He pointed out that the British Parliament had twice acted to regulate its slave trade and he predicted 'by the third Blow it will inevitably fall'.[14]

With the help of the eminent committeemen and their female 'honorary and assistant' members he distributed 1000 copies of the famous slave-ship plan, 500 copies of Wadström's illustrations of episodes in slaving and 1000 copies of his own *Impolicy*. The Archbishop of Aix was so horrified by the slave-ship drawing that he was nearly rendered speechless. Mirabeau ordered a wooden model of it for his dining room. It was a yard long with little carved figures of men and women painted black stowed tightly into it.

The beleaguered King expressed interest and Necker gave him copies of Clarkson's book in English and French as well as samples of African manufacture loaned by de Villeneuve, but the slave-ship section was thought to be too unsettling for him. Louis XVI was a virtual prisoner and unwell.

While Clarkson's various activities stiffened his friends in the cause, they also incited its powerful enemies. Clarkson became a personal target of abuse. Like other abolitionists he received a threat that he would be stabbed to death and it was whispered that he was a British government spy. In such dangerous times such stories had to be taken seriously. Lafayette, head of the Paris

National Guard, advised him to move to the Hôtel de York, nearer his own headquarters, and offered him the protection of the guard.

Early in his stay, Clarkson dined at Lafayette's table with six 'Deputies of Colour' from the rich sugar island of Saint Domingue (also called San Domingo then and now Haiti), all of whom were wearing the uniform of the Paris National Guard. He found them genteel and well-informed. They told him that since the whites of the colony were represented in the National Assembly, they were seeking equal representation for mulattoes. They were ardent abolitionists and knew and admired Clarkson's work. Later they visited him at his hotel and he learned of their deepening frustration as their hearing was repeatedly and mysteriously cancelled.

One of them, Vincent Ogé, threatened, 'We can produce as good soldiers on our estates as those in France. Our own arms shall make us independent and respectable.' Clarkson counselled patience and moderation 'as the best gifts I could leave them . . . for . . . with patience their cause would ultimately triumph'. They thanked him and gave him a souvenir trinket but he could see how unsatisfied they were.

'If the planters should persevere in their intrigue, and the National Assembly in delay, a fire would be lighted up in St Domingo, which would not easily be extinguished', he surmised.

Three months later Ogé returned home and led an unsuccessful uprising. The colonial authorities broke him on the wheel and cut off his head and a 'bloody war commenced'.[15]

Frequent letters to Wilberforce and to the Committee had kept his colleagues informed of his French sojourn until in February 1790 the Committee called him home.[16] As he made his farewells, Lafayette expressed Clarkson's own thoughts.

> He hoped the day was near at hand, when two great nations, which had been hitherto distinguished only for their hostility would unite in so sublime a measure [abolition]; and that they would follow up their union by another, still more lovely, for the preservation of eternal and universal peace. . . . Thus the revolution of France, through the mighty aid of England, might become the source of civilization, of freedom, and of happiness to the whole world. No other nations were sufficiently enlightened for such an union, but all other nations might be benefited by it.

Brissot saw him to his carriage. Although the sentiment was not wholly reciprocated, Clarkson had become attached to the highly moral young man who had the plain manner and appearance of a Quaker. Like Clarkson he was a prolific pamphleteer and like the Englishman, too, he was often quixotic and credulous. Brissot made fun of Clarkson's first essay on slavery for spending 20 pages proving that Africans were descended neither from Cain nor Ham and he cut the book severely in translation.[17] Clarkson judged everyone by his or her attitude to abolition and because they were all in the same sacred cause he could respect Mirabeau and overlook his moral defects, admire Lafayette and never see his limitations and cherish Brissot in spite of his priggishness. He treasured the letters of his French friends and when the Revolution had removed many of them, showed their writings to English friends, perhaps in some way to illustrate the idealism of the early days of the Revolution.

Clarkson was wanted at home to amass evidence for the resumed House of Commons inquiry but the hearings became bogged down by a slow parade of slave trade witnesses which lasted into April. Clarkson discovered that nine of the sixteen witnesses he had intended to produce were lost (one dead and eight at sea) and he spent three weeks on the road interviewing possible replacements, persuading three to come to London.[18]

A search for a single witness took another three weeks and it illustrates the astounding persistence of the man.[19] The background was this: conflicting pictures had been given so far of the method of obtaining slaves in the Calabar and Bonny Rivers. When slave ships lay offshore, fleets of well-armed canoes manned by Africans swarmed inland and returned with slaves to fill the ships. The traders said that the captives were purchased at African fairs or markets. Why, then, were the canoes armed and why were they not loaded with trade goods for barter?

Clarkson was told of one sailor who had been on such a slaving expedition. He was now in the navy on a ship out of commission but his name, rank and port were unknown. The challenge was irresistible: Clarkson 'felt myself set on fire'. No one but a zealot would have set out on such a wild-goose chase, but Clarkson obtained from Sir Charles Middleton permission to board every ship laid up in the royal docks and started his hunt at Deptford. He rode on to Woolwich, Chatham, Sheerness and Portsmouth and finally hurried to Plymouth, his last hope. He boarded, in all, 317 ships and interviewed all their skeleton crews before, on the frigate

Melampus, finding his man, one Isaac Parker, shipkeeper. Parker had indeed seen villages attacked and their inhabitants seized at gunpoint. Clarkson returned to London in triumph with Parker and five other witnesses found along the way.

When Parker was called and identified himself as a shipkeeper, the slave trade supporters in the committee room roared with laughter, Clarkson recounted later to a friend.

'Will you bring your 'Ship-keepers, Ship-sweepers, and Deck-cleaners in Competition with our Admirals and men of honour?' they demanded. Wilberforce, who conducted the examination with William Smith, replied coolly, 'Gentlemen, you have examined your Admirals and I will examine Isaac Parker and doubt not but there will appear as much Honour, as much Truth, and as much to the Point in the Evidence of Isaac Parker as in any, or all of your Admirals together'.[20]

The presentation of the abolition side was interrupted by a confrontation between Clarkson and Robert Norris of Liverpool.[21] Norris, stung by widely-circulated reports of his perfidy before the privy council, wished to justify his conduct, and Clarkson was urged to counter him. Norris claimed he had talked to Clarkson only out of courtesy to their mutual friend William Rathbone and accused Clarkson of asking him to recommend Falconbridge for command of a slave-ship, which Clarkson flatly denied. He testified to the important information Norris had given him and recalled the great confidence he put in it. He showed the committee his notebook: 'he dictated and I wrote . . . with his own pen and ink, and in his own room'. Clarkson felt he had the best of the match for Norris appeared to feel disgraced and 'never afterwards . . . looked the abolitionists in the face'.[22]

But the issue lost the attention of Parliament. Claims that emancipation was the real goal, that planters would be ruined (perhaps massacred) and that compensation would cost the nation untold millions gained ground. Rather than cut short testimony supporting his case, Wilberforce agreed to put off further action until 1791. The delay, the abolitionists told one another, was to make sure of victory next time.[23]

The session of 1790 found the Committee working tirelessly. Quarters were taken at the Parliament Coffee House to be closer to the Commons and to Wilberforce. The two Clarksons and William Dickson (Pitt called them 'white negroes', a phrase which Wilberforce adopted as shorthand in his diary but which, one suspects, those so designated would not have chosen) conferred with Wilberforce almost daily. When the House rose, everyone was exhausted. Clarkson had to dictate to clerks from his bed in the final days of the session.[24]

It was curious, however, that as the popularity of the cause flagged at Westminster it prospered in the country. The Committee had circulated the slave-ship drawing to great effect and another popular device appeared in William Cowper's poem, 'The Negro's Complaint', which the Committee published with a subtitle 'A Subject for Conversation at the Tea-table'. Thousands were sent out and the poem became a popular song.[25] Slavery was the topic of the day in drawing-rooms, pulpits and debating societies. Yet the Committee had received less than £220 during its third year and was in the red by £94 in July 1790.[26]

Clarkson undertook his interrupted tour through the north. It was to take him 7000 miles, last four months and be remembered as the 'most vexatious' he ever endured. It was harder than ever to find witnesses. He hoped for 100 and secured 20. 'I was disgusted . . . to find how little men were disposed to make sacrifices for so great a cause'. He was a victim to their whims as they blew hot and cold, forcing him to ride hundreds of miles back and forth in hope of a favourable decision. Some 'fled him as they would a wild Beast' and others held out for favours or patronage in return for cooperation. There were noble exceptions, such as the captain who told Clarkson, 'I had rather live on bread and water, and tell what I know of the Slave Trade, than live in the greatest affluence and withhold it.'[27]

As always, Clarkson found comfort in the homes of Quakers. At Yanwath near Penrith he spent a few days with Thomas Wilkinson, a farmer and poet. Sitting at Wilkinson's fireside, Clarkson described the state of the cause, Wilberforce's great exertions, Pitt's firm backing and his own experiences on the tour and in France. Wilkinson read the manuscripts of the interviews which Clarkson regularly forwarded to Wilberforce.

'I never in my Life saw a Man so devoted to any Cause as T Clarkson is to that which he has undertook', Wilkinson told a friend. 'He seems sensible his Constitution is wearing out fast, yet seems perfectly satisfied with being the slave of slaves, and would not Chainge it for any other. He says he should be thankful if he should be favoured to live out the ensuing Session of Parliament. . . . as he is a young man I hope he yet may see several years'.[28]

But victory eluded the abolitionists again in the spring of 1791 in spite of intense preparation. If we search today for an appropriate monument to Thomas Clarkson it stands in the mountain of evidence he accumulated. In addition to the 850 folio pages of the privy council report, there were by mid-1790 some 1300 pages of testimony delivered to the House of Commons, creating an invaluable source for historians. Clarkson believed that the accumulation of knowledge about this 'monstrous inequity' was good in itself and would inform posterity whatever use Parliament might make of it in his generation.[29]

For the 1790–91 session of Parliament, the Committee again took temporary rooms nearby, at 9 New Palace Yard.[30] In February 1791 Wilberforce moved that the House hear further testimony. The West Indian interest declared that the House had heard enough but Wilberforce pointed out that of the 81 days devoted to hearings so far, trade supporters had occupied 57. After a tussle, he won. Notifying correspondents to be ready to send up witnesses, Clarkson said, 'We expect great opposition . . . but we are not fearful as to the Event.'[31]

Examination began on 7 February with Wilberforce and Smith, as before, serving as counsel. The abolitionist witnesses were often browbeaten, called mercenaries and kept under stiff questioning for days. These were men who had left the trade on principle and Clarkson was proud to record that none was ever seen to 'prevaricate, nor to waver'. In its precise and shocking detail, their testimony rang more true than the 'airy' words of interested parties still in the trade or former guests of the planters.[32] When he wrote the history of the struggle, Clarkson named virtually all who had appeared before the privy council or a Commons committee – 69 heroes of the abolition.[33]

An abridgement of the evidence was rushed to completion by an extraordinary combination of Committee members, Wilberforce's friends and fellow MPs, and a copy was delivered to every MP before the debate came on.[34] The feelings of the abolitionists at this point were 'almost insupportable', Clarkson recalled, for in spite of every effort they could make, the cause was visibly losing ground in Parliament. Fear and prejudice took over. The times, too, were working against them. The French Revolution, now two years old, was terrifying the British propertied classes and kindling hopes among many less fortunate. 'The very book of the abridgment of the evidence was considered by many members as poisonous as that of the Rights of Man', said Clarkson.[35]

On 18 April 1791 Wilberforce introduced a bill to abolish the slave trade in a brilliant speech supported by Smith, Fox and Pitt. Lord John Russell and Colonel Tarleton of Liverpool led the opposition – 'a war of the pigmies against the giants of the House' – but a silent majority moved into the lobbies at 3.30 a.m. on 19th April and defeated the motion by 163 to 88.[36]

The Abolition Committee met a week later with full hearts and in 'solemn dignity'. It hailed the 'Illustrious Minority' and sent particular thanks to Wilberforce for his 'unwearied exertions' and to Pitt, Fox, Montagu and Smith for their 'virtuous and dignified cooperation'. It pledged that it would 'never desist ... till the commercial intercourse with Africa shall cease to be polluted with the blood of its Inhabitants'.[37]

In a letter to Mme Lafayette (titles were gone) Clarkson bravely forecast that it would be impossible next time to ignore the 'voice of the people'. As for France, he hoped 'that your Revolution will be established beyond the Possibility of being shaken by any human Power'. He added, 'There cannot be a more enviable thing ... than the Circumstance of seeing a great Nation free and happy.'[38]

In this friendly mood over the unsteady progress of the Revolution, Clarkson attended a dinner at the Crown and Anchor Tavern on 14 July 1791 to celebrate the second anniversary of the fall of the Bastille.

'What business had your friend Clarkson to attend the Crown and Anchor last Thursday?', Henry Dundas, the Home Secretary, inquired testily of Wilberforce. 'He could not have done a more mischievous thing to the cause you have taken in hand'.[39]

At Birmingham, the announcement of a similar dinner at which Joseph Priestley would preside had sent a Francophobe mob raging into the streets. Two Unitarian meeting houses were pulled down and Priestley's home with his library and scientific equipment was burned. The minister's fulmination and the Birmingham riots were not typical of the public mood in the summer of 1791 but they were a portent.

One ray of hope pierced the gloom of 1791. Months of planning to establish an abolitionist beach-head on the African coast came to fruition in an act of Parliament incorporating the Sierra Leone Company. It would be 'one of the greatest Wounds that the Slave-Trade ever received'.[40] It began as a rescue operation for the Province of Freedom which Granville Sharp had nurtured almost single-handedly for the last four years. In April 1790 the little settlement was destroyed in a dispute between an African chief and local slave traders. At the time Sharp was engaged in organising a British agency to trade with the settlers in African produce. It was called the St George's Bay Company after the great natural harbour at Sierra Leone.[41] Unable to get government help to relieve the scattered settlers, the Company sent some relief supplies. More would not be done by the 'mercantile Gentlemen' now involved until they were legally incorporated. This work was stimulated by the arrival in London of Thomas Peters as the delegate of black Loyalists now living in Nova Scotia who wanted to join the Province of Freedom. With 99 subscribers and a capital of £100 000 the Sierra Leone Company (as it was now called) received its charter from Parliament. Most of the Abolition Committee members took out shares as did benevolent merchants and bankers. Wilberforce and Clarkson each had 10 shares at £50 each and both were elected as directors.[42]

Shares were eagerly sought and Clarkson worried that some would fall into the hands of West India merchants. Tipped off that an attempt would be made at one subscribers' meeting to seat a West India director Clarkson hastily rounded up proxies from country shareholders and offended Wilberforce's good friend the Reverend Thomas Gisborne in the process. He asked Gisborne for his proxy without troubling to say why. Gisborne, who scarcely knew Clarkson at this point, complained to Wilberforce about this offhand treatment and the MP, who erred on the side of emollience, scribbled on the back of the letter – as if it were an old story to him – 'Gisborne justly suspicious of Clak's prudence – & resenting his impudence'.[43]

The nature of the colony was radically altered as evangelical businessmen replaced Sharp. To attract investors the government was taken out of the settlers' hands and placed in the Company's in London. Sharp had to accept a number of 'humiliating changes' or leave his infant colony destitute.[44] In August 1791, the Sierra Leone Company sent John Clarkson to Nova Scotia to arrange the transport of the black Loyalists. Of the two brothers, John was the one who was to realise their joint dream of seeing Africa. He became Thomas's eyes and ears as he investigated the slave trade, studied African society and guided the small Christian settlement in its first year.[45]

When Thomas Clarkson first read Benezet's *Some Historical Account of Guinea*, the opening words: 'Guinea affords an easy living to its inhabitants, with but little toil' made an indelible impression. His own research had reinforced the image of tropical fecundity. From everything he could learn, Africa offered boundless prospects for honourable ties to the western world once the distortion of the slave trade was driven out. The influential report he delivered to the Company proprietors, illustrated with maps and his tantalising specimen collection, quickened hopes that for once philanthropy would pay rich rewards.[46] He stuck closely to his brief of delineating the outlook in specific lines of trade and the 'civilising' role didn't enter until page 30 of his 36 pages when he observed that the same network of communication established to obtain 'all the Riches of Africa' would be the means for diffusing 'Precepts of Justice and extirpating the Trade in Men' and also opening the way to the Christian missionary.

Clarkson pictured shiploads of sugar, cotton, indigo, tobacco, oils, waxes and gums, spices and woods, gold and ivory leaving the bustling Sierra Leone waterfront for the London markets. Vineyards and whaling could be introduced. Coastal and river trading, even caravans of mules or camels, would link the colony to the great trade routes crossing Africa. He assured his audience of business-minded men that 'no Country affords a finer Prospect to the Merchant'. None of its products would be so profitable as sugar. If cultivated and manufactured by free men, not slaves, managed by men trained in the East – not the West – Indies who understood free labour, Sierra Leone sugar could show profits of 100 to 300 per cent.

Clarkson's Plan of Trade assumed that the Africans would be friendly, the slave traders indifferent, and the administrators sent by London competent, but the fact that none of these assumptions proved perfectly correct does not tarnish the fact that Sierra Leone survived its vicissitudes as the first British colony in Africa and the only one founded out of benevolence with the participation of blacks.

6

Raising the National Voice

I had the honour of seeing Mr Clarkson. My Brother went to Shrewsbury with the expectation of meeting him & they arrived here together about 10 o'clock at night. I was prepared to see with admiration a man who had now for some time given up all his own secular pleasure, & that too at a time of life when many think of little else, that he may dedicate his whole time to the glorious object of abolishing the African Slave trade – And, whatever his external appearance & manners had been it wou'd not have lessen'd my idea of him, as that was founded on the qualities of his head & heart which his conduct had established beyond a doubt – but I found him amiable & courteous in manners, above the middle size, well made & very agreeable in his person with a remarkable mildness of voice & countenance.

This is how Katherine Plymley on 20 October 1791 began her remarkable diary. 'Deeply interested in the abolition of the slave trade & impress'd with the most exalted idea of the character of Mr Clarkson', she decided, when he came to her village of Longnor in Shropshire for the first time, to 'assist my memory by written memorandums' on the progress of the movement and especially her brother's part in it.[1] She was 33 at the time, two years older than Clarkson, and her brother, the Reverend Joseph Plymley (later Corbett, after inheriting the large Longnor estate from an uncle) was a year younger. Until it ends in 1827, her diary is an invaluable aid to assessing Clarkson's character, accomplishments and impact in the country. It is also a welcome reminder that the abolition movement was far more than its leaders and blessed with numberless unheralded families like the Plymleys who devoted time and trouble to a controversial cause at no little cost to themselves. They supported, and sometimes guided the leading figures. Clarkson visited and heartened these enthusiasts while also attracting converts. Through him they learned the latest developments, the parliamentary prospects and the character of the public men involved. He in turn was strengthened by the knowledge and encouragement they passed on to him.

Soon after Clarkson's prize *Essay* was published in 1786, Joseph Plymley and his sister read it with interest and when the Committee was announced, Plymley offered his services. Early in 1788 he organised petitions from the clergy in each of the two Shropshire archdeaconries. The Committee sent material to him to insert in the Shrewsbury papers and he wrote occasional paragraphs himself. In London early in 1790 he met the Committee, attended the Commons inquiry to hear Clarkson testify and observed sessions of the House. In 1791 he was elected an honorary and corresponding member. When Parliament defeated the 1791 motion to abolish the slave trade, Plymley arranged a public meeting in Shrewsbury on 13 July to affirm the continuing concern for abolition in this part of Shropshire. The meeting followed the Committee's lead in thanking Wilberforce and others of the 'illustrious minority' and acknowledged also the service of previous labourers, 'especially the Rev Mr Clarkson whose early and indefatigable exertions' had led to widespread conviction that abolition 'is required not only by religion and morality but by every principle of sound policy'.

The ostensible reason for Clarkson's 1791 tour, which had him crisscrossing England and Wales and visiting Glasgow while Dr William Dickson travelled through other parts of Scotland, was to promote the use of a new easy reference work, an abstract he had prepared of abolition evidence. It was his fifth journey and he covered 6000 miles.[2]

What, in fact, both men did was to galvanise public opinion and lay the groundwork for an avalanche of petitions to coincide with the next parliamentary move in 1792. New committees were set up in Newcastle-upon-Tyne, Nottingham and Glasgow and public meetings were called.

'Of the enthusiasm of the nation at this time none can form an opinion but they who witnessed it', Clarkson wrote afterwards. 'There never was perhaps a season when so much virtuous feeling pervaded all ranks. Great pains were taken by interested persons in many places to prevent public meetings. But no efforts could avail.'[3]

Wilberforce seemed now to be convinced that only public clamour would move a Parliament driven, not by party discipline or universal suffrage but by landed and commercial interests. His original plan had been to move abolition shortly after Parliament met and then, after a predictable defeat, 'sound the alarm throughout the land'. With a huge manifestation of public support the abolitionists could 'carry something important' before the session closed. Later he decided to call for the petitions first, then move to abolish the slave trade. Supporters were to 'excite the flame as much as possible in a secret way' but not to allow it to do more than smoulder until he gave the signal.[4]

In his unaccustomed guise as a 'radical', Wilberforce did not throw caution to the winds. He had no desire to encourage 'political impulses' and thought that petitions could be confined to the 'educated and religious classes' at well-managed county meetings. He suggested that petitions be framed in such general terms that they could be signed by those who recoiled from the idea of banning the trade at once.[5]

On his travels, Clarkson also spread news of the Sierra Leone Company. The Reverend William Mason, preaching in York Minster after Clarkson left his city, 'contrived (by a sort of Lyrical transition in my sermon) not only to applaud the plan of that new Colony, but also to exhort my Audience to renew their petitions for the abolition'.[6]

'Who do you think we had in yesterday but T Clarkson who has been disseminating the Abstract through all the realm I trust with such effect that it will grow up & ripen to an abundant harvest', William Burgh reported to Wilberforce from York, enclosing money for his subscription to the Company. 'He has been writing to recommend rather than solicit Petitions to numerous Places & having visited many others is confident that in all of them he has succeeded.'[7]

Clarkson spent a week in York. He gave William Tuke 'most satisfactory information concerning the Sierra Leone Comp^y which if Parliament should still refuse will probably in a few years oblige the West India Planters not only to abolish the Slave Trade but slavery itself . . . or find themselves under the necessity of selling their produce for Loss.'[8]

He stayed in Shropshire only two days before departing for Birmingham, Chester and Liverpool. When he sent word from Worcester that he was coming, Plymley hastily invited members of the local abolition committee to dinner the next day. Clarkson spent the morning writing and when he met the company at 3 o'clock he gave a 15-minute talk to lead off the discussion. At tea the conversation continued in the same vein and it was only after the guests had left and Clarkson had retired to write for an hour, then walk in the garden, that he joined the rest of the family for a general chat as they sat down to a 9 o'clock supper. The regularity of his habits intrigued Katherine Plymley and he showed 'those little courtesies which make society pleasing', she found. He was so simple and modest in manner that he made one 'almost forget the superiority of his character'. She said he was easier to talk to than anyone she had ever known.

Clarkson and Plymley were to leave at 7 a.m. the next day to call on the generous Quaker ironmaster, William Reynolds, at Coalbrookdale. When Katherine and her sister Ann came down at that hour Clarkson was alone in the parlour, having risen at 6 a.m., written several letters and drunk a basin of milk. Her brother had only just gone into his dressing room. 'If I had known Mr Plymley wou'd not have been quite exact', Clarkson said to the ladies, 'I cou'd have written some letters.' He could still write one or two, Katherine ventured, and 'whilst he went for his papers, Ann & I with pleas'd alacrity ran for a table & desk. . . . When he sat down to write . . . he said, "now we shall gain time if you will seal the letters". I felt elated with the thought of doing any thing for him & answer'd that I will, & think myself honour'd by so doing'.

Back at Longnor after the excursion, Clarkson dined and was taken by chaise to Shrewsbury to have tea with other abolitionists. Plymley had many connections at Chester and planned to join Clarkson there in a few days. When Clarkson left Shrewsbury, plans were complete for organising petitions, seeking witnesses, circulating publications and keeping the issue in the local press, beginning with selections from the evidence. It was agreed to pay the local editor a half-guinea a week for regular space and weekly after Clarkson's visit, items appeared in the *Shrewsbury Chronicle*.

Katherine filled pages of her 'Memorandum Books' with Clarkson's observations and political gossip, such as:

The King is not with us & all the Princes are against us. They are all brutes, except the Prince of Wales . . . he I believe has some tenderness in his disposition. But he is persuaded to think favourably of the Slave trade. Fox has not his ear now.

I . . . am entirely convinced [Mr Pitt] is hearty in the cause but the divisions in the cabinet were so great that it was impossible for him to do more than an individual, for he cannot issue out a treasury letter unless the cabinet are unanimous, cou'd he have done that we shou'd have carried it, for many of the members wou'd have voted, had he pleas'd, that black was white.

Very many members having been brought to promise the West India planters to vote against the abolition, perhaps over a bottle, & had never read the evidence, when they . . . heard the arguments on the other side . . . wou'd have wished to have voted contrary to their engagements . . . but the planters were at the bar reminding them of their promise. They were therefore desirous to wipe off the stigma . . . & voted in favour of . . . the Sierra Leone Company.

Clarkson's comments on the French Revolution were scrupulously recorded, too. 'France will be the first country in the world', said Clarkson, and Katherine Plymley put him down as a 'favourer of liberty in every respect'. Burke's *Reflections on the French Revolution*, the first substantial criticism of the trend in France, had been published a year before, answered shortly by Thomas Paine's *Rights of Man*, and opinions tended to harden around one extreme view or the other. Clarkson felt that Burke, advocate for American independence and a highly respected legislator, had given an inaccurate account of affairs in France during the period of his own stay there while Paine 'has not at all exaggerated' but 'may have colour'd higher & not gone beyond the truth'.

Meeting people of all classes on his travels, Clarkson thought he knew the nation's mind and he had discovered far greater interest in the Revolution in 1791 than in the year before. A year ago those who mentioned it at all thought it would fail. This year, in general, they spoke favourably of it.

It was exactly the same in the American war, the Reverend Theophilus Houlbrooke, one of the guests at Longnor, remarked. Only the 'more enlighten'd & thinking minds' approved the colonists' independence at first 'but now that they have . . . establish'd their freedom almost all . . . think that they were in the right.'

Clarkson indicated his sympathy for the French when he met the Reverend Hugh Owen and others at Shrewsbury. Plymley had dropped him at Owen's house and only learned afterwards of the shock he gave his brief acquaintances. The group at Owen's 'happen'd to be of high monarchical principles, & having conceiv'd a horror of Revolutions were quite alarm'd'. Although Clarkson had said he was only reporting views he had collected on his tour, they described him as a 'revolutionist'. Plymley was worried that such talk would make organising petitions much harder and called on each of them to assure them that Clarkson was far from wishing for a British revolution.

When he joined Clarkson at Chester, he suggested it might be better to avoid the topic of the French Revolution. 'Our object is quite abstracted from all political parties & we must be careful how we involve it with any other question'.

The artless Clarkson, who had stopped in Staffordshire to see Wilberforce at Gisborne's home, replied, 'It is singular that almost the first word Mr Wilberforce said to me was this: "O Clarkson, I wanted much to see you to tell you to keep clear from the subject of the French Revolution & I hope you will".' He referred (not by name) to Dundas's protest about Clarkson's presence at the Bastille Day dinner three months before. Wilberforce had also heard criticism from his friend and mentor Dr Isaac Milner who, after a long talk with Clarkson, wrote Wilberforce: 'I wish him better health, and better notions in politics; no government can stand on such principles as he . . . maintains. I am very sorry for it, because I see plainly advantage is taken of such cases as his, in order to represent the friends of Abolition as levellers. . . . levellers certainly are friends of Abolition'.[9]

At Chester, therefore, Clarkson was mute on France but everyone else where they supped with abolitionist friends chatted happily about it, well-wishers all. Clarkson murmured afterwards that he, perhaps, could safely have joined in, but Plymley wouldn't have it; it would be even more improper in such company for 'they cou'd be so glad of the sanction of your name they wou'd mention your opinion every where'.

'I shou'd think it was quite consistent with an enemy to Slavery to rejoice in the French having acquir'd liberty', Clarkson persisted. 'But', said his friend, 'there are prejudiced people who cannot see *that*.'

So long as Clarkson had any reason to hope that the French would act on abolition in the new climate, he refused to condemn the Revolution. The Plymleys never doubted that he abhorred violence and hoped for reform, not revolution, in his own land. Katherine concluded that the 'intense reflection he has so long given to the evils of slavery & his ardent desire to promote the good of his fellow creatures may lead him strongly to wish every government may be so constituted that each individual may enjoy as equal a share of freedom as possible'.

For a man of 31, Katherine thought, Clarkson looked quite worn and when she asked about his health he told her with 'mild chearfulness' that it was 'quite gone'. He seemed to be developing an ulcer and needed to eat at frequent intervals. He delighted the Archdeacon's children by taking their questions seriously. Panton was inspired to start reading Clarkson's first *Essay* and when it was time to leave, with the chaise at the door, Clarkson abandoned his habitual punctuality to loiter with them. Panton, aged 6; Josepha, 5; and Jane, 4, crowded around him begging him to stay to rest or to return soon.

'Perhaps no child was ever more caress'd than Jane', her aunt wrote, 'yet she appear'd to think she cou'd not (after he was gone) too often tell us where he stood when he took leave of her & put his arms around her neck.' Whenever afterwards she put together the children's wooden map puzzle Jane would kiss Cambridgeshire because it was where he came from.

Among innovations that distinguished the abolitionist campaign of public agitation was the boycott of West Indian slave-grown sugar. Like petitioning, it did not originate with Clarkson but he grasped the idea enthusiastically and exploited it without asking or receiving the Committee's sanction. After the Commons defeat of April 1791 it was one clear way that people could protest.

According to Clarkson, the voluntary ban on sugar was inspired by a pamphlet by William Bell Crafton of Tewkesbury followed by another from William Fox of London which had even more dramatic results. Many other pamphleteers joined the chorus, including Thomas Cooper of Manchester who had thought of it as early as 1787.[10] The general message was simple. The slave trade was morally evil and the people had the remedy in their own hands. Britain consumed more sugar than the rest of Europe together. If a family using five pounds a week (and a similar equivalent of rum) would abstain for 21 months the murder or slavery of one fellow creature would be prevented. Abstention by 38 000 families would stop the slave trade. Parliament might see fit to 'license inhumanity' but the people did not have to be accomplices.

Clarkson ran into Fox's *Address to the People of Great Britain* early on his 1791 tour and was astounded at its impact on readers. In some places as many as 500 families promptly gave up sugar and rum. When he returned to London he sent out a circular letter over his own signature ('I write merely as an individual') urging its readers to promote the *Address* everywhere as an adjunct to petitioning. It would reach people who would never read the collected evidence and it was cheap – a halfpenny a copy or less if bought in quantity.[11]

If in the end petitions should fail again, the boycott would slash government revenues until the people's demand was satisfied. 'Is the cabinet divided against us, and was that the reason of our late defeat?' Clarkson asked. 'If this little book, on a wider circulation should produce but its usual effects, that cabinet must at last concur on the question!'

Having heard this from Clarkson himself the Plymleys had already given up sugar when the circular reached Longnor but Plymley got a Shrewsbury bookseller to order 500 copies. 'We observ'd lately Panton's shoes look'd very brown & found he had given orders that they shou'd not be black'd because he understood Sugar was used in the composition', Katherine wrote.

The Wedgwoods ate East Indian sugar or none, when that was not to be had. William Allen gave up sugar in 1790 and his ban lasted 43 years. Arthur Young's family abandoned sugar for honey, as many did, and the American art of making sugar from the sap of the maple tree was hailed. The Reverend Rochemont Barbauld of Hampstead took his own East India sugar with him when he went out to drink tea so that he would not have to accept any made by slaves. The Babingtons and most of their Leicester friends stuck to East Indian sugar and William Smith gave up sugar entirely and missed it very much.[12] A Birmingham grocer found his sugar sales cut by half in four months, another in Hackney by a third. 'Anti-saccharine principles spread much in France', Cooper reported in his tract.[13] Sugar abstainers were sometimes called anti-saccharists.

'There was no town, through which I passed, in which there was not some one individual who had left off the use of sugar', Clarkson recalled of this movement. He, of course, touched no sugar 'stained with Blood'. 'They were of all ranks and parties. Rich and poor, churchmen and dissenters had adopted this measure. . . . In gentlemen's families, where the master had set the example, the servants had often voluntarily followed it; and even children . . . excluded with the most virtuous resolution, the sweets . . . from their lips.'[14]

He calculated 300 000 persons refused West Indian sugar and there is no reason to doubt it. It is harder to tell whether it made much difference to the slave trade, sugar merchants or government revenues. The Saint Domingue rebellion cut off sugar exports to France, gave a new market there to British traders and pushed prices up, so some families abstained out of necessity. However, imports of East Indian sugar did rise and all those who spurned West Indian crops had the comfort of not sharing the guilt of slavery.[15]

Wilberforce was never happy about direct action and he feared the sugar boycott would alienate moderate opinion. 'Yet it was not without a struggle that the more violent of his followers obeyed his temperate counsels', his sons say in their biography of their father.[16] Perhaps because of his vacillations, the Committee took no stand until June of 1793 when it resolved to recommend that friends abstain from West Indian sugar and rum. In August, the Committee recanted and dropped all action. Finally in June 1795, the Committee with Wilberforce present, exhibited its disenchantment with parliamentary processes by resolving that so long as the slave trade continued 'a decided preference' should be given to East Indian sugar and substitutes should be found for such other exports from the slave colonies as rum, cotton, coffee, cocoa and chocolate.[17]

Petitions calling for abolition poured into Parliament in the opening months of 1792. The gathering-in of the appeals was directed by Clarkson from the Committee headquarters. The cause now depended 'on the virtue of the Community at large'. If Westminster spokesmen were supported by the 'voice of the people' they would prevail over the 'confined Views and narrow prejudices of our opponents', Granville Sharp told correspondents.[18]

Clarkson signed circular letters in mid-January alerting correspondents to the rough timetable for this session and requesting them to send in petitions as soon as they read that Wilberforce had notified the House of his intention to move for the abolition of the slave trade. He specified that the *prayer* of the Petitions should be for the *Abolition of the Slave Trade*.[19] Through March the Committee members diligently prodded supporters and publicised the petitions as they flowed in. They answered attacks as swiftly as they were made, denying yet again that they sought emancipation of the slaves.[20]

News of an uprising in Saint Domingue created the worst

problem. Just as Clarkson had predicted, word of the Revolution in France could not be kept from the slaves in French colonies. In the richest sugar island of the Caribbean – the pearl of the Antilles – unrest spread to the slaves who began in August 1791 to kill masters and burn plantations.[21] The revolt was taken by some as proof that the doctrine of 'rights' was everywhere dangerous. Fears that the carnage would spread to British possessions amounted to panic in some quarters. Wilberforce was pressed to postpone his motion 'on all hands, except by W Smith and the committee who hear little of the matter'.[22]

William Mason of York realised he could not give up 'after the Petitioning Spirit has spread so much. . . . Yet I with sorrow own to you that I have the greatest fears for its success. The St Domingo business . . . has & will affect the Sentiment of many in the house as it has certainly done of many out of it'. He added, 'You will be astonished to know . . . how many there are . . . that either will not or cannot discriminate the abolition of the Slave Trade from the Abolition of Slavery in the West Indies.'[23]

The West India Committee published an account of the insurrection from the planters' viewpoint and Clarkson replied in a paper published by the Abolition Committee in February 1792.[24] He placed the Saint Domingue troubles against a background of slave insurrections before 1786, none of which could have been inspired by a British abolitionist movement. The slave trade, however, could be blamed, for by it thousands 'fraudulently deprived of the Rights of Men' were poured yearly into the islands.

In Shropshire, Joseph Plymley like loyal adherents elsewhere, worked feverishly.[25] When Clarkson's paper on Saint Domingue came in the post he had 650 copies printed for immediate use in the canvass for petition signatures. Clarkson's first letter was followed in rapid succession by others urging 'pray come forward early' and the ardent cleric was engaged in almost ceaseless activity, writing letters, riding around to friends, giving dinner to fellow toilers. Meetings for the county and towns were set up. In the towns the petitions (most of which he wrote) were signed at meetings. For the counties of Shropshire and Montgomeryshire, sheets of parchment were carried around for signature by gentlemen and freeholders 'of weight and credit'. The Shropshire petition reached the House of Commons with 464 signatures and it was nine-and-a-half feet long. Shrewsbury collected 300 names. Each day's press brought news of other petitions arriving in London. Edinburgh's was signed by 9000, Glasgow's by 13 000 and Manchester's by 20 000.

A total of 519 petitions – by far the largest number so far submitted to the House on one subject and in one session – flooded into the Commons. They came from every county, 310 from England, 187 from Scotland and 20 from Wales. Two arrived too late to count. They 'breathed the voice of the people'. The last one – from the livery of the City of London, delayed by various ruses – was delivered breathlessly minutes before Wilberforce began his speech on 2 April.[26] This was the zenith of the public campaign.

Having business in Cambridge, Joseph Plymley decided to take in London, too, so that he could hear Wilberforce make the motion to abolish the slave trade. On Monday, 2 April 1792 he was in the gallery at 11 a.m. and like most of those present he did not leave until the House rose at 7 a.m. next day.[27] Wilberforce began his speech at 6 p.m. and the last speaker, Pitt, ended his 12 hours later. Clarkson was not there. He had tipped a doorkeeper 10 guineas to let in thirty friends of the cause but either failed to save a ticket for himself or couldn't bear to watch. He therefore did not hear the generous tribute Wilberforce pointedly paid to his somewhat controversial colleague as a 'Gentleman whose services in the whole of this great cause can never be over rated'.[28]

For all their certainty that they spoke for the British people, the abolitionists could not shake off an underlying unease. They needed 'good votes as well as good words' from Pitt, as Dr Baker put it.[29] In winding up the debate, Pitt made a thrilling speech supporting Wilberforce. It was thought to be the best of a brilliant lot from the abolitionist side and one of the greatest ever heard in Parliament.[30] The Committee sent 10 000 copies all over the kingdom.[31]

Wilberforce and his supporters thoroughly demolished the arguments purporting to show the value of the trade to Britain. They referred frequently to the collective voice of the people. The defenders of the trade raised the spectre of Saint Domingue and ridiculed the petitions. 'Itinerant clergymen [Clarkson], mendicant physicians [Dickson], and others, had exorted signatures from the sick, the indigent, and the traveller', charged Liverpool's Tarleton.[32]

Then to the consternation of the abolitionists, Henry Dundas proposed an amendment to insert the single word 'gradually' in

Wilberforce's motion. A powerful politician and a secretary of state, Dundas was speaking for the first time on the issue. He protested that he was a warm friend to abolition and differed with Wilberforce only in the means to the end. Yes, the trade should be banned, and probably slavery, too, but moderation must be the rule. The Commons agreed and by 230 to 85 pledged itself 'gradually to abolish' the British slave trade.[33] After a few skirmishes the House fixed 1796 as the year when the trade would end, but it was never to be implemented.[34]

Clarkson and Wilberforce agreed that abolition had no greater enemies than the gradualists and of these Dundas was the most crafty. A Yorkshire abolitionist dubbed him 'Secretary Gradual' and charged that he was attempting to 'bamboozle us, but we won't be bamboozled'. Wilberforce in hindsight judged that it was 'to the fatal appeal [of gradual Abolition] that we chiefly owed the defeat of our first assault and the twenty years' continuance of the murderous traffic'.[35]

The Commons bill was duly transmitted to the Lords who, facing the issue for the first time, stalled in the familiar fashion by voting to examine witnesses. Seven advocates of the slave trade testified before the inquiry was adjourned until 1793. They could easily prolong it indefinitely and probably a majority intended to do just that. Clarkson sent a letter to the Committee's stalwarts on 21 July urging them, 'Pray beat about your Neighbourhood' for anyone who had been to Africa or the West Indies and set out again to find fresh witnesses to replace those now dead or gone away. Dr Dickson again headed for Scotland.[36]

When he reached Longnor on 28 October Clarkson was obviously ill. The journey had been plagued with mishaps and once more he had risked his life. Crossing the Bristol Channel from Ilfracombe to Swansea he had been tossed about in a small boat by a storm and was left badly bruised and chilled. His face was still swollen and painful from the buffeting he had endured.

Furthermore, it had been almost impossible to locate new witnesses for the Lords. With the prospect of the trade being banned in four years' time, every experienced hand was employed and three times as many ships as sailed the year before were now in the hated commerce.

Plymley (who had been elevated to Archdeacon two months earlier) accompanied Clarkson into North Wales and parted with him at Oswestry. Clarkson wanted to press on to Bangor by coach.

It was full, so he climbed on the top. His coat was soaked from the rain of the night before and a servant, also travelling on the outside, offered his master's cloak which Clarkson gratefully pulled around him as the coach drove off.[37]

7

Bitter Times

The shadow of France darkened Clarkson's travels in the autumn of 1792 as the second and bloodier phase of the Revolution began. Prussia and Russia invaded in August, the King sent the army south and in undefended Paris, the mob stormed the Tuileries, killed the Swiss Guard and set up a rebel commune. The royal family were prisoners.

The Convention which replaced the National Assembly in one of its early acts conferred French citizenship upon Clarkson, Wilberforce, Joseph Priestley and Tom Paine and a number of other famous foreigners including George Washington who *'par leurs écrits et par leur courage, ont servi la cause de la liberté et préparé l'affranchissement des peuples'*. It was the last honour Wilberforce wanted and to offset the bad publicity he attended a public meeting to raise money for emigrant French priests. Clarkson was probably of two minds, but is unlikely to have repudiated the tribute, believing as he persisted in doing, that the French would 'soon' abolish the slave trade.[1]

He no longer paraded his views in unfamiliar company but still succeeded in alarming his more conservative colleagues. Earlier in the year he had inquired around confidentially for friends of the Revolution willing to contribute to a fund for the National Assembly. A letter to William Reynolds mentioned £100 000 as the target. Samuel Hoare, the Committee's treasurer, fretted that 'what may be only meant as his own private sentiments, will be construed into an opinion of our Committee'.[2]

Clarkson's hopes died hard. In November he was justifying the reported violence in Paris on the grounds of the King's 'duplicity'.

'He makes little doubt out that an Excellent Republic will be established on ye Ruins of Despotism & arbitrary Power', Elihu Robinson, a Quaker friend of Eaglesfield, wrote in his diary after he had given Clarkson a night's lodging. The idea that the government emerging in France would be a lighter burden upon the people appealed to him strongly.

He apprehends the engines of ye new government will move round with very little Expences & there will be such a saving in ye Sallaries of ye great officers of state compared with those of this Nation that a very moderate taxation will only become necessary.[3]

No year of Clarkson's life began more dismally than 1793. Louis XVI was sent to the guillotine on 21 January, a profoundly shocking event to all sections of British society, and France declared war on 1 February. Against such consequential events it was impossible to compete for public attention and although the Committee exerted itself to alert friendly MPs to be present, Wilberforce's motion that the Commons take up the abolition question lost in February, and in June a bill to stop British merchants from supplying slaves to foreign markets failed by the ignominious margin of 31 to 29.[4] Members were scarcely bothering to sit through the slave-trade business any more.

The Duke of Clarence tried his best to keep abolition off the Lords' calendar, with his usual vehemence branding the abolitionists (and Wilberforce by name) as 'fanatics and hypocrites'. He was so 'miserable an orator', Clarkson observed caustically, 'that it is a disadvantage to any cause he supports'. The Lords continued their desultory examination of slave-trade witnesses but to the seven heard the year before were added only seven more and the session ended.[5]

The early months of 1793 were clouded further by the unexpected rebuff to John Clarkson's hopes. He returned on leave from Sierra Leone only days after the outbreak of war with France.[6] He was unaware that some directors of the Sierra Leone Company had decided to replace him with William Dawes, a straitlaced marine officer, and Zachary Macaulay, a protégé of the Clapham Sect and a severe young man whose first job had been on a Jamaica plantation. John Clarkson's achievement in arranging the migration of more than 1100 black Loyalists from Nova Scotia and, as their much-loved governor, laying the foundations of the new society in West Africa were never publicly acknowledged.

He had every reason to believe, when he sailed to Nova Scotia in 1791, that while forwarding the cause of abolition he might also advance his career. He had devoted much time to abolition work and was elected to the Committee with Wilberforce in 1791. Wilberforce was exceptionally fond of John Clarkson, as the letters he sent during his mission showed, and he had more than once promised to use his influence to obtain a naval promotion for him.

As Wilberforce told John's mother, 'I am bound to him by the Ties of an affection which I trust will last for Life & it will afford me the sincerest & highest pleasure to be instrumental in placing him in a Situation which . . . would be likely to conduce to his comfort.' To John he had written, 'if I have any opportunity of serving you in the Line of your profession I shall be truly happy to embrace it' and, on another occasion, 'what I would do in the case of a brother or any near relation . . . I would do in yours'.

Both Thomas Clarkson and Wilberforce had tried to get a captaincy for John but in the period after the American war, junior officers longing for promotion were two a penny. Following his exploits in re-establishing the colony at Sierra Leone, Thomas believed his brother had an even greater claim and when nothing happened he sent a scathing letter to Wilberforce.[7]

Although by printing parts of it, Wilberforce's sons hoped to demolish Clarkson's reputation, the letter that Clarkson dashed off and Wilberforce's spirited reply, furnish evidence of a far more robust and interesting relationship between the two leaders of the cause than the biographers meant to convey. In the frank exchange, Clarkson was impetuous and tactless, Wilberforce devious and kind, but both are secure in their mutual regard.

The Wilberforces used Clarkson as an example of the trials their father suffered from place-seekers, but influence was everything then and Wilberforce no novice at using the system. One of the penalties for his close friendship with Pitt was to be badgered by appeals.

In the bits of his letter that were printed, Clarkson declared he could not understand why Wilberforce was making no headway with Lord Chatham, first lord of the Admiralty and brother of Pitt, about John's promotion. He went on, 'My opinion is that my Lord Chatham has behaved to my brother in a very scandalous manner, and that your own timidity has been the occasion of his miscarrying in his promotion.'

'Letters will not do', he added sternly, 'and unless personal applications be made you will not serve him.'

Wilberforce's reply (printed in full) blamed Clarkson's heat on 'tender solicitude' for a beloved brother. He dodged the point about calling on Chatham but defended his general policy of hoarding what influence he had for 'opportunities of public service'. He was used to the language of disappointed suitors but had not expected it from Clarkson. However he was glad Clarkson had written so freely and responded in kind so that nothing would 'interrupt the cordiality of our connexion; for unfeignedly do I return your assurance of sincere esteem and regard'. In a conciliatory passage of classic Wilberforcean grace, he added:

> We have long acted together in the greatest cause which ever engaged the efforts of public men, and so I trust we shall continue to act with one heart and one hand, relieving our labours as hitherto with the comforts of social intercourse. And notwithstanding what you say of your irreconcileable hostility to the present administration, and of my bigoted attachment to them, I trust if our lives are spared, that after the favourite wish of our hearts has been gratified by the Abolition of the Slave Trade, there may still be many occasions on which we may co-operate for the glory of our Maker, and the improvement and happiness of our fellow-creatures.

When the letters were penned in late August 1793, Clarkson was in the throes of mental and physical breakdown. He was worried about money as expenses ate into his slim fortune. Rather than borrow, he sold his shares in the Sierra Leone Company to trusted friends and distanced himself further by resigning as a director when the board consulted the government for political guidance before responding to a proposal from the French Convention to protect Sierra Leone shipping. Clarkson believed the colony should be independent of any quarrel between the two powers.[8]

To his illness and chronic fatigue were added distress at the war and the course of the Revolution. Bleakly he went through the motions of planning yet another tour in search of fresh witnesses for the House of Lords inquiry.

Clarkson was realistic enough to know that two or three years of struggle at least lay ahead and it frightened him to think that he might not survive that long.[9] He arranged to leave London in early September. On medical advice it was to be a journey on horseback limited to 600 miles and at a pace of not more than 10 miles a day, with plenty of rest and cold baths. 'He sends his baggage from one large town to another & travels with a few things in his pocket . . . quite alone', Katherine Plymley heard.[10]

Before setting forth, Clarkson unburdened himself to eight

friends and associates, among them Archdeacon Plymley and Wilberforce.[11] The letters differed slightly but the agonised tone was the same. It was the pathetic outpouring of a conscientious mind thrown into turmoil by a rather sudden realisation of his predicament. Exalted ideas of honour and duty which had guided Clarkson for fully seven years were now threatened by the prospect of financial ruin if he carried on with his life's work. He could see no way out of his dilemma, he could only describe it.

He presented his crisis with touching candour. 'My mind has been literally bent like a Bow to one gloomy subject', he wrote.

> The Anxiety . . . the Mental & Bodily Labour connected with it, the vexations, disappointments . . . these, with writing, travelling, sitting up till two or three in the mornings . . . have contributed to make inroads in my Constitution. . . . The whole nervous System has been affected by them. I am often suddenly seized with Giddiness & Cramps. I feel an unpleasant ringing in my Ears, my Hands frequently tremble. Cold Sweats suddenly come upon me. My Appetite becomes all at once ravenous, and, if not almost immediately gratified, I am ready to faint. I find myself weak, easily fatigued, & out of Breath. My recollection is also on the Decline. . . . I feel myself too almost daily getting worse & worse.

If this were all, with care and attention, he probably could prolong his working life except for the drain on his purse. He had spent £1500 so far in the cause, dipping into capital when his income did not stretch far enough, and, as he told Archdeacon Plymley privately when they met, he would have only £1200 left by Christmas.[12]

Clarkson only had himself to blame for his major extravagance, which was sending 'whole Coaches full of Seamen' to London in a futile effort to prosecute cases of barbarous treatment. He had to pay for their lodgings in case they might be needed to testify. The Committee had no funds for such bills. Certain Committee members, notably Samuel Whitbread, had helped[13] but before his letter descended upon them his friends could not have guessed the continual demands made on Clarkson by supporters. Some of the persons brought to London for parliamentary hearings, for example, were not satisfied with the Committee's allowances and Clarkson made up the difference 'lest the Cause should suffer'.

He was continually asked for money by persons who helped procure petitions or evidence. 'Travelling on this Subject I am considered as the Ostensible Person. Mr Wilberforce is unknown for he has no dealings with them. Our Committee escapes also ... & therefore I am the Person applied to ... whose finances are but as a mite compared with those of others, who are conspicuous in this Cause.'

He felt forced to tell them that many who offered help were not 'actuated by pure motives'. They 'eagerly embraced the Opportunity of serving us' in hope of positions or rewards. Having no patronage to give, Clarkson resorted to his own purse. If he retired now, he had enough to live an 'obscure Life'. He asked their advice, whether to carry on (towards ruin and an untimely grave) or to retire, tormented in his own mind and censured by others for abandoning the cause.

To some of his friends, Clarkson mentioned another complication. He could not and would not '(from certain scruples best known to myself) follow the Profession for which I was originally designed'.

Almost as soon as he had read Clarkson's letter,[14] Archdeacon Plymley set out for London to catch Clarkson before he left on his tour. They supped on 3 September and arranged to meet again in Shropshire. 'He is rather better', Plymley assured his family, 'but has too much cause for complaints of all kinds.'

His friends had reacted so sympathetically that Clarkson was comforted and calmed, and ready to let the matter rest. The Archdeacon had other opinions. 'If he retired the cause was absolutely lost ... though Mr Wilberforce knows more of the subject than all the committee together, yet his knowledge is as nothing compared to Mr Clarkson's, who is the link by which it is all managed. Whatever any one know, he knows, by which means he is able to conduct it all.'

The Archdeacon met Clarkson in November at Bishop's Castle, spending two days with him in the neighbourhood of Welshpool, and saw how ill he still was. He would talk animatedly and then appear lifeless with exhaustion. Back at Longnor, Plymley wrote a long letter to Wilberforce suggesting that 'true friends' of the cause and of Clarkson rescue him from 'pecuniary difficulties, since he has given his health & everything to the cause'. Plymley proposed a subscription since Clarkson had ruled out any application to Pitt for a public reward or sinecure. Wilberforce concurred and promised that on his return to London for the new Parliament he would speak to a few friends about it.[15]

The idea of a fund to replace Clarkson's capital occurred also to six of the seven others to whom Clarkson had turned for advice. By 22 January 1794 when he relayed their thoughts to Plymley, the only one Clarkson had not heard from was Wilberforce.[16] Clarkson unhesitatingly accepted the idea of a subscription. Having been contributing 'both fifties & hundreds myself' for years, he said, there seemed nothing improper about being on the receiving end. There was the recent precedent of the £1800 raised on Wilberforce's behalf to pay a legal bill resulting from the trial of Captain John Kimber. 'If he with a large fortune condescends to this, I feel less delicacy in accepting it myself.'[17] Kimber had been named by Wilberforce in the 1792 debate as the Bristol slave-ship captain responsible for a vicious killing of a 15-year-old slave girl. He was tried for murder in June that year in the Admiralty high court and acquitted, to general amazement.[18] The chief witnesses against him, his surgeon William Dowling and the surgeon's mate, Stephen Devereux, were then charged with perjury. They were tried in February 1793, the former found guilty and the latter acquitted although they had given exactly the same testimony. The costs were charged to Wilberforce who proposed a subscription be opened to pay them.

Dowling and Devereux were a great expense to Clarkson during 1793 and partly responsible for his despair when he appealed to his friends. They harried him with abusive letters and upbraided him for starting the investigation of the slave trade in the first place. He was constantly giving them money. Finally Clarkson got Devereux a job on a ship at Sierra Leone and one of the Lloyds of Birmingham gave Dowling £100 to start a new life in America.[19]

Presumably the Wilberforce subscription succeeded. Clarkson's did, too,[20] but not without his own intervention, and this lack of delicacy made some of his friends, even the devoted Miss Plymley, shrink a little. Once convinced the subscription was fair, Clarkson worked as hard for himself as he would have done for others. It was not selfishness but simplicity, a family friend judged. 'In the habit of acting chiefly for others, he acted for himself as if he were another.'[21]

The fund lagged after the first £500. Wilberforce, who had undertaken to contact most of the prospective donors, was busy with other matters. 'Add to which', Clarkson admitted to Wedgwood, 'that entertaining the Notions of Liberty I do, & having totally left the Church, I am as such a political Apostate, that even those who know my Labours in this Cause . . . would not subscribe a single Shilling to anything that personally related to Me'.[22]

Sir Richard Hill received an anonymous letter asserting that Clarkson was a Jacobin and a republican. Plymley told him Clarkson's services spoke for themselves and he belonged to none of the reform societies.[23] Lord Muncaster raised Clarkson's 'principles' with Wilberforce, who remained loyal in spite of Clarkson's chivvying about the slow pace of donations. He replied to Muncaster in a kindly, slightly condescending way:

> The truth is he has expended a considerable part of his little fortune, and though not perhaps very prudently or even necessarily yet I think, judging liberally, that he who has sacrificed so much time, and strength, and talents, should not be suffered to be out of pocket too. We should not look for inconsistent good qualities in the generality of men. Clarkson is ardent, earnest, and indefatigable, and we have benefited greatly from his exertions.[24]

The £1500 was, at Clarkson's suggestion, placed in a Shrewsbury bank and the interest sent periodically by Plymley until about 1803 when the capital was transferred to Clarkson.[25]

It was not enough to be silent now when either British or French politics were talked of. The label of Jacobin – meaning any radical or even reformer – was hung on anyone who did not explicitly support Church and King.

One of the Abolition Committee's first collaborators, Thomas Walker of Manchester, was an early victim of the new treason and sedition acts but Clarkson did not hesitate to call on him when he was in the area in November 1793. Walker had been charged with high treason. 'I have no business in Manchester', Clarkson wrote him, 'but wishing to see you on . . . the impending Tryal, and to go over some points which it may be useful to the Cause to ascertain, it is my Intention to visit you. . . . I am on Horseback. I don't wish it to be known that I am at Manchester, and should therefore like to ride up to your House, and spend the day with you, and be off the next morning.'[26]

Walker was a long-time advocate of parliamentary reform who had become president of the Manchester Constitutional Society formed in opposition to the local Church and King Club. The reformers were a tiny minority in a town where 'No Jacobins Admitted Here' signs hung in the taverns. Walker's house was besieged by mobs four times, and on the last occasion, his friends had gathered there armed with guns to defend themselves. This brought charges against Walker and six others of attempting 'with force of arms' to overthrow the government.[27]

At the trial in Lancaster the following April, the seven, defended by Thomas Erskine, were acquitted to Clarkson's delight but the cost of nearly £3000 almost bankrupted Walker.[28] Six months later Erskine defended Thelwall, Hardy and Tooke with other members of the London Corresponding Society in the more celebrated treason trials in London. They, too, were acquitted. Had they been found guilty, Clarkson intended to settle in America, 'for if it was look'd upon to be treason to belong to such popular societies as the constitutional society or the society of the friends of the people . . . no one was safe'.[29]

The abolition movement was particularly vulnerable since it relied heavily on whipping up public opinion to force a drastic change of course on a reluctant Parliament. Even to seem to yield to public sentiment could be seen to be dangerous. The wave of enthusiasm which had been generated in 1791 and 1792 receded and proceedings in Parliament faltered in the face of the implacable delaying tactics in the House of Lords. When a foreign slave trade bill passed the Commons in 1794 the Lords' excuse for not acting upon it was that witnesses were still being examined. Two more were questioned before the peers abandoned any pretence of interest.

Even the Abolition Committee found it hard to get a quorum and gave up its rooms in the Old Jewry. It met but twice in each of the next three parliamentary sessions and stood adjourned on 12 April 1797 for seven years – until May of 1804.[30]

Following the 1794 parliamentary session, Clarkson left London for the country, after his usual habit, but this time with little business to do, taking a route north and west which led to Penrith and the farm of his Quaker friend Thomas Wilkinson where he planned to rest and repair his shattered health.[31] Thanks to the kindness of friends his mind was eased. His brother was married and settled as manager of a Whitbread estate at Purfleet in Essex and his sister Anne was engaged to marry a wealthy clergyman, the Reverend John Leroo of Long Melford in Sussex. He was a 'violent aristocrat' in Clarkson's lexicon but otherwise a good match.[32]

The rest cure was a happy idyll. Wilkinson farmed a 40-acre freehold at Yanwath near Eamont Bridge, occasionally helped at harvest time by the two sisters who shared the house he called the Grotto.[33] He was one of the great influences in Clarkson's life, a poet, a constant reader and a landscape architect who installed rustic seats for the better enjoyment of his favourite views, with one of his sonnets inscribed on a slate nearby.[34] Wordsworth wrote a sonnet to Wilkinson's spade. Once a year, Wilkinson rode or walked to London (nearly 300 miles) usually accompanied by Elihu Robinson, to the Friends' Yearly Meeting. He had little education. 'An old woman in the next village taught me to read,' he recalled, 'and a few weeks to write, and a few weeks to learn arithmetic, were what I got.'[35]

Here Clarkson breakfasted with the family at 7 a.m., dined at the unfashionably early hour of 12.30 and went to bed at 9 p.m. after an evening of comfortable talk at the fireside. He imbibed a medicine impregnated with iron, probably the one recommended by Wilberforce from a Manchester physician. He shed his clerical dress. ('When one has not the emolument, there is no necessity to retain the odium', he remarked somewhat cryptically to Wilkinson.)[36] He worked alongside his host in the fields, groomed his own horse, and grew thinner, tougher and well-tanned. The frenzy of the last few years gradually fell away.

Clarkson fell in love with the Lake District at first sight and, when he spoke of abandoning further ambitions once the slave trade was abolished, and withdrawing into obscurity, he meant to Ullswater. This enthusiasm was shared by Wilberforce who had first seen the region when still a Cambridge student[37] and very likely the two had compared impressions before Clarkson chose his retreat. While Clarkson was there, Wilberforce wrote their mutual friend William Smith that 'To live in such a Country seems almost like a continual Turtle feast.'[38]

The Lake District was the popular destination of tourists searching for the picturesque and, of all its delights, Ullswater offered the 'happiest combination of beauty and grandeur', Wordsworth said in his *Guide*.[39]

Several months before, during that wretched summer of 1793, Clarkson had asked Wilkinson to look around for a bit of land as his refuge. Wilkinson found a 35-acre property on the lake near

Pooley Bridge, just three and a half miles from Yanwath. Clarkson bought it in 1794 with 1000 guineas, most of his remaining capital. Fourteen acres with a farmhouse called Woodside were let at 40 guineas a year and there was woodland to crop. The 21 acres on the shore, with a brook cascading into the crystal water of the lake, would be the site of his first home. He had a right of common to procure stone and slate nearby and planned to build a cottage.

'Awful times are approaching & those will be safest who are found in cottages', he had said.

'We have lately had the Benevolent Thos Clarkson staying with us', Wilkinson wrote a friend, 'and perhaps we may spend our days near one another. He has purchased a beautiful situation on our fine Lake of Ullswater. . . . I certainly consider him as an Acquisition to our Neighbourhood'.[40]

Clarkson rode to his land each day, feeling a 'spring in my veins' every time he approached. He dreamed of the house. It would be of rough cast stone, roofed in local slate, with large casement windows framing views across the water to the blue mountains which lifted towards the majestic peak of Helvellyn. It would be utterly plain with a door in the centre of the front, one window on each side and three windows above. When construction began, Clarkson laid the stones of the front himself.[41]

He shared in the life of the neighbourhood, conversing mainly with the 'poor & humble' who, he decided, had much to teach him. Wilkinson recalled that 'there were at least ten poor families to whose comforts he administers; his benevolence takes in every creature of every kind. . . . He has been begging round the neighbourhood for a poor man who had lost his cows.'[42]

Visiting the Plymleys in Shropshire on his way back to London in November 1794, Clarkson could not stop talking about the beauties of Ullswater, and his simple enchantment delighted these warm friends. They had to ask pointblank to get any news at all of the abolition strategy for 1795 from the man who had been so obsessed before.

Katherine drew the plans for his house and the Archdeacon gave him lessons in sketching so that he could record the lakeland prospects. He was a slow pupil, never satisfied with 'superficial knowledge' and he carefully wrote down the rules of perspective in his pocket memorandum book. He practised by drawing horses and dogs for the children and these sketches, after he was gone, were carefully dipped in milk to preserve them. They strolled around the Longnor gardens to help him decide what bushes and trees to plant. He wanted only 'cheerful' ones – yews and cypresses were out.

Although Clarkson had always loved the country and never stayed in London a day longer than necessary, it was Wilkinson who turned his thoughts to farming. It is easy to imagine how persuasive an example he would be when he could write, after a harvest, to his great friend Robinson:

> Yesterday I parted without regret from a close acquaintance, I set by my Sythe for this Year, and have got through as well as my Neighbours. I have often this season seen the dark blue Mountains before the sun, and his rising often embroider them with Gold; I have had many a good sleep in the shade among fragrant Grass and refreshing Breezes and though closely engaged in what may be thought Heavy work was sensible of the enjoyment of Life. Ah my Friend as thou beautifully Remarks, 'great is the Difference between Wearyness of Body and Anguish of Mind'.[43]

'When we have got an House to be sure we must have a Wife, that is also determined on', said Wilkinson while building Clarkson's house in the spring of 1795.[44] Clarkson seemed to be the last to know that he would marry Catherine Buck of Bury St Edmunds. The Plymleys had heard, in September 1794, from Wilberforce that Clarkson was to marry a 'very amiable & sensible young Lady at Bury' but when he was taxed to tell them about it, Clarkson would only say that he had been getting congratulations on that score for the last two years. Yes, there was a 'very amiable woman to whom he has been attached a long time' but what with his labours in the cause and his precarious private affairs the relationship had gone no further.

Then he grew coy about the object of his attentions. He intended to marry when he settled at Ullswater, true, but he was not yet certain who the bride would be. She had to be someone 'whose mind shall be so enlightened as to prove a pleasing companion to him, & yet one who . . . will find pleasure in that sort of retirement to which he looks forward, & with the simple conveniences that his small fortune can procure'.[45]

That was Catherine.

8

'My dearest Catherine'

Few historical figures have left us a better statement of their thoughts on women than Thomas Clarkson, whose views, although recorded in his study of Quakerism, he applied to the world. He believed in women's liberation from the conventions of 'idle parade and show'. He believed that women should be educated in general knowledge as well as in housekeeping and should have a public as well as a private scope for self-expression. The fact that Quakers alone, in his time, gave women a public place (as ministers) represented to him a 'new era in female history'. His discourse on the ministry of women in the Society of Friends is as clear an argument, on theological grounds, for the ordination of women as any advanced today.[1]

Christianity, in his view, was the first force acting to make women important in society. When it abolished polygamy it 'made one woman dearer than another, and of course every individual woman of consequence . . . raising them from the rank of slaves to that of the companions of men'. But in practice, 'Women are still weighed in a different scale from men. Their education is still limited, as if their understandings . . . were incapable of high attainments. If homage be paid to their beauty, very little is paid to their opinions.'

He deplored the tradition of his day and class whereby women spent their youth acquiring trivial talents to amuse themselves and others: 'the education they receive marks the inferior situation for which they are considered to be designed. Formed like dolls or playthings, which are given to children to captivate by outside appearances, they are generally rendered incapable of exhibiting great talents, or of occupying an important station in life . . . it seems to have been reserved for the Quakers . . . to insist upon that full practical treatment and estimation of women which ought to take place wherever Christianity is professed.'

He drew a biting contrast between Quaker women and those in fashionable society. '[Y]ou do not see them lavishing their caresses on lap-dogs, to the contempt of the poor and miserable of their own species. You never see them driving from shop to shop to make up a morning's amusement by examining and throwing out of order the various articles of tradesmen, giving them great trouble, and buying nothing in return. You never find them calling upon those whom they know to be absent from their homes, thus making their mimic visits, and leaving their useless cards. . . . Their pursuits are rational, useful and dignified . . . a model for the employment of time.'

Clarkson's respect for women of sense and sensibility is manifest in Katherine Plymley's account of their friendship and when he fell in love at last it was with a woman of similar intellect and a 'most loving heart'. He met Catherine Buck at the home of her uncle, Joseph Hardcastle, Hatcham House, New Cross, then a Surrey suburb and now part of Greater London. Hardcastle was a Methodist, cotton importer, philanthropist and fellow director of the Sierra Leone Company and Clarkson often stayed with him to escape at night from the City.[2]

She was the eldest child of William Buck, a prosperous yarn-maker at Bury St Edmunds, and his wife Sarah Corsbie, whose sister was married to Hardcastle. Their acquaintance ripened in the hectic year of 1792 when Clarkson was 32 and Catherine only 20. In the Hardcastles' parlour, she had first seen the shackles and thumbscrews, the cloth and spices of his treasure chest. She threw herself into his work by copying sheets of evidence and lists of questions for MPs. His love for her was still another element in his collapse the following year, for he could not hope to marry Catherine if he impoverished himself much further. He discussed his suit with her father in 1793 and formally proposed in May of 1795 on a visit to Bury on his way back to the Lake District.[3] From the evidence we have, it was the first love affair for both of them.

She was a vivacious young woman, a gifted conversationalist, with 'dark bright eyes twinkling in her delicate mobile face which smiled all over'. She was a voracious reader and celebrated among her friends for expounding in a 'dashing manner upon the reigning theory of the day'. She wrote in an equally spirited style, signing letters with 'Love in a lump' or recommending a visitor who could live on a 'Knat's Toe'. She was popular in West Suffolk ballrooms but prized as much for her wit as her beauty. 'An hour with Mrs Clarkson', recalled a young friend, 'was a time to remember.'[4]

One of Catherine's early conquests was Henry Crabb Robinson, son of a tanner who lived in Southgate Street near her own home in Westgate Street in Bury St Edmunds. He was the same age as her brother John and three years younger than she. Her father's house was a gathering place for liberal-minded, mostly nonconformist Burians and it was through Catherine that Robinson discovered the French Revolution. The young people formed what one of them, Sarah Jane Maling, described as a 'glorious tribe of *intrepid thinkers*' who read, debated and addressed one another as *'citoyenne'* and *'citoyen'* and scattered French phrases all over their letters. Of the two young women, Sarah Jane regarded herself as the more 'democratic' and did not mind being called a 'Tom Pain in petticoats'. Sometimes she claimed to detect in Catherine a 'spirit of Aristocracy'.[5]

Henry Robinson, who went on to become a German scholar, first English war correspondent, barrister and, above all, diarist and friend of the principal literary figures of the day (to many of whom he was introduced by Catherine) liked to recall how Catherine took charge of his mind in his youth. He judged that 'her excellence lay rather in felicity of expression than in originality of thought. She was the most eloquent woman I have ever known, with the exception of Madame de Stael. She had a quick apprehension of every kind of beauty, and made her own whatever she learned'.[6]

She felt sorry for any boy who had no sister (she had four brothers) and made it her business to reproach him for 'slovenliness in dress, as well as rudeness of behaviour. But at the same time she lent me books, made me first acquainted with the new opinions that were then afloat, and was my oracle till her marriage with the then celebrated Thomas Clarkson.' He used to look 'up to you & Sarah Jane as to my elder Sisters & was proud to be your disciple. . . . I recollect the days . . . When republicanism was the first virtue and a smack of infidelity the first essential ingredient to wit or Understanding!!!'[7]

She told him once 'of all those whom I knew in childhood or youth, you are the only one who has retained any likeness to myself'.[8] Her sympathy for the French Revolution, the great determining event in their generation, reflected Clarkson's own. She had a presentiment at Christmas of 1791 that its promises would not be fulfilled and when it took an ominous turn in August 1792 she, like Clarkson waited anxiously for each day's papers and wept for the misery and 'blindness of Mankind'. The fate of Brissot and others of his moderate faction tore at her heart.[9] The war fever in 1793 prompted these thoughts to Henry Robinson:

> The Aristocrats find that their all is at stake & are willing to risk everything. In the meantime the Commerce of the country is gone.... The lower orders of the People are degraded into slaves, the rest are deluded. Despotism has been long forging chains for us & its secret machinations have not been without effect. 50 years ago the measures that are now submitted to without a murmur wou'd have raised the voice of millions to oppose them.[10]

Those who met them during their courtship thought Catherine Buck and Thomas Clarkson were perfectly matched. They spent a few days in Cambridge with a party of friends. The Plymleys were told by a man who met them how spirited Catherine was, 'a great politician & her sentiments ... are in perfect unison' with Clarkson's. She argued 'with great strength & vivacity yet with most perfect good humour'. Katherine Plymley had heard before that 'Ladies in general on the eastern side the Kingdom are well versed in politics & converse with freedom on the subject.'[11]

Charles Berns Wadström, when the Plymleys dined with him in London, said he had never seen a couple more suited. James Phillips, however, had heard that she was an infidel and tried to talk Clarkson out of the marriage for fear of the consequences of giving his children such a mother. As something in her favour, they heard that Catherine sang very well.[12]

Clarkson finally told his pious friends in Shropshire what many others already knew, that he had abandoned the idea of seeking ordination as a priest. 'I have left the Church, after due examination, I mean as a Clergyman only ... my reasons concern only myself', he wrote. 'I shall be obliged to you therefore if you will omit the title of revnd: when you direct to me. Wilberforce & all my friends have left it off at my request. I know how you are too liberal to blame me for doing what I verily believe to be right myself.'[13]

Clarkson considered carefully what further use he could be to the cause before he married and moved to the Lake District to write and to farm. The commitment was no less but his base, the Committee, was dormant. It was illegal to hold a meeting of more than fifty people and the press was closed to abolitionist propaganda. Any attempt now to 'rouse the People' would be opposed by some abolitionists themselves as an effort to destabilise the government. They were willing to leave matters until peace returned.

After a Committee meeting on 14 January 1796, Clarkson signed a circular letter summoning supporters to make sure that friendly MPs were in the House when Wilberforce asked leave to bring in a bill which would fix the end of the slave trade at 1 March 1797.[14] On 21 January he and Catherine Buck were married by licence in St Mary's Church at Bury St Edmunds, where the life-size angels supporting the great hammer-beam roof blessed them as they had Catherine's parents more than a quarter century before. The Reverend Robert Edward Garnham, fellow of Trinity College, Cambridge, curate of Hargrave and Nowton and one of Catherine's dearest friends, read the service. Sarah Jane Maling, Catherine's father and her uncle Joseph Corsbie were their witnesses.[15]

Pleasantly engaged in a round of visits to family and friends, the bridal couple remained in and near London until April. 'Dull, uncomfortable & *discontent*' after her best friend's departure, Miss Maling teased William Buck by drinking toasts to 'Catherine and Thomas Clarkson' over his protest that gentlemen came first.[16]

Wilberforce won leave to introduce the bill which passed its second reading. Then, in a singularly dispiriting finale, it was lost on 15 March on third reading by a paltry four votes. At least a dozen abolitionist MPs were out of town or at the new comic opera. 'Enough at the Opera to have carried it', noted Wilberforce. 'I am permanently hurt about the Slave Trade.'[17]

'[T]o have all our endeavours blasted by the vote of a single night', Clarkson wrote, 'is both vexatious & discouraging.' Reluctantly he turned the cause over to the 'goodness & justice of Providence' for the time being.[18]

A case has been made in recent writings that the abolition suffered right along from Wilberforce's political ineptitude and the 1796 defeat has been cited as an example of his failure to rally his supporters behind him, but Clarkson was blamed this time by James Phillips, for one. Clarkson was not on hand on 15 March. 'Had he been in Town this unfortunate decision on Mr Wilberforce's motion wou'd not have happen'd, he would have ferreted out the members & seen that they were in their places.' Phillips complained that Clarkson had been in a trance since his marriage.[19]

His retirement, which even he in his history of the movement implies was forced by ill-health at least two years earlier than this, was clearly forced upon him by the times. His political hopes – if his friends' surmises are correct – were also frustrated. It was thought that he yearned for a place in some non-violent, reformist British 'revolution'. They watched him withdraw to the country with disbelief. 'Thee canst not think, whatever Clarkson may fancy, that he will remain in retirement. He can not give up politics', was one view.

'I think him born for public use', said Miss Plymley firmly. '& I look forward to the time when he shall be again engaged in benefitting mankind, though not perhaps in the way that he has imagined, for in a revolution ... I greatly fear ... that he would soon fall a victim to the factious & ambitious'.[20]

From his bench in the House of Commons Wilberforce kept the subject of the slave trade from vanishing completely during the next few years and Clarkson maintained some contact with his old colleagues through letters and visits to the south. After Wilberforce married in 1797 there was a jolly reunion breakfast in Old Palace Yard.[21]

But to return to the Clarksons as newly-weds, they set out for Ullswater on 1 April 1796 and moved unhurriedly from one hospitable house to the next behind their horse Button. Like her husband, Catherine always felt better 'in the air & travelling'.[22] The cottage was not quite finished and their first year was spent in the farmhouse, Woodside, while painters and plasterers completed the home they named Eusemere Hill.

Early one October morning, Clarkson rode into Pooley Bridge to post a letter to William Buck.

> Pooley Octob. 19. 96
> three in the morning
>
> Dear Sir
>
> I have but just time to inform you that my dearest Catherine was this morning delivered of a fine Boy & that both She and the Infant are well –
>
> You shall hear from Me by the next post – Few People experience such an easy Labour as she has done.
>
> Very affectionately yours
> Tho⁵ Clarkson[23]

This was quickly followed by a note from Catherine herself two days later.

My dear Parents

I write these few lines to shew you how well I am. I have been out of Bed to day without experiencing the least fatigue. My Nurse suits me in all respects – I shall write my Mother a long letter when they will allow me – My little Babe has sucked & found milk for the first time this even[g].

C Clarkson[24]

To which Clarkson added, 'My wife wishes her mother immediately to send her a Receipt for Children who may be griped.'[25]

To some of the affluent friends and relations who visited them in a steady stream, the cottage looked small and the Clarksons 'very poor' and they seemed to lead a rather bohemian 'peasant life'.[26] Their little boy, named Thomas, grew up on oatmeal porridge and ran about 'without cap or hat, without shoes or stockings & with very few cloaths'. They did not attend church but read at home, a practice which sent Archdeacon Plymley and his son Panton away to Lord Muncaster's magnificent house and orthodox religious habits a day early. Clarkson expressed his opposition to the new wartime taxes by avoiding as many as possible. He had neither clock nor watch in the house and followed the farmers' example in exchanging his two-wheeled chaise for a pleasure cart.[27]

The visiting Archdeacon was rather amused by Clarkson's earnest application to farming. He grew wheat, oats, barley, red clover, tares and turnips and pastured sheep and Scotch bullocks. In 1798 he leased another farm to expand operations and he bought and sold in Penrith market. Every detail was supervised and much of the work performed by Clarkson himself. With Thomas Wilkinson's aid he dug his own garden.[28]

'Mr Clarkson sums up the evidence for & against his hen-pens, his duck crews & goose house & its convenience with the same detail & precision he sum'd up the evidence on the Slave trade: he will make a very good farmer', Plymley concluded, 'but it will be both by labour of body & mind'.[29]

Clarkson recorded his new craft in a 'most regular & minute journal', complete with index.[30] On farming, he waxed as near to lyrical as he could get in prose. A sample:

The bud and the blossom, the rising and the falling leaf, the blade of corn and the ear, the seed-time and the harvest, the sun that warms and ripens, the cloud that cools, and emits the fruitful shower, – these and a hundred objects afford daily food for the religious growth of the mind. Even the natural man is pleased.... But the spiritual man ... sees none of these without feeling both spiritual improvement and delight. It is here that he converses with the Deity in his works.

He was fond of William Cowper's *Contemplation of a Country Life* and quoted it in his study of the Quakers:

> O friendly to the best pursuits of man,
> Friendly to thought, to virtue, and to peace,
> Domestic life, in rural leisure passed! . . .[31]

The Clarksons talked less and less of abolition and the little of politics that intruded made Catherine's heart ache. The man to whom writing was as natural as breathing discovered one day that there was only a single sheet of paper in the house and he appropriated it for a letter to his father-in-law.[32]

'The life we lead here suits me exactly', Catherine told her family on a day when there was little other news. 'It is regular & tranquil. My Husband enjoys good Health & spirits. My little Boy is ye sweetest fellow you ever saw. Every thing about us is improving & flourishing.'

She ran the dairy, churned butter and made cheese and sheep salve. When they put in nearly an acre of potatoes she 'planted one fourth part of them with my own Hand'. She directed the landscaping and started to study botany. Before Tom was 3 she began to teach him his letters, an uphill task. 'Round 0 is ye summit of his attainments & we can't get a step further', the grandparents learned.[33]

During the bad weather and poor harvests that plagued all the country towards the end of the century, Clarkson bore his vicissitudes 'as patiently as a lamb'. After the bitter winter and spring of 1799, 'There is hardly a blade of grass to be seen', Catherine reported. 'The Hay is all consumed & the Cattle are dying everywhere of hunger. This is ... actual fact. We don't expect to have above half our quantity of lambs. The old Ewes do pretty well but the two year old sheep have no milk for their lambs & the nights are so cold that they perish as soon as they are dropt.'[34]

The Clarksons' contentment with Ullswater was flawed only by the distance from their families and lifelong friends which bred in

Catherine a loneliness never overcome by long visits back and forth. She was unusually close to her parents and when Clarkson's mother died in October 1799 at the age of 64 his grief was intensified by the fact that he had been unable to reach Wisbech during her short last illness.[35] They planned in time to settle permanently in the south.[36]

When the Wordsworths and Coleridges moved into the Lake District they became instant and welcome new friends, together forming a 'richly gifted band'[37] that came to be known in later years as the Wordsworth circle. The newcomers may have met the Clarksons as a by-product of the romantic escapade of Priscilla Lloyd, daughter of Charles Lloyd, the Birmingham banker and abolitionist, who fell recklessly in love with her brother Charles's Greek tutor, Christopher Wordsworth, brother of the poet, during the Christmas vacation of 1798. They were engaged on 10 days' acquaintance but could not marry until Wordsworth found a living. Priscilla, 'mad with passion', as her father put it, was packed off to the Clarksons for safekeeping and spent six months in 1799 at Eusemere Hill.[38]

The first known meeting between Wordsworth, Coleridge and the Clarksons was in November 1799 when the poets spent a day at Eusemere. Wordsworth was looking for a home for himself and Dorothy, his sister. Coleridge was in high spirits and talked a great deal. He sat on a stump on the shore of Ullswater and described the view in his notebook: 'That round flat backside of a hill with its image in the water made together one absolutely indistinguishable form, a kite or paddle or keel turned towards you. The road appeared a sort of suture. I never saw so sweet a sight.'[39]

In a letter to Priscilla, now back at Bingley, Catherine told her about her future brother-in-law. William Wordsworth 'was more reserved but there was neither hauteur nor moroseness in his reserve. He has a fine commanding figure is rather handsome and looks as if he was born to be a great Prince or a great General. He seems very fond of C laughing at all his Jokes & taking all opportunities of showing him off & to crown all he has the manners of a *Gentleman*. I know how my Husband would laugh were he to see this last Sentence. . . .'[40]

The Wordsworths moved into the Town End cottage at Grasmere in December 1799 and the Clarksons came for a rainy weekend the following autumn. It was the beginning of frequent letters and visits between the two houses. The women were instantly friends and grew to love one another more dearly than most sisters. In 1800, Catherine was 28, a year younger than Dorothy; Wordsworth was 30 and Clarkson 40. Wordsworth was entering the years of his greatest work and Catherine, with her appetite for the new, appreciated his genius long before the multitude. Urging her friend Robert Garnham to buy both volumes of *Lyrical Ballads*, Catherine remarked, 'I am fully convinced that Wordsworth's genius is equal to the Production of something very great, and I have no doubt that he will produce *something that Posterity will not willingly let die*, if he lives ten or twenty years longer.'[41]

Clarkson and Wordsworth shared many qualities, in manner and appearance, for a start. Wordsworth was tall and grave, often silent in company, said Hazlitt, who also spoke of the 'severe, worn pressure of thought about his Temple, a fire in his eye. . . .' Both men were educated for the clergy at St John's, Cambridge, and both had chosen other vocations. Both had travelled in revolutionary France and had been enthusiastic over its prospects. Both preferred country life to any worldly advantage that might have been gained in a town.[42]

Clarkson also appreciated poetry; reading it was one of his few relaxations. He had written 'some trifles' when young, like most young people.[43] When poets took up the slave trade as a subject he was doubly moved and quoted them extensively in his works, especially Cowper. He himself excited poetic imaginations with his heroic exertions.

Clarkson was the first to link Wordsworth's poetry with the Quakerism which was his chief study in the Eusemere Hill years.[44] The Friends believed that the Spirit of God was given as a guide which spoke directly to the soul and also through material objects and daily occurrences. Writing just after the turn of the century when the poet was not yet acclaimed, Clarkson pointed out that 'William Wordsworth, in his instructive Poems, has described this teaching by external objects in consequence of impressions from a higher power, as differing from any teaching by books, or the human understanding, and as arising without any motion of the will of man, in [a] beautiful and simple manner.'[45]

The bonds between the Clarksons and the Wordsworths – William, his sister and, soon, his wife Mary – created, in effect, an extended family in which each cared deeply for the smallest news of the others, wherever they lived. At times they spoke of living together. The Wordsworths named a daughter for Catherine and although their son Thomas was named after Mary's brother Tom Hutchinson 'we do not forget the two Thomas Clarksons in calling him by his name'.[46] Much of what is known today about the Wordsworths lies in the wonderfully warm and garrulous letters addressed to Catherine by Dorothy. Unfortunately fewer of Catherine's replies survive. When the families were separated by distance, the Clarksons' silhouettes were requested, to hang over the Town End mantel.[47]

The flavour of the friendship permeates Dorothy's Grasmere journal.[48] Eusemere was a natural refuge for her at critical periods in her life, and one in particular gave us all something to savour. William left Dorothy with the Clarksons when he went to ask Mary Hutchinson to marry him. He returned for her and they set out for Grasmere on 15 April 1802. Catherine had intended to walk with them as far Watermillock but was driven back by a furious wind.

When we were in the woods beyond Gowbarrow Park we saw a few daffodils close to the water-side [Dorothy wrote in her journal]. We fancied that the lake had floated the seeds ashore, and that the little colony had so sprung up. But as we went along there were more and yet more; and at last, under the boughs of the trees, we saw that there was a long belt of them along the shore, about the breadth of a country turnpike road. I never saw daffodils so beautiful. They grew among the mossy stones and about them; some rested their heads upon these stones as on a pillow for weariness; and the rest tossed and reeled and danced, and seemed as if they verily laughed with the wind, that blew upon them over the lake; they looked so gay, ever glancing, ever changing. . . . There was here and there a little knot, and a few stragglers a few yards higher up, but they were so few as not to disturb the simplicity, unity and life of that one busy highway.[49]

While Dorothy and William were in France in August, to see Annette Vallon and his daughter before marriage, the Clarksons borrowed the cottage at Town End and it was there that Charles and Mary Lamb, on their single visit to the north, met and stayed with them a night or two.[50]

As the intimate friend of the Wordsworths at this time – they were 'three persons and one soul' – Coleridge, too, became attached to the Clarksons and was especially susceptible to Catherine's enduring charm. He described his devotion extravagantly in letters to Henry Crabb Robinson. He loved Catherine 'even as my very own Sister, whose Love for me with that of Wordsworth's Sister, Wife, and Wife's Sister, form almost the only Happiness I have on earth'. And a few years later: 'to feel, not only how *much*, but *how* I love and esteem her, reconciles me to my own nature, when I am least contented with it. Had she been my Sister, I should have been a great man. . . . I never saw a Woman yet, whom I could so imagine to have been of one parent with me at one Birth, as Catherine Clarkson & she has all, that is good in me, and all that is innocent in the peculiar dying parts of my nature would to God! I had what she has besides – & which I have not her sacred magnanimity.'[51]

Coleridge was both acerbic and affectionate when he spoke of Clarkson. It appears that he is also the only one of Clarkson's friends who called the majestic abolitionist 'Tom'. His single-mindedness fascinated the poet for, even in this quiescent period for the cause, the abolition was never entirely out of his mind.

'I once asked Tom Clarkson whether he ever thought of his probable fate in the next world, to which he replied, "How can I? I think only of the slaves in Barbadoes!"' Coleridge added, obviously thinking of the evangelical motives of the other great leader of the cause, 'Does Mr Wilberforce care a farthing for the slaves in the West Indies, or if they were all at the devil, so that *his soul were saved*? As there is a worldliness or the *too-much* of this life, so there is *another-worldliness*, or rather *other worldliness*, equally hateful and selfish with *this worldliness*.'[52]

Robert Southey, who joined the Lakes dwellers in 1803, was also affected by the 'man who so nobly came forward about the Slave Trade to the ruin of his health – or rather state of mind – and to the deep injury of his fortune'. Introducing him to a friend by letter, Southey wrote of Clarkson, 'if you do not find him a very pleasant man I am sure you will be interested with him on this account. It agitates him to talk upon the subject – but when he does – he agitates every one who hears him.'[53]

In 1803, Catherine's health began markedly to fail. Without seeing the new baby at Grasmere she left with her son in early July for the Buck home in Bury St Edmunds to consult the family physician. Dorothy's letter with a lock of Johnny's hair followed her. 'My ever dear Friend', her postscript read, 'may God restore you to health &

may you come back to us with a Body as fit for enjoyment among these noble & quiet Mountains & vales as your heart is.'[54]

But she made no progress and leaving Tom, now 7, with his grandparents and his aunt at Long Melford, she went to Bristol and Dr Thomas Beddoes, who was thought by many to be the best doctor in England. A talented chemist and medical pioneer, he was a man of such 'republican' views that he had been forced to resign his lectureship at Oxford and had established a practice at fashionable Clifton near the famed Hot Wells.[55] From her letters, it seems that Catherine had a liver disorder. There is no clue to her problem in Beddoes' special interests for they were so broad. Her suffering was intense and friends wondered that she did not die of pain alone.[56] Clarkson joined her in November 1803 and she was gaining ground when he returned to Ullswater the following February but a relapse kept her in Bristol until the summer. Her mother died suddenly in July of a paralytic stroke and her father brought Catherine back to Bury St Edmunds in August.[57]

The medical advice was that Catherine should not live again in the colder climate of the Lakes and (surely reluctantly) Clarkson arranged to sell their home to Lord Lowther. He made it neat for its new owner and gave Catherine's writing box to Dorothy, along with one of her hens and a cock. '[H]ow dearly do I prize it!' Dorothy wrote, much moved to see it again.[58] Each time she went back to Eusemere, she lamented the absence of her friend, as she thought of the first night she had come there with William – 'little Tom first put into trousers, your dear husband Mr Clarkson . . .'. 'Could you but have heard the thrushes and seen the thousand primroses under the trees!' she said after a return visit with Sara Hutchinson; 'the Lake was beautiful and all about the house neat and flourishing – need I say how full our hearts were? Ellen [Bewsher, the Clarksons' servant] gave us a kind welcome. We drank tea by the kitchen fire and had nice bread and everything comfortable. We went upstairs and when we entered the drawing room the view from the window struck upon us both in the same moment in the same way, as if it were an unearthly sight, a scene of *heavenly* splendour.'

During his weeks alone at Eusemere, Clarkson continued work on his *Portraiture of Quakerism* which he had begun at Wilkinson's fireside. It was published in 1806 but largely completed before he returned to abolition work in 1804. No outsider knew more about their 'living manners' and his was the first book to explain the principles and peculiarities of the sect to the world at large. He was admittedly partial to them, as the first friends of abolition, but not blind to imperfections and he cited criticisms of them and deviations from the purity of their system as he went along.[59]

Quakers watched his progress with some anxiety but as he finished each volume he gave it to Thomas Wilkinson and others for their unsparing comments. 'He wishes it to be as perfect as may be', Wilkinson said. 'One would like to help T Clarkson what one could, as the Love of Truth, justice to our Society, and general Usefulness to Mankind are what have led him to the Undertaking.'[60]

His wife shared his interest, attended the Penrith meeting several times and read George Fox's journal. Her friends thought they saw a change from her 'free thinking' past. 'She is become a religionist and a believer', Henry Robinson's brother reported. 'Her faith receives little or no aid from written revelation – but God has spoken to her heart in a most sublime and mystical manner. In short she is of a species of Quaker.'[61]

9

The Trade Abolished

Clarkson's retirement ended in May 1804 and he resumed his seat with a revived Abolition Committee in June. He had been away for eight years and for seven of those the Committee itself had slumbered. Signs proliferated that the cause was 'secretly gaining ground'.[1]

Increasingly reliant on anti-abolitionist votes to maintain unity in wartime, Pitt was no longer a keen advocate but the political atmosphere was better for the cause. France, whose experiment in democracy had so frightened the establishment in Britain was now a despotism under Bonaparte that few in Britain wanted to copy. The panic over 'Jacobins' and reformers had subsided and further to destroy liberal sympathies, Bonaparte had restored the French colonial slavery which the Convention had abolished in 1794. Britain had captured most of the French West Indian islands (returning slavery to them in the process) and commercial circles worried little now about competition in production. To add to all that, a hundred Irish members had entered Parliament under the 1800 Act of Union, most of them friendly to the idea of abolition of the slave trade.[2]

It was also clear by now that West Indian interests were not going to cooperate in any plan for gradual abolition and this, plus the knowledge that the planters were heavily engaged in illegal trading with the United States instead of fulfilling their obligations to supply and buy from the mother country, eroded toleration for them.[3]

Remarkably, eight of the original twelve members of the Committee were still available 17 years on: Sharp, Dillwyn, Hoare, Harrison, Lloyd, Richard Phillips, Sansom and Clarkson. Its strength was to rise to 40 for the final push in the abolition campaign and in 1804 were added the first of a new generation of notable activists in the persons of Henry Brougham, Zachary Macaulay and James Stephen, the latter already established as an influential adviser to Wilberforce as well as his friend and brother-in-law.[4]

The last chapter in the struggle to abolish the slave trade was written mostly in Parliament and no large-scale effort was undertaken to stir up vehement public pressure. After all, laws censoring speech and assembly were still in effect. The Committee now acted more quietly and selectively. Victory was not inevitable, even in the changed climate, as the abolitionists, toughened by repeated rebuffs, should have known. Several preliminary skirmishes took place.

Wilberforce introduced an abolition bill on 30 May 1804 and with Irish and some moderate West Indian support it passed all stages in the Commons and was carried to the Lords on 28 June. On Lord Grenville's advice that, with the session so far advanced and so many friends of the abolition already gone home, they would be defeated if it came to a vote, the measure was 'hung up till next year'.[5]

This was Wilberforce's first direct liaison with Grenville, who had fallen out with Pitt but who was essential to the abolition in the Upper House. In going, as it were, over Pitt's head to make sure of Grenville's continued support, Wilberforce confessed to an ignorance of parliamentary processes that might help to explain in part the repeated failure of abolition measures in that chamber. Bishop Porteus had told him only the evening before, he said in a flattering note to Lord Grenville, 'that in the House of Lords a bill from the House of Commons is in a destitute and orphan state, unless it has some peer to adopt and take the conduct of it'.[6]

In 1805, Pitt advised delay, but the abolitionists – brushing aside bitter experience – expected no trouble getting a bill through the Commons which had so readily passed one the previous session. They lost by 7 votes, a mortifying margin. Pitt was silent during the preceding debate.

Wilberforce was totally unprepared for this: 'Sad work! ... I could not expect the defeat, and all expressed astonishment.' Both his and Clarkson's assessments, however, were that their side had been careless. Wilberforce blamed 'Great canvassing of our enemies, and several of our friends absent through forgetfulness, or accident, or engagements preferred from lukewarmness.' Clarkson found that nine supporters, never absent in any previous vote, were away, confident that the motion was safe, and now sat 'on the Stool of Repentance'. Of the Irish supporters in the previous year, only a handful attended this time. Eternally sanguine, Clarkson decided all these 'accidental' causes of defeat could be remedied.[7]

So, in a cheery frame of mind, Clarkson set out once more quietly to collect a small band of useful witnesses should they be needed for the next battle in the long war. He dared to hope it would be the last. 'It was now almost certain, to the inexpressible joy of the committee, that the cause, with proper vigilance could be carried in the next session.'[8]

Afterwards, and for the first time, Clarkson looked back on one of his journeys round Britain as an 'extraordinary success'. He reported to the Committee by letter on 9 July 1805 that old friends remained faithful but that there was work to be done among young people. They knew little about the cause since for several years the Committee had not circulated books and there had been no reports of debates in Parliament. But the 'rising generation' was interested and could be educated to become enthusiastic.

He suggested that it might be useful to put out a small pamphlet wholly devoted to an explanation of slaving operations in Africa to go with the one Stephen was writing on the horrors of West Indian slavery. Some such emphasis on the slave trade would help to underline their objective of abolishing the trade but not emancipating the slaves. The Committee, in the event, acted on Clarkson's alternative proposal and issued a new abridgement of evidence.[9]

For some of his 1805 tour Clarkson had his wife with or near him and when they reached Longnor in Shropshire in late June she was welcomed heartily by the Plymleys. The Archdeacon had inherited the family estate from an uncle in the autumn of 1804, taken the name of Corbett and moved his family across the road to Longnor Hall. His sisters, Katherine and Ann, remained at Bank House. Katherine discovered Clarkson to be kinder, more amiable than ever and, happily, in somewhat better health, but, as her affectionate eye observed, he often seemed exhausted and still needed frequent small meals.[10]

Clarkson told her it was a miracle that his wife had survived her illness. She had joked about dying 'chearfully & with elegance' but when she spent the early part of June with Dr Beddoes at Bristol he had decided that she was now well enough to make the journey.

Their plan was to settle Catherine in a cottage at Grasmere near the Wordsworths while Clarkson travelled in the northwest and Scotland. They would return south in the winter. Their Tom was at school in Bury St Edmunds under his grandfather's care.[11]

This was the first time that Katherine Plymley had met Clarkson's wife and any doubts created by what she had heard before were swept away; her hero had found a worthy mate.

'She is very sensible, truly modest & unassuming, plain in her person but with so good an expression that conversing with her we soon cease to think her plain. She is able to appreciate Mr Clarksons merit, & fully sensible of it – "I am indeed" said she one day to us "very proud of him". He is strongly attached to her, very anxious about her health & attends himself to all her medicines.' He wheeled Catherine about the garden, familiar to him from his nocturnal walks, and reminisced about former visits for her benefit. Coleridge had sensed in Clarkson's personality this need to serve those he loved.[12]

Clarkson spoke of his book on the Quakers and while he was away with the Archdeacon in Montgomeryshire in search of two surgeons once employed on a slave ship, the women and older children of the Longnor households read the manuscript, passing chapters from one to another, 'Uncommonly interesting', was Katherine's judgement. '"I think it will do good"' said Clarkson, with the simplicity that is so pleasing a part of his character.'

Knowing that Clarkson was sometimes suspected of being 'inclined to the Unitarian opinions', his friends kept him under surveillance at both services in Longnor church on the Sunday. The 'infidel' Catherine pleased them by attending family prayers and Clarkson went the extra mile when he joined the Archdeacon's catechism class. It was observed that he participated in those parts of the service that the Unitarians could not and the considered view was that 'Whatever his private opinions may be, he is very pious & possesses true Christian charity, so does Mrs Clarkson.'

Clarkson had reactivated local committees at Bristol, Gloucester, Tewkesbury and Worcester and after further stops on abolition business at Liverpool, Ashton-under-Lyne and Lancaster, the Clarksons reached Grasmere in late July. Lodgings had been taken for them at Robert Newton's house near his small inn, only a short walk from the Wordsworths' at Town End. 'We have a little Parlour to ourselves, & a good Kitchen for my Wife's Maid & a Cook, whom we have hired. A good Bed Room also for ourselves, & a comfortable one for the two Maids', Clarkson told Archdeacon Corbett in his thank-you letter.

The reunion in the Lakes lasted into November of a 'glorious autumn'. In the course of it, Clarkson's sister Anne Leroo died. There is almost nothing in surviving Clarkson papers about her but the fact that he saved and showed to Wordsworth the letters she wrote while his son was with her speaks of a close bond.[13]

Dorothy Wordsworth rejoiced at the long interval with her dearest friend and she found Catherine, in spite of her frailty, 'cheerful and often lively and even merry and the cause of mirth by our fire side', although the slow walk to Town End often left her pale and worn.[14]

One August day, at the Wordsworths' for tea, Clarkson related a pathetic story about Charles Gough, a young Manchester volunteer with a company of militia at Ambleside, who had gone off alone to fish, and had died on Helvellyn. Three months later a shepherd found the body – a bundle of clothes with a few bones inside them – attracted by the movements of a small brown spaniel bitch. A watch, a fishing rod and a pocket book which contained a 'disownment' of him as a Quaker for having joined the volunteers helped to identify the young stranger. Clarkson wrote a friend at Manchester to break the news to his anxious mother. When she was found, the faithful little spaniel was wild and weak, having lived on snails and grass. Out of the tragedy came Wordsworth's 'Fidelity'.[15]

Part of the time, when Clarkson was away, Catherine stayed with the Coleridges at Greta Hall near Keswick and she also visited other old friends.[16] But the highlight of her stay in the Lakes was the copying, in a beautiful small clear hand, of Dorothy's 'Recollections of a Tour made in Scotland' which was written after she and William with Coleridge had returned 'for the friends who ought to have been with us'. A note by the copyist attached to the work read:

This copy of my beloved friend's Journal was begun at Grasmere the beginning of September and finished at Patterdale this day (the 1st of November 1805). When I began the work I scarcely indulged the hope of finishing it myself, my health being so indifferent that every little exertion of mind or body fatigued me exceedingly; but instead of a difficult task I have found it the easiest and pleasantest employment that I ever engaged in; and though the possession of such a treasure makes me very happy, yet I am sincerely sorry that my work is ended. The whole . . . was written in bed, and the whole by myself except the title-

pages and the divisions of the work which were written by
George Hutchinson, brother of my two dear friends Mrs Wordsworth and Sara Hutchinson, and the title on the first page of the
work, which my Husband had the kindness to interrupt himself,
when he was exceedingly busy in his own work, to write for me.
– C C[17]

Clarkson got back to London shortly before the death of William
Pitt rocked the political world. Although he had lately done little
for abolition, Clarkson always denied the lost Prime Minister was
insincere because he knew that Pitt's hands were tied by three of
his most powerful cabinet ministers. Clarkson also hinted that
royal intervention ('a difficulty, still more insuperable ... but
which is much too delicate to be mentioned') in 1791 made
everything Pitt did useless.[18] All the same, the change to an
administration led by Grenville with Fox as Foreign Secretary must
have been exceedingly welcome.

Its first move was a bill to confirm the 1805 Order in Council
(prised out of Pitt by Wilberforce) banning the slave trade to
captured colonies. 'We have rather more friends in the Cabinet
than formerly', Clarkson wrote on the circular sent to friends of the
cause as the Abolition Committee moved into action to promote a
'spontaneous' lobbying of MPs. They would not again take it for
granted that their supporters would turn up to vote. 'But the
Prince of Wales appears the great obstacle at present'. Wilberforce,
however, got word through William Smith that the Prince 'had
given his honour to Fox, not to stir adversely'.[19] In poorly attended
sessions the bill passed both houses and received the royal assent
on 23 May, the first act in the 19-year struggle that 'dismembered
this cruel trade'. Clarkson estimated that it alone would save 35 000
Africans 'from being annually torn from their Country'.[20]

Government men, not Wilberforce, led in Parliament now but
there was close consultation on strategy. Fox next asked the
Commons to affirm a resolution declaring the African slave trade
'contrary to the principles of justice, humanity and policy' and that
steps would be taken to abolish it. By an overwhelming 114 to 15,
this was agreed. In the Lords, it carried by 41 to 20. Lord Grenville
thus won the first condemnation of the trade in the upper house.

It was now 'universally believed ... that the Slave-trade had
received its death-wound', said Clarkson, and Wilberforce actually
was congratulated prematurely on reaching his goal. Two more

steps were taken in his momentous 1806 session. Wilberforce's proposal that the King seek international negotiations to end the slave trade was adopted in both houses and, to stop merchants from fitting out new vessels to dash to the African coast for their 'last harvest', a bill providing that no ship could clear a British port for the trade unless previously used for the same purpose by the same owner became law on 21 July.[21]

Hardly had the Committee expressed its joy and gratitude to those who made these victories possible than Fox died, and the movement lost one of its oldest and most eloquent advocates.

> I never heard whether Mr Fox, when he came into power, made any stipulations with His Majesty on the subject . . . but this I know, that he determined upon the abolition of it . . . as the highest glory of his administration, and as the greatest earthly blessing which it was the power of the Government to bestow,

Clarkson wrote. On Fox's deathbed, Clarkson was told, abolition was 'even nearer to his Heart than the Peace, which he was endeavouring to make'.[22]

During the parliamentary recess, Wilberforce decided to write his first treatise on the slave trade. It was not a subject he had ever raised in Yorkshire in 22 years as a county MP but he chose to call it a *Letter on the Abolition of the Slave Trade Addressed to the Freeholders and Other Inhabitants of Yorkshire*. Like Clarkson he believed much had been forgotten in the nearly two decades since the question came before Parliament and many new MPs as well as the whole younger generation were uninformed. He intended his book to be distributed early in the 1807 session and it was.[23] But the writing was interrupted when a snap election which threatened his seat was called in October by Lord Grenville to increase his parliamentary troops while the memory of Fox was still warm. He and Earl Fitzwilliam, leader of the Whig interest in Yorkshire, were eager to recapture at least one Yorkshire seat, both of which were held now by Pittites, Wilberforce and Henry Lascelles, son of the Earl of Harewood, owner of Barbados sugar plantations and, of course, slaves.

Wilberforce was not a natural choice to represent the realm of Yorkshire and he was anathema to large sections of nobility and gentry because he came from a mercantile family, had relatively little land and owned no country seat. He knew it and never took re-election for granted. He worked hard as a constituency MP for the 20 000 electors who formed the largest body of voters in Britain, and abolition was not of great use to him on the hustings. One reason for writing his *Letter* was to explain why 'this question has occupied so large a share of my parliamentary life'.[24]

In practical political terms, Wilberforce and the slaveholding Lascelles were a compatible team.[25] They worked and voted together on everything but abolition. During the 1806 session, they sat together on an inquiry into the woollen industry which reported in favour of the new system of factory production which was bound to destroy the domestic pattern of small clothiers weaving at home which prevailed in the West Riding. Lascelles's unabashed support for the rising factories earned him the undying hatred of the West Riding clothier-freeholders, and there were a lot of them.

When Wilberforce's carriage entered Yorkshire he discovered that the Whigs had put up a third candidate, Walter Fawkes of Farnley Hall, a landed aristocrat of an old Yorkshire family, a patron of J. M. W. Turner and agricultural improver, a convinced abolitionist and a moderate parliamentary reformer. In short, the kind of Whig Grenville wanted in Parliament.

The awful news signified a contest which would be ruinously expensive. The lordly Whigs were tempted to force the issue to get rid of Wilberforce 'for he's poor & durst not contend'. However, Grenville pointed out that Wilberforce had been 'uniformly friendly' to his government while Lascelles was a decided enemy and he urged Fitzwilliam to canvass for Wilberforce and Fawkes. As word spread that a contest loomed in Yorkshire, Clarkson, Richard Phillips and William Allen began writing letters to secure votes for Wilberforce.[26]

Abolition was an election issue everywhere and in Yorkshire it was Fawkes who fought Lascelles on that ground. 'Friends of the Abolition' took out newspaper advertisements cautioning electors to back only candidates who favoured it.[27] In some places, resolutions were adopted at public meetings. The cause won in Yorkshire when Lascelles withdrew after the canvass, mostly thanks to the angry West Riding clothiers, showed Fawkes and Wilberforce leading. They were elected by acclamation in the Castle Yard at York. In all, Grenville made a net gain of 40.

Twenty years after the organisation of the London Committee and the start of the great public campaign, the British slave trade was outlawed. Lord Grenville masterminded the victory which had eluded the abolitionists for so long. He started where the move could expect the most opposition, in the Lords, with a bill in January 1807 to stop the trade to British colonies on grounds of justice, humanity and sound policy. He opposed a delaying inquiry but several last-ditch petitions came from West Indian, London and Liverpool shipping and planting spokesmen. Grenville addressed the Lords for three hours on 4 February, concluding with a handsome tribute to Wilberforce. He was determined to succeed and his canvassing of support had been meticulous. The bill sailed through the Lords triumphantly by 100 (including 28 carefully-arranged proxies) to 34. It passed a third reading without a division and reached the Commons on 10 February.[28]

The Committee conducted an intense lobbying of MPs from a rented headquarters at 18 Downing Street during February and March. Everyone available had his list of members to canvass. 'A terrific list of doubtfuls', Wilberforce noted at one point, 'yet I think we shall carry it. . . . How popular Abolition is, just now! God can turn the hearts of men.'[29]

When the crucial debate took place, members actually competed for a chance to be heard. For the first time, Wilberforce heard a fellow Yorkshire MP support his side, albeit with a passion the senior member termed 'too much studied'. Fawkes wound up with a eulogy to Wilberforce. Although it was Grenville's men who put the measure through, MPs remembered Wilberforce's unremitting advocacy until, after a fulsome tribute from Sir Samuel Romilly, he was reduced to tears. Spokesmen for the trade could do little more than denounce the 'popular clamour'. The trade was abolished by a resounding 283 to 16, probably the biggest majority recorded on any issue where the House divided, Clarkson thought.[30]

The vote was taken in the early hours of 24 February and Clarkson spent much of the day writing notes with the tidings to friends around the country, as he had done when the Lords decided the issue. His message was much the same to all: 'My joy is so full & my gratitude so great, to the Parent of all mercies, that I can only give you the plain and simple statement of our brilliant victory', he said of the first triumph. And of the Commons decision he said, 'our efforts were blessed by Providence last night. . . . I want words to express the joy I feel'. To some he added, 'I shall attend a Committee to day to deliberate upon a Plan for securing our Victory after which I shall leave London, with a Heart full of gratitude to the Parent of all Mercies that he had been pleased thus to render a Portion of my Life useful to my oppressed fellow Creatures.'[31]

Yes, in spite of the general euphoria, the Committee met that day, and it agreed that as the question of compensation had arisen, a pamphlet Clarkson had prepared in the course of the session should be circulated at once, his *Three Letters . . . to the Planters and Slave-Merchants Principally on the Subject of Compensation.*[32]

Certain amendments now required action in the Lords which, when taken by 23 March, caused Grenville to congratulate his fellow peers on the 'most glorious measure, that had ever been adopted by any legislative body in the world'. The ease with which despite a Cabinet made up of 'jarring parties' and a hostile court he had carried the day was the subject of admiring comment which contrasted – unfavourably – Pitt's inability to prevail on his most servile colleagues. Grenville's achievement, furthermore, was on the very eve of his dismissal. He had incurred the wrath of George III for a Catholic emancipation bill and was ordered to deliver up the seals of office by 11.30 a.m. on 25 March. 'There was an awful fear through the kingdom, lest it should not receive the royal assent before the ministry was dissolved' but as the clock struck 12, 'just when the sun was in its meridian splendour to witness this august Act, this establishment of a Magna Charta for Africa in Britain, and to sanction it by its most vivid and glorious beams, it was completed', as Clarkson told it.[33]

The tributes to Clarkson came 'out of doors' as you would expect. His image all over the country – that of a solitary, dedicated traveller, the tireless author of tracts, risking everything, including his life for the cause – made him the hero of poets, liberals, romantics and the American antislavery leaders who were beginning to arise. At the passage of the Abolition Act, Wordsworth saluted his friend with this joyous sonnet:

> *To Thomas Clarkson*
> Clarkson! it was an obstinate hill to climb:
> How toilsome – nay, how dire – it was, by thee
> Is known; by none, perhaps, so feelingly:
> But thou, who, starting in thy fervent prime,
> Didst first lead forth that enterprise sublime,
> Hast heard the constant Voice its charge repeat,
> Which, out of thy young heart's oracular seat,

First roused thee. – O true yoke-fellow of Time,
Duty's intrepid liegeman, see, the palm
Is won, and by all Nations shall be worn!
The blood-stained Writing is forever torn:
And thou henceforth wilt have a good man's calm,
A great man's happiness; thy zeal shall find
Repose at length, firm friend of human kind![34]

But beginning with the tributes paid him in Parliament, even more public acclaim greeted Wilberforce, portrayed as 'God's instrument', and a saintly symbol for succeeding generations. Even Clarkson, a man of little vanity, thought of a medal that might be struck to commemorate the act with a profile of Wilberforce on one side and some kind of device on the other.[35]

A fear that the newborn Abolition Act might be repealed arose with the sudden change in government back to Pittite control. The King's peremptory dismissal of the Grenville government over a Catholic issue was immensely popular. The elderly Duke of Portland was put in but his hold on Parliament was so slim that a new election had to be called. 'No Popery' became the most potent battle-cry of the campaign but the outcome in Yorkshire was watched as a referendum on abolition.[36]

Walter Fawkes decided not to stand again and the Earl Fitzwilliam's precocious heir, Lord Milton, was launched in the Whig interest. Lascelles of Harewood House was a candidate, of course, and Wilberforce's fate hung in the balance as the two great houses fought for the county seats in the most uproarious, expensive election ever conducted in Britain. Harewood and Fitzwilliam each spent at least £100 000. A nationwide subscription was opened to save Wilberforce, who did not want to exhaust his own fortune on the fray, and more than £64 000 poured in from 2800 donors, chiefly, it would seem, abolitionists. He ran a frugal campaign with many volunteer helpers and spent only about half the sum collected.

Lord Milton was on record as an abolitionist. Lascelles now insisted that he would never vote to repeal the act, but political scribblers suspected his conversion. Wilberforce as usual did not exploit his abolition colours; the votes of sympathisers were already his. Friends combed the country for non-resident voters who could go to York. 'Have you any votes in Manchester for Yorkshire, whom you could engage for Wilberforce?' Clarkson asked John Wadkin. 'It is absolutely necessary that he should be in Parliament – He will be a Host, in Case any Attempt should be made to reverse the late Bill. . . . He desires only to be in Parliament, till he can see this great Measure out of danger'.[37]

By far the greatest hazard to Wilberforce, and the issue that pained him most, was the rumour that he had formed a coalition with his former colleague Lascelles to defeat a brother abolitionist, Lord Milton. When the rumour reached London, recent allies such as Lord Howick and Samuel Whitbread were furious. Howick called him a 'little rogue' and Whitbread threatened 'little Wilberforce will pay dear for his shabbiness'.[38]

The poll for Yorkshire lasted 15 days and on 5 June 1807 Wilberforce and Milton were elected. As in 1806 Lascelles was beaten by the fierce opposition of the West Riding clothiers determined to hold on to their way of life and their political independence. Wilberforce topped the poll but he had hoped for a nearly unanimous endorsement. He estimated the coalition rumours cost him 8000 votes.

It was his sixth election, and only contest, for the county and it left him 'thin and old beyond his years'. In 1811 he decided to give up the county seat for reasons of health and family. Lord Calthorpe offered him a pocket borough at Bramber and he was returned from there in 1812 without stirring from his holiday retreat.

10

The Problems of Victory

Many months before the Abolition Act passed, Clarkson began his personal history of the movement. His knowledge was unique and friends told him it would be a pity if it died with him. Chary of being lumbered with unsold copies, Clarkson encouraged advance subscriptions but when the book came out in May 1808 it went very well at a guinea for the set of two volumes. Nearly 4000 copies were bought before it was advertised.[1]

He called it the *History of the Rise, Progress, and Accomplishment of the Abolition of the African Slave-Trade by the British Parliament* and dedicated it to the nine of the twelve members of Grenville's Cabinet who supported the 1807 bill and to the memories of Pitt and Fox.[2]

'There will not be one copy to be had in the Kingdom in two Months Time', Clarkson predicted happily to the stalwart North Shields abolitionist, Henry Taylor, to whom he dispatched 30 copies, 'and Paper being now 40 per cent advanced there cannot be another edition at the same price.' The next edition would cost 24 shillings.[3]

There is no other contemporary published record of the origin and growth of the British anti-slave-trade movement, which makes Clarkson's history invaluable. It is also his autobiography though it covers but a short period in a long life. In a Prospectus, Clarkson referred to it as a book of history and biography such as would 'please young Persons'.[4] Judges of Clarkson's historical view should bear in mind that he wrote as the originator of the movement outside Parliament. His view is that of the country and the Committee. He is best on the historical background to and the early stages of the public campaign. His detailed account of his investigations at the slave ports is enthralling, and he provides a useful summary of each major debate, but the details of ministerial policy and parliamentary tactics are not here, although Clarkson sheds light on them. The story is weakest from the late 1790s to 1807. His severest critics were those who entered the movement latest and cared least about its history. They were also Westminster-orientated, and blamed his choice of emphases on egotism.

Clarkson's is a story of the eternal conflict between good and evil – a 'two-volume morality play', as David Brion Davis called it. Dorothy Wordsworth enjoyed it as she would a novel and couldn't put it down. Little wonder that among the reprints and editions which followed was an abridgement for Sunday School children in the United States. 'We are taught by it, most impressively, that nothing which ought to be done, should be deemed impracticable; that a few noble spirits may excite a whole nation to action . . . and finally triumph over evils the most enormous and appalling which have ever afflicted mankind', was an appreciative American comment.[5]

Coleridge had a preview and told Southey:

> I have read the sheets of the 1st vol of dear Mr Clarkson's History of the Abolition etc. The grave intensely common commonplace, the mild and genial dulness of the first 3 pages, disappoints one most delightfully, for all the rest is deeply interesting, written with great purity as well as simplicity of Language, which is often vivid and felicitous (as the monthly Rev would say) and nothing can surpass the moral beauty of the manner in which he introduces himself and relates his own maxima pars in that Immortal War – compared with which how mean all the conquests of Napoleon and Alexander![6]

When he sent his review of it to the *Edinburgh Review*, Coleridge expanded on his feelings about the author.

> I do not hold Clarkson's fame dear because he is my friend, but I sought and cultivated his acquaintance, because a long and sober inquiry had assured me, that he had been, in an aweful sense of the word, a benefactor of mankind: and this from the purest motives. . . . He, if ever human being did it, listened exclusively to his conscience, and obeyed its voice. . . . Such a man I cannot regard as a mere author. I cannot read or criticise such a work as a mere literary production. The opinions publicly expressed and circulated concerning it must of necessity in the author's feelings be entwined with the cause itself, and with his own character as a *man*. . . . I know that any sarcasms or ridicule

would deeply wound his feelings, as a veteran warrior in a noble contest, feelings that claim the reverence of all good men.[7]

The review as printed outraged Coleridge because Francis Jeffrey had altered both his tribute to Wilberforce and his defence of Pitt. The tampering was the more offensive because Coleridge had no sympathy with Wilberforce and objected strongly to Pitt's policies, and Clarkson's evidence had forced him to change both opinions. Jeffrey inserted a 'nauseous and most false ascription of the Supremacy of merit' to Wilberforce and vilified Pitt's sincerity.[8] Clarkson refused to allow Coleridge to 'expose the transaction'.[9]

Wilberforce had not read it when, thanking Clarkson for a complimentary copy, he promised to 'assign it a distinguished place in my Library' in remembrance of Clarkson's 'persevering Exertions'. His sons asserted that he refused to read it 'lest he should be compelled to remark upon it'.[10] He must have read it by 1814, however, when he gently complained to Clarkson that justice had not been done to James Stephen. Clarkson took the criticism in stride, explaining that by 1807 he had scarcely met Stephen, and was, in fact, 'never introduced to him in my Life'. And Wilberforce surely had read it when some years later he told a correspondent that the *History* 'though so far accurate as that nothing is said ... which is not true & still more is not *intended* to be so, yet by no means conveys a just conception of all that deserves commemoration'. The deficiency was in the latter years of the struggle. 'Nevertheless I know not any other connected account.'[11]

The slight attention given Stephen continued to rankle in the Clapham Sect but Clarkson's excuse was valid. Stephen's chief contribution was as a private adviser to Wilberforce rather than work with the Committee and there was no record for Clarkson as historian to deal with. He might have taken notice of Stephen's writings, however, which began to appear in 1802. It can be argued that Stephen, like Macaulay and Brougham and other later adherents, belong to the next period of abolitionist activity. Clarkson saw a need for a third volume but by the time it should have been written, with the abolition of slavery, he felt too old to undertake it.[12]

The passage of the Abolition Act coincided with the winding up of the Sierra Leone Company as the colony of black settlers was turned over to Crown rule and in its place arose the African

Institution with much the same Claphamite leadership. The new Institution would watch over the execution of the law, seek a ban on the slave trade by foreign powers and promote the 'civilization and happiness' of Africa. Clarkson was on the temporary committee and became a director after the inaugural meeting on 14 April 1807 but his name would have been left out of the vote of thanks to forerunners if it had not been for the vigilance of William Smith. Clarkson's name was vital, however, for any such body to have public credence. The patron and president was the 31-year-old Duke of Gloucester, nephew of the King. Macaulay was the first secretary and Henry Thornton treasurer.[13]

Clarkson now lived at Bury St Edmunds, yet he took part in the Institution's affairs where he could be useful and his concern mounted as it became apparent that the slave trade would not be destroyed by the triumphant act of 1807 so long as there existed a market for slaves. At his suggestion, a committee was set up to keep surveillance on British and foreign ports. After one two-day visit to Liverpool, Clarkson conceded that evasions were 'deplorably numerous'. 'We always expected this, when the Act passed ... but we always had a hope that ... we should be able, in a course of years, to suppress these outrages – we now know all the tricks & subterfuges and we know the authors, we know under what flags the mischief is continued; we know the haunts of the marauders, their employers &c &c & we hope to do them away one after another, till we have cleared the Coast', said the old campaigner. With William Smith and Wilberforce he served on another committee to collect data on slavery in the British colonies.[14]

In these years, William Allen, the brilliant manufacturing chemist and Quaker philanthropist, became Clarkson's most influential friend and collaborator. Ten years Clarkson's junior, Allen was elected to the Abolition Committee in 1805 but from the beginning of the public campaign he had been an ardent supporter. Clarkson loved Allen like a brother and believed him to be the 'greatest man in Europe'.[15] He found a second home in Allen's establishment at Plough Court off Lombard Street. The two had met in 1794 but it was four years later that Allen recorded the first visit in his diary: 'That apostle of humanity, Thomas Clarkson, supped and lodged with me this evening.'[16]

Clarkson would announce his impending arrival to be an 'Inmate in your Family, when we may again unbosom ourselves to each other' and the room over the kitchen would be made ready. 'It was called the study . . . and he had to go up and down to it by a very dark staircase', Catherine Majolier Alsop, a child in the house then, recalled. Clarkson wrote much of his *History* there, and Mrs Alsop remembered being sent on explicit errands for him: 'Now, you French girl, go down into the shop, or into the counting-house, and ask Daniel, or Cornelius or John Barry, for two or three sheets of paper, one good pen, and two or three wafers. . . . I used to fancy that he went about the house with his eyes shut, for I have often had to get out of his way, so as not to be stumbled over . . . he was very near-sighted. He never used spectacles, and when he read or wrote his nose almost touched the paper'. She listened entranced as he spoke in company of the slave trade and slavery. 'Then his whole frame would become animated; his countenance . . . would be lighted up, and that noble enthusiasm which enabled him to go through so much self-denying labour, become visible in every feature.'[17]

What Clarkson called Allen's all-encompassing love for all mankind found expression in science, education and practical philanthropy until Allen had a list of causes to rival Wilberforce's. In 1811 he added a periodical to stimulate good works. He called it the *Philanthropist* and Clarkson became a regular writer and reviewer.[18]

Sierra Leone was something they must have talked about as they walked from Plough Court to Suffolk Street where the African Institution board met and through the *Philanthropist* Allen began to take up the cudgels for the often-maligned settlers, to the annoyance of some of the men who used to run the Sierra Leone Company. Perhaps the most influential among them now was Zachary Macaulay, a former governor, and partner in Freetown's largest trading company. Government policy towards the colony was largely guided by them and through their influence Sierra Leone was chosen for the vice-admiralty court to adjudicate cases of slave-ships seized on the high seas. The Freetown population was swollen by an influx of 'liberated Africans' as the people rescued from the slavers came to be called. Questions began to arise over the apprenticeship system (Macaulay's invention), by which they were presumably integrated, and the colony's compulsory militia service. Were these just new forms of slavery?

During its 16 years of existence, the Company had conspicuously failed to interest the settlers in substantial trading and in farming for export. One reason was that markets and credit were firmly in the hands of white merchants, licenced and initially subsidised by the Company. The emergence of Paul Cuffe, an American Quaker of African and Indian descent and a prosperous shipbuilder and trader from Westport, Massachusetts, seemed providential to Allen and Clarkson; he was a 'man made on purpose' for promoting the interests of Africa.

Cuffe sailed to Sierra Leone in 1811, with a plan to establish trade links and to help American free blacks settle there, after corresponding with Allen and the African Institution. Wilberforce helped to get the necessary permits for him from the Board of Trade.[19]

Cuffe made an excellent impression on the Institution's directors during his visit to London but that body was barred by its rules from engaging directly in commercial operations and could not give him the injection of capital he needed.[20] So, to forward the promising plan of trade, in January 1814 a gathering of old abolition friends at Plough Court started the 'Society for the purpose of Encouraging the Black Settlers at Sierra Leone, and the Natives of Africa generally, in the Cultivation of their Soil, by the Sale of their Produce'. Clarkson became chairman, Allen secretary and Samuel Hoare, Jr, treasurer.[21] The Society offered a direct trading connection between Britain and the Friendly Society of Sierra Leone that Cuffe helped to establish on his return visit there. When the news reached Freetown, there was 'joy on every countenance', James Wise reported. Among its next consignments the Society sent Clarkson a gold ring for his writing hand in gratitude for his 'trouble . . . in the cause of our emancipation'.[22]

Using chartered space, the cooperating societies traded African produce for manufactured goods until 1819. The failure of the Friendly Society of Sierra Leone to survive longer had much to do with continuing white commercial domination and the hazards of war and sea. Clarkson's final account showed the Society at Freetown in debt by £779 which was settled for £500 in view of such misfortunes as shipwreck and plunder.[23]

On Cuffe's plan for new settlers from America, the Institution could do more. It was willing to help pay their expenses and arrange land for a 'few very choice persons' – not more than 12 to 18. The war with the United States delayed the project until 1816 when Cuffe brought seven families to Sierra Leone.[24] Clarkson saw the interval as an opportunity to get Sierra Leone itself to rights so that mistakes of old which had antagonised the settlers would not be repeated with the new arrivals.

Proposing an inquiry, Clarkson told Allen, 'We have ourselves found out the existence of a *hateful monopoly*, which shows us *why this Colony has not like many others improved with time.*' Black merchants should have equal rights with white, differences of religion should be respected (it was possible some of the newcomers would be Quakers) and the enforced militia service should be reconsidered.[25]

This was not the first time an inquiry had been asked. The first Crown governor, brash young Thomas Perronet Thompson, who was recalled in 1810 when he began denouncing the mismanagement legacies of the Sierra Leone Company, had wanted one and was successfully ignored.[26] In 1813 the *Philanthropist* published a long critique of the seventh African Institution report which acidly observed that while Sierra Leone plainly languished, praise continued to be heaped on everyone connected with its business or government. (It was not written by either Allen or Clarkson but undoubtedly reflected their views.)[27] This brought down on Allen the wrath of the Institution hierarchy, starting with the Duke of Gloucester.[28]

Pressure for an investigation increased when the chief justice of the court at Freetown, Robert Thorpe, came home with fresh complaints. The Friendly Society had recommended him as their spokesman, therefore Allen and both Clarksons listened to him. They also interviewed others returning from the colony.[29] Thorpe was a venomous critic of Macaulay, charging that his apprentice system exploited liberated slaves and that his trading company profited by his influential position in London.[30] The Clarksons and Allen did not accept Thorpe's more virulent charges but did believe mistakes had occurred and the settlers had suffered for them.[31]

As Clarkson was not always in town, Allen became the prime mover for the inquiry which he formally proposed to the board on 7 December 1813. A committee of board members was named and it met on 15 December. Henry Brougham was chairman and Clarkson, Wilberforce, Thornton and Macaulay were among the members. After 22 long sittings, and many witnesses, the committee issued a report exonerating the policies of the Sierra Leone Company and denying the existence of a white trading monopoly. The failure of the Institution to do more for the colony was put down to lack of resources and the need to concentrate on enforcement of the slave-trade ban.[32]

'I expected nothing and was not disappointed', said Thorpe. 'They considered it would be dangerous to impeach the management, curtail the patronage, or contract the mercantile interest of an old directing servant and friend.'[33]

From their long and close association, Wilberforce was used to being at odds with Clarkson, but he was genuinely distressed at Allen's behaviour and thought him misled by Clarkson. He liked Allen and once told him – in a kindly but nonetheless bigoted way – that he wished 'your religious principles and my own were more entirely accordant'. After all the Quakers had done, said another Friend when he heard about this remark, Wilberforce and his colleagues should be convinced 'that we are, as we are willing to admit they may be, real genuine Christians'.[34]

In his diary Wilberforce wrote on 11 February 1814, 'poor Allen made his speech – How weak a defence for Philan[t].... All his prejudices & Errors, manifestly orig[ly] from Clarksons Tom & Jno, & great mischief from Thorpe & from his only talk[g] & read[g] on one Side. Am sad to see so fair & so kind a man so misled.' He grieved for the hurt to Macaulay's reputation, 'Yet he will come pure out of the fire.'

A report even more favourable to Macaulay would have emerged but that Brougham had softened it to 'let down Allen & his friends easily'. Had Macaulay demanded vindication, and got it, Allen and the Clarksons would have resigned from the African Institution and a 'mischievous rent have been made'.[35]

Allen did not enjoy angering such men as Wilberforce but he saw it as his duty to stand by the 'poor black settlers – they have few to take their part'.[36]

The *Philanthropist* continued to print articles on the circumstances of the African colonists and Clarkson contributed a lengthy 'History of the Colony of Sierra Leone', the most detailed account published in the lifetime of those involved, to dispel the cloud of mystery that hung over its origins.[37]

The diverse actors in the abolitionist drama were, however, united again in 1814 in an effort to prod the European powers to ban the slave trade. The long war ended. Louis XVIII came to the throne in France and Napoleon was exiled to Elba. Having urged the government to insist that France abolish the slave trade (which the war had effectively ended anyhow) as a condition for the restoration of any colonies, the abolitionists were cruelly shocked at the Treaty of Paris which allowed France to continue the slave trade for five years and returned the colonies with no strings. Wilberforce did not join in the welcoming cheers for Lord Castlereagh, the foreign secretary, and he told the Commons the treaty the secretary had brought home was a death warrant for thousands.[38]

The next opportunity to remove the offending article would be at the Congress of Vienna, due to open in November. A huge public rally was held at Freemasons' Hall on 17 June while the Russian emperor and King of Prussia were in London. Clarkson was so elated by the meeting, which resolved to petition Parliament (the document attracted 39 143 signatures in four days) that once more he began to believe the 'Tide will be turned'.[39] Every opportunity was seized to lay the abolition case before the foreign leaders and both Wilberforce and Allen were granted audiences by the charismatic Russian emperor.

Clarkson had copies of the abstract of the evidence on the slave trade 'decently bound' and presented to the Emperor and to the King of Prussia to read on their long route to Vienna. Later, when the Emperor, on a rough crossing to Calais, became violently ill and a courtier sympathised, the ruler pointed weakly to a drawing of the slave ship, 'It is that book . . . which has made me more sick than the sea.'[40]

Clarkson was called upon to coordinate a public outcry. 'My dearest Love', he wrote Catherine with vast enthusiasm:

Our great Committee has met, and we are beginning Business, I trust, very effectually in procuring Petitions so that perhaps in a week we shall have 5 or 600, and in a subsequent 7 days, 3 times as many more. If we *exert our Voices*, we are *sure to find a Change at the ensuing Congress. If we do not* we must leave Matters as they are, i.e. *Desolation & Misery to Africa for 5 Years*, and, if *for that time, then perhaps for 20 or 30 more, as no one can say, when it will end, if it be once suffered to be renewed.*[41]

There was a clamour from abolitionists around the country, unwilling to 'be answerable for the guilt' of doing nothing. Wilberforce was now an enthusiast for petitioning, and called on his friends in various towns to express their deep disappointment at the treaty. Clarkson set up a headquarters at the New London Tavern, Cheapside, and sent out 2000 letters with the form of words to be used in appealing to Parliament.[42] To the old Abolition

Committee lists were added names from Wesleyan leaders, who also joined in the letter-writing task. The first days had been chaotic, the hastily-formed group proceeding '*without any order*, and contrary to what the good old Slave Committee would have done', Clarkson told his wife in one of his daily scribbles, 'but yesterday William Allen, myself, and two Quakers [Richard Phillips was one of them] were occupied in a System of organization, by which Labour would be properly distributed throughout. . . . This Morning I expect to see all the Departments at their proper Work.'

Since it would take several weeks to channel the 'Voice of England' to ministers, he decided to bring Catherine and their son to London. While she visited her sister, 'Tom can give us a little assistance by sitting for an Hour or two at my Elbow & see our Work going on.'[43]

The astonishing total of 861 petitions voted at public meetings and signed by 755 000 people was laid before Parliament and, backed by this outpouring, Wilberforce easily carried an address to the Prince Regent and an amendment to an address on the peace which kept the subject open for renewed consideration after the Vienna meeting. The Prince, not noted for favouring abolition, wrote to the French king to say he would regard it as a personal favour if the article were given up.[44]

The African Institution committee climaxed a summer of feverish agitation with an appeal, signed by Clarkson, for funds to carry on its work and the old Abolition Committee, with Clarkson under another hat and in another chair, held one of its rare meetings and donated £240.[45]

Sometimes Clarkson must have seemed like a 'loose cannon' as he popped up with one idea after another, heedless of protocol or practice. Now he decided that he could do some good for the cause at Vienna when the European powers met and one has a certain sympathy for Wilberforce when he expressed shock.[46] Clarkson proposed to go as a delegate of the African Institution and the Duke of Gloucester seemed to approve. The Duke of Wellington, ambassador to France, and Lord Castlereagh also encouraged Clarkson when he put his plan to them. Both Clarkson and Macaulay furnished Wellington with books and background reading before he left for Paris.[47]

Clarkson prepared an address to present to each ruler at Vienna. 'You yourselves have been great sufferers', he reminded them.

'Some of you have been in exile in a foreign country. But divine providence has restored you to your former comforts. . . . Make the signing of the definitive Treaty memorable by proscribing the execrable Slave Ship from all parts of the world. In so doing you will show your gratitude to God for the Blessings you have received, and in a way most acceptable to Him'. He kept the tract to 32 pages so that the busy potentates could master the subject in half an hour.[48]

Wilberforce was adamant that Clarkson should not go to Vienna and they argued on two successive Sundays at Wilberforce's London home. Clarkson gave in 'for no other reason than because it is your wish', but was clearly nettled. Privately he thought Wilberforce was being far too timid but he allowed himself to be persuaded that Castlereagh must be left to take full credit or blame for whatever happened.[49]

Clarkson insisted, however, that he would go to Paris to see what could be done, by circulating his works and talking with prominent figures, to encourage the government to cut off the slave trade sooner than the treaty provided. Few of the Amis des Noirs had survived the Revolution (those who did had no influence in the new government) and the slave-trade issue had faded out of sight. There was deep suspicion that British cries for abolition hid some self-serving purpose.[50]

He took Catherine with him and the change of air and scene was a tonic. They stayed at the Hôtel du Helder and while Clarkson plunged happily into work for some 14 hours a day Catherine polished her French at the theatre and visited gardens, galleries and museums with the compatible Henry Crabb Robinson. Sometimes she helped with her husband's voluminous correspondence. They all attended the English church services at the Duke of Wellington's and Clarkson was able at last to introduce his wife to the Marquis de Lafayette and Bishop Gregoire.[51]

When the Comte de St Morys, a friend who had been in exile in England, an arch royalist but a warm abolitionist and a great help to Clarkson in distributing his tracts, chided him for seeing so much of 'those people', Clarkson replied very seriously, 'I know but two classes of persons – the friends and the enemies of Africa. All the friends of Africa are my friends, whatever they may be besides. You and Monsieur LaFayette are the same in my eyes.'[52]

Clarkson was cordially received by the Duke of Wellington who had mastered his briefing papers on the road to Paris. He had presented a copy of Clarkson's address to Louis xviii[53] and he passed on the advice he had received from Talleyrand and the King that in view of the deep antagonism towards Britain, the best thing to do would be to show the 'literati of Paris' the horrors of the slave trade and they would set the tone for the country. The French slave-trade interests were powerful and the public, if left ignorant of the facts, would support them. The King told Wellington that 'I can no more abolish the trade against the will of the people of France than the King of England can continue it against the will of the people of England', and that he would welcome a 'current of popular feeling' which would allow him to ban the trade. Under these circumstances, Wellington urged Clarkson to proceed 'in our good old English fashion'.[54]

Accordingly the address was printed and widely circulated. Clarkson remembered that his *Impolicy of the African Slave Trade* had been published in Paris 25 years ago and rummaged through bookshops until he found a copy which could be reprinted. The censor cleared it in record time of twelve hours and the Duke used his diplomatic pouch to bring over the blocks for the slave-ship diagram so that it could be included. Soon a copy was in the hands of every legislator. From this and other offers of help, including those from persons whom he had never known before, Clarkson was persuaded that an abolition committee could easily be re-established.[55]

In conversations with Wellington, Lord Holland, the Russian ambassador and others Clarkson learned that the French government was willing to ban the slave trade from the Senegal to the Volta rivers and might outlaw the trade entirely but could not, from public sentiment, do it unconditionally. Clarkson discussed with Wellington the possibility of ceding Mauritius, St Lucia or Tobago in return for abolition and found that the British government was prepared to pay large sums to Portugal and Spain to stop their slave-trading.

All this and other gleanings from his mission, Clarkson reported in a long confidential letter which he sent to a few co-workers. He saw a link to the petition campaign in the energy now displayed in British officialdom. 'No other satisfactory answer can be given why Administration was so apparently indifferent to the subject when the treaty was made and why so interested since.'

Wilberforce and Stephen were horrified at what they regarded as Clarkson's indiscretion in describing conversations with the ambassador. Clarkson, for his part, was indignant at their suspicions that he intended to publish the document. Lord Grenville, however, acknowledged it graciously and rejoiced to hear of so much being done to bring the issue before the French public. He suggested some other avenues to pursue.[56]

In Vienna, the Congress confined itself to a declaration that the slave trade was the 'desolation of Africa, the degradation of Europe, and the afflicting scourge of humanity.'

11

Of Friends and Family Matters

In the autumn of 1806 the Clarksons settled in Bury St Edmunds, the ancient Suffolk market town 72 miles from London where Catherine grew up. While abolition remained his chief concern, Clarkson once more combined his research and writing with farming on land leased nearby.

They took a genteel house in St Mary's Square at the end of Westgate Street where the widowed William Buck and Catherine's sister Anne lived in the family home. Three of her brothers were settled in the area and the fourth, John, in London. They were in the parish of St Mary's Church where they had married and where, in the shady graveyard that stretched to the Abbey ruins, her mother was buried.

The house was of recent fashionable construction in pale brick with red-brick dressings. They lived in a 'very comfortable & respectable way'. Servants were about six guineas a year, plus tea and sugar.[1]

Dorothy Wordsworth thought that her dear friends might have lived 'more to your own satisfaction in London – you might have chosen your own society, and that of the best, and you need never have had more than you liked, which is not possible always to help in a country town' but that, she conceded, was 'out of the question, he disliking it so much'. The house, however, as Catherine described it, was 'all that could be desired in a town house, and how cheap!'[2]

The Clarksons became regular churchgoers, surprising her dissenting friends but not the Wordsworths, who adopted the same practice at about the same time. But, 'you have no business at Church in winter', Dorothy warned Catherine, alarmed to hear that she had attended on four successive Sundays, 'and . . . you are more likely to catch cold there than anywhere else'.[3]

It amused the Grasmere family to learn that their somewhat

unconventional friend had become 'so great a work woman & a member of a committee too! You married Ladies come high', Dorothy wrote. Catherine was involved with a lying-in charity that supplied baby linen to the poor.[4]

'Bury is grown very fine', Catherine told them on another occasion. 'We have Lords & Ladies & rich widows & *poor gentry* like us make no figures amongst them. Yet I must say that considering how little Mr C lays himself out to please such folks he is very much thought of here.'[5]

Tom's education had been a factor in the choice of Bury. Clarkson believed that the notoriously rough and rowdy public schools tended to 'harden the heart & corrupt the morals' and he was convinced that abolition would not have been defeated year after year if most members of Parliament had not been to public schools.[6] He enrolled Tom as a day pupil in the scholastically sound King Edward vi Grammar School in Northgate Street. Tom was to take prizes for essays in each of the three years before he went up to Trinity College, Cambridge, in 1814 and as a fifth-former he earned the distinction of having his verses published. 'It *is* a feather in his cap', his mother boasted, 'for the like was never done for any fifth form boy before,'[7] In his last year at the school he stood fourth among top boys. His headmaster was Dr Benjamin Heath Malkin, well-known then in literary circles, and the under-master was the Reverend Samuel Tillbrook, a family friend and later Tom's tutor at Cambridge.[8]

The Clarksons' son was much loved by their friends who noticed his strong resemblance to his mother and used such phrases as 'modest & obliging' to describe him pleasingly to his parents.[9] Mary Lamb had him in mind when she wrote her nursery classic, *Tales from Shakespeare*. In a Christmas letter when he was 9 she sent greetings to 'our old friend Tom, whom we do not like a bit the worse for being a little tall, a little awkward, and not over passionately addicted to literature'. A year later she was glad to hear his learning was progressing slowly. 'Indeed I have reasons for wishing him a little backward in that respect, for I have a little book I mean to send him and the printer has been so long bringing it out I began to fear Tom would attain so much knowledge as to outgrow the use thereof, and Tom's approbation of my first production was one of the things I built upon.'[10]

How one would have loved to witness the escapade in which small stout Mary in her bonnet and full dark skirts helped weedy young Tom rob a cherry tree on the Lambs' first visit to the Clarksons at Bury St Edmunds in June 1807. 'Of all the places I ever saw Bury has made the liveliest impression on my memory', said Mary Lamb. But the long-anticipated visit ended sadly. In a moment of madness in 1796, Mary had stabbed her mother to death and the fits of insanity returned at intervals all her life. One took her at Bury St Edmunds, and Charles hurried her back to the asylum at Hoxton. Bury 'passed away as like a dream', he wrote Catherine. 'But I have some recollections of a great deal of kindness & hospitality, abruptly terminating. . . . I know you will grieve for us, but I hope my sister's illness is not worse than many she has got through before.'[11]

When Tom Clarkson decided, after two years at the university, not to sit for an honours degree, Wordsworth, who had left Cambridge without a degree, admonished him like an uncle: 'Know thyself, look into the goodly garden of thy own mind, and pluck up the weeds, for it is yet springtime, early spring with thee, before they have choked the fragrant flowers and the profitable Herbs. Bestir thyself and be a Son worthy of thy never to be forgotten Father.'[12] Tom migrated to Peterhouse where Tillbrook was and dutifully received his BA in 1818.

In a society with no state-aided education whatsoever, illiteracy was, of course, widespread. Like William Allen, Clarkson had no fears of mass education and welcomed the plan devised by Joseph Lancaster to teach large numbers cheaply and rapidly and without any religious bias. He joined other leading Burians to open a school on Lancaster's plan for 200 children in 1811. Urging one like it for Shrewsbury, he told Archdeacon Corbett it could cost as little as seven shillings per boy, less in a larger school.[13]

Clarkson also helped to found the Suffolk Auxiliary of the British and Foreign Bible Society, a favourite philanthropy of many abolitionists.[14] Less popular, shunned by evangelicals and treated as attacks on property, were the efforts he espoused, again with William Allen, Thomas Fowell Buxton and Richard Phillips, among others, to reform the penal code and in particular to reduce the use of the 'wicked . . . & impolitic Punishment of Crimes by Death'. A 'little society' to this end was set on foot in April 1808 at a time when capital punishment was just the crowning evil of a barbaric criminal code. More than 200 offences – from stealing property worth five shillings to forgery and murder – carried the death penalty.[15]

Clarkson's quarrel with capital punishment was that it was unchristian and ineffective. In spite of it, crimes were rising rapidly. Because of it, prosecutions were not always brought, witnesses would not come forward. No less important was the fact that the death penalty 'is irremediable and all human tribunals fallible'.[16]

There was not room in Clarkson's life for many causes but one other should be mentioned. This was pacifism. It was only after the French wars that it took public form. The first meeting of what became the Society for the Promotion of Permanent and Universal Peace took place in June 1814 with Clarkson's brother John in the chair. The host was, as so often, William Allen at Plough Court.[17]

Clarkson may have been the 'Friend of Peace' in Bury St Edmunds who in the *Philanthropist* the next year proposed a campaign of public education on the values of abandoning war but it was June 1816 before the Peace Society was publicly announced to a war-weary Europe. Robert Marsden, a stockbroker, was chairman; John Clarkson treasurer and Thomas Clarkson the best-known figure among the 20 Anglicans, Dissenters and Quakers who made up the committee.[18] An auxiliary started up in Bury St Edmunds. Clarkson wrote one of the Peace Society's first publications, *An Essay on the Doctrines and Practice of the Early Christians as They Relate to War*, in which he pointed out that the early church was pacifist, and it was only after corruption set in during the third century that Christians became soldiers and adopted the concept of a 'just' or 'holy war'.[19] This and other peace tracts were attacked as highly subversive, especially by the evangelical *Christian Observer*.[20] The Society made quiet progress, meeting privately for its first ten years and emerging with a public gathering in 1826. As Clarkson and Richard Phillips saw it, the Peace Society proposed a shift in public sentiment comparable in its depth to the abolition of the slave trade.[21]

Clarkson first dealt with the doctrine of pacifism in his important study of Quakers. The three-volume work, published in 1806, has a special interest for historians. In Clarkson's time the Quakers differed from their countrymen more than many foreigners in their language, dress and informality. A hundred years later, most of the outward differences had gone and the Society had adopted that 'conformity to the World' against which its prophets had warned.[22]

To the biographer it also reveals something of Clarkson's own

religious preferences. We know that he was a committed Christian
but he defies categorisation. Most previous writers have either put
him in the Clapham Sect with Wilberforce or labelled him a
Quaker. The latter has more substance; the Society often seems his
spiritual home. When in 1815 the Tsar Alexander I asked him
point-blank whether he was a Quaker, Clarkson replied that he
'was not in Name, but I hoped in Spirit; I was nine parts out of ten
of their way of thinking'. The Quakers reciprocated his regard. His
was one of the few pictures allowed in their homes.[23]

He remained in the Church of England, yet rejected ordination
as a priest, clerical clothes and the title 'reverend'. He left no
explanation of his conduct but inferences were and can be drawn.
The established church in his day was an integral part of the ruling
class and the clergy (his saintly father an exception rather than the
rule) notoriously lax. Church positions were often sinecures distributed by patronage to the well-connected. It was the age of the
fox-hunting parson, the hard drinker and high liver who abandoned his parish (or parishes) to a curate and enjoyed rank and
fortune in society. Clarkson and Archdeacon Corbett agreed that
the clergy did not have or earn respect; their object seemed to be to
'enjoy the revenues of the church as little encumber'd with its
duties as possible'.[24]

Clarkson had a horror of being 'servile' or doing 'unhandsome
things' for money. The use of the church to climb materially and
socially was demeaning and he was repelled from an early age by
the idea of being paid for performing religious duties, as if in
'trade'. (It was also a Quaker tenet that ministers should not be
paid and one reason the sect objected to tithing.) Even Catherine
could not follow his puritanical reasoning. When Samuel Whitbread, among others, wanted to present Clarkson with a living she
thought he might well have taken it and done much good. He
carried his 'delicacy' to a romantic length, she ventured to think.[25]

Someone closer to his time said of Clarkson, 'He believed that
Christianity in its sublimest discoveries can be reduced and
embodied in the lives and actions of its professors. It entered into
his whole being, and constituted the great presiding and controll-
ing power of his mind and conduct.'[26]

Since writing was one of his trades, Clarkson was glad that it
paid. He received £600 – 'a famous sum' – for the work on
Quakerism, leading Dorothy Wordsworth to comment, 'We may
now fairly call you rich people.' 'Alas! poetry is a bad trade', she

observed, sending congratulations, 'and William's works sell slow-ly.' Clarkson estimated a clear profit of £1700 on the first edition and the book reached a third edition within a year.[27]

In writing of pacifism, Clarkson had used the example of Pennsylvania under William Penn where the native Indians and the British colonisers managed to live in a harmony unfamiliar in other settler lands. His next major literary work was a lengthy biography of Penn, published in 1813.[28] It was a critical failure, though the best book on Penn so far.

'Was there ever such a book as Clarksons life of Wm Penn!' wrote Robert Southey to John Murray, who had sent him a copy to review.

> really in respect of Clarkson . . . it is best to leave his volumes unnoticed. . . . If I could make a life of Wm Penn that would be in any degree interesting, the better way would be so to do, and to avoid all criticism – but it must needs be a dull task. . . . like the multitude I had given him credit for being a great man till Clarkson undeceived me. . . . Nevertheless, if it must be reviewed I will do what I can, and serve it as we do a calfs or cods head – conceal its insipidity by aid of the sauce.

In the event, the *Quarterly* carried no review.[29]

Unfortunately, the *Edinburgh Review* did – a long one.

'It is impossible to look into any of Mr Clarkson's books without feeling that he is an Excellent man – and a very bad writer', it began.

> Feeling in himself not only an entire toleration of honest tediousness, but a decided preference for it upon all occasions . . . he seems to have . . . forgotten, that though dulness may be a very venial fault in a good man, it is such a fault in a book as to render its goodness of no avail whatsoever. . . . With all his philanthropy, piety, and inflexible honesty, he has not escaped the sin of tediousness, – and that to a degree that must render him almost illegible to any but Quakers, Reviewers, and others who make public profession of patience insurmountable. He has no taste, and no spark of vivacity – not the vestige of an ear for harmony – and a prolixity of which modern times have scarcely preserved any other example. . . . he has great industry – scrupulous veracity – and that serious and sober enthusiasm for his

subject, which is in the long-run to disarm ridicule. . . . above all, he is perfectly free from affectation; so that, though we may be wearied, we are never disturbed or offended – and read on, in tranquillity, till we find it impossible to read any more.[30]

The Wordsworths rushed to Clarkson's defence. The Edinburgh reviewers were a 'vicious set', said Dorothy. 'Whenever Mr Clarkson is deeply interested he writes well and *must write* well. – and in the flatter parts of all [his] works there is always a pleasing simplicity and good sense which the Edinburgh Reviewers can neither understand nor value.'[31]

Clarkson's hopes of becoming an academic historian were disappointed. When in 1807 the professor in modern history at Trinity College died, Clarkson applied for the coveted post which was in the gift of the government and he asked Wilberforce and other parliamentary friends to speak to Lord Grenville on his behalf. His study of the Quakers had been published only a few months before and he suspected that he might be turned down as one of them. But Lord Henry Petty, the new MP for Cambridge, thought the greater hazard was the large number of applicants from within the university.[32] It was Clarkson's second and last attempt to return to scholarly life. In 1791 he applied for a fellowship at St John's but an applicant thought to be a better mathematician won the post.[33]

Clarkson's other trade, of course, was farming. He was more of a gentleman farmer now, employing a bailiff, but it was he who decided the rotation of crops, bought and sold the cattle and sheep and took samples of corn to market.[34] He would drive visitors out to the farm in one of the little 'ass curricles' or 'dickey carts' then popular with the gentry of Bury St Edmunds. When they stayed with the Clarksons in 1815, William and Mary Wordsworth nearly bought a curricle and pair for £25. Later Catherine could not convince Samuel Tillbrook to drive one to the Lakes for them. 'I am sure [it] would take him down better than his old pony but he has a prejudice against asses & I believe thinks that we who are in favour of them are asses ourselves', she wrote to Mary Wordsworth.[35]

Long visits as well as uninhibited letters maintained the bonds between the Clarksons and their Lakeland friends. Sara Hutchinson came to Bury St Edmunds in the early summer of 1807 and the following year Mary Monkhouse had the same opportunity to 'know, & love and feel, the goodness of such a noble Creature, as [Mrs Clarkson] most truly is'.[36] In 1809 Clarkson, now 49, took his 12-year-old son to the Lakes for a summer walking tour, each of them with 'shoes made on purpose'.[37] It was Dorothy Wordsworth's turn to come to Bury St Edmunds in 1810 and, leaving William at Coleorton with Sir George and Lady Beaumont, she set off for Cambridge where Clarkson met her coach. Next day he showed her the university town, perhaps too helpfully. Dorothy fell silent before the beauty of the Newton statue in Trinity Chapel while an organ played background music but 'dear Mr Clarkson did now and then disturb me by pointing out the wrinkles in the silk stockings, the buckles etc etc all which etceteras are in truth worthy of admiration'. They dined, saw King's Chapel, set off in Clarkson's gig, drank tea at Newmarket and arrived at Bury St Edmunds at 9 o'clock.[38]

Dorothy stayed eight weeks. She liked the house in St Mary's Square – it was the 'same as being in a village' – and she enjoyed the clean and pretty town and 'though the neighbourhood is not very interesting we have had very pleasant walks. Mrs Clarkson does not walk. She rides upon a pony and I walk by her side. . . . We pass our time very pleasantly – chiefly amongst ourselves, for Mrs Clarkson does not keep much company though she has a large acquaintance.'[39]

Still a semi-invalid, Catherine habitually rose at noon after spending the morning in bed, sitting up in a pale dressing gown and neat cap, surrounded by piles of books and papers. She breakfasted there, wrote her letters and kept the household accounts.[40]

The Clarksons entertained at dinner or tea, dined out, too, and spent many an evening playing whist. But it was a quiet home. It was not unknown for Clarkson to fall asleep after dinner while Catherine and Henry Robinson kept themselves awake by playing piquet. Catherine enjoyed reading aloud, especially from any new publication of Wordsworth or Coleridge. 'I hear of parties here and there but I have not been to any yet', Catherine remarked. 'I wish it was more the fashion for people to meet in a public room for I like to go out in an Evening.' There was a gentlemen's coffee room in the town but no assembly rooms where cards and refreshments could be had.[41]

Catherine Clarkson was a passionate admirer of Wordsworth's poetry. She was incensed, although not surprised, at the poor welcome which greeted *The Excursion* in 1814. It sold slowly and the critics were cool, sometimes savage. Had Wordsworth written in prose, she declared, he might have become the founder of a sect and sent missionaries all over the world.[42]

The work was dismissed as dull and yet Tom Clarkson pleased his mother (and Wordsworth) by staying up all night to read it, and at 18, he usually preferred 'flowery soft sounding verses'.

'Your anecdote of Tom, that he sate up all night reading William's poem gave me as much pleasure as anything I have heard of the effect produced by it', Dorothy wrote. 'I must say I think it speaks highly in favour of Tom's feeling and enthusiasm that he was so wrought upon.'[43]

The Wordsworths were kept waiting for Clarkson's impressions (there seems to be no record of them) and wanted him to write or arrange a review in the *Philanthropist* to encourage rich Quakers to buy copies. When Catherine sent her thoughts for a review, Dorothy called the 'receipt' excellent 'and we pray you earnestly to do the work yourself . . . and not be over nice. . . . You cannot but satisfy others, and will do the sale of the Excursion service, that is all we care about.' The review – anonymous, but it could have been Catherine's – in the *Philanthropist* praised the poet's 'sublime and beautiful imagery' and promised that from 'Philanthropists the Poet will meet with that consideration and esteem which those who have a deeper insight into the human heart will be ready to bestow'.[44]

Their letters did not always dwell on things of the mind. Dorothy wrote about making over Tom's nankeen trousers for Johnny Wordsworth and Catherine sent her housekeeper's receipt for the spot on 'dear little Willy's head'. She was sure (and Catherine was regarded by all as an 'excellent Doctoress') that it wasn't ringworm.[45]

The death in 1812 of her namesake, whom she had never seen in the four short years of her life, soon followed by that of Thomas Wordsworth, the 'darling of the house' brought forth some of the most anguished exchanges in the all-too-frequent sharing of family tragedies. In the Clarksons' case it was the ravages in John Clarkson's brood that were so heartbreaking. Of his ten children only four survived him. After the Wordsworth children died, Catherine made a surprising comment: 'Of all accidents or misfortunes to which humanity is liable none brings its own peculiar consolation so quickly as this – a dead infant is a *beautiful* sight. A little child leaves behind it none but pleasurable recollections.'[46]

When Wordsworth wrote to tell Catherine about the little girl's death, he signed the letter, 'my dear Friend and now our only dear living Catherine, most Tenderly yours, Wm Wordsworth'. Dorothy sent Catherine 'a morsel of your dear God-daughter's hair – all that you have ever seen of her'.[47]

The Clarksons remained close to Coleridge, too, in the years after Eusemere. In 1806 when he returned from Malta, Clarkson, then in London for the last months of the abolition campaign, helped him retrieve his luggage and papers from the ship and customs and Coleridge escorted Catherine home to their new house at Bury St Edmunds where he stayed a few days before joining the Wordsworths at Coleorton. As Clarkson remained in London, Coleridge carried on by letter a metaphysical discussion they had begun about what is the spirit of God and what is the soul? Some of the ideas floated reappeared in *The Friend* and they are the essence of Coleridge's later *Aids to Reflection*.[48]

When Coleridge delivered his lectures at the Royal Institution in 1808 – his 'bread and cheese employment' – Catherine urged Henry Robinson to attend them and to advertise them among his friends. She introduced Robinson to Coleridge by letter and Coleridge left a free ticket for him as a token of his love for Catherine. Robinson provided Catherine with a resumé of each lecture. The series over, Coleridge stopped again at Bury St Edmunds for a month on his way to Grasmere.[49]

On that visit, Coleridge was making plans for a weekly magazine (*The Friend*) and enlisted Clarkson's help in signing up subscribers.[50] Hardened by his own battles with printers and booksellers, Clarkson undertook to do much more, and bombarded Coleridge with advice.[51] He urged Coleridge first of all to delete 'Dress, Dancing, Music' from his prospectus else the 'Quakers might take fright'. He advised on price – few would object to a shilling a copy but few would pay more – and on how to avoid heavy stamp duties. He and Basil Montagu helped procure steady paper supplies. Clarkson strongly recommended Coleridge employ a printer rather than handle it himself, or he would find booksellers unwilling to take his work. He particularly counselled that Coleridge have at least 30 essays written before he printed one, but Coleridge launched his prospectuses without a line written. The Wordsworths had scant hopes for his success. Were he not under their roof, said Dorothy, he would be as much a 'slave to stimulants' as ever.[52]

Coleridge grumbled about Clarkson's interference: 'Had I conceived Mr Clarkson's Business to have extended beyond the matter of Subscribers and Prospectuses he is the last man, God bless him! with whom I should have troubled you', he wrote Daniel Stuart in February 1809, 'for he has never more than one thought in his brain at a time, let it be great or small. I have called him the moral Steam-Engine, or the Giant with one idea – Heaven knows! how well I love and how very highly I revere him. He shall be my Friend, Exemplar, Saint – any thing only not my Counsellor in matters of Business.'[53]

Clarkson almost despaired of Coleridge's project when in June 1809 with *The Friend* barely begun, Coleridge decided to print a volume of poems. 'What enemy adverse to your comfort and future happiness, could have proposed to you the wild prospect (*burthened as you are . . .*) of keeping you in eternal hot water in *point of money matters* by recommending you to print your *Poems at this particular time?*' he protested. Sell the poems to Longman, he pressed, for the 100 guineas offered and pay the paper bill for *The Friend*. 'You can write fresh poetry almost as fast as you can speak.'[54]

Clarkson sent out hundreds of prospectuses and obtained at least 70 subscribers but Coleridge was far from grateful. Those solicited thus privately said 'yes' to avoid saying 'no', then did not pay up, he complained to his generous friend Lady Beaumont as his high hopes ebbed.[55] He was aggrieved when Clarkson suggested he was charging too much at a shilling a sheet – 'a serious sum for a person to *bestow* upon an author'.

'Pity that Mr C had not added – "when there are so many other *objects* of distress that have equal or stronger claims on the charitable"' Coleridge wrote bitterly. He continued, 'I struggle to forget that [Mr Clarkson] would be a case more in point, if an original coarseness of mind had not made the labours and toils of beneficence less difficult to him, than they would have been to a man of equal benevolence, but of a finer tact and more exquisite sensibility. Still, his example shows what *one* good man may do when he goes to work in right earnest'.

The visionary enterprise proceeded erratically for 28 issues, then died in 1810.[56]

The quarrel between Coleridge and Wordsworth nearly broke

Catherine's heart. It arose from Wordsworth's remark to a mutual friend which Coleridge interpreted to mean that he had been a nuisance in the Wordsworths' home, which he had made his own for some time.[57] Catherine instinctively sided with Wordsworth – there might be something stern in his manner but his conduct had always been 'affectionate & forebearing' – while Coleridge's 'gloomy fancies or wild dreams' let him think the worst of even his best friends, she told Henry Robinson, who was to help, in the end, to repair the rift.[58] The poets did not meet for many months and the break in their creative friendship never fully healed. When Coleridge did not rush to his friends after the death of their small son Thomas, Catherine, in London, decided to see him. She had received no answer to a note and, urged on by letters from Grasmere, called upon Robinson to escort her to his lodgings.[59]

The interview with Coleridge in March 1813 must have been deeply affecting to them both. She came away fearful that he had not long to live. 'It is frightful to me to think of losing him whilst his mind seems so utterly estranged from all its best feelings', she said, but she was glad she had seen him – it gave her strength to face 'the agony which I shall have to bear whenever it pleases God to remove him from this world – It cannot be so great as that which I suffered for the extinction of his poetical life'. Coleridge did not yet realise that the cause of failure lay in himself. He had said to her, 'Catherine I shall soon be a poet again you will make me a poet'; but she thought, 'It is past and I know by experience that there is a virtue in the strength of love which makes a thing endurable that else would break the heart.'[60]

It was at such times that Catherine felt most keenly her isolation in Bury St Edmunds, a prisoner of poor health. She was Clarkson's confidante, sometimes his amanuensis, but he was often absent. They had never appeared together in public until the installation of the Duke of Gloucester as chancellor of Cambridge University in the summer of 1811. She read *The Times* and *Courier* daily but depended on her husband to feed her 'insatiable craving' for other public news and on Henry Robinson for the 'tittle tattle' of the lecture halls and London drawing-rooms.

As she passed her 39th birthday, she told her childhood friend, 'I am still only a great baby without the simplicity of that period of life & my value a zero. The more I reflect upon what I see around me & feel within me the greater & more awful does the mystery of life appear – a mystery which no process of thought can abate.

Happy they who run on their course evenly with time, whom neither ambition, nor disappointed affection, nor bodily disease, nor the working of a dissatisfied mind force into enquiry of why? wherefore? cui bono?'[61]

Of Clarkson at about the same time we have William Hazlitt's impression in the portrait he painted at Bury St Edmunds when his subject was 51. Catherine thought the face 'most beautifully painted & there is a freedom in the whole Picture very creditable for Hazlitt'. Twenty years before, von Breda gave us an author in powdered wig and velvet coat. Hazlitt presented a self-assured provincial gentleman in tweeds, one curl of dark hair fallen over his brow, his lips thoughtfully pursed. He sits before a bare wall without a shred of conventional furniture or drapery. It is the only surviving Clarkson portrait in which he is not holding a quill pen.[62]

12

Two Emperors

In the interval between the victory over the British slave trade in 1807 and the start of the antislavery campaign in the 1820s Clarkson served his cause chiefly on the international stage. This is an extraordinary fact, for Clarkson was a private citizen of very moderate means. He held no public office, had limited access to government departments, commanded no political or religious faction and dispensed no patronage. He did not even make his home in the capital. His position as a director of the African Institution gave him a quasi-official status, perhaps, but he had become a kind of institution himself, distinguished by far-flung contacts and a voracious appetite for information and hard work.

Napoleon Bonaparte returned from Elba in 1815 and in his Hundred Days abolished the slave trade (which he had re-established in 1802 after the Revolution had banned it) perhaps in a gesture to win British goodwill. But it may have been, as Lafayette for one believed, that he acted to court popularity with his own people, more ready now than it was supposed the year before to approve such a step. Perhaps for similar reasons, the restored monarchy did not rescind the abolition but since the law was never promulgated, French slaving continued, along with the trade of Portugal and Spain.[1]

Having worked on his French with a master for several months, Clarkson returned to Paris in September 1815 with the sole object of speaking to the Tsar Alexander I at the new gathering of Allied sovereigns.[2] Great hopes were attached by abolitionists to the enigmatic 38-year-old autocrat, educated in eighteenth-century humanitarian philosophy, who was known at this time for his piety. It was said his knees wore the mark of constant prayer.[3] The fact that feudal Russia had no African slave trade gave him freedom to act on the subject of abolition, for which he had argued at the Vienna Congress, unsuccessfully.

Clarkson was inspired to approach him because of the Emperor's serious interest in Quakerism.[4] In London in 1814 he had amazed everyone by asking to attend a Friends meeting and William Allen had been conscripted to lead him to one. Later the Emperor received Allen, John Wilkinson and Stephen Grellet (their hats firmly on their heads) and questioned them for two hours. He agreed entirely that worship 'was an internal and spiritual thing' and declared he was 'one in sentiment with us . . . though, from his peculiar position, his practice must be different', Allen said. Before sailing from Dover the Emperor and his sister, the Duchess of Oldenburg, paid a surprise call on a Quaker family, looked all round the neat home and took tea.

Clarkson thought the opportunity to see him might never come again. He consulted the Duke of Gloucester who replied with a letter of introduction to the Emperor whom he had met the year before.[5] A complete set of his works was sent by Clarkson to Alexander and he used his Quaker connections in requesting an audience. He gave this letter with the Duke's to Baroness Krudener, at whose Paris home the Emperor often called of an evening to discuss religion. He read them in her presence and when he spotted the names of Allen, Wilkinson and Grellet promised to find time for Clarkson.[6]

This time Clarkson travelled with his son, who was now 19. While he awaited Alexander's return from reviewing his troops, Clarkson introduced Tom to old friends and favourite sights.[7] They dined with Helen Maria Williams and called on the Duke of Wellington. The Comte de St Morys took the youth to the King's chapel to watch His Majesty at mass and another friend took him to the opera. With Tom's university tutor, Samuel Tillbrook, Clarkson visited the British camp and was delighted to meet a Bury St Edmunds lad of the 52nd guards regiment. He wrote Catherine a long letter about French politics. He was perturbed that the mere 35 000 electors of France, sick of Bonaparte, had returned an aristocrat-laden Chamber of Deputies likely to try to restore feudal privileges.

He captured the atmosphere of Paris filled with liberating armies when he told his wife about the three Polish lancers serving the Emperor of Austria who slept in the yard of the Hôtel du Helder beside their horses and of the coachmen (attached to a Russian general) who washed the carriages, fed the horses and 'laid *themselves down to sleep all night* on the Stones in the open air – an easy way of maintaining Servants – what w^d our English Servants think of this'. It was so hot in Paris that September that Clarkson himself had to sleep with his windows wide open all night.

On 23 September Clarkson was ushered into the Emperor's presence.[8] 'I felt a little embarrassed as to what I ought to say, but I was instantly relieved ... by the affability & condescension of the Emperor' who took his hand and addressed him in English. He was honoured that Clarkson had come from England expressly to see him. He had always believed the slave trade an outrage against human nature but when he read Clarkson's books and saw the print of the slave-ship, he was further determined to do his utmost to 'wipe away such a pestilence from the face of the Earth'.

The audience lasted more than an hour. Clarkson voiced the gratitude of all abolitionists for so powerful a friend and described their disappointment that the Congress at Vienna had not proclaimed the slave trade piracy. Alexander agreed that it would have done the collective governments honour to do so, but the powers there had a single object, the 'Future Safety, Peace & Tranquility of Europe', and harmony was essential. He believed abolition would prevail in the long run. He invited Clarkson to write him with suggestions for achieving it.

Alexander inquired after the Quaker trio and told Clarkson his conversation with them was among his most agreeable memories.

Abruptly he asked Clarkson whether he were a Quaker. 'I replied, that I was not so in name, but I hoped in spirit, I was nine parts in ten of their way of thinking. They had been Fellow Labourers with me in our Great Cause, the more I had known them, the more I had loved them. The Emperor said (putting his hand on to his breast) "I embrace them more than any other People; *I consider myself as one of them!*"'

An opportunity to help a free black state came in 1815 when Clarkson received a letter from Henry Christophe, the visionary black ruler of independent Haiti (or Hayti, as it was spelled).[9] His interest, of course, dated to meetings in 1789 with Vincent Ogé in Paris. After the failure of Ogé's revolt and a series of race-wars the blacks won their freedom.

Henry Christophe had fought with Toussaint l'Ouverture and Jean-Jacques Dessalines. Toussaint died in a French prison; Dessalines after proclaiming himself emperor in 1804 was murdered, and Christophe as commander of the army took control of the north, while Alexandre Pétion, his mulatto rival, became president of a southern 'republic'. In 1811 Christophe made himself Henry I, King of Hayti. Energetic and ambitious, he surrounded himself with tutors and advisers and established a prosperous and orderly state under an absolute monarchy. Under a new code of law, he broke up large plantations, developed irrigation and created a disciplined army.

Haiti lived under a threat that the French would try to reclaim it. When the monarchy was restored in France, still supporting slavery and the trade, King Henry vowed to make his country Protestant and English-speaking. He also hoped for trade and international recognition, which was universally withheld. He turned to the British abolitionists, writing first to Wilberforce in 1814 and to Clarkson soon after.

Typically the two Englishmen responded differently and each in character. 'Wilberforce was the missionary, eager to bring the light of the true Protestant religion ... to the interesting but inferior Negroes of Haiti. Clarkson ... filled the role of colleague and collaborator, showing from the earliest days a genuine excitement and sincerity in setting about obtaining a public recognition of complete equality for the Haitians – as human beings and as a nation', a modern biographer of King Henry concluded.[10]

Wilberforce believed the introduction of 'true religion' would be the 'greatest of all benefits' to Haiti, supported Henry's dreams of an English-speaking Protestant nation and defended him against charges of tyranny.[11]

Clarkson was enthralled at the prospects not only in religion and language but agriculture, commerce, diplomacy and the possibility of giving asylum to 'free people of colour' from the United States. He became Haiti's European adviser. He covered reams of paper with his fine handwriting, painstakingly devoted to the task. Clarkson accepted that progress came slowly; Henry wanted to accomplish in one generation what it had taken Europe centuries to achieve. Much of their exhausting correspondence (some of Clarkson's letters ran to 30 pages) was published in 1952.[12]

Henry proposed to put schoolmasters into every community and a university at the capital. He provided Wilberforce with £6000 for expenses and with the combined efforts of Wilberforce, Clarkson and Allen (and the British and Foreign School Society of which Allen was treasurer) teachers using the Lancasterian system of mass education were supplied and schools soon set up with 2000 pupils.[13] A Royal College was founded in 1818 when William Wilson and George Clarke, experienced teachers, were recruited

1a. (*above left*) The earliest known portrait of Thomas Clarkson, 1788, by Carl Frederik von Breda.

1b. (*above right*) Richard Phillips, shown here at 75, was around 30 when he helped Clarkson to work out the strategy for the national movement to abolish the slave trade.

1c. (*below left*) William Allen, close friend and collaborator, whom Clarkson called the greatest man in Europe.

1d. (*below right*) William Wilberforce by George Richmond, after Sir Thomas Lawrence.

2. Clarkson with his treasure-chest of samples of African produce and manufactured articles, his map of Africa and busts of Wilberforce (*left*) and Sharp. By A. E. Chalon.

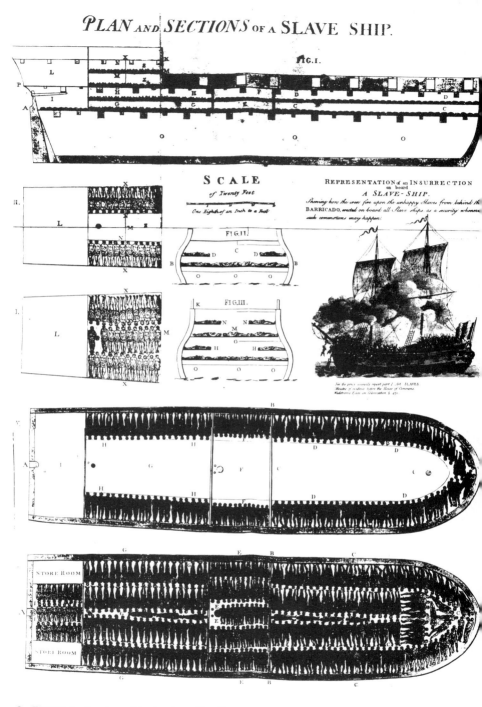

PLAN AND SECTIONS OF A SLAVE SHIP.

FIG. I.

SCALE
of Twenty Feet

One Eighth of an Inch to a Foot

FIG. II.

FIG. III.

REPRESENTATION of an INSURRECTION on board
A SLAVE-SHIP.

Shewing how the crew fire upon the unhappy Slaves from behind the
BARRICADO, erected on board all Slave ships, as a security whenever
such commotions may happen.

STORE ROOM

STORE ROOM

3. This plan of a slave ship developed by Clarkson and his co-workers shocked the public
when it appeared in 1789. It shows just how 482 slaves could be packed into the
Brookes of Liverpool for the six-to-eight week voyage to the West Indies. The *Brookes*
had actually carried 609 on one voyage.

4. Clarkson in 1811, by William Hazlitt. Engraved by T. S. Engleheart.

5. Catherine Buck Clarkson, in her only known portrait, possibly by A. E. Chalon.

6. Clarkson at the time of the 'Wilberforce affair', a portrait by Samuel Lane commissioned by Wisbech Corporation.

7. Clarkson at 80 addressing the 1840 world's antislavery convention, with his daughter-in-law Mary Clarkson and grandson Thomas (*left*). Pictured near the podium, are Joseph Sturge (*beneath Clarkson's uplifted arm*) and William Allen (*below Clarkson*). The American women delegates were brought out of the gallery for artistic reasons by the painter Benjamin R. Haydon.

Thomas Clarkson,
Playford Hall. Aug. 31.1846, aged 87

8. Thomas Clarkson and Playford Hall, autographed less than a month before he died. A widely-circulated lithograph.

by Clarkson. Clergymen, doctors and even two ploughmen followed the teachers to Haiti.[14]

Since Clarkson's services to King Henry are so well described
elsewhere, only one or two points need be touched on here. He
introduced the King to the Society of Friends through Stephen
Grellet, who made a preaching tour of the West Indies in 1816.
Clarkson wrote, 'Whenever you see a Quaker, you see a friend to
the distressed.'[15] He encouraged the King to replace his 40 000-
man army with a militia and give the disbanded soldiers land to
carry out his agricultural schemes.[16]

Colonisation plans for the growing number of free blacks were
being broached in these years in the United States. A Philadelphia
convention in 1816 debated the merits of setting aside land on the
American frontier for a black colony. It was contentious, and
Clarkson's opinion was invited.[17] The next year he was asked to
support the fledgling American Colonization Society to sponsor a
home for freed slaves on the west coast of Africa.[18] He believed the
slaves should stay in America as full citizens and that any plan for
them must have their free consent.[19]

As his knowledge of Haiti and trust in King Henry grew, he saw
there a possible home for 'free people of colour' who wanted to
migrate, and he corresponded on the subject with Prince Sanders
(or Saunders), an American black and one of the first teachers sent
to Haiti, and Robert Vaux of Philadelphia. If Congress would
supply money and diplomatic protection, Haiti, with some liber-
alisation of its laws, would be preferable to Africa, he had decided.
He discussed all this in letters to Henry as well.[20]

Partly to serve the King's international interests, Clarkson determined to attend the European Congress at Aix-la-Chapelle in the
autumn of 1818. His chief object was to press once more for an
internationally enforced ban on the slave trade. He began prepara-
tions in January and February with letters to the Emperor
Alexander.[21] He told Lord Castlereagh that he would attend as a
'humble Individual' unconnected with government 'in obedience
to my own feelings'.[22]

This time Clarkson's volunteer mission was not opposed by
Wilberforce. Although he believed that the presence of a politician
or office-holder (such as himself or Stephen) might embarrass the
Foreign Secretary, 'Clarkson seems formed by Providence for the
purpose. . . . he will be more acceptable than most to the Emperor

Alexander, and we may depend upon his being in earnest. . . . He would be regarded as half Quaker, and may do eccentric things with less offence than you or I could.'[23]

Clarkson discussed his plans with Wilberforce and accepted his alterations to the short tract he proposed to circulate. His companion this time was his 19-year-old nephew, John Brassey Clarkson, and they arrived at Aix on horseback on 28 September 1818 after a 'delightful ride'.[24] The conference had been called to ratify an agreement to withdraw the Allied army of occupation, under Wellington's command, from France. Five nations were there – Austria, Britain, France, Prussia and Russia – 5000 visitors were expected and the town was *en fête*. The Clarksons were lucky to find two airy bedrooms in a quiet street (rue St Jacques).

'We propose to dine every day at a Table d'Hote among Frenchmen, Germans & others', Clarkson informed his wife. 'I expect to hire a servant today, who speaks French to attend us, & to do our Errands.'[25]

He lost no time in calling on Castlereagh and Wellington and by 3 October had been told privately that although the slave trade was not on the agenda, it would be discussed.[26] His presence was useful in several ways, for when the French objected to charges in his circulated pamphlet about the renewal of the slave trade in Senegal, Clarkson could furnish Castlereagh with eyewitness testimony without delay.[27] The address to the sovereigns was sent to London by the *Times* correspondent and printed in instalments on 16 and 17 October. Amongst the hangers-on, dandies and lobbyists who thronged the town, the correspondent had been happy to see a 'better representative of our countrymen in the person of Mr Clarkson'.[28]

An audience with the Emperor was difficult to fix. He was away part of the time, then sent word that he was ill. When he was not writing to Wilberforce or his wife or diligently spreading his views, Clarkson showed his nephew a grand time. The Duke of Wellington wangled a ticket for him to the burgomaster's grand ball and John reported that of the 1000 guests none was so splendid as Castlereagh, kitted out in a coat encrusted with diamonds that 'cost 9000 Guineas at Rundles'. Clarkson, who hated taxes, grumbled, 'I doubt the poor English People shall have to pay for this fine Coat'.[29]

Together uncle and nephew attended one of the great dinners (this one given by Clarkson's banker) and Clarkson with his plain tastes and uneasy stomach was alternately impressed and appalled.

'We were kept eating for 3 hours & a half, till we were actually as much tired and wearied with eating, as a man with hard Labour', he told Catherine.[30] 'I calculate that each person ... had his Plate changed five & twenty times, and 25 multiplied by 30 would make 700 dishes for the cook and servants to wash. . . . every German Lady ate and drank as much as did every German Gentleman. There could be no Lady that did not drink a full bottle of wine. The wines too were most delicious & innumerable in their sorts. The [Hock] was more delicious than any I had ever tasted. . . . The Sweet Meat & Confectionery were handed round to us every three or four minutes. . . . In the intervals in order to sharpen the appetite, little Pieces of boiled Salmon & other fish were handed about, savoury, and tempting one to eat further. . . . splendid and luxurious as everything was, I never was so tired of anything in my life.'

Clarkson was the only private person admitted to Alexander's presence during the conference. He was summoned on 11 October and received at 9.30 at night 'with all the tokens of an old & familiar friend'. This time the Emperor brought Clarkson a chair and took another 'so that we sat opposite to each other, knee to knee, and face to face'.[31]

For more than an hour they ranged over the slave trade and King Henry's plans and fears of French invasion. 'This good man's efforts must not be allowed to be undone', said the Emperor. Clarkson presented an address from the Peace Society with a bound set of its tracts. (Alexander hoped to replace war with arbitration and started the first disarmament talks held among European powers.) Clarkson's gifts were an assortment of African articles which Alexander admired greatly.[32]

There was no agreement at Aix on the abolition question because the European nations would not open the door to outside interference with trade. Again at the Congress of Verona in 1822, British efforts were defeated. With unabated persistence, the two most prominent British abolitionists, Wilberforce and Clarkson, had once again sent appeals to the European powers. Clarkson called his *The Cries of Africa . . . or, a Survey of that Bloody Commerce Called the Slave-Trade*.[33] Both wrote directly to the Emperor of Russia and these missives were delivered by William Allen who felt moved to go to Vienna and see Alexander on his way to Verona.

'He smiled when he took Clarkson's letter, and said, "That is Clarkson's writing"', Allen recounted. To read Allen's description of his four long interviews with Alexander at Vienna and Verona in September and October of 1822, to realise how affectionately the Emperor behaved, how he remembered Allen took no sugar in his tea, how they knelt and prayed together, is to understand better why the abolitionists looked to the Russian ruler as their best hope for international action to ban the slave trade.[34]

Clarkson's optimism could survive on morsels. It smacked of *naïveté* to his critics but it made every effort seem worthwhile in itself. He left Aix-la-Chapelle with a light heart – the cause had been given a 'lift'.[35]

He sent a report to King Henry and advised him to write to the Emperor Alexander who had shown such interest in Haiti. Clarkson would send it by diplomatic channels. It might open an 'Intercourse between a white and a black sovereign founded on Christian Benevolence' and a new era.[36]

In 1819 King Henry asked Clarkson to become his ambassador to France, to seek for him French recognition in return for a commercial treaty.[37] As a British subject Clarkson could not accept the honour nor could he, and those he consulted, see the advantage of such a move to Haiti. Their advice was to carry on without a treaty.[38] However, Clarkson went to Paris in 1819 and 1820 as Henry's friend to gather information. To Baron Frederich Turckheim at the Ministry of Marine and Colonies, Clarkson expressed freely what Haiti had suffered at France's hands. 'The French name is odious in Hayti', he wrote. 'Think for a moment of the misery, which France inflicted upon this unhappy Island under the reign of Bonaparte. How many hundreds were hunted down, and given alive to blood-hounds. . . . How many hundreds were confined in the holds of ships, and purposely suffocated there by the fumes of brimstone! How many hundreds were taken out to sea, and thrown overboard, or purposely sunk with the vessel itself!'

He established that France would not try to regain Haiti by force and that the French, especially merchants and ex-colonials, remained deeply antagonistic to any 'liberal proceedings towards Negroes'.[39]

In a long letter to 'My Friend' on 10 July 1820, Clarkson advised Henry to have a pamphlet prepared to inform an ignorant French public of Haiti's historic troubles and recent achievements. 'I have only to add', he concluded, 'that if I can be useful to you and to your country at any other time ... you may command my services.'[40]

When it reached the Palais de Sans Souci, the King was dead. He had suffered an apoplectic fit during mass in August and was left half-paralysed. His army, discontented at his growing despotism, rebelled in October. He said farewell to his family and shot himself, legend says, with a golden bullet. His two sons were bayoneted but the Queen and her two daughters were spared.[41]

General Boyer (who succeeded Pétion in 1818) marched into Henry's kingdom and was declared president of both the northern and southern provinces. With Boyer's army came one Captain Robert Sutherland, age 26, an adventurer son of a British merchant, and in the summer of 1821 he accompanied Madame Marie-Louise Christophe (as she was now called) and her two daughters, Améthiste and Athénaire, to London. General Boyer had directed them to Clarkson and he with others of the African Institution supervised their arrangements and finances.[42]

Their arrival nonplussed the abolitionists. Macaulay told his wife of their 'somewhat sombre aspect' (they being 'coal black' and in deep mourning) and assured her that Mme Christophe 'is not likely to come near us. But if she had you might have rested perfectly easy on the score of morals.'[43] Clarkson later remarked that there was a 'sort of shrink at admitting them into high society'.[44] But the ladies were shy in their turn 'from their fear of being confounded with Africans. I can pity their weakness', said Clarkson, 'few can bear to be reminded of any circumstances in their history which may be thought degrading.' Perhaps they were thinking of the degradation of slavery associated with blacks. Henry was born free and his Queen was the daughter of a black slave-owner.[45]

Clarkson and his wife invited the three women and their maid to spend a month at Playford Hall while Captain Sutherland searched for a permanent home. 'A more delightful family never entered a person's house', Clarkson remarked. However, the bumptious Sutherland dismayed him by suggesting that they stay indefinitely as paying guests.[46]

Catherine's hesitation melted away when she saw how happy the Christophes were in the quiet of Playford and the 'hateful idea of taking money' was smoothed over by an arrangement that when the family left, Sutherland would give Clarkson whatever he considered to be reimbursement for extra expenses after the first month. In his plain way, Clarkson gave all the details to Macaulay so that he and Wilberforce would 'not give me credit for a generous action'. The extra expenses for a 20 weeks' visit came to £103 19s 10d.[47]

'Clarkson is the noblest gull that ever breathed', Henry Crabb Robinson remarked to Dorothy Wordsworth. The Emperor Alexander had gulled him and so had Henry Christophe 'and so will scores to the end of the chapter'.[48]

The Clarksons genuinely loved and admired their Haitian guests, who had survived the rebellion because of a long history of charitable acts for orphans, the aged and the poor.

'Like all Haytian females [Mme Christophe] is distinguished by a *douceur*, an humanity, which shudders at violence', William Wilson testified. 'It is the men only, who are sanguinary.' In his letter Wilson commented that the King probably acted from self-interest all his life. On the margin, Clarkson wrote, 'I do not believe this.'[49]

Although Wilberforce, like Macaulay, helped look after the Christophes' finances[50] it was nearly a year before he met them. In April 1822, just before they left Playford, he invited the Haitian refugees to dine, taking pains to see that Catherine Clarkson came with them for 'it is obviously of great Importance to females so entirely unacquainted with our manners, characters &c &c to have with them a friend of their sex'. He added, 'I am sure I should be cordially glad to render them any Benefit & so would Mrs W also But I have no time to spare, & she has not at present Spirits to undertake an office which would require a considerable share of them.'[51]

When Catherine and the Christophes arrived, Wilberforce had just time to scribble a note on a letter he was franking: 'Dinner is just going on the table with an ex-Queen and 2 Ex-Princesses with others of inferior note for guests.'[52]

Immense curiosity surrounded the visitors, whose exotic appearance on the streets of Ipswich is still recalled.[53] When Clarkson told the family at Longnor that the Haitian princesses were 'most charming young ladies', he was asked, 'Are they black?' 'As black as ink', he replied easily. He showed friends little notes they wrote to him as specimens of their excellent French and proudly exhibited the silk pocket handkerchiefs they made for him.[54] The papers called Playford a royal residence and the Wordsworths were agog.

'If you could see the lively picture I shaped to myself of the Sable

Queen sitting with her sable daughters beside you on the sofa in my dear little parlour at Playford you would thank the newspapers for being so communicative!' Dorothy wrote. 'Sara says "No! they will sit in the great room" . . . now my fancy espies them through the window of the court upon the larger sofa – them and you – and your dear Husband talking French to them with his old loving-kindness.'

On the previous Sunday afternoon, when the talk was of 'Mr Clarkson's . . . kindness to the distressed Negro Widow and her Family', William and Sara Hutchinson composed a parody on Ben Jonson. 'Oh! how they laughed! I heard them into my Room upstairs', Dorothy added,[55] copying the lines:

> Queen and Negress chaste and fair!
> Christophe now is laid asleep,
> Seated in a British chair
> State in humbler manner keep
> Shine for Clarkson's pure delight
> Negro Princess, Ebon bright!
>
> Let not 'Wilby's' holy shade
> Interpose at Envy's call,
> Hayti's shining Queen was made
> To illumine Playford Hall
> Bless it then with constant light
> Negress excellently bright!
>
> Lay thy Diadem apart
> Pomp has been a sad Deceiver
> Through thy Champion's faithful heart
> Joy be poured, and thou the Giver
> Thou that mak'st a day of night
> Sable Princess, ebon bright![56]

No proper thanks were returned from Playford Hall and three months later Dorothy 'fancied that our joke . . . had been displeasing to you'.[57]

By the autumn of 1822, the Christophes had moved to a cottage near Hastings where it was hoped Mme Christophe's rheumatism would improve. After three years of England's weather they took 'affectionate leave' of the Clarksons and settled in Pisa in Italy.[58]

There in 1840 Sir Robert and Lady Inglis found them by tracking down a rumour that a 'Russian Princess, but quite black' lived near. Mme Christophe did not at first recognise Sir Robert, who had grown fat. When she did, she embraced them both in floods of tears and asked after the Clarksons. She seemed lonely and to be living on her English memories. Athénaire was dead. Améthiste died, too, both unmarried, and Mme Christophe followed them to the grave in 1851.[59]

13

The Slaves Set Free

It is entrancing to find in the brittle documents that record historic occasions a glimpse of domestic life. Thus, fresh from an interview with the Duke of Wellington at Aix-la-Chapelle in 1818, Thomas Clarkson directed his wife to have three pigs slaughtered and cured and promised her black silk stockings from Brussels.[1] And while he packed for Paris and an audience with the Emperor Alexander in 1815, he also was negotiating the family's removal from Bury St Edmunds to Playford, a tranquil straggling village only four miles from Ipswich and less than thirty from Bury.

His new landlord was the Earl of Bristol, who had made up his mind not to let Playford Hall and its 340-acre farm to anyone but Clarkson.[2]

In making the move, Clarkson had the priceless help of Arthur Biddell at Hill Farm, then a tall, plain-spoken young man of 33 who was to become a noted Suffolk agriculturalist and land-valuer. He was also a reader and a Shakespearian scholar. Clarkson used to say Playford would not be worth living in without him.[3]

The village lay in a hollow with St Mary's Church perched above it on a steep bank. The poet Bernard Barton thought Playford typified the 'landscape lovely, soft and serene' of East Suffolk.

> And, if nature can boast of charms for thee
> Thou wilt love it, and leave it not.[4]

The Earl's generosity was not boundless – Clarkson was to take care of all repairs and when he and Catherine walked round the ancient moated Hall just before he left for Paris, he saw one or two ceilings coming down, wainscoting falling off and eight or nine windows to be replaced. The roof was leaking and the moat-wall needed repair. New 'stoves' were required for all the best rooms.[5]

But it was a wonderful house in an arcadian setting, cupped in green fields. The spring-fed brook that drifted through the moat meandered off through the valley between banks edged with wild forget-me-nots. A curving drive lined with elms and chestnuts led through a small park to the Hall, which was entered over a low bridge, through iron gates and across a courtyard. As built in Elizabethan times, the house was three-sided with a row of columns on the fourth side of a square. Now only the main body and one wing remained, forming an L-shaped structure of massive red-brick walls with many chimneys and a small bell turret. It was clothed in honeysuckle, Virginia creeper and magnificent grape vines. Behind the house were stables, a coachhouse, cattle yards, sheds, granaries and a large barn. Two stew ponds near the house had held fish since the Middle Ages.[6]

Preceded by three wagon-loads of belongings, the Clarksons moved into Playford Hall in the bitter January of 1816. 'They were in good spirits', reported Henry Crabb Robinson who saw them off, but he thought it a 'calamitous change' for the couple.[7] Others were apprehensive too. 'What is the use of farming for you beyond what is just sufficient to keep Mr Clarkson employed?' Dorothy Wordsworth had wanted to know, 'and Twenty acres would serve the purpose as well as 300.' If 'Mr C had had two cows and a horse', she insisted another time, 'they would have furnished him with sufficient employment to withdraw him from fancies and cares that might sometimes oppress him in his study or by his fireside.'[8]

But visitors soon established the fact that the Clarksons were well content. As the squire of Playford, Clarkson had new duties, for he arranged tenancies and livings, executed the poor laws, even supervised the emigration to Canada of several poor families in search of a new life. Catherine looked after the village school and, after reading everything in print on the subject, devised its teaching-plan. She delighted in the flower gardens surrounding the Hall and Clarkson enjoyed looking up from his writing table in the ground-floor study to see her happily employed with the gardener in the beds and borders.

They kept Christmas in the old way. A 'dole' of beef and pork and a faggot of wood to cook it on went to every cottage, and parties for tenants, servants and schoolchildren were held in the baronial kitchen, decorated with mistletoe and holly.[9]

To her friends' surprise, Catherine, who loved society, bloomed in what others felt to be a lonely place. Sara Hutchinson complained mildly of the dullness there: without an effort 'we might die of the vapours'. She must have been the sunniest of their

visitors. She loved Clarkson for being so 'nice and droll'. His
foibles, his sudden quizzing remarks sent her into peals of laughter, 'and he does not dislike being laughed at', she discovered,
'indeed he often says things for the purpose of making us merry
with him – though he *never* laughs himself & seldom smiles
even'.[10]

He was still a stickler for punctuality and they lived 'as regular as
the sun'.

> Mr C puts his watch upon the Table the moment supper is over –
> & from time to time consults it & reports progress till half past 10
> – when Mrs C & I retire together & she stays ten minutes with
> me by my fire – and by 11 we are in bed – at 8 I am called and Mr
> C gives me a second hollow if he passes my room door, & I am
> always ready by the time the Urn arrives so that he has not a
> moment to wait & we suit mightily – indeed to his great dismay,
> I have been down twice before him.[11]

By the time Clarkson became involved in the antislavery campaign of the 1820s, Catherine had taken over the management of
the farm. She might reproach herself to literary friends for 'such
low pursuits' but it set Thomas free 'to follow the noble impulses of
his better nature'. To say that either of them 'farmed' is somewhat
misleading, for the bailiff who came with them from Bury St
Edmunds had the day-to-day responsibility. In late years, Catherine's farming amounted to a Sunday morning's ride over her acres
in a bath chair. Nevertheless, she took pride in her contribution
and talked as knowledgeably of the dipping and feeding of sheep
as she did of Wordsworth's poems. 'My farm has done well & only
gives me healthful occupations', she observed in the early days.
'Ld Bristol has been to see us & was so surprised & delighted that
he could not contain himself – He jumped about like good Mr
Wilberforce.'[12]

When, after her husband's death, she had to fill in the census
return for 1851, Catherine firmly listed herself not as 'Independent', as gentry usually did, but as 'farmer of 340 acres employing
16 men and 6 boys'.

'Out of the way' characters continued to interest the Clarksons,
among them Benjamin Laroche, a young French refugee who
helped Catherine translate Clarkson's *Cries of Africa* when he was
preparing for the Verona Congress. Laroche was sent to Playford

by Lafayette after being sentenced to prison for his anti-royalist writings. He was 24 and the Clarksons thought his work extraordinary for his age. Catherine nursed him for six weeks after he fractured a leg in a riding accident. During his exile, Laroche started a magazine on English charitable work, *Le philanthrope chrétien*, and Clarkson, of course, was put to work soliciting subscriptions. He applied to 20 and got two, one of them his brother's.[13] Laroche stayed for several months and was soon followed by the Christophe family.

The future of their only child claimed attention, as well. Tom left Cambridge in 1818 at 21 and after a happy fortnight's shooting went up to London to read law with a friend of Henry Robinson.[14] In less than a month, he was stricken with smallpox. Catherine was called to his bedside. It was weeks before she could write to Dorothy Wordsworth one of those harrowing accounts of sickness and suffering that distinguish the correspondence of that day. When she reached him, Tom's body was 'completely excoriated by the bursting of the postules – I had three or four hours work dabbing with milk & water before his shirt could be removed & the stench was so dreadful that I was completely poisoned by it. It occasioned violent retchings & ended in Diarrhea. Elizabeth [her maid] who took my place was seized in the same way but by the time she got very bad I was better', she said – and much much more.[15]

Tom remained clearheaded and patient, 'often merry – never sad', and when he could be moved from his lodgings he was taken to his Uncle John Buck's home to convalesce.[16]

Neither parent expected great things from Tom. Clarkson was pleased that he was 'not at all extravagant . . . very abstemious and he has no vices' to which, on recording the words in his diary, Robinson added three exclamation points. Their old friend knew that Tom had wearied of whatever dissipations Cambridge then offered and he thought Tom likely to fall into those of London if not under the eye of his father's connections. Robinson, a contented bachelor, became his inconspicuous guardian.[17]

As Catherine described her son, he was a chip off the old block: 'He has a vast share of that property which in a good cause is called perseverance, in a bad one obstinacy.' She worried that Clarkson's public reputation might lead to unwarranted expectations of his son whom she persisted in calling an 'overgrown schoolboy' until he was 23 years old.[18]

Tom, however, began to show marked symptoms of ambition. He hired his own chambers at No 1 Pump Court, Temple, and became a special pleader. His cousin, John Brassey Clarkson, a rising young stockbroker, told Tom's parents what Tom had not, that he had 18 regular and well-satisfied clients and worked like a horse.[19] After he was called to the bar, he began practice on the sprawling northern circuit and Clarkson – not encouraged by Tom – sent word to solicitor friends and colleagues who might supply a useful introduction or a brief.[20] Later, through Henry Brougham, who had become Lord Chancellor, young Clarkson was appointed a magistrate of the Thames police court.[21]

Tom was impatient to be settled for he wanted to marry and his choice of bride could not have pleased his parents more. Catherine had sung the praises of John Clarkson's third daughter for many years. At two-and-a-half, Mary was the 'greatest beauty I ever saw'. At five she was the 'darling of the flock'. She grew up to become 'as charming & as perfect a young creature as can be imagined'. Robinson added his compliment, 'an elegant girl with great sweetness'.[22]

The engagement dragged on for four years. 'Why does not the marriage take place?' the Wordsworths wanted to know. 'Thus people wait till "All the life of life is gone"', said Dorothy.[23]

Mary's father apparently withheld his consent on the grounds of his nephew's want of fortune but another reason might have been that the John Clarkson family was so often in mourning. His promising son died unexpectedly at the age of 25 and less than a year later his youngest daughter succumbed to a lingering illness. She was 14.[24] In April 1828, just before his 64th birthday, John Clarkson died of heart disease and Thomas lost his close friend, partner in many enterprises and most stimulating companion – the whole family's 'fountain of innocent mirth'. All four of his daughters married the following year.[25]

The grandson of the two brothers was born in July 1831 and named Thomas. Mary brought him to Playford when he was three weeks old. She stepped out of the carriage 'as fresh as a flower, took the babe from the Nurses arms & presented it to me by whom it was transferred to its grandfather', Catherine wrote happily to the Wordsworths. She could hardly wait for the nurse, with her prejudices against air and water, to go.

'You may think of us sitting out of doors with the babe lying in his little basket. What a blessing that he has come whilst his dear grandfather has eyes to see him & his grandmother strength to handle him.'[26]

Clarkson never entered much into Suffolk politics nor was he generally regarded as a party man although he favoured the Whigs, parliamentary reform and such schemes as the founding of London University (University College now) to help 'do away Bigotry, and to increase Liberal Ideas'. He accepted the office of steward when the county nobility and gentry turned out to celebrate 'Mr Fox's Birth-day'.[27]

But his intervention in the 1818 contest in Westmorland caused more of a flutter in the family for it pitted him against Wordsworth. Henry Brougham was standing in opposition to the two sons of Lord Lonsdale, and Clarkson was asked to use his influence among the Quakers. He gave Brougham's committee a letter declaring the 'abolute necessity' of keeping Brougham, author of a bill to make the slave trade a felony, in the Commons. Wordsworth, having become a robust Tory, was incensed, but also grateful that Clarkson was not on the spot to do more damage.[28]

'It is my honest opinion that well-intentioned Enthusiasts . . . are of all men living the persons who are most likely to do mischief when they meddle with legislation or Politics', he pontificated to Lord Lonsdale. 'He is an intractable man, deservedly noted for his integrity – and his countenance would, among a certain class, have strengthened the opposition Party. Besides he is of incredible activity, and unwearied perseverance in whatever he undertakes. We want such a Man on our side.'[29]

Clarkson's letter was beautiful, said Dorothy and a feather in the opposition caps, but he did not understand that most of the county was 'ready for revolution' and needed only enough people like Brougham to set about it.[30]

Actually Clarkson did the least he could for his abolitionist friend, since the Lowther interest also supported the cause. He got Sara Hutchinson to warn Wordsworth of his predicament. She bet Clarkson one pound of snuff to two that Brougham would lose, as he did.[31] The incident seemed to do the friendship little harm but, Catherine confided to Robinson, it was curious to find the Wordsworths 'so thoroughly torified'.[32]

At the end of his *History*, Clarkson had written, 'Who knows but that emancipation, like a beautiful plant, may, in its due season, rise out of the ashes of the abolition of the Slave-trade.'[33]

Since 1807 the abolitionists had evaded the thought of freeing the slaves. They had clung to the delusions that the slave trade could be destroyed while a market for them existed anywhere and that the abolition of the trade – supposing it could be enforced – would eventually undermine the system of slavery. They saw, however, that the traffic continued under foreign flags and slavery flourished.[34]

The unfinished business was faced during 1822 and in January 1823 a cautiously named Society for Mitigating and Gradually Abolishing the State of Slavery throughout the British Dominions was formed.[35] New and younger men led the new campaign but the old leaders, Wilberforce and Clarkson among them, gave the movement invaluable continuity.[36] By now Wilberforce had chosen his parliamentary heir, the able and energetic Thomas Fowell Buxton, and in two years' time would leave the House of Commons.[37]

'I had no merit whatsoever in originating the society', Clarkson recalled. William Allen simply told him, 'We have . . . put thy name on the Committee in the midst of those, with whom thou has always delighted to work.'[38]

But Clarkson's thinking had paralleled that of others and in 1822, after a roundabout jaunt with Catherine to the Lakes, Scotland and Yorkshire, he began to write his first pamphlet on the abolition of slavery. To some, it ranked among his most powerful arguments.[39] He gave it the interminable but explanatory title of *Thoughts on the Necessity for Improving the Condition of Slaves in the British Colonies, with a View to their Ultimate Emancipation, and on the Practicality, Safety, and Advantages of the Latter Measure*[40] and in it Clarkson opened war on a new front. He had become convinced that slavery in the colonies was illegal because it was maintained by laws which were contrary to the British Constitution and thus violated colonial charters, for example, laws permitting arbitrary punishment by owners and the refusal to admit testimony of slaves in courts.

Slavery was based upon misrepresentation, false assumption and fraud, he asserted. Here and elsewhere Clarkson argued for Parliament's right to intervene in colonial affairs. He also stressed the practical benefits of emancipation, a word which still evoked fears of violence and insurrection. In a speech he was to use in organising local committees, Clarkson argued that the root cause of uprisings was slavery, not freedom. But emancipation would come in careful stages until the slaves were christianised and civilised to the rank of free peasants. 'Nothing so insane' as immediate emancipation was in view.[41]

The illegality of slavery was a theme used by Buxton in May 1823 when he introduced a motion that slavery ought to be abolished – gradually. After the first debate on slavery in the Commons, the Liverpool government went so far as to make amelioration of slavery official policy but left it to the colonial assemblies to enact the necessary laws.[42]

Macaulay took note of Clarkson's talent as organiser as well as polemicist and in March 1823 he wanted Clarkson in London. 'We need him much for the organisation of our Society', he told Catherine Clarkson. 'I have been unable to attend to it. W Allen is engrossed with other matters. And there is no one who will take a lead.'[43]

Clarkson tested the waters in Suffolk to stir up support for Buxton's motion. The results were cheering. At Ipswich he and his banker friend Richard Alexander collected signatures of both Whigs and Tories, 'an Event which has not taken place for the last 35 years', he told Macaulay. 'I have no where been refused. It seems only to *ask* & to *have*.'[44]

He urged a national mobilisation of public opinion so that if the colonial legislatures refused to act or dragged their feet, 'all the Island would be ready to petition Parliament'.[45] James Cropper, a Liverpool Quaker merchant and perhaps the country's earliest advocate of emancipation[46] came to Playford to discuss how to do it. Their ideas were submitted to a grateful Anti-slavery Committee in June 1823. Clarkson offered to take to the road again to resurrect the old abolition network of some 70 local bodies and to establish new ones. He guessed the operation would take a year and Cropper offered to pay for it with £500 from his own pocket. Only Clarkson 'could or would spare the time . . . and they could not think of employing a stranger'.[47]

This tour, although it took Clarkson some 10 000 miles in two journeys lasting eight and five months, was neither so hazardous nor exhausting as his earlier researches had been. Where Quakers had paved the way before, he now had ready access to Church of England, Wesleyan and Scottish clergy and hundreds of names were produced by the Bible and Church Missionary Societies. By the summer of 1824, there were 230 auxiliaries covering 800 towns and 777 petitions had been sent to Parliament. On this groundswell, the Anti-slavery Society held its first public meeting in Freemasons' Hall on 25 June 1824.[48]

Clarkson discovered that the planters and their friends were not idle. He found their 'furious, scurrilous and false' (and free) publications in libraries, reading rooms and coffee houses. They predicted mayhem and economic ruin if the slaves were freed. Abolitionists were condemned as traitors by those won over by such prophecies.[49]

His paramount finding, however, was that the country was ready for emancipation. 'It is every ones opinion, that SLAVERY is to fall. . . . *this Idea* pervades all England & Wales'.[50]

His travels were a positive cordial to Clarkson personally. 'He looks worn & older than he is, but his mind is as ardent as ever, he has the spirits & the sociability of youth', observed Katherine Plymley when he reached Shropshire. He looked 'ten years younger' when he arrived at Tom Hutchinson's farm in Wales, Catherine was told. 'They were quite charmed with his cheerfulness and good looks.'[51]

The cause languished for several years while the government waited for the West Indians to adopt a proposed new code of laws. Clarkson busied himself nagging the London committee to set out a plan of action for localities, furnishing information to MPs, writing 'fugitive pieces' for periodicals and conducting a massive correspondence. 'If I work hard today', he told William Smith in July 1826, 'I shall finish my three hundred and twelve letters which I am writing to our correspondents . . . about Petitions.'[52] He became chairman of the Ipswich branch committee.

By 1830 impatient younger abolitionists pushed the Society into rejecting gradualism and setting the goal of immediate emancipation. More than 2000 crowded into Freemasons' Hall for a grand antislavery rally in May. Wilberforce came, exceedingly frail, for what was to be his last public appearance, and Clarkson called the meeting to order and moved that Wilberforce take the chair 'as the great Leader in our cause'. Wilberforce accepted with equal grace. 'I could have been called to take this chair by no person more dear to me than my valued friend and fellow-labourer. . . . I cannot but look back to those happy days when we began our labours together; or rather when we worked together – (for he began before me) – and we made the first step towards that great object, the completion of which is the purpose of our assembling this day.'[53]

Under a new Agency Committee, organised by Cropper and Stephen's son George, paid lecturers were employed for the first time to hold public meetings at which the horrors of slavery were exposed in the most passionate terms. In one year the number of local branches shot up to 1300. Between October 1830 and April 1831, in response to a call from the Anti-Slavery Society for the 'entire Abolition of Colonial Slavery', 5484 petitions fell upon Parliament.[54]

Although it took until 1833, the outcome was no longer in doubt. The bill which passed under Earl Grey's administration extended freedom to slaves as of 1 August 1834. It had two controversial features: a transitional apprenticeship period and compensation to owners totalling a startling £20 000 000.[55]

Clarkson was 'inexpressibly thankful' to have lived to see the day. 'The twenty millions will have been well laid out, if it will secure the cordial cooperation of the planters. . . . I wish the apprenticeship had been two years shorter. But we cannot always have what we wish. The subject was one of extraordinary difficulty. . . . our eyes have seen a great salvation, and we have had a hand in it too', he wrote William Smith.[56]

In an exchange of letters with Buxton, Clarkson laid out in great detail how the Society should now proceed to watch over the enforcement of the law. He wrote in a scrawl which, increasingly large and unsteady, had been replacing his normal neat hand for some time. The cataracts which had been forming over his eyes had left him nearly blind. He ended his letter, 'I have not been able to read a word of what I have now written.'[57]

14

The Wilberforce Affair

The joy and thankfulness that surrounded passage of the Emancipation Act was clouded by the death of Wilberforce in July 1833. It was a grievous, even if not unexpected, blow to Clarkson. For 46 years they had sunk their personal differences over religion, politics, even tactics, in a remarkable partnership.

'My dear old Friend', Wilberforce had opened one of his last letters to Clarkson. 'I am unaffectedly glad that a Circumstance has happened which gives me Occasion to write to you, because I thereby have an opportunity of assuring you, that tho it is so long since there has been any Intercourse between us, you & your's still occupy a constant place in my friendly remembrance & I beg when you reply to my Letter you will inform me how you & Mrs Clarkson & all ye family are going on in all the particulars of which an old friend naturally wishes to be inform'd.' He ended 'with every good Wish for you & yours, in time & for Eternity – My dear Old friend, Ever sincerely your's.' He must have been thinking of their earliest days, for he addressed the letter to the 'Revd Thos Clarkson'.[1]

Catherine broke the news of Wilberforce's death as carefully as she could. Clarkson locked the door of his study and his wife and daughter-in-law heard him 'in an agony of grief weeping and uttering loud lamentations'.[2] After a day or two Clarkson wrote – a line at a time, not seeing what he wrote – a note of condolence to Mrs Wilberforce who responded with a detailed account of her husband's last months and news of all her family. 'He seems to have never been happier in his life than in the last twelvemonth & he suffered very little pain even at the last', Catherine wrote the Wordsworths. '. . . His second son Robert is about to publish a Memoir. I wish that he may do it well. The young man sent here expecting to receive Vols of Letters. Those which we have sent will I think surprise him especially some to my Brother Clarkson.'[3]

Ramsay, Sharp, now Wilberforce. Writing to William Smith soon afterwards, Clarkson expressed the loneliness of the survivor: 'Of the old Committee only Richard Phillips and Myself now remain. Of the original Parliamentary Labourers (Wilberforce being dead) You only are left.' The new allies acquired on his emancipation tours were acquaintances of but a few hours. He had so outlived his contemporaries that where once he knew more than half the members of both Houses of Parliament personally, he now could count his Westminster friends on the fingers of one hand.[4]

But imminent blindness threatened a greater isolation for a man who spent nearly every waking hour reading or writing. Typically Clarkson refused to give in, consulted London's leading eye specialist and waited for darkness to fall completely so that an operation could be performed on his cataracts. His 'old occupation' (abolition) was gone but he was launched on a new programme, 'what he calls "My own Thoughts on Religion"'.[5] For a year or two he had been able by applying belladonna to the lower lids to see enough to write in the morning hours. Catherine (or whatever guest could be commanded) read to him.

'You may fancy us in the Study every Evening. I lying on a little couch just made for the purpose with the book on my knee & poor Dr Ramsden's Candlestick which has a shade like a pent house on one side on the table my Husband sitting on the other side the fire ... with fire-screen & a Shawl upon his knees on account of the Rheumatism the light of the candle being completely obscured to him.' She was then reading the Old Testament with Dr Adam Clarke's notes.[6]

Sara Hutchinson on a long visit in early 1834 was his secretary for his research into the 'way in which men first acquired their knowledge of God'. She spent her mornings with Clarkson, working until 12 or 2 as the case might be, and her afternoons with Catherine for a 'duty walk in the Garden or a drive ... in the Carriage'. She was a godsend, he assured her, for 'poor Misses is worn out' by reading, writing and looking up references. 'Twenty pages only for you to copy Sara', he would say, 'I have saved them for you' and the 20 would swell to 28 before they finished.[7]

Dear Mr C is quite an old man – he pokes about with his hands like blind Bartimeus in Raphaels cartoon of which there is a print in one of the penny mags. He is just the same in all other respects his peculiarities strengthened rather than weakened – I am watched as a cat watches a mouse & am obliged to do his bidding. . . . he is engaged in a very interesting work I have no doubt, on religion – & Mrs Clarkson reads the Bible & takes notes at his suggestion . . . for an hour every evening.[8]

Sara was a particular favourite of both Clarksons. She regularly knitted yarn stockings for him and he, in turn, cured her corns as he had vanquished his own and many others in Playford parish with 'Denmers Brunswick corn plasters'.[9]

The operation on his right eye (the left remained blind) in May 1834 was a success and Clarkson at 74 was possibly the best, certainly the most obedient patient Mr Tyrell of 17 Bridge Street, Blackfriars, ever had.[10] He gave Lord Bristol a minute account of the experience. The operation took 59 seconds and was no more painful than bleeding. He had rested in bed one day, sat up the next. 'When I left home . . . I was put into a Post Chaise like a Log of Wood. . . . but before I left London . . . I found my Way alone . . . on foot from Finsbury Circus to Gracechurch Street'. It seemed almost a miracle and on his first Sunday at home he asked the vicar to give public 'Thanks to God in my Name . . . for his Mercy, his great Mercy, in the partial Restoration of my Sight'.[11]

He threw himself even more intensely now into his theological studies with the scholarly zest that had distinguished him at Cambridge. He believed he broke new ground in proving – against the new wave of Tractarian thinking at Oxford – that mankind could know God only through revelation. He believed that God's first revelation was not to Moses on Mount Sinai, but to Adam at the Creation. During the centuries that mankind lost knowledge of the true God, not all the genius of the ancient philosophers could rediscover him. The faith was restored by revelation through Jesus Christ. Clarkson published his findings in 1836 to combat the 'fatal errors now daily propagated' that mankind could know God by 'light of nature or their own reasoning'.[12] His *Researches Antidiluvian, Patriarchal, and Historical* was admired by friends – Quakers and churchmen alike. He said he wrote it to be useful, not for gain, which was just as well since the booksellers were telling him that 'infidel works and works which may be called Trash sell freely' while religious and grave tracts were left on the shelves.[13]

Although he wrote (for Mary and her son, chiefly) some other religious notes, his only other published work in this field was an *Essay on Baptism, with some Remarks on the Doctrines of the Nicene*

Church, on which Puseyism is built. In it he argued that baptism, although commended by Christ, had in itself no power of salvation, as the Puseyites believed.[14]

Meanwhile the Clarksons underwent several severe tests of faith. It was a season of deaths. Sara Hutchinson died in July 1835 of rheumatic fever. Mary Wordsworth could not bring herself to write of the loss of her sister 'to *you* dearest Mrs Clarkson who loved her so well, & knew so well what you loved'. Catherine could only think that Sara had been taken to heaven as a 'reward for her superior goodness'.[15] Their old Lakes circle was already decimated by the death the year before of Coleridge, the loss of Lamb six months later, and the living death of Dorothy Wordsworth, victim of pre-senile dementia. Two years after her illness set in, Catherine Clarkson read over 'heaps' of Dorothy's letters. 'What a heart and what a head they discover! What puffs we hear of women, and even of men, who have made books and done charities, and all that, but whose doings and thinkings and feelings are not to be compared with hers!'[16]

Very little can be found in surviving Clarkson papers about the greatest blow of all. On 9 March 1837 their only child was thrown out of his gig and killed instantly.[17] He was 40. In one bleak note to Lord Brougham Clarkson said, 'My Son has been taken from me.'[18]

Catherine touched on her heartache in a letter to Henry Robinson. 'It is true that under the infliction of so sudden & so sharp a blow I was at first incapable of receiving consolation from any earthly source.' Called upon to console her husband, her daughter-in-law and the 5-year-old child, she had been forced to 'forget that I was a mother. Yet I am a mother at heart & I feel that the greatest Luxury I could experience would be if I could go to some solitary place for a short time to bewail my only child.'[19]

Neither parent was told the full story of the fatal accident. Robinson had been summoned by Tom Clarkson's friends for the painful task of identifying his bloody remains at the Clerkenwell Workhouse. He quickly learned that a woman 'not of good character' had been with him in the gig. Abetted by Joseph Hardcastle and John Buck, Robinson moved swiftly to keep the circumstances, as revealed at a coroner's inquest, out of the newspapers. A sum of £7 was distributed, a sovereign to those who wrote nothing and half as much to those who left the woman out of their stories.[20]

A wholly gratuitous blow was delivered from a quarter Clarkson was least likely to fear. By slow degrees from 1834 onwards he learned that Wilberforce's sons intended to use their father's biography to destroy the reputation of the one person whose own stature threatened their image of Wilberforce's supremacy in the abolition campaign.

He had responded to Robert Wilberforce's initial request for Wilberforce letters with simple enthusiasm, but had to tell him that there were far fewer than they might expect because much of his communication with Wilberforce had been face to face. He referred the brothers to his *History* for the origins of the movement, his own journeyings, Wilberforce's parliamentary activities and the like. He offered to be of any help he could in a generous, encouraging letter (dictated to Catherine by her nearly sightless husband) which called attention to Wilberforce's 'prodigious labour'.

In his own hand he added, 'I am glad that you are going to write your Father's Life. Such a Life ought to be made known to instruct, but it will be a most laborious Task . . . for his private life was as full of glorious Labour and as splendid as his public one.' He sent five Wilberforce letters to himself and 11 from Wilberforce to his brother, which John's widow had preserved. He withheld Wilberforce's last three letters as they dealt with a still controversial subject (the American Colonization Society).[21]

Robert and Samuel read the *History* with dismay, discovering that their father did not originate the slave trade abolition campaign and that its 'glories were divisible among many'. It 'gradually dawned upon them, and was impressed by friends to whose judgment they most properly deferred, that to do their father justice' they must dispute its general tenor.[22]

Two of these friends were Zachary Macaulay and James Stephen the younger. The former, who knew full well from Clarkson's correspondence that Clarkson never paraded his own merit, accused Clarkson of 'egotism and partial views' although many of his 'facts are correctly stated'.[23]

The other, convinced that his father (who had died in 1832) had been neglected in Clarkson's brief summary of the late stage of the struggle, attacked fiercely. (The fact that Clarkson skimped his own contributions to the final part of the campaign was ignored on all sides.) Stephen advised Robert to reject any help from Clarkson and to tell him 'you find it impossible to abstain from statements & remarks hostile to his pretentions'.

'There is no question on which I am more clear than the

necessity of your reclaiming for your Father the hardly earned
Laurels of which Clarkson has but too successfully laboured to
deprive him', Stephen declared, adding, that although he was 20
when the slave trade was abolished he had never heard of
Clarkson's existence until, at a public meeting celebrating passage
of the act, William Smith proposed a vote of thanks to him. The
younger Stephen labelled Clarkson an English Jacobin and
asserted that 'by alarming George the 3^d, Mr Pitt & the whole race
of anti-Jacobins, I believe that Clarkson did as much to frustrate
and delay the abolition, as he ever did to promote it'.

Furthermore, according to Stephen, Clarkson had tried to 'ex-
clude every one else from any share in the honour. It is a public
duty to put down this Charletanerie. With you it is an urgent
private duty. It is especially necessary to give Clarkson direct
notice of your intention, and to preserve, with a view to publication, any correspondence which may pass between you.'[24]

The slighting of Stephen was coming to appear the most reckless
act of Clarkson's long career, and there had been nothing wilful
about it.[25] The younger generation neither knew nor cared.

Wilberforce's close friend Thomas Gisborne advised the Wilberforce brothers not to give Clarkson a bellicose warning that they
were going to answer his book. Like the others now determined to
disparage Clarkson's account, Gisborne knew nothing of the
origins of the campaign, though he understood Clarkson was a
'zealous intelligent & indefatigable Pioneer'. He should be coun-
tered with 'simple facts' shorn of controversial remarks.[26]

Robert Wilberforce's reply to Clarkson's packet of letters was
cool. He had found in Clarkson's *History* 'much which excites in
me great surprise'.[27] Consciences perfectly clear, the Clarksons
probably thought that was a compliment until July 1834 when
Robert flung down the gauntlet.

'The impression which ... your History ... is calculated to
convey, is that my Father was originally engaged in it by you &
that he was subsequently a sort of Parliamentary agent of whom
you availed yourself. Now that neither of these statements is
correct I have abundant evidence'. Samuel, who would write this
section, would be compelled to contradict Clarkson. 'I do not say
this Sir from any feeling of disrespect towards you but on the
contrary because I am unwilling that you should only learn along
with the Public at large the tone which the writer of my Father's life

must needs take. . . . in a manner as free as possible from all insult & unkindly feeling.'[28]

This letter reached Playford not long after Clarkson returned from his cataract operation. 'Now is it not provoking that the first use wh my Husband put his eye to should be such a dirty job as this', Catherine exploded to the Wordsworths. He took it quietly but agreed that they should consult the few survivors – Richard Phillips, Archdeacon Corbett, William Smith – who could corroborate Clarkson's view of history.[29]

In the month of August 1834 when all abolitionists should have been heralding the emancipation in the British West Indies, Clarkson put his good eye to greater strain by writing at length to Robert Wilberforce. No one had to his knowledge drawn such inferences from his *History* before. When the book was published in 1808, five members of the old committee, including Wilberforce, were still alive and could have instantly exposed any errors. In the next 25 years, although Wilberforce wrote Clarkson perhaps a hundred letters and saw him at least fifty times, he had uttered no criticism, other than to pass along a suggestion that Stephen had been given less than his due.[30]

Robert retreated from insinuations that Clarkson had lied but appeared to have decided to attack him on the slippery ground of 'conclusions which you appear to me to have conveyed' and 'such Impressions as I derived'. They would try to write 'nothing but what is fair & christian'.[31]

'We must wait . . . till we see what the Mountain will bring forth', Catherine said at one point in the long running preamble. 'Perhaps after all it may be only a little mouse.'[32]

But the five volumes which the Wilberforces published in 1838 vindicated Clarkson's worst fears that he would be forced to reply. How far the memoir was Christian, I must leave to others to decide. That it was unfair to Clarkson is not disputed. Where possible, the authors ignored Clarkson; where they could not they disparaged him. In the whole rambling work, using the thousands of documents available to them, they found no space for anything illustrating the mutual affection and regard between the two great men, or between Wilberforce and Clarkson's brother.[33] They had room, however, to exploit two highly personal incidents, involving Clarkson's letters about his financial subscription and his plea for his brother's promotion. These were written when Clarkson was shattered in mind and body. The Wilberforces' use of them attracted almost universal condemnation at the time.

The Wilberforce *Life* was preceded by several weeks by an article by James Stephen in the *Edinburgh Review* in which it was alleged that Clarkson was 'remunerated' for his work. This and several other misrepresentations were altered in the October issue under pressure from Lord Brougham.[34]

The exchanges which were the forerunners of publication of the *Life*, given here for the first time, reveal an unpleasant and narrow fanaticism. It was said that Samuel Wilberforce could not respect Clarkson because he had dropped the title 'reverend'. The publication in 1838 by sheer accident of Wordsworth's sonnet to Clarkson was understood to have stimulated Stephen's malignity. The year before in a book on Charles Lamb, Sergeant Talfourd had paid tribute to Clarkson as 'the true annihilator of the slave trade'.[35]

Even Clarkson, who found it much easier to forgive than to quarrel with the children of his reverend friend, spoke of the 'malignant Jealousy' which caused them to treat him so shamefully that he was goaded into fighting back in his 79th year. He called his *Strictures on a Life of William Wilberforce* the only book he had written 'with feelings of unmingled pain'.[36] Henry Crabb Robinson loyally devoted most of the summer to helping him with it. The public response was a triumph for Clarkson and the Clarksonites, as they described themselves. 'We have done all we could to save their fathers reputation – They have established ours', said Catherine.[37] The press response was gratifying, with one paper going so far as to say that 'Everyone of common sense knows that the merit was Clarkson's and not Wilberforce's.'[38]

Proposing that antislavery bodies speak up, one supporter asserted that 'It will be criminal ingratitude to leave this dying lion unprotected to receive all the kicks these young things choose to give him' and deputations made their way to Playford to present addresses.[39] A new edition of Clarkson's *History* was planned, with a preface by Brougham.[40] The Central Negro Emancipation Committee commissioned Henry Room to paint a portrait and Thomas Taylor was inspired to write Clarkson's first biography.[41] The Common Council of the City of London by unanimous vote gave Clarkson the freedom of the City as a 'grateful testimonial' to one 'who had the merit of originating, and has the consolation of living to witness, the triumph of the great struggle for the delivrance of the enslaved African' and commissioned a marble bust by Behne to put beside one of Granville Sharp.[42] In April 1839, accompanied by a delighted Robinson as 'Cls squire having buckled on his armour and accompanied him into the field', Clarkson received the freedom of the City at the Mansion House, with proud Catherine looking on. After short speeches by the Lord Mayor and Chamberlain, the frail old abolitionist responded in a 'tone of voice so sweet as to be quite pathetic. There was a graceful timidity mingled with earnestness – an evident satisfaction very distinguishable from gratified vanity. Everybody was pleased.'[43]

Even the *Christian Observer*, the Evangelical organ, although critical of Clarkson's *History* and his politics, expressed regret at the disparaging remarks made about him in the *Life*. 'Both were earliest, and both were best, in their respective spheres', the writer said diplomatically.[44]

Wordsworth was overjoyed and gave Robinson treasured compliments for the *Strictures*. Clarkson's vigorous defence 'is scarcely less than wonderful, and the candour with which he admits the imperfections and deficiencies of his book, must endear him still more to his friends, and to the sound-hearted portion of the community.'[45]

The Wilberforces lived 'so shut up in a circle of their own'[46] that they may not have sensed or cared about the wave of public disapproval. Much later, however, Macaulay's son, meeting Robinson at the Reform Club, claimed he had disapproved of the Wilberforces' conduct from the start. He had, from his father's close association with the senior Wilberforce, a 'hereditary respect' for them, believed them to be pious and sincere but 'incapable of anything generous or liberal or kind'. In his view it had been 'most ungenerous to treat so eminent a person of his years and after such a life, in such a way'.[47]

James Stephen, 'staggered ... by the apparent unanimity with which parts of the Book, and therefore of the Review of it, would appear to be condemned', squirmed uncomfortably as he advised Samuel Wilberforce to drop the controversial personal letters in a future edition. He admitted a strong bias against Clarkson, believed his cousins were bound 'to reduce him to his real level', and 'Yet truly can I say that it gave me heartache to think of the pain which the old man would have to endure.'[48]

With appalling incomprehension of the seriousness of their act, Samuel sent a 'soothing' letter to Clarkson, expressing concern for any hurt they might have inflicted upon him.[49] Their next opportunity to strike came in a Preface to Wilberforce's correspondence which the sons published in 1840. They had denied themselves a 'slashing rejoinder' to the *Strictures* but were eager to get on with 'cutting up Crab Robinson severely, and Clarkson not a little'.[50]

With breathtaking effrontery, Samuel Wilberforce sent the new book to Clarkson with a note to say he hoped that it removed any painful impressions. Clarkson's kindly reply that the 'confirmation of peace with you & your Brother was really to me most agreeeable news'[51] is equally ludicrous, for the Preface amounted to a renewed attack.

The authors boasted of selling 30 000 copies of the *Life* as if that proved they were right. They dealt with Clarkson's few charges of inaccuracy in a way that retracted nothing. (Clarkson did not complain of the way he had been 'written out'.) They thought he had a 'predisposition to receive offence' and indignantly denied that they had meant any harm. They made a scarcely veiled threat that they might do even worse damage to Clarkson if 'piqued into publishing what they deemed it better to suppress'. This did bother Clarkson and he unsuccessfully tried over several years to find out what this was and get his letters back. At last Robert told the Clarksons that he had been 'compelled to burn' the relevant materials.[52]

The Wilberforces were not reluctant to tell others what small coinage of insult they held back. Robert cited to Lord Brougham, as an example of their delicacy, the substitution of a dash for Clarkson's name in a quotation from M. Sismondi commending a pamphlet by Wilberforce and describing Clarkson (who had written another) as *'un mauvais écrivain'* beyond the help of a translator.[53] Patty Smith learned that 'if obliged' the Wilberforces would print correspondence with Lord Muncaster in which he applied the words 'importunate beggar' to Clarkson.[54]

In 1844 Clarkson received what he took to be an apology, six years after publication of the damaging memoir. He was well past 84 when Archdeacon Robert and Bishop Samuel Wilberforce co-signed a letter which said,

> As it is now several years since the conclusion of all differences between us, and we can take a more dispassionate view than formerly of the circumstances of the case, we think ourselves bound to acknowledge that we were in the wrong in the manner in which we treated you in the Memoir of our Father. . . . we are conscious that too jealous a regard for what we thought our Father's fame, led us to entertain an ungrounded prejudice

against you & this led us into a tone of writing which we now acknowledge was practically unjust.[55]

Luckily, Clarkson had lived long enough to reply. He told Robert the letter was 'highly gratifying' though it awakened painful memories. It was unnatural for him to be at odds with the children of a 'dear departed friend whom I loved and revered'. He harboured no unfriendly feelings towards them, he knew how hard it was to admit error, and their letter would enable him to satisfy even his sternest champions 'that you have done every thing that we could desire'.[56]

No apology was ever made public, but the Bishop after Clarkson died 'graciously' told Catherine that they would not object to this letter being included in any memoir of her husband.[57] 'I don't like to tell them', said Catherine, sending a copy of the latest Wilberforce letter to the Wordsworths, 'that there are positively no Documents for a memoir'.[58]

Does any of it matter now? Yes.

The problem raised by the Wilberforce *Life* was identified by Henry Robinson. Not one in a hundred readers of the *Life* would be able to compare its account of the abolition campaign with Clarkson's *History*, published 30 years before.[59] The *Life* has been treated as an authoritative source for 150 years of histories and biographies. It is readily available and cannot be ignored because of the wealth of original material it contains. It has not always been read with the caution it deserves. That its treatment of Clarkson, in particular, a deservedly towering figure in the abolition struggle, is invalidated by untruths, omissions and misrepresentations of his motives and his achievements is not understood by later generations, unfamiliar with the jealousy that motivated the holy authors. When all the contemporary shouting had died away, the *Life* survived to take from Clarkson both his fame and his good name. It left us with the 'simplistic myth of Wilberforce and his evangelical warriors in a holy crusade'.[60]

15

The Father-Figure

To American abolitionists Clarkson was 'more intimately, & *endearingly*, associated with the holy cause' than any other Briton. His works filled their library shelves. He was an honorary member of nearly every antislavery group formed in his time, and age made him a legend.[1]

Through his many American correspondents, Clarkson followed the rise of antislavery in the United States with great attention but even he underestimated the bitterness of their internal quarrels and the passions which sent mobs into the streets. All agreed that slaveholding was evil; the abolitionist disputes were over methods of ridding the nation of it.[2]

He was drawn into the rancorous controversy over the American Colonization Society, established to encourage the manumission of slaves (with compensation to their owners) and their emigration to Liberia, when Elliott Cresson arrived in 1831 to raise £100 000 for the new West African settlement.[3] It was crucial to obtain endorsements from Wilberforce and Clarkson, and one of the persuasive arguments employed was that Liberia could help drive out the continuing slave trade. Various American colonisation schemes had been put before Clarkson and he had shown moderate interest, although he never understood why freed blacks could not be given land and citizenship within the vast United States.

Wilberforce saw some benefits in the ACS plan, as he told Clarkson by letter.[4] After his own session with Cresson, Clarkson virtually endorsed it, under a mistaken impression that the Society believed in emancipation 'of all the slaves now in the United States', as well as in using Liberia to help end the slave trade and promote African civilisation. His letter to Cresson, as printed in America, however, made no reference to emancipation and committed Clarkson simply to the voluntary emigration of the 'colored population of the United States'.[5]

Cresson must have seemed exceptionally plausible. He was a Quaker and Clarkson knew that the American Friends, with few exceptions, rejected the ACS which was supported in the South as a way to remove free blacks and thus reduce the risk of insurrection. Other Americans had also told him that blacks would not go to Liberia, voluntarily.[6]

His 'endorsement' brought William Lloyd Garrison, at the age of 27 the rising star of American antislavery, to Britain in 1833.[7] In every country where an abolition movement appeared, someone was designated its 'Clarkson' and in the United States that was the fiery Garrison.[8] (There was no Wilberforce in the United States Congress.) After serving a printer's apprenticeship, Garrison had founded the *Liberator* in 1831 and with it the struggle to free American slaves truly began.[9]

'On this subject I do not wish to think, or speak, or write with moderation', Garrison declared in his first editorial. 'No! no! Tell a man whose house is on fire, to give a moderate alarm; tell him to moderately rescue his wife from the hands of the ravisher; tell the mother to gradually extricate her babe from the fire into which it has fallen: – but urge me not to use moderation in a cause like the present.'[10]

In 1832, with friends, Garrison founded the New England Anti-Slavery Society (later the Massachusetts Anti-Slavery Society), more militant than any previous group, which demanded total and immediate abolition of slavery without strings. One of his first pamphlets denounced the American Colonization Society as racist and impractical.[11]

To secure his leadership claims, Garrison needed British recognition. He had followed the antislavery campaign in Britain and read the speeches of Buxton and Brougham. He was impressed by the British identification of slavery with sin. When Clarkson and Wilberforce, the 'wisest and best men of their age', agreed that immediate emancipation was the only hope for Britain and its colonies, America must follow.[12] He came ostensibly to raise funds for a manual labour school for black youth[13] but mainly to confront Cresson and the ACS which seemed to have won over the venerated Clarkson and perhaps Wilberforce. At a public meeting on 10 June 1833, with James Cropper presiding, Garrison charged that Clarkson had been duped by Cresson, and Cresson admitted that this was so. Cropper told another meeting that Wilberforce now regretted saying anything favourable to the ACS.[14]

Cropper had condemned the ACS in a public letter addressed to Clarkson, prompting Wilberforce to suggest to Clarkson that they should adopt a common position. For his part, Wilberforce hoped the ACS could do 'great good' if means could be found to prevent its use to prolong slavery.[15] Clarkson's replies do not seem to survive.

Garrison went to see Wilberforce at Bath in June, only a few weeks before he died. He was feeble, his head drooped on his breast but his mind was clear and in a 'silvery cadence' he said that he abhorred the idea, propagated by the ACS, that blacks could not be raised to equality with whites within the United States.[16] Wilberforce and eleven others, including Buxton and Macaulay, signed a protest against British support for the Society which Garrison carried proudly back to Boston.[17] One name was missing. Garrison had failed to budge Clarkson. He had gone to Playford in July 1833 with his travelling companion, the Reverend Nathaniel Paul, a black Baptist minister from Albany, New York, and protégé of one of Clarkson's correspondents, Lewis Tappan. Garrison – of all people – was awed into silence in the presence of his hero.[18]

Clarkson recounted for him his conversations with Cresson and repeated his hope that the ACS would assist abolition in America. He could not regard it as evil, without better proof, but he had refused an honorary membership. *'I occupy neutral ground'*, he insisted.

Garrison argued that the ACS deflected support from antislavery and catered to prejudice. He claimed that the few so far embarked for Liberia did not go 'cheerfully and voluntarily'. Clarkson was not wholly persuaded.

'That Colonization Society has been a troublesome concern to us', Catherine reported.[19] 'Mr C has been annoyed above measure. It belongs to America to settle the question. The scramble for my Husband's sanction has been earnest.' She judged Garrison's side 'lays most hold on the feelings' but it was 1840 before Clarkson finally changed his mind about the ACS and apologised to Garrison for being hoodwinked. Garrison was 'overjoyed to think that the dear old man has publicly abandoned that wicked combination'.[20]

Clarkson was obviously impressed with Garrison's spirit and dedication but watched with dismay his growing fanaticism, as did such American abolitionists as the Reverend Henry Ward Beecher who believed that if Garrison had only balanced his ability with the 'moderation and urbanity of Clarkson, or the deep piety of Wilberforce, he had been the one man of our age'.[21] But Garrison and his followers boycotted elections (for a government based on force which kept people in chains), assailed churches for their institutional complicity, opened their ranks to women, stood against war, the death penalty and the convention of keeping the Sabbath holy. They called for the northern states to secede from the Union.[22] A schism in the Massachusetts society was followed by the breakup of the American body into the American Anti-Slavery Society (the Garrison wing) and the American and Foreign Anti-Slavery Society with most of Clarkson's correspondents such as the pious Lewis Tappan, guiding spirit of the AFASS; Gerrit Smith, J. G. Birney, Theodore Weld, the Reverend Joshua Leavitt and Judge William Jay.[23]

Clarkson grieved over the American quarrel and refused to take sides. 'Standing in the very conspicuous situation I do, as at the head of the cause', he could only 'from the bottom of my heart wish both Parties success'.[24] He tried unsuccessfully to convince the Americans that they should not mix abolition with other subjects. 'This cause is a pure and holy cause, and must be kept unspotted as far as it is possible.... [The Americans] should abstain from all political as well as fanatic excitements.'[25]

The British movement suffered inner stress, too, as factions differed over new directions. The most divisive issue was the West Indian apprenticeship system, due to last until 1838 for domestic and 1840 for field-hands. It was not working. Reports of abuses streamed in from the islands and were brought to the government's attention to little effect,[26] until Joseph Sturge, a Birmingham corn merchant and another of those remarkable wealthy Quaker businessmen who served the cause so well, seized the leadership. A radical and reformer now in his forties, Sturge was known to Clarkson for antislavery activities and also as an early member of the Peace Society which his father had helped to found.[27] In the winter of 1836 Sturge sailed to the West Indies to see the situation for himself and his book, *The West Indies in 1837* created a sensation with its first-hand evidence that, whatever the intentions, apprenticeship was not improving life for the supposedly free blacks.[28]

Sturge was the key figure in founding the Central Negro Emancipation Committee, which inspired a series of lobbies and rallies to prod government to act. During the festivities attending the first state opening of Parliament by young Queen Victoria in November 1837, a deputation marched to Downing Street with a petition to end 'coerced labour'.[29] Local committees were reactivated and petitions were called for. In February 1838, Buxton and William Allen were in a delegation which presented a petition against apprenticeship to the Queen signed by 449 000 women.[30]

As other demands flooded both Houses of Parliament, the Central Committee asked the 'oldest Veteran in the cause' to send one signed simply by himself. It suited some of the latter-day abolitionists to say that Clarkson's advice was seldom heeded and his writings seldom read but Buxton, at the height of the scandal over the Wilberforce *Life*, assured him, 'It is no compliment to say that the Public will pay more attention to your opinions, than to those of any other man.'[31]

Clarkson's petition was carried to the Lords by Brougham and the Commons by Dr Stephen Lushington. In it he contended that since colonial legislatures, abetted by magistrates, had failed, especially in Jamaica, to carry out emancipation in the spirit of the Act, the contract was broken and Parliament should end apprenticeship on 1 August 1838.[32] This petition campaign produced 2143 with 511 399 signatures.[33] The colonial assemblies, reading the writing on the wall, abolished apprenticeships as of that date. 'I hope . . . our work is complete', wrote Allen in his diary.[34]

It never was for Clarkson. He wrote regularly to Buxton and Brougham – supplying and seeking information on slavery – and gave Brougham a passionate protest against the government's adoption of a proposal by W. E. Gladstone ('of a notorious slave-holding family') to allow the importation of 'hill coolies' from India to work on plantations in British Guiana, a Crown colony Clarkson characterised as a 'sink-hole of cruelty and oppression'. To Clarkson, this augured a new slave trade. Brougham had his letter printed in several papers.[35]

In the next few years, in spite of a catalogue of ailments that began or ended most of his letters, Clarkson drove his pen as steadily as he ever had done.

Old Clarkson is really a wonderful creature [Henry Crabb Robinson told Mary Wordsworth in 1844]. There he is in his 85th year as laborious and calmly strenuous in his pursuits as he was fifty or sixty years ago. . . . writing letters assiduously both to private friends & for the press and all for his Africans. He is happy in this that he really cannot see difficulties or dangers or doubts in any interest he has embraced or in any act he has to do

– No one ever more faithfully discharged the duty of *hopeing*. . . .
He does not believe that Texas will be united to the States. He
will not see that France and America are doing all in their power
to get rid of their reciprocal obligations to annul the Slave trade –
However obstinate the hill may be to clime, he toils on and has
no doubt of reaching the summit.[36]

In his last year, Clarkson himself said, 'I long very much to be
well again . . . because I cannot endure an *idle Life*'.[37] Joseph Soul,
secretary of the British and Foreign Anti-Slavery Society and often
on the receiving end of Clarkson's advice, told him, 'Your constant
& unwearied application in the good cause of truth & liberty is very
cheering & delightful. I am told by some of my friends that I work
too hard, but I point to you as an example & tell them it is better to
wear out than to rust out. . . . You seem to write more vigorously &
continuously now than you did in 1840.'[38]

British abolition had settled down in 1839 into the British and
Foreign Anti-Slavery Society with Joseph Sturge again the driving
force, although he held no office for several years.[39] The leadership
was predominantly Quaker and the overall tone moderate. Clarkson was a vice-president and attended such sessions of the
committee as his health allowed. He was referred to as president in
1842 and until his last days signed the Society's official letters and
documents, sometimes correcting them. 'Dehumanizing', he wrote
to the secretary in 1841, 'there is no such word in the English
language – but is a coined word, but may pass'. [40] Many of his
letters were published in the *Anti-Slavery Reporter*. Confined as he
largely was to Playford, it is astonishing to see how well-informed
he was. He read widely – more accurately, as his eyes faded, he
was read to by his able wife and daughter-in-law cum niece, Mary,
who now with her son lived at Playford Hall. Both gave priceless
service as copyists and secretaries but it is surprising to find so
many late letters in Clarkson's own increasingly crabbed handwriting, complaining that he couldn't see how to load his pen and
begging forgiveness for the ink blobs.

During the day he was attended by Mary Sheldrake, one of the
family that served the Clarksons for so many years. But from 7
p.m. 'or a little after I must read', Catherine said.[41] They got
through quantities of things – histories, tracts and sermons on the
controversies of the day, literature, often poetry. Clarkson corresponded with the Reverend David Jonathan East about the Niger

expedition and subscribed for five copies of East's *Western Africa* – doubting that he would live to read it, but he did.[42] When a delegation from the Wesleyan Missionary Society visited him on a fund-raising tour for African schools, Clarkson undertook to review a forthcoming book by one of them, the Reverend Thomas B. Freeman, who used to be head gardener for one of his neighbours and started his career teaching other servants to read. The review of *Journal of Visits to Ashanti* was written 'under great bodily Pain' (rheumatism was a torment to him) and published as a fourpenny tract.[43]

Clarkson's intellectual curiosity never faltered. Four months before he died he was finding *Ancient Egypt* by George R. Glidden, the American consul there for 25 years, a source of constant delight. The deciphering of the hieroglyphics 'opens a new world of history', he marvelled.[44]

Its sights now set upon abolishing slavery throughout the world, the British and Foreign Anti-Slavery Society sponsored a 'general convention' in London in June 1840. It was a measure of how far the African cause had come since 1785, when Clarkson took it up and the royal family stoutly supported slavery, that also in 1840 Prince Albert made his first public appearance before a related body, the African Civilization Society, and shared a platform with abolition leaders. The royal consort, as president, was welcomed by 'thundering applause' and made a short, suitable speech. A letter from Clarkson was read to 'long & lasting cheering'.[45]

Clarkson ventured into London a few days later for the general convention and his old heart must have been gladdened as he accepted a silent standing tribute from 5000 delegates and observers from Britain, the United States, Canada, France, the West Indies, Haiti, Spain, Switzerland and Sierra Leone who filled Freemasons' Hall on 12 June 1840.[46] The American antislavery poet, John Greenleaf Whittier, called it a 'world's convention' in an ode he wrote for the occasion.[47]

Clarkson was voted president of the convention on a motion of William Allen, seconded by the American James G. Birney, and in the hush requested in deference to his age and frailty he was led to the platform by Joseph Sturge followed by 'his dead son's beautiful wife' Mary (prudently armed with a smelling bottle and phial of wine) and his only grandchild Tommy, 9 years old that day.[48] Clarkson had wanted the boy with him 'that he may be initiated in the good cause and to be brought up as my successor, if a successor should ever be wanted.'[49]

Clarkson, now 80, introduced himself as the *'originator* and . . . now unhappily the only surviving Member' of the 1787 committee to two of whose members, Wilberforce and Smith, he paid tribute before exhorting the convention: 'Take courage, be not dismayed, go on, persevere to the last.' Ahead lay the 'extirpation of slavery from the *whole world'*. He attacked specifically the American cotton planters who held more than 2 000 000 of their fellow beings in 'the most cruel bondage'. He urged all justifiable means to make them feel the consequences of their guilt, including underselling them in the markets of Europe with the produce of *'free tropical labour'*.[50]

Then to the deep annoyance of American delegates,[51] Clarkson omitted an expected reference to British India which was much on their minds. He may have been advised by the more conservative British leaders to avoid the subject, but he made the entire speech available afterwards and it was printed as a leaflet. In the censored section he made the point that the East India Company, with abundant land and free labour at its disposal, could produce cheap cotton enough to drive the United States cotton from the market. If India were cultivated as it might be, *'it is all over with American slavery'*. [52]

He spoke with 'dignity, clearness & feeling – tears I believe ran down his cheeks, as they did from most eyes', Mary Clarkson reported to Catherine. As he pronounced a benediction the great audience murmured 'Amen'. 'The women wept – the men shook off their tears', the painter Benjamin Haydon remembered, 'it was many minutes before I recovered . . . and this was the moment I immediately chose for the picture.'[53]

The audience held back until Clarkson had finished and Sturge had thanked them for their stillness, whereupon a 'shout & clapping which shook the building began & lasted for several minutes, with waving of hats & handkerchiefs', Mary continued. 'When this had a little subsided J Sturge took the dear Boy forward & introduced him . . . to the meeting, the shouting & cheers & emotion seemed to be doubled, but I was near to fainting.'[54]

In history the 1840 convention is remembered for the 'woman question'. Among the visiting Americans were seven women delegates chosen by Garrisonian branches of the American Anti-Slavery Society. Clarkson had no sooner tottered out of the hall the first day than a bitter debate over seating them began. The BFASS in sending out its first invitations had not thought to specify 'men only', but when they reached Freemasons' Hall the women were refused tickets. Wendell Phillips argued that affiliated organisations should be able to send whom they pleased, under their own rules. The alarmed British hosts, however, treated the gathering as a British meeting with a few friends thrown in and stuck to their own rules and customs, and the revolutionary Americans were soundly defeated in a vote.[55]

The women were allowed to sit in a railed gallery where, when his ship arrived belatedly, Garrison defiantly joined them, a silent inflexible spectator, with Lucretia Mott and the others who would found the women's rights movement.[56]

Clarkson's views are not known but on the Sunday following he sent a note to the women's boarding house asking to call in recognition of the 'obligation which our sacred cause owes to the American Ladies' and their 'sacrifice' in leaving their families and risking the danger of the sea to serve it. He brought Mary, Tommy and a few friends and was received by about 40 Americans, male and female. Mr and Mrs Mott were invited back to Hatcham House for a late supper and to meet Catherine.[57]

There was a craze at this time for Clarkson's autograph and locks of his snowy hair. So many asked for snippets that evening that someone remarked he was in danger of losing it all. 'Never mind', said Clarkson, 'shear away'. Her uncle's head was 'half cleared of his hair', said Mary, who did the shearing, and Tommy also had a 'good portion taken off his'. Mary also meted out slips of paper with phrases from speeches and Clarkson's signature.[58]

Pilgrims to Playford always claimed an autograph and a lock, and once Clarkson posted to Gerrit Smith in New York a 'few other Hairs' to add to the curl he already had and prized so much.[59] Joseph Sturge kept a supply of autographs as gifts to friends, especially Americans, and just a month before Clarkson died, Sturge acknowledged a new supply which had come with a note to 'Dear Joseph Sturge':

'I finished a few autographs for you yesterday', it said, 'and meant to go on with them to day, but alas this day found me so ill, even near unto Death that I fear I can do no more for you – may God bless you and your heavenly Cause'. It is almost the last letter he ever wrote.[60]

Benjamin Haydon, who made the large historical painting of the world's convention, sketched the three Clarksons at several sittings in town and at Playford. 'Clarkson has a head like a Patriarch, & must have been in his Prime a noble figure', said this keen observer, '. . . but there is a nervous irritability, which is peculiar. He lives too much with adorers, especially Women.'[61]

His account of Clarkson at Playford is one of the best contemporary sketches we have of the man in old age.

After the Women retired to Bed, I sat with him. He had his watch on the table, a bottle of Ale standing on a stool before the Fire . . . two boxes of Pills on the table, one marked A (aperient), another S (sedative), and he poured the hot Ale into a tumbler (quite hot) with a mixture without which, he said he got no sleep. [Haydon found Clarkson's absorption with his debilities rather tiresome.] A Servant came in at a certain time by his watch to strap his legs, which he suffered much in many years ago, but now . . . only bracing by cold water & strapping was necessary. As he seemed impatient at my staying beyond a certain time, I went to bed.

At 10 next morning, after his usual breakfast of bread and milk, Clarkson called in the servants to watch Haydon make the first stroke of the painting. When it was done he told them, 'There now, that is the first stroke; come in again in an hour, & you shall see the last'.

Haydon formed this opinion:[62]

Though Clarkson is a gentleman by birth & was educated like one, he is too natural for any artifice. He says what he thinks, does what he feels inclined, is impatient, childish, simple – hungry & will eat, restless & will let you see it; punctual & will hurry, nervous & won't be hurried, positive & hates contradiction, charitable, speaks affectionately of all, even of Wilberforce's Sons, whose abominable conduct he lamented, more as if it cast a shadow over the Father's tomb, than as if he felt wounded from what they had falsely said of himself.

The completed painting with its 138 portraits (a 'waggon load of heads', said one critic, 'poor as a work of art but interesting')[63] was exhibited in May 1841 in the Egyptian Hall, Piccadilly, where Catherine went alone one day to see it. She stayed two hours; it was the 'most wonderful thing I ever saw'.[64]

Clarkson told Haydon about a 'voice' that awakened him one night some five months after the convention dispersed. 'You have not done all your work. There is America!' it said. He sat up in bed and the subject of his next pamphlet came into his mind. If Clarkson really did hear a voice, it was his guilty conscience speaking, for the Americans he met in London had urged him to write the pamphlet and he forgot it until his rude awakening. He called it *A Letter to the Clergy of Various Denominations and to the Slave-Holding Planters in the Southern Parts of the United States.*[65]

Seven-tenths of the clergy in America, he had been told, supported slavery, even defended it from their pulpits. 'They go so far as to say, that there is *no sin* in Slavery . . . and that the Scriptures . . . sanction it. It has fallen to my Lot at the age of 81, when Quiet and Repose are actually needed by me, to be fixed upon to take up my Pen again, and to answer these Wolves in Sheeps Clothing'.[66]

He told Lady Bunbury it would be his last work, for his doctors had warned that he must give up all writing. 'My Mind', he insisted, 'is literally worn out.'

For another five years he turned out tracts and each, he declared, was the last he should ever do. 'Would you think it possible . . . that now on the eve of going into the eighty-fourth year of my age, I should have been obliged to work *eight hours* a day for the last three years to forward our cause', he groused happily to his good friend the Reverend John Charlesworth in 1843. 'But there has always been something or other rising up to call me into action.' Something always occurred to keep him 'constantly in *hot* water'.[67]

He wrote on baptism, as we know, and reviewed Freeman's book. He produced a paper extolling emancipation in the West Indies to support Lord Brougham's opposition to further imports of workers from Africa.[68] His last published work returned to his early compassionate concern for the conditions of British mercantile seamen. He could not have *'died easy'* without taking up their cause again.[69] He was credited with influencing the terms of the 1842 Ashburton extradition treaty so that fugitive slaves who had escaped to Canada were exempt from its provisions.[70] He contributed his wisdom to a study the French were making on the effects of emancipation and sent regular messages to antislavery gatherings. He wrote a kind of 'farewell address' for the 1843 antislavery convention but was persuaded not to try to go to London and it was read from the chair.[71]

In making American churches his target, Clarkson agreed with the American historian of antislavery William Goodell that pre-judice was fostered in them[72] and he liked to believe that he had altered the 'tone' of the debate there. Lewis Tappan said that 'tens of thousands' read his works. Joseph Sturge took copies of the *Letter to the Clergy* with him when he sailed to the United States in 1841 and Clarkson sent his work regularly to his correspondents who in turn saw that it was reprinted or published in their local papers. Clarkson kept everything short, pocket-sized, easy and cheap to circulate.[73]

Clarkson's *Letter to Such Professing Christians in the Northern States of America as have had no Practical Concern with Slave Holding* was reprinted from Texas to New York and brought Clarkson into touch with Cassius M. Clay, the largest landholder in Kentucky, who had recently become an abolitionist and planned to free his slaves.[74] It also produced a rejoinder from South Carolina's governor James Henry Hammond, to whom a copy was sent by Clarkson's new son-in-law, Willoughby W. Dickinson, the Playford curate. In two public letters, Hammond denounced Clarkson's warnings of divine vengeance and his call to northern Christians to break the South's political domination and charged him with ignoring the plight of the poor and exploited classes in Britain. 'Raise them from the condition of brutes, to the level of human beings – of American slaves at least', he taunted. 'We accept the Bible terms as the definition of our slavery, and its precepts as the guide for our conduct.'[75]

Nothing irked Clarkson and his friends more than the use of the Bible to defend slavery and Clarkson repeatedly argued against the notion that slavery began with Abraham.[76] In one of his least-known pamphlets, *On the Ill Treatment of the People of Colour in the United States, on Account of the Colour of their Skin*, he blamed prejudice on slavery which made a black skin synonymous with inferiority. The daily humiliations suffered by free blacks were costing America its good name.[77]

Clarkson's reputation as an authority on American slavery brought him in 1841 a curious compliment in the form of a request for information from the as-yet-unapologetic Archdeacon Samuel Wilberforce who was writing the *History of the Protestant Episcopal Church in America*. Clarkson replied freely and sent books on the American churches from his library.[78]

Clarkson had needed much persuasion before he consented to Mary Clarkson's marriage to the 26-year-old curate of Playford,

Willoughby Dickinson, who has been mentioned above, though Mary got Dickinson's promise not to leave Playford so long as the elderly Clarksons lived. Catherine gradually discovered that he was an 'amiable and inoffensive' fellow and Clarkson detected a certain cleverness, in time. Mary and her uncle jointly decided to enter Tommy in the reformed Rugby School, where he was very happy. During his holidays, his grandfather and stepfather tutored him alternately.[79] Clarkson seemed to live for the boy. On one of his restless nights he asked Catherine for a sweet thought to go to sleep upon. 'Think of your little grandson', she said. 'Yes, that will do.'[80]

January of 1846 brought the Clarksons' fiftieth wedding anniversary on 'not a very bright day'. The winters were hard for him now and Clarkson kept to his bedroom with a good fire and his writing table shielded from draughts by a large screen. He was wheeled from sofa to bed wrapped in a blanket. His confinement and his painfully swollen legs made him equally irascible. On fine days the servants carried him downstairs for an airing in a garden chair on wheels. When summer arrived he could struggle downstairs himself but the heat threw him off his food. His sensibilities were more tender than ever.[81]

The news of the suicide of the artist Haydon with whom he had spent so many interesting hours affected him deeply, coming so soon as it did after the death of Buxton. The loss of William Allen in 1843 was a heavy blow. They last met at Playford in 1841 and Allen said of their parting, 'I was affected on taking leave of T C, and said "The Lord bless thee;" it came from my heart and went to his; he quite wept. We have been dear to each other for nearly half a century, and it is doubtful whether we shall ever meet again.'[82] Neither could have expected the younger man to go first.

Some days Clarkson could receive company and write busily. On others he lived 'under a cloud'. Catherine had to ration his visitors and caution his correspondents that at times he was unfit to write for publication. He could even forget the schism in the American antislavery ranks.[83] But it would scarcely be fitting for Clarkson, who had spent a lifetime in controversy, to leave the world placidly, and he didn't.

Impetuous always, William Lloyd Garrison did not wait to learn whether Clarkson could see him when he took the 'train of cars' to Ipswich on 20 August 1846. His letter asking for an interview reached Playford Hall at 9 o'clock that morning, and it was followed by Garrison before 1 p.m. With him were the British firebrand George Thompson and the eloquent Frederick Douglass, the former slave who had been captivating British audiences for the last year. Garrison was in Britain to help set up a breakaway Antislavery League, headed by Thompson.[84]

Clarkson greeted them affectionately. Douglass recalled, 'We found the venerable object of our visit seated at a table, where he had been busily writing a letter to America against slavery. . . . he took one of my hands in both of his, and, in a tremulous voice, said "God bless you, Frederick Douglass! I have given sixty years of my life to the emancipation of your people, and if I had sixty years more they should all be given to the same cause"'.[85]

They dined and just before the Americans left, Garrison saw Clarkson alone. He carried away, as Catherine later learned, an unfinished paper which argued for the secession of the northern states as a means of withdrawing legal sanction of slavery, a Garrisonian position. The 'Last Thoughts of Thomas Clarkson on the Subject of Slavery' were given to the world by the London *Patriot* on 1 October. Clarkson was made to seem a wholehearted supporter not only of Garrison's wing of the American movement but of the Garrisonians within Britain as well, in conflict with his own BFASS. At an uproarious public meeting in Norwich, Thompson flourished the document crying, 'Here it is blotted & blurred by the blind old man.'[86]

Catherine tried, to no avail, to get the document back, but Garrison insisted he must preserve it 'as a token of his regard for my antislavery services'. As she feared, doubts rose in some BFASS minds that Clarkson, at the end, had defected to the radicals. She assured them this was not so.[87]

After all the pain and grief he had known, during a life of great fulfilment, death came easily to Clarkson. He was bedridden only a week and died at 4 o'clock on the morning of 26 September. He told Catherine he had no fear but it hurt him to leave her and Mary and 'his voice faltered & he could not name the Boy'.[88] In his last hours he said, 'I am very happy I am constantly engaged in prayer. . . . I do not wish to have my mind disturbed from praying.' He wondered what his last thoughts would be. Catherine replied, 'I hope, my dear, of your God and Saviour.'

'He took his draught and went to sleep, and awoke in the last struggle', as a friend described the deathbed. 'He raised his hands together and his eyes turned upward and then uttered, "Come,

come, come, my Beloved." He then tried to speak to each one around him, but his words could not be understood, and he expired.'[89]

Catherine said later, 'He was such a grand piece of clay that the persons employed went out of the room backwards as if in the presence of a monarch'. Only a 'thin Veil' divided her from her husband of 50 years and 'in no long time', she felt, she would pierce it.[90]

The press rained tributes upon him and eulogies were delivered from pulpits on both sides of the Atlantic. His *History* was ransacked for anecdotes of his early heroic days. The unparalleled length of his service, the purity of his motives and his lack of ostentation inspired the poets, and verses galore hailed the lost apostle for peace, freedom and justice.

A Quaker in the Lake District concluded his homage:

> A name that scatters light
> And teaching on his times, proclaims abroad
> How one just man may serve truth, peace and right,
> By faith that works for God.[91]

Clarkson was buried in the family vault near the south chancel door of Playford church. The site is marked by a simple palisade of iron railings on which hang three pretty marble plaques with the names of Thomas and Catherine and their son between. Mary Dickinson planted honeysuckle inside the rails, like that which climbed over Playford Hall. Later she placed a marble memorial in the chancel with Clarkson's bust in bas relief, 'to unite her own memory with the memory of those she so dearly loved' – her uncle and aunt, her first husband and her only son.

The funeral at Playford on 2 October 1846 was as utterly simple as Clarkson had wanted it to be.[92] The day was calm and grey with leaves falling and rustling underfoot as the cortège of six carriages bearing only family members and neighbourhood friends followed the hearse from the Hall and wound through the village to the church where the bells were tolling. The horses carried no plumes and the hearse no escutcheon. Clarkson's grandson, aged 15, was chief mourner. His widow, by custom, remained in seclusion at home. Representing Clarkson's long public life were his constant correspondents, the past and present secretaries of the British and Foreign Anti-Slavery Society, Joseph Soul and John Beaumont.

Joseph Sturge came from Birmingham in a private testimony of grief. Six of Clarkson's farm-workers walked on either side of the hearse and the house-servants followed.

The route was lined with villagers who joined the procession and filled the church to overflowing. The Reverend Thomas D. West, vicar of Rushmere who held the Playford living, began the burial service as the heavy lead-lined oak coffin was borne by the labourers up the steep steps and pathway to the church door. In the silent funeral parade and at the church were a number of Friends, who, on this occasion, removed their hats.

The press made much of the unusual simplicity of Clarkson's funeral. His faith embraced two traditions, the Church of England and the Society of Friends, and probably for this reason he was not honoured, as other antislavery leaders had been, with a memorial and service in Westminster Abbey. His funeral combined an Anglican rite with a Quaker procession, stripped of all outward show.

The Quakers did not believe that tombstones were a proper way of honouring the dead; instead, 'If you wish to honour a good man ... let all his good actions live in your memory.... show, by your adoption of his amiable example, that you really respect his memory.'[93]

So talk of a statue in the Abbey was quickly squelched as offensive to Quaker friends, and Catherine refused permission for a monument over his grave, defying complaints over 'how unhandsomely I have disposed of my Husband's body!'[94]

She did not object when George Biddell Airy proposed a monument at the church door, but the plain obelisk of Aberdeen granite was not erected until 1857, a year after her death. The activity in arranging a subscription for it was a nice tribute from Airy, Arthur Biddell's nephew and later Sir George, whose genius was spotted by Clarkson when the boy came to Playford. Clarkson tutored him in classics and helped him enter Cambridge as the first step in his road towards becoming the eminent astronomer royal.[95]

Feeling the need to provide the public recognition Clarkson did not claim, others placed monuments, too. A memorial was unveiled in 1879 near Wadesmill in Hertfordshire, at the spot where Clarkson in 1785 resolved that something must be done about the slave trade. It was the gift of Arthur Giles Puller, MP and landowner, of Youngsbury.[96] Wisbech Corporation a year later spent £2000 on a glorious monument by Gilbert Scott in the town centre. Beneath the statue of Clarkson are bas-relief panels of Granville Sharp and William Wilberforce and the kneeling slave in his chains.

In 1853, Harriet Beecher Stowe, the celebrated author of *Uncle Tom's Cabin*, travelled to Britain and made a pilgrimage to Playford Hall to see Clarkson's frail widow and his grave. She found 'just such a still, quiet, mossy old church as you have read of in story books, with the graveyard spread all around it, like a thoughtful mother, who watches the resting of her children'. The churchyard grass was long and spotted with daisies, the grave carefully tended and planted with flowers. It was a 'lazy dream of peacefulness and rest'.[97]

Notes

Abbreviations used in source notes:
DNB *The Dictionary of National Biography*
BM Add Ms British Museum Additional Manuscript
CO Colonial Office paper
PRO Public Record Office
The place of publication and location of libraries is always London unless otherwise indicated.

Dedication page quotation from Ralph Waldo Emerson's essay, 'Self-Reliance', in *American Scholar* (New York, 1893).

1 The Man and the Cause

1. [Henry Crabb Robinson], review of *Life of William Wilberforce, Eclectic Review*, III (1838), 678.
2. Diary of Katherine Plymley, Corbett of Longnor Papers, Shropshire Record Office, Book 19; Folarin Shyllon, *James Ramsay the Unknown Abolitionist* (Edinburgh, 1977), p. 85.
3. Alexander Crummell, *The Man: The Hero: The Christian! A Eulogy on the Life and Character of Thomas Clarkson* (New York, 1847), p. 22.
4. Charles James Fox, for one, was willing, as he said in the House on Pitt's motion and earlier privately: C. J. Fox to T. Walker in Blanchard Jerrold (ed.), *The Original*, Vol. I (1874), pp. 106–7.
5. S. T Coleridge to D. Stuart, 13 February 1809, BM Add Ms 34 046, f. 76.
6. H. C. Robinson to W. Wordsworth, 22 April 1842, in Thomas Sadler (ed.), *Diary, Reminiscences and Correspondence of Henry Crabb Robinson*, Vol. III (1869), p. 169.
7. Plymley Diary, Books 2, 3, 21, 25; Recollections of Julia Smith, William Smith and Family Papers, Cambridge University Library, Add 7621.
8. Robin Furneaux, *William Wilberforce* (1974), p. 10; John Pollock, *Wilberforce* (1977), p. 8; Mary Carr, *Thomas Wilkinson: A Friend of Wordsworth* (1905), p. 36. At William Allen's establishment in 1823 Wilberforce weighed 76 pounds including his iron brace: Martha Braithwaite (ed.), *Memorials of Christine Majolier Alsop* (1881), p. 67.
9. Robert Isaac Wilberforce and Samuel Wilberforce (eds), *Life of William Wilberforce*, 2nd edn, Vol. IV (1839), p. 126; Ford K. Brown, *Fathers of the Victorians: the Age of Wilberforce* (Cambridge, 1961), pp. 70, 108.
10. Reginald Coupland, *Wilberforce* (Oxford, 1923), p. 37; Furneaux, *Wilberforce*, pp. 10, 288; author's unpublished study, 'The Great Yorkshire Election'.

11. Furneaux, *Wilberforce*, p. 287.
12. Thomas Clarkson, *History of the Rise, Progress, and Accomplishment of the Abolition of the African Slave-Trade*, Vol. I (1808), pp. 271–2. A facsimile was printed in 1968.
13. David Richardson, 'Profits in the Liverpool Slave Trade: the Accounts of William Davenport 1757–1784', in Roger Anstey and P. E. H. Hair (eds), *Liverpool, the African Slave Trade, and Abolition* (Liverpool, 1976), pp. 60–90.
14. T. Clarkson to A. Haldane, n.d. [1845], Thomas Clarkson Papers, St John's College Library, Cambridge University; Earl Leslie Griggs, *Thomas Clarkson the Friend of Slaves* (1936), p. 24n. Clarkson told a friend collecting autographs that he had destroyed 'Boxes after Boxes of Papers for the Sake of Making Room': T. Clarkson to T. Thompson, 5 May 1823, Boston Public Library, Ms Eng 183 (43).
15. M. M. Linnell to A. Clarkson, 17 December 1932, in Correspondence and Researches of Mr and Mrs Augustus Clarkson, held by Mrs A. M. Wray.
16. C. Clarkson to E. Shewell, 9 November 1846, Clarkson Papers, Wisbech and Fenland Museum.
17. Griggs, *Thomas Clarkson*. Thomas Taylor published *Biographical Sketch of Thomas Clarkson, MA, with Occasional Brief Strictures on the Misrepresentations of Him Contained in the Life of William Wilberforce* in 1839 and James Elmes, *Thomas Clarkson: a Monograph, Being a Contribution Towards the History of the Abolition of the Slave-Trade and Slavery* appeared in 1854.
18. St Peter and St Paul Parish Registers, Wisbech Museum.
19. H. Lawrence White, *History of Wisbech Grammar School* (Wisbech, 1939). Also for Wisbech and the school, Neil Walker and Thomas Craddock, *History of Wisbech and the Fens* (Wisbech, 1849), pp. 188–205. A roundel on the Old Grammar School commemorates the birthplace of Clarkson, the 'Friend of Slaves'.
20. Genealogical material from Ellen Gibson Wilson, *John Clarkson and the African Adventure* (1980), pp. 3–8 where the family history is given in more detail.
21. William Smith (ed.), *Old Yorkshire*, Vol. I (1881), p. 129; Jennifer Tann, 'Survey of Thirsk, Yorkshire', in *Industrial Archaeology*, Vol. IV (1967), 232–47; Thomas Langdale, *Topographical Dictionary of Yorkshire* (Northallerton, 1822); William Grainge, *Vale of Mowbray: Historical and Topographical Account of Thirsk and Its Neighbourhood* (1859), pp. 80, 83, 126, 148; [J. B. Jefferson], *History of Thirsk* (Thirsk, 1821), p. 59; Edward Baines, *History, Directory and Gazeteer of the County of York*, Vol. II (Leeds, 1823); [Daniel DeFoe], *Tour Through the Island of Great Britain*, 8th edn, Vol. III (1778), p. 181.
22. St Mary's Parish Registers, Thirsk.
23. Thomas Zouch, *The Good Schoolmaster, Exemplified in the Character of the Reverend John Clarke MA* (York, 1798); George Poulson, *Beverlae, or the Antiquities and History of the Town of Beverley*, Vol. I (1829), pp. 452–69; Wilson, *John Clarkson*, pp. 4–5.

24. J. A. Venn (ed.), *Alumni Cantabrigiensis* (Cambridge, 1953), part III, Admissions to St John's.

25. See Wilson, *John Clarkson*, pp. 7–10 for more on Clarkson's maternal lineage.

26. Parish Registers, Wisbech. Anne Clarkson seems to have been older than Thomas but her birth was not recorded in any of the area parish registers searched. No birth-date is on her gravestone in Holy Trinity Church, Long Melford.

27. C. Clarkson to E. Shewell, 31 March 1836, Wisbech Museum.

28. C. Clarkson to E. Shewell, 8 November 1846, Wisbech Museum.

29. Clarkson, *History*, Vol. I, p. 8: Thomas Clarkson, 'My Speech at Exeter Hall 24 June 1840', Clarkson Papers, BM Add Ms 41 267A, f. 201.

30. Wilson, *John Clarkson*, p. 10; Griggs, *Thomas Clarkson*, p. 24.

31. Wilson, *John Clarkson*, pp. 11–12.

32. [DeFoe], *Tour*, Vol. I, pp. 68–9; Samuel Pepys, *Diary*, 18 September 1663; William Cobbett, *Rural Rides*, Vol. II (1930 reprint of 1912 ed.), pp. 239–40.

33. Michael F. J. McDonnell, *History of St Paul's School* (1909).

34. Ibid., pp. 358, 361.

35. Robert Barlow Gardiner (ed.), *Admission Registers of St Paul's School, 1748–1876* (1884), pp. 161, 403; McDonnell, *History*, p. 294; J. E. B. Mayor (ed.), *Admissions to the College of St John's, the Evangelist* (1882); Edward Miller, *Portrait of a College* (Cambridge, 1961), mentions a 'Robert Clarkson' as a graduate who became a notable reformer, p. 70.

36. Plymley Diary, Book 20; Wilfred Airy (ed.), *Autobiography of Sir George Biddell Airy* (Cambridge, 1896).

37. Venn, *Alumni*, Part II.

38. Clarkson, *History*, Vol. I, pp. 206, 207; Chester W. New, *Life of Henry Brougham to 1830* (Oxford, 1961), p. 23.

39. Peter Peckard, *Justice and Mercy recommended, particularly with reference to the Slave Trade* (Cambridge, 1788); Thomas Clarkson, *Essay on the Slavery and Commerce of the Human Species, Particularly the African* (1786), p. 254; Clarkson, *History*, Vol. I, pp. 203–4.

40. Clarkson, *History*, Vol. I, pp. 93–6; Wilson, *John Clarkson*, p. 44; Roger Anstey, *Atlantic Slave Trade and British Abolition 1760–1810* (1975), pp. 242, 246. Seymour Drescher, *Capitalism and Slavery: British Mobilization in Comparative Perspective* (1986), p. 60 says the *Zong* case got little publicity in spite of its horror.

41. Clarkson, *Essay*, p. xxvi.

42. Clarkson, *History*, Vol. I, p. 207.

43. Ibid., pp. 208–9.

44. Peckard, *Justice*, p. ix.

45. Drescher, *Capitalism*, p. x.

46. Clarkson, *History*, Vol. I, p. 210.

47. Clarkson, *History*, Vol. I, pp. 210–11.

48. C. Clarkson to E. Shewell, 9 November 1846, Wisbech.

49. W. Wordsworth to H. C. Robinson [c. 5 May 1838] in Alan G. Hill (ed.), *Letters of William and Dorothy Wordsworth, Later Years, Part III* (Oxford, 1982), p. 581.

50. Julia Smith Recollections; Plymley Diary, Books 2, 3, 4, 12, 13; John Purcell FitzGerald, *Quiet Worker for Good, a Familiar Sketch of the late John Charlesworth* (1865), pp. 93, 94; 'Clarkson's Autobiography', *Christian Observer*, LXVI (1866) 482–3, 488.

51. Plymley Diary, Book 12.

52. Ibid., Books 21, 25, 56; FitzGerald, *Quiet Worker*, pp. 93, 94; Recollections of Julia Smith.

2 The Originator

1. Thomas Clarkson, *History of the Rise, Progress and Accomplishment of the Abolition of the African Slave-Trade*, Vol. I (1808), pp. 210–12.

2. Diary of Katherine Plymley, Corbett of Longnor Papers, Shropshire Record Office, Book 64; C. Clarkson to E. Shewell, 31 March 1836, Clarkson Papers, Wisbech and Fenland Museum.

3. Clarkson, *History*, Vol. I, pp. 212–13.

4. Ibid., pp. 213–14, 216. Trained in the classics (and the published essay retains notes in both Latin and Greek) Clarkson felt awkward in English composition. He worked from his original long version (an abridgement to meet competition rules for length had won the prize) and added material gained from his new friends. Thomas Clarkson, *Essay on the Slavery and Commerce of the Human Species, Particularly the African* (1786), pp. xxii–xxiii.

5. David Brion Davis, *Problem of Slavery in the Age of Revolution, 1770–1823* (Ithaca, NY, 1975), pp. 213ff. on the Quaker ethic and antislavery; Clarkson, *History*, Vol. I, pp. 213–16.

6. Ibid., pp. 117–28. Woods' book was *Thoughts on the Slavery of Negroes* (1784). Porteus preached in February 1783 to the Society for the Propagation of the Gospel in Foreign Parts on conditions among West Indian slaves and proposed a legal code to protect them and encourage conversion. It previewed Ramsay's first essay: Folarin Shyllon, *James Ramsay the Unknown Abolitionist* (Edinburgh, 1977).

7. Roger Anstey, *Atlantic Slave Trade and British Abolition 1760–1810* (1975), pp. 201, 203–5, 212–13, 226–30; Patrick C. Lipscomb III, 'William Pitt and the Abolition of the Slave Trade', PhD thesis, University of Texas (1960), p. 73.

8. Clarkson, *History*, Vol. I, p. 216; Ellen Gibson Wilson, *John Clarkson and the African Adventure* (1980), p. 6; G. Sharp to Rev. Dr Sharp, 23 September 1791, introducing Clarkson as very sensible and worthy of any civility and 'I believe related to my father's old relation Rev Mr Clarkson of Silkston nr Rotherham': Granville Sharp Papers, Hardwicke Court, when consulted; now deposited at Gloucestershire Record Office.

9. Clarkson, *History*, Vol. I, p. 216.

10. Ibid., pp. 84–5; Dale H. Porter, *Abolition of the Slave Trade in England, 1784–1807* (Hamden, Conn., 1970), p. 31 n. 3; John Pollock, *Wilber-*

force (1977), pp. 10, 11; Reginald Coupland, *Wilberforce* (Oxford, 1923), p. 74. David Hartley, Whig MP for Hull, first introduced the subject of slavery in 1776, proposing rights of jury trial for slaves in preparation for gradual abolition. His motion failed. In 1780 young Wilberforce replaced Hartley as MP for Hull, but Hartley was returned in a by-election in 1782.

11. Clarkson, *History*, Vol. I, p. 217.
12. Phillips's biography by his daughter makes no such claim: Mary Phillips, *Memoir of the Life of Richard Phillips* (1841). Phillips joined the Friends formally in 1789 and became a minister in 1791. He was involved in many charities for the sick, poor and imprisoned.
13. The Essay was dedicated in flowery fashion to the Earl of Portmore, Viscount Milsintown, whose domestic chaplain (purely honorary, apparently) Clarkson had become on leaving Cambridge. As the Earl never appears again in Clarkson's recorded life, it is not possible to explain the connection. Portmore attended St John's well ahead of Clarkson. His eldest daughter was Lady Scarsdale who became an early abolitionist.
14. Clarkson, *Essay*, pp. 38–9, 137, 249, 252, 256.
15. Porter, *Abolition*, pp. 32–3; W. Smith to C. Clarkson, 1 August 1834, Clarkson Papers, William R. Perkins Library, Duke University. Catherine's memory was that the *Essay* 'set the whole country in flames': C. Clarkson to W. Smith, 18 August 1834, Duke University.
16. Copy of Clarkson's *Essay* with his endorsement in Thomas Clarkson Collection, Trevor Arnett Library, Atlanta University.
17. Clarkson, *History*, Vol. I, pp. 211, 218, 196.
18. Ibid., pp. 219–22. For Langton, DNB; *Gentleman's Magazine* (1801), p. 1207. Johnson bequeathed his Polyglot Bible to Langton and said of him the world did not hold a 'worthier man'. He succeeded Johnson as professor of literature at the Royal Academy. When Johnson died in 1784 he left Langton £750 to arrange an annuity for his black servant Barber. For Lady Scarsdale, see note 13. Dr Baker held the living at the Scarsdales' home, Kedleston in Derbyshire.
19. Clarkson, *History*, Vol. I, pp. 101–4; Shyllon, *Ramsey*, pp. 18ff.; Anstey, *Atlantic Slave Trade*, pp. 248ff.
20. Clarkson, *History*, Vol. I, p. 103.
21. Ibid., pp. 222ff.; Pollock, *Wilberforce*, pp. 50–51; Shyllon, *Ramsey*, p. 84.
22. Clarkson, *History*, Vol. I, pp. 224–5.
23. Thomas Clarkson, 'My speech at Exeter Hall', 24 June 1840, BM Add Ms 41 267A, f. 201.
24. Clarkson, *History*, Vol. I, p. 223.
25. Ibid., pp. 225–30.
26. Ibid., p. 229.
27. Ibid., p. 228–9.
28. Ibid., pp. 233, 236.
29. Clarkson was hailed as the originator at the first world's antislavery convention 23 June 1840: BM Add Ms 41 267A, f. 212. Among other descriptions are 'lecturer' (he rarely spoke in public); 'stipendiary

secretary' (to Wilberforce), 'henchman', and 'field representative' or 'field agent'. These titles are taken from James Walvin, 'Freeing the Slaves: How Important was Wilberforce?' in Jack Hayward (ed.), *Out of Slavery, Abolition and After* (1985), p. 35; Robert Isaac Wilberforce and Samuel Wilberforce (eds), *Life of William Wilberforce*, 2nd edn (1839), Vol. I, p. 152; Sir George Stephen, *Antislavery Recollections* (1854), p. 86; Ernest Howse, *Saints in Politics* (1952), p. 21; Earl Leslie Griggs and Clifford H. Prater (eds), *Henry Christophe and Thomas Clarkson, a Correspondence* (Berkeley, Calif., 1952), p. 63. Sir James Stephen, *Essays in Ecclesiastical Biography*, Vol. II (1849), p. 245 says Clarkson (not named) was paid a 'reasonable salary' and this error is perpetuated by Leslie Stephen in the authoritative DNB's piece on Wilberforce in which Stephen says the Committee 'employed' Clarkson to collect evidence. John Campbell Colquhoun, *William Wilberforce: His Friends and His Times* (1867), pp. 369–70, fancied Clarkson as a 'pioneer' [foot soldier] or 'quartermastergeneral' to Wilberforce's 'commander-in-chief'.

30. Clarkson, *History*, Vol. I, pp. 231, 232.
31. Ibid., p. 233.
32. Ibid., pp. 234–6, 256. Sir Herbert Mackworth was MP for Cardiff; Lord Newhaven, an Irish peer; Lord Balgonie a Scottish peer, son of pious parents, who married a daughter of John Thornton of Clapham.
33. Clarkson, *History*, Vol. I, p. 236; Peter Fryer, *Staying Power. The History of Black People in Britain* (1984), pp. 42–3, 44–7; Porter, *Abolition*, pp. 8, 28–9.
34. Clarkson, *History*, Vol. I, pp. 24–5.
35. Ibid., p. 220.
36. Ibid., pp. 237–8. The specimen chest with some contents survives at the Wisbech and Fenland Museum. One of Clarkson's lifelong themes was to be that the slave trade degraded and distorted relationships between the British and the African rulers and that abolition would open a vast African market to the great benefit of both sides. See Christopher Fyfe, 'Reform in West Africa: the Abolition of the Slave Trade' in J. F. A. Ajayi and Michael Crowder (eds), *History of West Africa* (1974), pp. 30–56 for Afro-European relations and the obstacles presented by the slave trade.
37. Clarkson, *History*, Vol. I, p. 238.
38. Ibid., p. 239. Wilberforce used his influence to gain access for Clarkson to London customs house documents: G. Rose to W. Wilberforce, 27 September 1787, Wilberforce Manuscripts, Bodleian Library, Oxford University, d 17 f. 8.
39. Clarkson, *History*, Vol. I, pp. 243, 248.
40. Ibid., pp. 247, 248. Clarkson was told of one plantation which had not bought a slave in 40 years: 'Benjamin Kaye's Journal to and at Yearly Meeting, London, 1787', *Journal of the Friends Historical Society*, XXI (1924), 56.
41. Clarkson, *History*, Vol. I, p. 245.
42. Anstey, *Atlantic Slave Trade*, pp. 203, 212–13; Davis, *Problem of*

Slavery, p. 233. His whole discussion of the Quaker ethic and transatlantic antislavery is illuminating, pp. 213ff.

43. 'Benjamin Kaye's Journal', p. 56.
44. [Henry Crabb Robinson], review of *Life of Wilberforce*, in *Eclectic Review*, III (1838), 680.
45. Differing versions of the meeting are found in Wilberforce *Life*, Vol. I, pp. 147–51; Coupland, *Wilberforce*, pp. 76–81; Robin Furneaux, *William Wilberforce* (1974), pp. 70–71; Pollock, *Wilberforce*, pp. 52–5 and Clarkson's *History*, Vol. I, pp. 241–2, the only contemporary version.
46. C. I. Latrobe, *Letters to My Children* (1851), pp. 21–3.
47. Furneaux, *Wilberforce*, pp. 71–2; Clarkson, *History*, Vol. I, p. 241.
48. Ibid., pp. 243–4.
49. Anstey, *Atlantic Slave Trade*, pp. 250–51 summarises such influences. Wilberforce *Life*, Vol. I, pp. 147ff. provides an unreliable account as to dates and the sequence of events, relying at crucial points on notes from memory. Most accounts of Wilberforce's early interest mention a letter written as a schoolboy to a York newspaper but so far no one including the present writer has been able to find it.
50. Wilberforce, *Life*, Vol. I, divorces Clarkson completely from the committee on p. 151.
51. Stephen, *Antislavery*, p. 79; Furneaux, *Wilberforce*, p. 287.
52. Clarkson, *History*, Vol. I, p. 249. Dr Gregory, author of *Essays Historical and Moral*, one of which supported Ramsay's arguments on slavery and pointed out how destructive the slave trade was to British seamen. He proposed that Parliament abolish both: Clarkson, *History*, Vol. I, pp. 98–9.
53. Ibid., pp. 239–40.
54. Ibid., pp. 250–51.
55. Ibid., p. 251.
56. Wilberforce, *Life*, Vol. I, pp. 129–38; Ford K. Brown, *Fathers of the Victorians* (Cambridge, 1961), pp. 83, 84; David Owen, *English Philanthropy 1660–1960* (Cambridge, Mass., 1964), p. 98.
57. Clarkson, *History*, Vol. I, p. 273.
58. John S. Harford, *Recollections of William Wilberforce* (1864), p. 138.
59. Clarkson, *History*, Vol. I, p. 251.
60. Furneaux, *Wilberforce*, p. 72.
61. Clarkson, *History*, Vol. I, p. 252.
62. Ibid., pp. 252–4. Although his fellow guests did not know it, Wilberforce already had pledged himself to Pitt and Grenville: Furneaux, *Wilberforce*, p. 72. This decision was made at Pitt's home on 12 May, according to Pollock, *Wilberforce*, pp. 57–8, but Pollock alone fixes the date of the Langton dinner as 13 March 1787, based on an entry in Boswell's ms diary (p. 317 n. 25). Clarkson's *History*, the Wilberforce *Life* and Furneaux agree on the sequence of events. Pollock believes 13 March, as that entry carries the 'only mention of Clarkson in the diary', but it is unlikely to have been the only meeting between Clarkson – a frequent visitor to Langton – and Boswell, the companion and biographer of Langton's friend Dr

Johnson. The really remarkable thing about the entry quoted by Pollock as fixing the date of the fateful dinner is that it does not mention Wilberforce and it does list Malone who is not in Clarkson's guest list.

63.   T. Clarkson to R. Wilberforce, 12 August 1834. Wilberforce Manuscripts, Bodleian Library; C. Clarkson to H. C. Robinson, 15 September 1843, Henry Crabb Robinson Letters, Dr Williams's Library.

3   At the Perilous Fountainhead

1.   This meeting with Clarkson was on 19 May according to the Calendar of the Diaries of William Dillwyn, Vol. II, 1781–90, National Library of Wales, Aberystwyth, or three days before the Committee was launched. Thomas Clarkson, *History of the Rise, Progress, and Accomplishment of the Abolition of the African Slave-Trade* (1808), Vol. I, p. 255, suggests the Quakers met on the 21st and the new Committee the following day.

2.   Clarkson, *History*, Vol. I, p. 255.

3.   Ibid., pp. 255–7; Minute Book of the Committee of the Society for Effecting the Abolition of the Slave Trade, BM Add Ms 21 254, 22 May 1787. Where possible, Clarkson's account had been checked against other sources. The accuracy of the organisational details supplied by his *History* has not been challenged.

4.   Clarkson, *History*, Vol. I, p. 256. One missing person on the new Committee was James Ramsay who refused to join because of the controversy swirling around him but put his knowledge at their disposal: J. Ramsay to S. Hoare, 11 August 1787, Thomas Clarkson Collection, Huntington Library, San Marino, California; Committee Minute Book 5 July 1787. Although Richard Phillips did not become a Friend until 1789 he may be counted as one here.

5.   Committee Minute Book during 1787.

6.   Robert Isaac Wilberforce and Samuel Wilberforce, *Life of William Wilberforce*, 2nd edn (1839), Vol. I, p. 152. Clarkson is not mentioned as a Committee member. Frank J. Klingberg, *Anti-Slavery Movement in England* (New Haven, Conn., 1926), p. 73 makes Wilberforce 'chief adviser', says Clarkson 'was directed by' the Committee (p. 73n) and calls him its 'indefatigable field agent' (p. 75).

7.   As in W. Wilberforce to W. Eden, 18 January 1788, in *Journal and Correspondence of William Lord Auckland* (1861), Vol. II, p. 307. Typical of the misunderstanding of the structure of the campaign is Trevelyan's reference to the 'systematic propaganda begun by Sharp and Wilberforce': George Macaulay Trevelyan, *Britain in the Nineteenth Century* (1967), p. 51.

8.   Committee Minute Book for 1787; Clarkson, *History*, Vol. I, pp. 258ff., map and text.

9.   Several have been noted. Among the others, Sansom was a merchant, Harrison a barrister, Woods a merchant and woollen draper, Lloyd from a metal-working and banking family. See also David Brion Davis, *Problem of Slavery in the Age of Revolution 1770–1823*

(Ithaca, NY, 1975), pp. 233, 234, 235; Ellen Gibson Wilson, *Loyal Blacks* (New York, 1976), p. 184.

10. Clarkson, *History*, Vol. I, pp. 271–2.

11. Committee Minute Book, July–November 1787.

12. [Thomas Clarkson], 'Notes Respecting the late Mr Granville Sharp', the *Philanthropist* III (1815), p. 391; E. C. P. Lascelles, *Granville Sharp and the Freedom of Slaves in England* (1928), p. 70, says Sharp's reluctance to take the chair may have reflected uneasy doubt about being there at all, rather than humility.

13. G. Sharp and Rev. Dr Sharp, 3 November and 13 July 1787, Granville Sharp Papers, Hardwicke Court (now Gloucestershire Record Office). The Committee Minute Book never shows anyone 'presided' until, after a long period of inactivity, the Committee was revived in 1805. The old habit of taking turns continued. On only five occasions did anyone take the chair: 14 May 1805, Richard Phillips; 1 June 1805, Zachary Macaulay; 17 October 1806 and 9 July 1819, T. F. Forster, and 2 July 1814, Thomas Clarkson at the Committee's next-to-last meeting. All BM Add Ms 21 256.

14. Thomas Clarkson, *Portraiture of Quakerism as Taken from a view of the Moral Education, Discipline, Peculiar Customs, Religious Principles, Political and Civil Oeconomy, and Character of the Society of Friends* (1806), Vol. I, pp. 298–319.

15. G. Sharp to Rev. Dr Sharp, 3 November 1787, Sharp Papers; Clarkson, *History*, Vol. I, pp. 282–9; Roger Anstey, *Atlantic Slave Trade and British Abolition 1760–1810* (1975), pp. 255–6; Davis, *Problem of Slavery*, pp. 408–10.

16. Lascelles, *Granville Sharp*, p. 7; Prince Hoare, *Memoirs of Granville Sharp, Esq.* (1820), Vol. II, p. 234; W. Tooke, 'Memoir of the late Granville Sharp, Esq.', *Gentleman's Magazine* (1818), pp. 489–92.

17. J. Cartwright to G. Sharp, 15 October 1787, Clarkson Collection, Huntington Library.

18. Committee Minute Book, 31 January 1792, BM Add Ms 21 256; Clarkson, *History*, Vol. I, pp. 317–18.

19. Ibid., p. 277; Committee Minute Book, 24 May 1787, BM Add Ms 21 254.

20. Committee Minute Book, 24 May and 7 June 1787, BM Add Ms 21 254.

21. Clarkson, *History*, Vol. I, pp. 289–91; Committee Minute Book, 24 May, 12 and 22 June 1787, BM Add Ms 21 254. F. E. Sanderson, 'The Liverpool Abolitionists' in Roger Anstey and P. E. H. Hair (eds), *Liverpool, the African Slave Trade, and Abolition* (Bristol, 1976), pp. 196–238 cites the 12 June minutes (p. 207) as showing the Committee 'who authorised his tour' had misgivings about Clarkson's fitness for the task. The minute has the Committee resolving that he should 'proceed as soon as convenient to Bristol' etc. and communicate by letter with the treasurer, with no evidence that the approval was not wholehearted. One member, John Barton, expressed his own doubts to a Liverpool friend (see below).

22. 'Benjamin Kaye's Journal to and at Yearly Meeting, London, 1787',

Journal of the Friends Historical Society XXI (1924), p. 56; Diary of Katherine Plymley, Corbett of Longnor Papers, Shropshire Record Office, Book 3.

23. Thomas Clarkson, *Strictures on a Life of William Wilberforce* (1838), p. 79.
24. Anstey, *Atlantic Slave Trade*, pp. 264–5.
25. Clarkson, *History*, Vol. I, pp. 289–90.
26. Plymley Diary, Book 13.
27. C. Clarkson to H. C. Robinson, 21 January 1845, Henry Crabb Robinson Letters, Dr Williams's Library.
28. Clarkson, *History*, Vol. I, p. 319.
29. Ibid., p. 292.
30. Thomas Clarkson's Journal 25–7 June 1787, Thomas Clarkson Papers, St John's College Library, Cambridge University, a fragment of the record Clarkson kept of the tour. After writing the *History* the rest probably was destroyed: Prospectus for a Work on the Slave Trade, 30 June 1814 [1807], Huntington Library, HM 35528.
31. Ibid.
32. Alexander Pope quoted in Walter Minchinton, *Port of Bristol in the Eighteenth Century* (Bristol, 1962), p. 12.
33. Ibid., pp. 1, 3; Leonard Nott, 'Bristol and the Slave Trade', typescript adapted from a 1973 thesis for WEA extramural studies, Bristol University, for the BBC Bristol Religious Unit; Peter Marshall, *Anti-Slave Trade Movement in Bristol* (Bristol, 1968), p. 15.
34. Clarkson, *History*, Vol. I, pp. 294–5; Marshall, *Anti-Slave Trade*, pp. 1–2; C. B. Wadström, *Observations on the Slave Trade, and a Description of some Part of the Coast of Guinea . . .* (1789), p. 227.
35. Clarkson, *History*, Vol. I, pp. 345–6, 365.
36. Ibid., pp. 327–30.
37. Ibid., pp. 338–41; Sheila Lambert (ed.), Parliamentary Papers, House of Commons Sessional Papers of the 18th Century (1973), Vol. 69, pp. 50–53, 125–6.
38. Clarkson, *History*, Vol. I, pp. 342–4.
39. Ibid., pp. 310–12.
40. Ibid., pp. 316–18, 359–64.
41. Ibid., pp. 427–35.
42. Ibid., pp. 322–5.
43. Ibid., pp. 348–53.
44. Ibid., p. 460; Mary Phillips, *Memoir of the Life of Richard Phillips* (1841), pp. 24–5; Committee Minute Book, January–February 1788, Bm Add Ms 21 254.
45. Clarkson, *History*, Vol. I, pp. 304–5, 326–7.
46. Anstey, *Atlantic Slave Trade*, p. 262; Clarkson, *History*, Vol. I, pp. 105, 107, 321.
47. Ibid., pp. 366–7; Marshall, *Anti-Slave Trade*, pp. 3, 5–6.
48. Clarkson, *History*, Vol. I, pp. 300, 302, 303–4.
49. Committee Minute Book, 7 and 21 August, 11 and 18 September, 16 October 1787.

50. Clarkson, *History*, Vol. I, pp. 365–6, 368–71; Ramsay Muir, *History of Liverpool* (1907), p. 192.
51. Clarkson, *History*, Vol. I, pp. 377, 395; Anstey and Hair, *Liverpool*, p. 5; Gomer Williams, *History of the Liverpool Privateers ... with an Account of the Liverpool Slave Trade* (1897), p. 570.
52. Clarkson, *History*, Vol. I, pp. 375–7.
53. Plymley Diary, Book 2.
54. Sanderson, 'Liverpool', pp. 197, 198; Clarkson, *History*, Vol. I, pp. 371–3.
55. Ibid., pp. 371, 372–3; Sanderson, 'Liverpool', pp. 204–5.
56. Clarkson, *History*, Vol. I, pp. 280–82; Sanderson, 'Liverpool', pp. 201–3, 211.
57. Ibid., pp. 203–4, 210, 228.
58. Ibid., p. 207. Barton, father of the poet Bernard Barton, resigned from the Committee when he moved to Hertford: Committee Minute Book, 9 September 1788.
59. Clarkson, *History*, Vol. I, pp. 385–8.
60. Ibid., pp. 388–9.
61. Ibid., pp. 373, 374–5, 395.
62. Ibid., pp. 392–3.
63. William Wallace Currie (ed.), *Memoir of the Life, Writings and Correspondence of James Currie* (1831), Vol. I, pp. 111, 112–26; Sanderson, 'Liverpool', pp. 209–10, 216, 234 n. 66. Wilberforce, replying to something similar from Currie which his biographers place in 1792, said, 'I trust you have done me the justice to acquit me of having adopted any such indiscriminate and false judgment as that you oppose.' He believed in a conciliatory approach to persons in the trade, he said: Wilberforce *Life*, Vol. I, p. 354.
64. *Gentleman's Magazine*, 1788, pp. 215–16; Gilbert Francklyn, *An Answer to the Rev Mr Clarkson's Essay on the Slavery and Commerce of the Human Species ...* (1789), pp. viii–ix.
65. Clarkson, *History*, Vol. I, pp. 396, 397.
66. Ibid., pp. 396–9.
67. Ibid., pp. 400–2.
68. Ibid., pp. 404–6.
69. Ibid., p. 407.
70. Ibid., pp. 411–12.
71. Ibid., pp. 401–10; Sanderson, 'Liverpool', p. 234 n. 64.
72. Clarkson, *History*, Vol. I, pp. 378–82.
73. Ibid., pp. 410–11, 412.
74. Seymour Drescher, *Capitalism and Slavery: British Mobilization in Comparative Perspective* (1986), pp. 67ff.; Patrick C. Lipscomb III, 'William Pitt and the Abolition of the Slave Trade', PhD thesis, University of Texas (1960), pp. 153, 154; Clarkson, *History*, Vol. I, pp. 415–16.
75. Ibid., pp. 416–17; Plymley Diary, Book 65.
76. Clarkson, *History*, Vol. I, pp. 418–25, a summary of the sermon, one of only two he delivered and the only one of which there is a text.

77. Drescher, *Capitalism*, pp. 66, 70–73; Lipscomb, 'William Pitt', pp. 154–5; Committee Minute Book, 1 and 15 January 1788.
78. Clarkson, *History*, Vol. I, pp. 412–13; Committee Minute Book, 2 October 1787; Earl Leslie Griggs, *Thomas Clarkson the Friend of Slaves* (1936), p. 43.

4 People to Parliament

1. Thomas Clarkson, *History of the Rise, Progress, and Accomplishment of the Abolition of the African Slave Trade* (1808), Vol. I, pp. 436, 441ff.; Minute Book of the Committee for Effecting the Abolition of the Slave Trade, 22 and 27 November 1787, BM Add Ms 21 254; *Gentleman's Magazine* (1788), pp. 161–3.
2. Committee Minute Book, 8 January 1788; Clarkson, *History*, Vol. I, p. 437.
3. Ibid., pp. 436–40; Committee Minute Book, 5 February 1788.
4. Ibid., 5 July, 27 August and 16 October 1787; Wedgwood design information, Wilberforce Museum, Hull; Harriet Beecher Stowe, *Sunny Memories of Foreign Lands* (1854), p. 292; T. Clarkson to agent for Wedgwood, 27 August 1788, Wedgwood Manuscripts, Keele University Library; Seymour Drescher, 'Public Opinion and the Destruction of British Colonial Slavery' in James Walvin (ed.), *Slavery and British Society 1776–1846* (1982), p. 47; Clarkson, *History*, Vol. I, p. 450.
5. Clarkson's *Impolicy* was published in 1788. A useful summary is in Elizabeth Donnan, *Documents Illustrative of the History of the Slave Trade to America* (Washington, DC, 1931), Vol. II, p. lvii. Clarkson estimated the essay cost him £1000 and 10 months' work: Diary of Katherine Plymley, Corbett of Longnor Papers, Shropshire Record Office, Book 65.
6. Clarkson, *Impolicy*, pp. 50–53, 30–34, iii–iv, 36–49, 53; Dale H. Porter, *Abolition of the Slave Trade in England 1784–1807* (Hamden, Conn., 1970), p. 63.
7. Clarkson, *Impolicy*, pp. 23–6.
8. Ibid., pp. 7–8.
9. Clarkson, *History*, Vol. I, pp. 470–71; Roger Anstey, *Atlantic Slave Trade and British Abolition 1760–1810* (1975), p. 267; Committee Minute Book, 16 and 26 February 1788; Robert Isaac Wilberforce and Samuel Wilberforce, *Life of William Wilberforce*, 2nd edn (1839), Vol. I, p. 166.
10. Clarkson, *History*, Vol. I, pp. 442, 443; Committee Minute Book, 12 June 1787.
11. Clarkson, *History*, Vol. I, p. 425.
12. Ibid., p. 465; Committee Minute Book, 22 January 1788.
13. Clarkson, *History*, Vol. I, p. 459; Committee Minute Book, 7 August 1787.
14. Clarkson, *History*, Vol. I, p. 445.
15. Ibid., pp. 454–6; Nicholls, *Letter to . . . the Society . . . for . . . Effecting the Abolition of the Slave Trade* (1787).

16. Clarkson, *History*, Vol. I, pp. 447–8; Committee Minute Book, 30 October 1787.

17. Clarkson, *History*, Vol. I, pp. 459, 460; John Newton, *Thoughts Upon the African Slave Trade* (1788); James Dore, *Sermon on the African Slave Trade* (1788); Seymour Drescher, 'Capitalism and Abolition: Values and Forces in Britain, 1783–1814' in Roger Anstey and P. E. H. Hair (eds), *Liverpool, the African Slave Trade, and Abolition* (Bristol, 1976), p. 186; *Gentleman's Magazine* for 1788 typically carries numerous slavery-related articles; Betsy Rodgers, *Georgian Chronicle: Mrs. Barbauld and Her Family* (1958), pp. 110–11; Patrick C. Lipscomb III, 'William Pitt and the Abolition of the Slave Trade', PhD thesis, University of Texas (1960), p. 150.

18. Clarkson, *History*, Vol. I, pp. 444, 451, 495, 566 and Committee Minute Book *passim*.

19. Clarkson, *History*, Vol. I, pp. 571, 491.

20. Petitions had been used to some extent in the parliamentary reform movement begun by the Yorkshire Association. James Walvin, 'The Public Campaign in England Against Slavery, 1787–1834', in D. Eltis and James Walvin (eds), *Abolition of the Atlantic Slave Trade* (Madison, Wis., 1981), pp. 64, 65; Lipscomb, 'William Pitt', pp. 151–4.

21. Wilberforce, *Life*, Vol. I, pp. 160–61; Robin Furneaux, *William Wilberforce* (1974), p. 107.

22. Clarkson, *History*, Vol. I, p. 491; *Gentleman's Magazine* (1788), p. 460; Seymour Drescher, *Capitalism and Slavery: British Mobilization in Comparative Perspective* (1986), p. 74; Drescher, 'Capitalism and Abolition', p. 25.

23. James Walvin, *England, Slaves and Freedom 1776–1838* (1986), p. 110; Drescher, *Capitalism*, p. 75; Peter F. Dixon, 'Politics of Emancipation: The Movement for the Abolition of Slavery in the British West Indies 1807–33', DPhil thesis, Oxford University (1971), p. 111. See also, E. M. Hunt, 'North of England Agitation for the Abolition of the Slave Trade, 1780–1800', MA thesis, University of Manchester (1959). Clarkson, *History*, Vol. I, pp. 467–8, gives names of some leaders of the petition movement. Peter Marshall, *Anti-Slave Trade Movement in Bristol* (Bristol, 1968), pp. 6–7; Wilberforce, *Life*, Vol. I, pp. 160–61; Blanchard Jerrold (ed.), *The Original* (1874), Vol. I, pp. 106–7.

24. Marshall, *Anti-Slave Trade*, pp. 6–7; *Gentleman's Magazine* (1788), pp. 175, 311–12, 416; Dixon, 'Politics', pp. 109, 111, 112.

25. Wilberforce, *Life*, Vol. I, p. 166; Porter, *Abolition*, pp. 34–6, 46.

26. Jerrold (ed.), *The Original*, pp. 106–7. In May 1788 Fox said in the Commons that he was glad the subject was in Wilberforce's hands knowing the 'purity of his principles and character': Clarkson, *History*, Vol. I, p. 507.

27. Wilberforce, *Life*, Vol. I, pp. 67ff.; Furneaux, *Wilberforce*, pp. 76, 78–9; John Pollock, *Wilberforce* (1977), pp. 78, 79–81; Porter, *Abolition*, p. 46; A. S. Byatt, *Wordsworth and Coleridge in Their Time* (1970), p. 90.

28. Clarkson, *History*, Vol. I, pp. 471–4; Plymley Diary, Book 1.

29. Clarkson, *History*, Vol. I, pp. 476–9, 484; Robert Norris, *Short Account of the African Slave Trade* (Liverpool, 1788), p. 13.

30. Clarkson, *History*, Vol. I, pp. 481–2.
31. Ibid., pp. 489, 491. C. B. Wadström, *Observations on the Slave Trade* was published by the Committee in 1789, Committee Minute Book, 15 July 1788, BM Add Ms 21 255. Sharp, Clarkson, Ramsay and Richard Phillips witnessed Wadström's redemption of a young African in early May. The youth, Peter Panah, had been kidnapped and sold by an English trader and reached England under complex circumstances. After paying the trader who held him £20 (to avoid litigation) Wadström had baptised and educated Panah but he died of consumption before Sharp could arrange his passage to Sierra Leone.
32. Walker and Cooper sat in on Committee meetings 25 April and 20 May 1788, Committee Minute Book.
33. Ibid., 8 April 1788; Clarkson, *History*, Vol. I, pp. 500–501; Lipscomb, 'William Pitt', p. 215; Wilberforce, *Life*, Vol. I, pp. 170–71.
34. Committee Minute Book, 22 and 29 April and 6 and 13 May, 1788; Clarkson, *History*, Vol. I, pp. 502–3.
35. Ibid., pp. 504ff.
36. The debate account follows Clarkson, *History*, Vol. I, pp. 507–24 unless otherwise advised.
37. Porter, *Abolition*, p. 38; Lipscomb, 'William Pitt', pp. 225–6.
38. Clarkson, *History*, Vol. I, pp. 524, 526; Committee Minute Book, 13 May 1788; Porter, *Abolition*, p. 33.
39. Clarkson, *History*, Vol. I, pp. 528ff.; Lipscomb, 'William Pitt', pp. 239ff.
40. Clarkson, *History*, Vol. I, pp. 545–50, 560; Porter, *Abolition*, pp. 41, 43–4, 47; Lipscomb, 'William Pitt', pp. 241, 255–60; Anstey, *Atlantic Slave Trade*, pp. 269–70.
41. Clarkson, *History*, Vol. II, pp. 184–5.
42. Furneaux, *Wilberforce*, pp. 80–83.
43. Clarkson, *History*, Vol. II, pp. 13–16; Sheila Lambert (ed.), *Parliamentary Papers, House of Commons Sessional Papers of the 18th Century* (1973), Vol. 69, pp. 73–4, 142–3, 144–56; summarised in Porter, *Abolition*, p. 63; Anstey, *Atlantic Slave Trade*, p. 265; Daniel P. Mannix and Malcolm Cowley, *Black Cargoes, a History of the Atlantic Slave Trade 1518–1865* (1963), pp. 150–52.
44. For the Sierra Leone settlement story, Ellen Gibson Wilson, *Loyal Blacks* (New York, 1976), pp. 139–73; James W. St G. Walker, *Black Loyalists: the Search for a Promised Land in Nova Scotia and Sierra Leone 1783–1870* (1976); Stephen J. Braidwood, 'Initiatives and Organisation of the Black Poor 1786–1787', in *Slavery and Abolition* III (1982). For overall Sierra Leone history, Christopher Fyfe, *History of Sierra Leone* (1962).
45. Wilson, *Loyal Blacks*, p. 168; Ellen Gibson Wilson, *John Clarkson and the African Adventure* (1980), p. 53; Prince Hoare, *Memoirs of Granville Sharp Esq.*, 2nd edn (1828), Vol. II, p. 104.
46. Davy's Suffolk Collection, BM Add Ms 19 173, ff. 41–2. The von Breda portrait was published 23 May 1789: Plymley Diary, Book 34. It was left to the National Portrait Gallery by Henry Crabb Robinson

and now hangs in the Wordsworth Museum, Grasmere with others of the Wordsworth Circle.

47. Committee Minute Book, 15 and 29 July, 12 and 26 August 1788; Clarkson, *History*, Vol. I, p. 572.

48. Committee Minute Book, 10 and 17 June, 22 July, 26 August 1788; Clarkson, *History*, Vol. II, pp. 3–4.

49. Ibid., p. 8.

50. Ibid., pp. 9–10.

51. Ibid., p. 11.

52. Ibid., pp. 4–7.

53. Ibid., pp. 29, 111–15; Committee Minute Book, 17 March, 21 and 28 April 1789; C. B. Wadström, *Essay on Colonization, Particularly Applied to the Western Coast of Africa* (1794) carries the 'Description of a Slave Ship' showing the results, with a man given a space of 6 feet by 1 foot 4 inches; a woman 5 feet by 1 foot 4 inches; boys 5 feet by 1½ feet and girls 4 feet 6 inches by 1 foot.

54. Clarkson, *History*, Vol. II, p. 12.

55. Ibid., pp. 16–20; Lambert (ed.) *Parliamentary Papers*, Vol. 69, pp. 50–55. Clarkson seems to have squeezed in eight more witnesses, in fact, as several are identified as being produced by him while the report was being written. Committee Minute Book, 10 and 14 February, 10 March 1789; Marshall, *Anti-slave Trade*, pp. 9–10.

56. *Parliamentary Papers* (1789), Vol. 84, *Report of the Lords of the Committee of Council*; Wilberforce, *Life*, Vol. I, pp. 210, 211, 213, 214; Pollock, *Wilberforce*, p. 88; William Roberts, *Memoirs of the Life and Correspondence of Mrs Hannah More*, 2nd edn (1834), p. 156.

57. Clarkson, *History*, Vol. II, pp. 34–7; F. E. Sanderson, 'The Liverpool Abolitionists', in Anstey and Hair (eds), *Liverpool*, pp. 214–15; Porter, *Abolition*, p. 72; Marshall, *Anti-slave Trade*, pp. 11–12.

58. Clarkson, *History*, Vol. II. pp. 40–41; Wilberforce's speech 41–67, the twelve propositions 67–73, 103–8; Wilberforce, *Life*, Vol. I, pp. 218–20, 221–2; Porter, *Abolition*, pp. 72–3; Anstey, *Atlantic Slave Trade*, p. 271; Committee Minute Book, 19 May 1789.

59. Clarkson, *History*, Vol. II, pp. 115–17, with tribute to Ramsay; Folarin Shyllon, *James Ramsay the Unknown Abolitionist* (Edinburgh, 1977), p. 111; Bishop Porteus Occasional Memorandums and Reflexions, Ms 2103, Lambeth Palace Library, 10 July 1789.

60. Committee Minute Book, 28 July 1789; Clarkson's new pamphlet was *Essay on the Comparative Efficiency of Regulation or Abolition* as *Applied to the Slave Trade*; Clarkson, *History*, Vol. II, pp. 110–11, 109; Pollock, *Wilberforce*, p. 91.

61. Clarkson, *History*, Vol. II, pp. 119–20; 21–4.

62. Ibid., pp. 121, 122; Committee Minute Book, 14 and 28 July 1789.

5 The Shock of Revolution

1. Thomas Clarkson, *History of the Rise, Progress, and Accomplishment of the Abolition of the African Slave-Trade* (1808), Vol. I, p. 564.

2. John Cannon, *Parliamentary Reform 1640–1832* (Cambridge, 1973), p. 116.

3. W. Wilberforce to Abbé de la Jeard, 17 July 1789, quoted in John Pollock, *Wilberforce* (1977), pp. 91–2; Robert Isaac Wilberforce and Samuel Wilberforce, *Life of William Wilberforce*, 2nd edn (1839), Vol. I, pp. 227, 228; Robin Furneaux, *William Wilberforce* (1974), pp. 90–91; Lord Grenville to W. Wilberforce, 18 December 1787, Wilberforce Manuscripts, Bodleian Library, Oxford University, d 17 f. 9.

4. Clarkson, *History*, Vol. II, p. 122.

5. Earl Leslie Griggs, *Thomas Clarkson the Friend of Slaves* (1936), pp. 51–2; Wilberforce, *Life*, Vol. I, p. 229, implies that Wilberforce paid most of the cost but gives no source. Nor does Griggs, who says the expenses were shared.

6. Minutes of the Committee of the Society for Effecting the Abolition of the Slave Trade, BM Add Ms 21 254, 27 August 1787; Diary of Katherine Plymley, Corbett of Longnor Papers, Shropshire Record Office, Book 22; Ellen Gibson Wilson, *John Clarkson and the African Adventure* (1980), p. 48.

7. Clarkson, *History*, Vol. I, pp. 500, 446, 447; Committee Minute Book, 8 April 1788, BM Add Ms 21 255.

8. Committee Minute Book, 12 February 1788. Lafayette was convinced slavery should be abolished during the war in America. He and his wife bought a plantation at Cayenne in French Guinea in 1786 and started an experiment to free the slaves gradually. The plan was believed to have helped preserve harmony in that colony when other French possessions felt ripples of the Revolution. Through John Adams, American minister in London, Lafayette obtained books on slavery and the slave trade from Granville Sharp. When he joined Les Amis des Noirs, his wife became an 'honorary and assistant' member. Melvin D. Kennedy, *Lafayette and Slavery, from His Letters to Thomas Clarkson and Granville Sharp* (Easton, Pa., 1950), pp. 1–5, 29; Louis Gottschalk, *Lafayette Between the American and the French Revolutions (1783–1789)* (Chicago, 1950), pp. 228–9; Plymley Diary, Book 1; Clarkson, *History*, Vol. I, pp. 492, 466–7; Vol. II, pp. 123–4.

9. Edward D. Seeber, *Anti-Slavery Opinion in France during the Second Half of the Eighteenth Century* (Baltimore, 1937), pp. 160–61; Gaston Martin, *Histoire de l'Esclavage dans les Colonies Françaises* (Paris, 1948), p. 168.

10. Philip D. Curtin, *Atlantic Slave Trade: a Census* (Madison, 1969), p. 78; Roger Anstey, *Atlantic Slave Trade and British Abolition 1760–1810* (1975), p. 11; Kennedy, *Lafayette*, p. 7; Valerie Quinney, 'Decisions on Slavery, the Slave-Trade and Civil Rights for Negroes in the Early French Revolution', *Journal of Negro History* L (1970), 117–30.

11. Clarkson's Journal of his 1789 visit to France, Thomas Clarkson Collection, Trevor Arnett Library, Atlanta University, Atlanta, Georgia, described his first days there. It was written [1797] perhaps for publication, but the diary on which it was based is lost.

12. Account of visit to France based on Clarkson, *History*, Vol. II, pp.

123–66 unless otherwise noted. Also for this section, Quinney, 'Decisions on Slavery'; J. M. Thompson, *Leaders of the French Revolution* (Oxford, 1962); David Brion Davis, *Problem of Slavery in the Age of Revolution 1770–1823* (Ithaca, NY, 1975), pp. 93–100.

13. Thomas Clarkson, *Letters on the Slave-Trade, and the State of the Natives in Those Parts of Africa which are contiguous to Fort St Louis and Goree* (1791); T. Wilkinson to E. Robinson, 28 November 1790, Letters of Thomas Wilkinson and Elihu Robinson, Cumbria County Library, Carlisle.

14. T. Clarkson to A. Bouvet, 1 December [1789], Clarkson Collection, Huntington Library, San Marino, Calif.; Davis, *Problem of Slavery*, p. 400 n. 24; Griggs, *Thomas Clarkson*, pp. 54–5.

15. C. L. R. James, *Black Jacobins. Toussaint Louverture and the San Domingo Revolution* (1938), p. 56, writes that Clarkson helped to raise funds for Ogé to buy arms in the United States but does not believe it himself and no evidence has been found for this.

16. Wilberforce, *Life*, Vol. I, pp. 229–30; Committee Minute Book: Clarkson wrote 17 letters to the Committee between 27 August 1789 and 2 February 1790.

17. *Memoires de Brissot . . . sur Ses Contemporains et la Révolution Française publiés par son fils* (Paris, 1830), Vol. III, pp. 3–5.

18. Clarkson, *History*, Vol. II, pp. 162–8, 169, 178, 183; Wilberforce, *Life*, Vol. I, p. 261.

19. Clarkson, *History*, Vol. II, pp. 169–78.

20. T. Wilkinson to E. Robinson, 28 November 1790; Parker's testimony, Sheila Lambert (ed.), *Parliamentary Papers, House of Commons Sessional Papers of the 18th Century* (1973), Vol. 73, pp. 121–37.

21. Clarkson, *History*, Vol. II, pp. 181–3; *Parliamentary Papers*, Vol. 73, pp. 50–80; Wilberforce, *Life*, Vol. I, p. 270.

22. Clarkson, *History*, Vol. II, pp. 182–3.

23. Dale H. Porter, *Abolition of the Slave Trade in England, 1784–1807* (Hamden, Conn., 1970); slave trade arguments summarised pp. 55–62; Clarkson, *History*, Vol. II, pp. 194, 195–6; Committee Minute Book, 20 July 1790, BM Add Ms 21 256.

24. Committee Minute Book, 23 March and 20 April 1790, BM Add Ms 21 255; Wilberforce, *Life*, Vol. I, pp. 255, 264–5; Plymley Diary, Book 2; T. Wilkinson to E. Robinson, 28 November 1790.

25. Clarkson, *History*, Vol. II, pp. 187–92; Furneaux, *Wilberforce*, pp. 94–5.

26. Seymour Drescher, *Capitalism and Slavery: British Mobilization in Comparative Perspective* (1986), pp. 78, 214–15; Committee Minute Book, 20 July 1790, BM Add Ms 21 256.

27. Clarkson, *History*, Vol. II, pp. 196, 197; T. Wilkinson to E. Robinson, 28 November 1790.

28. Ibid.

29. Clarkson, *History*, Vol. II, p. 195.

30. Committee Minute Book, 28 September 1790, 1 and 23 February 1791.

31. Clarkson, *History*, Vol. II, p. 199; T. Clarkson to A. Alison, 20 January

1791, New York Historical Society.

32. Clarkson, *History*, Vol. II, pp. 200, 201; Porter, *Abolition*, p. 76.
33. Clarkson, *History*, Vol. II, pp. 202–6. Clarkson left his own name off the list.
34. Ibid., pp. 207–8.
35. Ibid., pp. 209–10.
36. Ibid., pp. 212–337; Wilberforce, *Life*, Vol. I, p. 299; Furneaux, *Wilberforce*, pp. 100–103. Clarkson watched the debate from the gallery. He had counted the vote in advance and knew that they would be defeated: Plymley Diary, Book 2.
37. Clarkson, *History*, Vol. II, pp. 339–41.
38. T. Clarkson to Mme Lafayette, 17 June 1791, Department of Rare Books, Olin Library, Cornell University, Ithaca, NY. He congratulated her on the Assembly's condemnation of slavery and ruling that children of free parents should be full citizens regardless of colour.
39. H. Dundas to W. Wilberforce, 18 July 1791, Wilberforce Papers, William R. Perkins Library, Duke University, Durham, NC. I have found no evidence that Clarkson went to the dinner but there is no reason to think he didn't.
40. Cannon, *Parliamentary Reform*, p. 126; T. Clarkson to Mme Lafayette, 17 June 1791.
41. For Province of Freedom, Ellen Gibson Wilson, *Loyal Blacks* (New York, 1976), pp. 158–73; and *John Clarkson and the African Adventure* (1980), pp. 53–4. Prince Hoare, *Memoirs of Granville Sharp* (1828), Vol. II, pp. 150–53, 154–6; Sharp's letters to Sierra Leone 27 September 1790 and 22 January 1791, PRO 30/8/363 with List of Names for [St George's Bay Company], n.d.
42. G. Sharp to J. Smith, 30 May 1791, PRO 30/8/310; C. B. Wadström, *Essay on Colonization, Particularly Applied to the Western Coast of Africa* (1794), pp. 341ff.; Hoare, *Memoirs*, Vol. II, p. 161; John Pollock, *Wilberforce* (1977), p. 10, says wrongly that Clarkson 'could have put up only a token share'. Henry Thornton MP, the banker, became chairman. He saw the Act through the Commons and was the colony's biggest backer, with 58 shares. His two brothers took another 24.
43. T. Clarkson to J. Wedgwood, 25 August 1791, in Katherine Eufemia Farrar (ed.), *Correspondence of Josiah Wedgwood 1781–1794* (1906), pp. 167–9; T. Gisborne to W. Wilberforce, 'Sunday', n.d., Wilberforce Papers, Wrangham Collection when consulted, now Bodleian Library, Oxford; W. Burgh to W. Wilberforce, 13 December 1791, Wilberforce Papers, Bodleian Library, Oxford University, d 15; Plymley Diary, Book 2.
44. G. Sharp to H. Beaufoy, 23 March 1791, Sharp Papers, Hardwicke Court when consulted, now Gloucestershire Record Office; G. Sharp to W. Thornton, 5 October 1791, in Hoare, *Memoirs*, Vol. II, pp. 157–9.
45. T. Clarkson to J. Clarkson, 28 August 1791, Clarkson Papers, BM Add Ms 41 262A and successive very long letters of guidance and encouragement.

46. Clarkson's report on African productions, BM Add Ms 12 131, f4ff.; also Clarkson Collection, Huntington Library; Philip D. Curtin, *Image of Africa* (Madison, 1964) for contemporary ideas of Africa and the founding of Sierra Leone, especially pp. 108, 115–16, 119, 129, 132–3.

6 Raising the National Voice

1. Diary of Katherine Plymley, Corbett of Longnor Papers, Shropshire Record Office. This immense document, made up of 137 small 'memorandum books', is a chronicle of a landed family with the abolition cause one important thread. Miss Plymley also kept records of her travels, reading and thoughts in another 80 notebooks. All of Clarkson's first visit to Longnor comes from Books 1, 2 and 3.

2. Thomas Clarkson, *History of the Rise, Progress, and Accomplishment of the Abolition of the Slave-Trade* (1808), Vol. II, pp. 348–9, 350–51.

3. Ibid., pp. 351, 352–3.

4. Robert Isaac Wilberforce and Samuel Wilberforce, *Life of William Wilberforce*, 2nd edn (1839), Vol. I, pp. 333–4.

5. Ibid., pp. 334–7.

6. W. Mason to T. Gisborne, 29 December 1791, Wilberforce Manuscripts, Bodleian Library, Oxford University, d 14 f 1.

7. W. Burgh to W. Wilberforce, 10 December 1791, Wilberforce Manuscripts, Bodleian Library, d 17 f 20.

8. W. Tuke to T. Palmer, 12 December 1791, Tuke Papers, Borthwick Institute of Historical Research, University of York.

9. Wilberforce, *Life*, Vol. I, pp. 316–17, 343; Robin Furneaux, *William Wilberforce* (1974), p. 109.

10. Clarkson, *History*, Vol. II, pp. 347–8. Crafton's pamphlet was *Sketch of the Evidence with a Recommendation on the Subject to the Serious Attention of People in General*. Fox's *Address to the People of Great Britain on the Propriety of Abstaining from West India Sugar and Rum*, Cooper's *Considerations on the Slave Trade; and the Consumption of West Indian Produce*, all published 1791. Cooper's was first published in *Wheeler's Manchester Chronicle* in 1787. Cooper, pp. 4, 14; Patrick C. Lipscomb, 'William Pitt and the Abolition of the Slave Trade', PhD thesis, University of Texas (1960), p. 140.

11. Clarkson's circular letter 7 January 1792, Wedgwood Manuscripts, Keele University Library; Katherine Eufemia Farrar (ed.), *Correspondence of Josiah Wedgwood 1781–1794* (1906), pp. 183–6; Plymley Diary, Book 4; Earl Leslie Griggs, *Thomas Clarkson the Friend of Slaves* (1936), p. 69.

12. Plymley Diary, Book 1; Elizabeth Isichei, *Victorian Quakers* (Oxford, 1970), p. 233; John C. Gazley, *Life of Arthur Young* (Philadelphia, 1973), pp. 276–7; W. Allen to J. Priestland, March 1791, Ms Box 7:10, Library of the Religious Society of Friends; Jacques Pierre Brissot de Warville, *New Travels in the United States of America* (1794), Vol. I, pp.

255–60; Betsy Rodgers, *Georgian Chronicle: Mrs Barbauld and Her Family* (1958), p. 133; Wilberforce, *Life*, Vol. I, p. 338.

13. Cooper, *Considerations*, pp. 15–16, and n.

14. Clarkson, *History*, Vol. II, pp. 349–50; Elihu Robinson Diaries and Memoranda, 13 November 1792, Ms Box R3/1–9, Library of the Religious Society of Friends.

15. Seymour Drescher, *Capitalism and Slavery: British Mobilization in Comparative Perspective* (1986), pp. 78, 79; *Morning Chronicle*, correspondence in December 1791.

16. Wilberforce, *Life*, Vol. I, pp. 338–40.

17. Minute Book of the Committee of the Society for Effecting the Abolition of the Slave Trade, BM Add Ms 21 256, 20 June and 16 August 1793; 25 June 1795. Wilberforce was elected to the Committee after the 1791 defeat. Before signing the Committee statement, Sharp asked Wilberforce whether he should soften the tone a little. No, said Wilberforce, 'let them take it': Plymley Diary, Book 35.

18. Clarkson, *History*, Vol. II, p. 352 says there was not a day for three months (except Sundays) 'when five or six were not resolved upon in some places or other'. Drescher, *Capitalism*, p. 80; G. Sharp to W. Elford, 29 December 1791, Clarkson Papers, Moorland-Spingarn Research Center, Manuscript Division, Howard University, Washington, DC.

19. T. Clarkson to J. Wedgwood, 19 January 1792, Wedgwood Manuscripts, Keele; Lipscomb, 'William Pitt', p. 157.

20. Committee Minute Book, 31 January 1792; Lipscomb, 'William Pitt', p. 160.

21. C. L. R. James, *History of Negro Revolt* (1938), pp. 6–10; David Geggus, 'British Government and the Saint Domingue Slave Revolt, 1791–1793', in *English Historical Review* XCVI (1981), 123.

22. Wilberforce, *Life*, Vol. I, p. 340.

23. W. Mason to W. Wilberforce, 20 February 1792, Wilberforce Manuscripts, Bodleian Library, d 17 f 23.

24. The West India pamphlet was *Particular account of the commencement and progress of the insurrection of the negroes in St Domingo*. Clarkson wrote *True State of the Case Respecting the Insurrection*. Committee Minute Book, 14 February 1792.

25. Plymley Diary, Books 4–7.

26. Drescher, *Capitalism*, pp. 80, 83; Clarkson, *History*, Vol. II, pp. 354–5. Liverpool Corporation spent £10 000 but sent no petition against abolition: Wilberforce, *Life*, Vol. I, p. 345. In all, the slave-trade advocates collected four petitions (one from citizens at Derby and the rest from groups or persons in the trade) and one from Reading seeking regulation.

27. Plymley Diary, Book 8.

28. *Debate on a Motion for the Abolition of the Slave-Trade in the House of Commons, on Monday the Second of April 1792* (1792), p. 15.

29. Plymley Diary, Book 8.

30. Clarkson, *History*, Vol. II, pp. 446–7; Furneaux, *Wilberforce*, p. 111; Wilberforce, *Life*, Vol. I, p. 346; Lord Auckland to Lord H. Spencer,

Journal and Correspondence of William Lord Auckland, Vol. II, p. 400; Griggs, *Thomas Clarkson,* p. 71.

31. Committee Minute Book, 10 June, 1792. The Committee seems never to have published a Wilberforce speech.

32. Clarkson, *History,* Vol. II, the debate pp. 355–448; *Debate . . . 1792.*

33. Clarkson, *History,* Vol. II, pp. 398–404, 415, 449; *Debate . . . 1792,* pp. 101–4; Dale H. Porter, *Abolition of the Slave Trade in England* (Hamden, Conn., 1940), pp. 81, 83. Dundas was ill when the question was raised in 1791. He controlled the votes of 34 MPs and 11 peers. David Brion Davis, *Problem of Slavery in the Age of Revolution* (Ithaca, NY, 1975), pp. 429–32, notices the confusion that arose upon Dundas's action. Dundas had no intention of introducing a bill for gradual abolition and Wilberforce would not do so. Fox finally forced Dundas to offer a bill and Pitt saw that it was passed. But in 1795 Dundas persuaded the House to put off the date of abolition to the end of the war with France.

34. Clarkson, *History,* Vol. II, p. 487; Wilberforce, *Life,* Vol. I, pp. 346, 348–9; Porter, *Abolition,* pp. 79, 83, 84.

35. Clarkson, *History,* Vol. II, p. 488; Wilberforce, *Life,* Vol. I, p. 351; H. Grimston to T. Grimston, 17 April 1792, Grimston Manuscripts, Humberside Record Office, DDG-R 43/12.

36. Clarkson, *History,* Vol. II, pp. 460–62; T. Clarkson circular letter, 21 July 1792, Wedgwood Manuscripts, Keele; E. Robinson to T. Wilkinson, 25 August 1792, Letters of Thomas Wilkinson and Elihu Robinson, Cumbria County Library, Carlisle.

37. Plymley Diary, Books 11–13.

7 Bitter Times

1. Letter from Ministre de l'Interieur, 10 October 1792, Clarkson Papers, BM Add Ms 41 262A; Robert Isaac Wilberforce and Samuel Wilberforce, *Life of William Wilberforce,* 2nd edn (1839), Vol. I, pp. 368–9. Earl Leslie Griggs, *Thomas Clarkson the Friend of Slaves* (1936), pp. 58–9, gives the full text of Clarkson's citation. Diary of Katherine Plymley, Corbett of Longnor Papers, Shropshire Record Office, Book 5 is the only authority for the information that Clarkson revisited France in August 1792 and spent three weeks in or around Lille.

2. Plymley Diary, Book 8; S. Hoare to W. Wilberforce, 20 February 1792 in Robert Isaac Wilberforce and Samuel Wilberforce (eds), *Correspondence of William Wilberforce* (1840), Vol. I, pp. 89–90; Griggs, *Thomas Clarkson,* pp. 70–71.

3. Elihu Robinson Diary, 13 November 1792, Library of the Religious Society of Friends, Temp Mss Box R 3/6.

4. Thomas Clarkson, *History of the Rise, Progress, and Accomplishment of the Abolition of the Slave-Trade* (1808), Vol. II, pp. 462–4. The Queen was executed in October. Sir Samuel Romilly called the vote disgraceful for sanctioning 'continual robberies and murders',

adding, as one sympathetic to French matters, that the Commons was not a National Assembly 'and certainly does not speak the sense of the nation' – another disgrace in his view: *Memoirs of the Life of Sir Samuel Romilly* (1840), pp. 425–6.

5. Ibid., p. 464; Roger Anstey, *Atlantic Slave Trade and British Abolition 1760–1810* (1975), pp. 330–32; Plymley Diary, Books 16, 21.

6. For John Clarkson, Sierra Leone and the Wilberforce relationship, Ellen Gibson Wilson, *John Clarkson and the African Adventure* (1980), pp. 79, 116–42; also Wilson, *Loyal Blacks* (New York, 1976), pp. 285–94.

7. Wilberforce, *Life*, Vol. II, pp. 38–44. The original letters in this matter do not seem to survive. Henry Crabb Robinson, in his review of the *Life* for the *Eclectic Review* III (1838) 685, raises the thought that the Wilberforce letter was never sent. Thomas Clarkson, *Strictures on a Life of William Wilberforce* (1838), pp. 74–5, 76; Griggs, *Thomas Clarkson*, pp. 173–4. None of the friendly letters from Wilberforce to John Clarkson, loaned to the sons for their biography, was used.

8. Using Clarkson's description of his symptoms, Mr John Mander, consultant surgeon of York, diagnosed his illness as nervous exhaustion or anxiety depression for which the modern treatment would be tranquillisers, antidepressants, and rest. Clarkson, *Strictures*, p. 74; Plymley Diary, Books 16, 17; T. Clarkson to J. Wedgwood, 17 June 1793 in Katherine Eufemia Farrar (ed.), *Correspondence of Josiah Wedgwood 1781–1794* (1906), pp. 215–16; Wilson, *John Clarkson*, p. 136; Wilson, *Loyal Blacks*, pp. 317, 333 n. 26. Unprotected by any international agreement, the Sierra Leone settlement was invaded and plundered by the French in 1794.

9. Plymley Diary, Book 18.

10. Ibid., Books 20, 21.

11. The others addressed were Josiah Wedgwood, Samuel Whitbread, William Smith, Matthew Montagu, William Burgh and Thomas Gisborne. The last two seem to be more Wilberforce's intimates than Clarkson's. Letter to J. Plymley in full in Plymley Diary, Books 18–19; to J. Wedgwood, a mutilated copy in Anti-Slavery Papers, Rhodes House Library, Oxford, Mss Brit. Emp. S18, C107; to M. Montagu, 28 August 1793, Huntington Library, San Marino, California, MO 710. Clarkson, *History*, Vol. II, p. 469, describes the symptoms. The Clarkson letter which prompted the subscription was first used in Wilson, *John Clarkson*.

12. Incomplete records show that the Committee reimbursed Clarkson for £148 5s 0d spent on his journeys up to mid-1788. His first tour to Bristol and Liverpool left him out of pocket by £150 and others would have been roughly similar. The Committee never had much to spend. Peak income from subscriptions was £2760 in the first year and most of it was spent on publications.

13. Clarkson, *History*, Vol. II, p. 471n.

14. Plymley Diary, Books 19–21 *passim*, for the family involvement.

15. Ibid., Book 22. Private subscriptions to help friends were not uncommon. C. J. Fox in 1793 was relieved of his debts by a

subscription which left him with a good income, for which he was very grateful: Henry Edward Lord Holland (ed.), *Memoirs of the Whig Party During My Time* (1852), Vol. I, p. 64. In 1801, Pitt's friends, including Wilberforce, raised £12 000 to pay his debts: Robin Furneaux, *William Wilberforce* (1974), pp. 243–4.

16.   Plymley Diary, Book 25; Wilberforce, *Life*, Vol. II, pp. 51–2 says nothing of Clarkson's original letter or Plymley's initiative and with the letters selected to be published, pp. 52–5, has fixed the tone for all later mention of the episode. On p. 51: 'Many were the sources of annoyance which this cause furnished for its leader. Thus in the course of this spring [1794] he [Wilberforce] had determined by a subscription amongst the adherents of the Abolition, to reimburse Mr Clarkson. . . . The conduct of such a business must, under any circumstances, have proved distasteful' and Clarkson aggravated this, the authors say. The use of the incident in John Pollock, *Wilberforce* (1977), p. 125 is particularly dismissive of Clarkson. The additional evidence about how the subscription began was first used in Wilson, *John Clarkson*, pp. 145–6.

17.   Plymley Diary, Book 23.

18.   Peter Marshall, *Anti-Slave Trade Movement in Bristol* (Bristol, 1968), pp. 18–21; Furneaux, *Wilberforce*, pp. 113–14; Dale H. Porter, *Abolition of the Slave Trade in England 1784–1807* (Hamden, Conn., 1970), p. 90; Wilberforce, *Life*, Vol. I, pp. 356–9. None of these mentions the subscription raised to pay the legal costs charged to Wilberforce.

19.   Plymley Diary, Books 11, 13, 15, 16, 19, 21, 23. It was widely reported that Kimber's acquittal came with the Duke of Clarence on the bench, applauding any testimony supporting the captain. He dined afterwards with the judges.

20.   Ibid., Book 30.

21.   Ibid., Book 24; Robinson, *Eclectic Review*, p. 685.

22.   T. Clarkson to J. Wedgwood, 18 April 1794, Wedgwood Manuscripts, Keele University Library; Frances Julia Wedgwood, *Personal Life of Josiah Wedgwood the Potter* (1915), p. 254; Farrar (ed.), *Wedgwood Correspondence*, p. 221; Griggs, *Thomas Clarkson*, p. 77.

23.   Plymley Diary, Book 27.

24.   Wilberforce, *Life*, Vol. II, pp. 52–3.

25.   Plymley Diary, Book 61.

26.   Blanchard Jerrold (ed.), *The Original* (1874), Vol. I, p. 54; David Brion Davis, *Problem of Slavery in the Age of Revolution 1770–1823* (Ithaca, NY, 1975), p. 375 and n. 35.

27.   Ibid., pp. 21–7; Archibald Prentice, *Historical Sketches and Personal Recollections of Manchester* (1851), pp. 5–10.

28.   Jerrold (ed.), *Original*, pp. 54–69, 74–5.

29.   John Cannon, *Parliamentary Reform 1640–1832* (Cambridge, 1973), pp. 129–31; Plymley Diary, Book 29.

30.   Alan M. Rees, 'Pitt and the Achievement of Abolition', *Journal of Negro History*, XXXIX (1954), 173; Clarkson, *History*, Vol. II, pp. 466–7, 468–9; Porter, *Abolition*, p. 47; Plymley Diary, Book 26; Wilberforce, *Life*, Vol. II, p. 18; Committee Minute Book. For an analysis

of the opposition to abolition, Anstey, *Atlantic Slave Trade*, pp. 286–320.

31. The following account of Clarkson's period in the Lakes is almost entirely from the assiduous Miss Plymley: Plymley Diary, Books 28–30.

32. Wilson, *John Clarkson*, pp. 10, 153.

33. For Wilkinson, Mary Carr, *Thomas Wilkinson: a Friend of Wordsworth* (1905), pp. 3, 11, 48–64. They might have met at the Yearly Meeting but Wilkinson rode around with Clarkson on his visit to the area in 1790 and organised a petition at Penrith market that got 1450 signatures. Griggs, *Thomas Clarkson*, pp. 79–80.

34. Maxwell Fraser, *Companion into Lakeland*, 2nd edn (1939), pp. 121–2.

35. Carr, *Thomas Wilkinson*, p. 3. Wordsworth's sonnet was entitled 'To the Spade of a Friend; an Agriculturalist' and composed 'that afternoon when you and I were labouring together in your pleasure-ground': W. Wordsworth to T. Wilkinson, November 1806, in Mary Moorman (ed.), *Letters of William and Dorothy Wordsworth, Middle Years* (Oxford, 1969), *Part I*, p. 105.

36. Wilberforce had sent him with a prescription to Dr Percival in Manchester: Plymley Diary, Book 21. Chalybeate medicines became well-known in the seventeenth century.

37. C. E. Wrangham (ed.), *Journey to the Lake District from Cambridge 1779* (Stocksfield, 1983), p. 15.

38. W. Wilberforce to W. Smith, 29 October 1794, Thompson Clarkson Collection 1/319, Library of the Religious Society of Friends.

39. Ernest de Selincourt (ed.), *Wordsworth's Guide to the Lakes*, 5th edn (1835, 1970 reprint), pp. 14–20.

40. T. Wilkinson to M. Leadbeater, 22 March 1795, Wilkinson Letterbook, Cumbria County Library, Carlisle.

41. Plymley Diary, Book 65.

42. Carr, *Thomas Wilkinson*, pp. 48–64; Griggs, *Thomas Clarkson*, p. 80.

43. T. Wilkinson to E. Robinson, 16 August 1789, Letters of Thomas Wilkinson and Elihu Robinson, Cumbria County Library.

44. Same to same 15 March 1795.

45. Plymley Diary, Book 30.

8   'My dearest Catherine'

1. Thomas Clarkson, *Portraiture of Quakerism* (1806), Vol. II, pp. 256–63 on the ministry of women; Vol. III from pp. 284ff. on women in general.

2. *Memoir of Joseph Hardcastle, Esq. . . . a Record of the Past for His Descendants* (1860), pp. 41ff.

3. C. Clarkson to W. Smith, 18 August 1834, Clarkson Papers, William R. Perkins Library, Duke University, Durham, NC; T. Clarkson to W. Buck, 10 September 1793, Thomas Clarkson Collection, Trevor Arnett Library, Atlanta University, Atlanta, Georgia; Diary of

Katherine Plymley, Corbett of Longnor Papers, Shropshire Record Office, Book 33.

4.   Julia Smith Recollections, William Smith and Family Papers, Cambridge University Library, Add 7621; T. Robinson to H. Robinson, 3 July 1804, Henry Crabb Robinson Letters, Dr Williams's Library; Herman Biddell, 'Thomas Clarkson and Playford Hall, Reminiscences and Recollections', Reference Department, Ipswich Borough Libraries, 1912, f. 53.

5.   Thomas Sadler (ed.), *Diary, Reminiscences, and Correspondence of Henry Crabb Robinson* (1869), Vol. I, p. 30; John Creasey, 'Henry Crabb Robinson Remembered', *Inquirer*, 4 February 1967; S. J. Maling to C. Buck, 10 September 1794 and 30 November 1793, Clarkson Papers, BM Add Ms 41 267B.

6.   Sadler (ed.), *Diary*, Vol. I, p. 30; Edith J. Morley (ed.), *Henry Crabb Robinson on Books and Their Writers* (1938), Vol. I, p. 2.

7.   Sadler (ed.), *Diary*, Vol. I, pp. 30, 31; H. C. Robinson to C. Clarkson, December 1804, Henry Crabb Robinson Letters; Edith J. Morley (ed.), *Correspondence of Henry Crabb Robinson with the Wordsworth Circle 1808–1866* (1927), Vol. I, p. 50; John Milton Baker, *Henry Crabb Robinson of Bury, Jena, The Times and Russell Square* (1937), pp. 42–3. 'Did he love Catherine Buck?' speculated an article on 'A Bury Celebrity'. 'He was devoted to her; she was his oracle. Their friendship ended only with his life': Suffolk County Record Office, Bury St Edmunds, HD 526/26/36.

8.   Sadler (ed.), *Diary*, Vol. I, p. 31.

9.   Baker, *Henry Crabb Robinson*, p. 59. Brissot de Warville and 19 others were guillotined in October 1793.

10.   C. Buck to H. Robinson, 16 October 1793, Henry Crabb Robinson Letters.

11.   Plymley Diary, Book 35.

12.   Ibid., Books 34, 35, 43. James Phillips gossiped that Catherine was heiress to £20 000 or £30 000 but nothing in surviving papers suggests her father was more than moderately well-off or that the Clarksons ever enjoyed that much money.

13.   Plymley Diary, Books 33, 34, 35. Granville Sharp regretted and disapproved Clarkson's decision against ordination.

14.   Minutes of the Committee of the Society for Effecting the Abolition of the Slave Trade, 14 January 1796, BM Add Ms 21 256. The Committee met with seven present at James Phillips's home: Plymley Diary, Book 40.

15.   St Mary's Parish Register, Suffolk County Record Office, Bury St Edmunds. William Buck of Norwich and Sarah Corsbie of Bury were married 11 December 1769.

16.   S. J. Maling to C. Clarkson, 29 April 1796, Clarkson Papers, BM Add Ms 41 267B.

17.   Plymley Diary, Book 43 and Journey to London 1796. Lord Muncaster told Plymley that 17 abolitionists were at the opera. Robert Isaac Wilberforce and Samuel Wilberforce (eds), *Life of William Wilberforce*, 2nd edn (1839), Vol. II, pp. 139–42; Thomas Clarkson, *History of the*

Rise, Progress, and Accomplishment of the Abolition of the Slave-Trade (1808), Vol. II, p. 473.

18. Plymley Diary, Book 43.
19. Fiona Spiers, 'William Wilberforce: 150 Years On', in Jack Hayward (ed.), *Out of Slavery: Abolition and After* (1985), p. 53; Plymley Diary, Book 43.
20. James Phillips quoted in Plymley Diary, Book 41; also Books 42, 48; Clarkson, *History*, Vol. II, pp. 471, 472.
21. C. Clarkson to W. Smith, 18 August 1834. Lord Muncaster was at the 'joyous meeting'.
22. Plymley Diary, Journey to London 1796; T. Clarkson to S. Buck, 6 April 1796 and to W. Buck, 'Monday 12' [1796], Clarkson Collection, Atlanta.
23. T. Clarkson to W. Buck, 19 October 1796, Clarkson Collection, Atlanta; Earl Leslie Griggs, *Thomas Clarkson the Friend of Slaves* (1936), p. 82.
24. C. Clarkson to Mr and Mrs Buck, [22 October 1796], Clarkson Collection, Atlanta.
25. T. Clarkson to W. Buck, 22 October 1796, Clarkson Collection, Atlanta.
26. Julia Smith Recollections.
27. C. Clarkson to W. Buck, 11 June 1797, Clarkson Collection, Atlanta; Plymley Diary, Books 47, 48.
28. T. Clarkson to W. Buck, 15 October 1798, Clarkson Collection, Atlanta, with a long list of questions on agriculture requiring expert answers; Julia Smith Recollections.
29. Plymley Diary, Book 48. Apparently Clarkson dressed the part of simple farmer, too, and Plymley, after seeing him in London, told his sister he looked slovenly and this would add to the prejudices of those who thought him too democratic: Book 51.
30. C. Clarkson to W. Buck, 5 May 1799, Clarkson Collection, Atlanta.
31. Clarkson, *Quakerism*, Vol. II, pp. 49–50.
32. T. Clarkson to W. Buck, 2 September 1798, and C. Clarkson to W. Buck, 11 June 1797, Clarkson Collection, Atlanta; Plymley Diary, Book 65.
33. C. Clarkson to W. Buck, 7 April 1799 and 11 June 1797; T. Clarkson to W. Buck, 3 September 1798, Clarkson Collection, Atlanta; Griggs, *Thomas Clarkson*, p. 84.
34. C. Clarkson to W. Buck, 5 May 1799, Clarkson Collection, Atlanta; Griggs, *Thomas Clarkson*, pp. 83–4.
35. Plymley Diary, Book 64; Notes on the Memoir of John Clarkson, Clarkson Papers, Huntington Library, San Marino, California; A. Clarkson to J. and S. Clarkson, 13 August 1799, Huntington Library; C. Clarkson to W. Buck, 7 April 1799 and 10 February 1800, Clarkson Collection, Atlanta.
36. T. Clarkson to W. Buck, 3 September 1798 and 22 January 1800, Clarkson Collection, Atlanta.
37. Julia Smith Recollections; Griggs, *Thomas Clarkson*, pp. 84–8.
38. Humphrey Lloyd, *Quaker Lloyds in the Industrial Revolution* (1975), pp.

222–5; C. Clarkson to P. Lloyd, 22 January 1800, quoted in Jonathan Wordsworth, 'Letters of the Coleridge Circle', *The Times Literary Supplement*, 15 February 1968, p. 164; C. Clarkson to W. Buck, 5 May 1799, Clarkson Collection, Atlanta; D. Wordsworth to J. Marshall, 10 September [1800] in Ernest de Selincourt (ed.), *Early Letters of William and Dorothy Wordsworth 1787–1805* (Oxford, 1935), p. 249.

39. Gerard Hartley Buchanan Coleridge, 'Samuel Taylor Coleridge Discovers the Lake Country' in E. L. Griggs (ed.), *Wordsworth and Coleridge* (Princeton, 1939), p. 149.

40. C. Clarkson to P. Lloyd, 22 January 1800.

41. Ernest de Selincourt (ed.), *Journals of Dorothy Wordsworth* (1959), Vol. I, p. 60; C. Clarkson to R. Garnham, 12 February 1801, Henry Crabb Robinson Letters, Dr Williams's Library.

42. William Hazlitt, *Spirit of the Age, or Contemporary Portraits* (1935 reprint of 1904 edn), p. 124; A. S. Byatt, *Wordsworth and Coleridge in Their Time* (1970), pp. 13–14.

43. Plymley Diary, Book 65. One of his wife's jokes made Clarkson seem less susceptible to poetry than she, and he may well have read poems more for substance than delight in imagery and form. When Bernard Barton addressed some verses to Clarkson, Catherine thanked him, observing her 'good man is so little of a poetical amateur that when he had a similar tribute once forwarded to him in the form of an ode, the poet was forced *to promise him a prose translation'*: John Glyde, 'Materials for a History of Woodbridge', Reference Department, Ipswich Borough Libraries.

44. Robert Woof, *Wordsworth Circle: Studies of Twelve Members of Wordsworth's Circle of Friends* (Grasmere, 1979), p. 17.

45. Clarkson, *Quakerism*, Vol. II, pp. 142–50.

46. D. Wordsworth to C. Clarkson, 23 July 1806, in Ernest de Selincourt (ed.), *Letters of William and Dorothy Wordsworth, Middle Years, Part I* (Oxford, 1969), p. 60. Thomas Wordsworth was born in 1806 and Catherine in 1808. They died six months apart in 1812–13.

47. Ernest de Selincourt, *Dorothy Wordsworth* (Oxford, 1933), p. 180; de Selincourt (ed.), *Journals*, Vol. I, and letters of 1800 onwards in the published Wordsworth volumes, including D. Wordsworth to C. Clarkson, 16 February and 28 December 1807, *Wordsworth Letters, Middle Years, Part I*, pp. 136, 137, 183–4, and D. Wordsworth to C. Clarkson, 5 January [1813], *Wordsworth Letters, Middle Years, Part II*, p. 63.

48. de Selincourt, *Journals*, Vol. I, pp. 96–8, 99–101.

49. Ibid., pp. 137–8, 139. William wrote 'I Wandered Lonely as a Cloud' in 1804.

50. E. V. Lucas (ed.), *Letters of Charles Lamb* (1935), Vol. I, p. 315, C. Lamb to T. Manning, 24 September 1802; Woof, *Wordsworth Circle*, pp. 34–5; de Selincourt, *Dorothy Wordsworth*, p. 150.

51. Earl Leslie Griggs (ed.) *Unpublished Letters of Samuel Taylor Coleridge* (1932), Vol. II, p. 49; Baker, *Henry Crabb Robinson*, p. 44.

52. [Thomas Allsop], *Letters, Conversations and Recollections of Samuel Taylor Coleridge* (1836), Vol. I, pp. 48–9. The implied criticism of

Wilberforce has been wrongly attributed to Clarkson, as by his friend Robinson, see Sadler, *Diary*, Vol. III, p. 74. In several years of reading Clarkson's papers I have never discovered any remark critical of his friend and colleague.

53. R. Southey to C. Danvers, 7 November 1803, in Kenneth Curry (ed.), *New Letters of Robert Southey* (New York, 1965), Vol. I, p. 335.

54. D. Wordsworth to C. Clarkson, 15 July 1803, Letters of Dorothy Wordsworth to Mrs Clarkson 1803–1830, BM Add Ms 36 997; de Selincourt, *Dorothy Wordsworth*, pp. 156–7.

55. Dr Beddoes was a feminist, especially interested in teaching physical hygiene to overcome the 'studied neglect' in female education, according to Jacques Barzun, 'Thomas Beddoes or Medicine and Social Conscience', *Journal of the American Medical Association* (April 1972), pp. 5–53. Also Dorothy A. Stansfield, *Thomas Beddoes, MD, 1760–1808, Chemist, Physician, Democrat* (Dordrecht, 1984), pp. ix, 1, 5, 74–5, 197; Byatt, *Wordsworth and Coleridge*, p. 90. Coleridge took part in his experiments for treating tuberculosis with nitrous oxide. Dr Beddoes established a Preventive Medical Institution teaching the virtues of cleanliness, diet, exercise and temperance to the 'Sick and Drooping Poor'. Most of his ideas are common practice now, but not his prescription of opium for Coleridge, de Quincey and Charles Lloyd.

56. S. J. Maling to C. Clarkson, 30 November 1803, BM Add Ms 41 267B; de Selincourt (ed.), *Letters of William and Dorothy Wordsworth*, 2nd edn (Oxford, 1967), p. 444.

57. Ibid., pp. 450, 487; T. Robinson to H. Robinson, 3 July 1804, Henry Crabb Robinson Letters, Dr Williams's Library.

58. de Selincourt (ed.), *Letters*, Vol. I, pp. 444, 471: Plymley Diary, Books 62, 64; D. Wordsworth to C. Clarkson, 18 July 1804, in de Selincourt (ed.), *Early Letters*, pp. 398–401; D. Wordsworth to C. Clarkson, 3 August [1808], *Wordsworth Letters, Middle Years, Part I*, pp. 259–63; D. Wordsworth to C. Clarkson, 9 May 1804, in de Selincourt, *Dorothy Wordsworth*, pp. 180–81.

59. Griggs, *Thomas Clarkson*, p. 79; Clarkson, *Quakerism*, Vol. I, p. vi; Elizabeth Isichei, *Victorian Quakers* (Oxford, 1970), pp. 152, 285.

60. E. Robinson to T. Wilkinson, 16 February 1803 and Wilkinson to Robinson, 7 March 1803, Letters of Thomas Wilkinson and Elihu Robinson, Cumbria County Library, Carlisle.

61. T. Wilkinson to E. Robinson, 7 March 1803; T. Robinson to H. C. Robinson, 8 September 1803, in Morley (ed.), *Correspondence*, Vol. I, p. 49.

9 The Trade Abolished

1. Minutes of the Committee for Effecting the Abolition of the Slave Trade, BM Add Ms 21 256; Diary of Katherine Plymley, Corbett of Longnor Papers, Shropshire Record Office, Book 52; Thomas Clarkson, *History of the Rise, Progress, and Accomplishment of the Abolition of*

the Slave Trade (1808), Vol. II, p. 495; *Life of William Allen* (1846), Vol. I, p. 69, diary for 10 May 1804.

2. Alan M. Rees, 'Pitt and the Achievement of Abolition', *Journal of Negro History* XXXIX (1954), 172–6; Roger Anstey, *Atlantic Slave Trade and British Abolition 1760–1810* (1975), p. 343; Patrick C. Lipscomb III, 'William Pitt and the Abolition of the Slave Trade', PhD thesis, University of Texas (1960), pp. 445, 447; Robin Furneaux, *William Wilberforce* (1974), pp. 239–40.

3. Dale H. Porter, *Abolition of the Slave Trade in England 1784–1807* (Hamden, Conn., 1970), pp. 124–8.

4. Committee Minute Book, 23 May and 6 June 1804; List of Members 29 April 1805.

5. Porter, *Abolition*, pp. 124–8; Lipscomb, 'William Pitt', pp. 452–9; Clarkson, *History*, Vol. II, pp. 476–94; Robert Isaac Wilberforce and Samuel Wilberforce, *Life of William Wilberforce*, 2nd edn (1839), pp. 164–88.

6. Wilberforce, *Life*, Vol. III, pp. 179–80. Perhaps Wilberforce was just being ingratiating and pretending ignorance of procedure.

7. Wilberforce, *Life*, Vol. III, pp. 211–12; Clarkson, *History*, Vol. II, pp. 495–9; Porter, *Abolition*, p. 129; Anstey, *Atlantic Slave Trade*, p. 345; T. Clarkson to T. Poole, 29 March 1805, Correspondence of T. Poole 1765–1837, Vol. II, BM Add Ms 35 344.

8. Clarkson, *History*, Vol. II, p. 501; Committee Minute Book, 29 April 1805.

9. Clarkson, *History*, Vol. II, p. 502; Committee Minute Book, 9 July 1805; Wilberforce, *Life*, Vol. III, pp. 197–203. The idea for a slave-trade pamphlet was first bruited by Wilberforce who suggested to Macaulay that 'our several white negroes' compile background material from published works on Africa. This pamphlet does not seem to have been published.

10. For the Longnor visit, Plymley Diary, Books 64 and 65, unless otherwise noted.

11. H. C. Robinson to T. Robinson, 1 March 1806, Henry Crabb Robinson, Letters, Dr Williams's Library; D. Wordsworth to C. Clarkson, 8 June 1805, in Ernest de Selincourt (ed.), *Early Letters of William and Dorothy Wordsworth* (Oxford, 1935), p. 499; T. Clarkson to J. Corbett, 15 April 1805, author's collection; T. Robinson to H. C. Robinson, 21 May 1805, Henry Crabb Robinson Letters.

12. Edith J. Morley (ed.), *Henry Crabb Robinson on Books and Their Writers* (1938), Vol. I, p. 35.

13. Ernest de Selincourt, *Letters of William and Dorothy Wordsworth*, Vol. I (Oxford, 1967), p. 445; monumental inscription Holy Trinity Church, Long Melford.

14. D. Wordsworth to Lady Beaumont, 7 August 1805, de Selincourt (ed.), *Early Letters*, p. 515, quoted in Robert Gittings and Jo Manton, *Dorothy Wordsworth* (Oxford, 1985), p. 149; D. Wordsworth to C. Clarkson, 9 October [1814], in Mary Moorman and Alan G. Hill (eds), *Letters of William and Dorothy Wordsworth, Middle Years, Part II*, p. 158.

15. Danvers Journal, 5 August [1805], BM Add Ms 30 929; T. Clarkson to J. Wadkin, 23 July 1805, Clarkson Letters, Wordsworth Library, Grasmere.

16. S. J. Maling to C. Clarkson, September [28, 1805], Clarkson Papers, BM Add Ms 41 267B; Ernest de Selincourt (ed.), *Journals of Dorothy Wordsworth* (1959), Vol. I, p. 413; vii, xviii.

17. Ernest de Selincourt, *Dorothy Wordsworth* (Oxford, 1965 reprint), p. 195. Catherine was staying with Captain and Mrs Luff at Patterdale.

18. Clarkson, *History*, Vol. II, pp. 503–6; Lipscomb, 'William Pitt', p. 513. The three opponents in Pitt's cabinet were Henry Dundas, Lord Liverpool and Lord Chancellor Thurlow.

19. Plymley Diary, Book 67; Committee Minute Book, 7 March 1806; Wilberforce, *Life*, Vol. III, p. 259; T. Clarkson to T. Poole, 8 March 1806, BM Add Ms 35 344; Anstey, *Atlantic Slave Trade*, p. 365.

20. Clarkson, *History*, Vol. II, pp. 507–9; David Brion Davis, *Problem of Slavery in the Age of Revolution 1770–1823* (Ithaca, NY, 1975), pp. 443–4; Anstey, *Atlantic Slave Trade*, pp. 368–74; Porter, *Abolition*, pp. 132–4; Plymley Diary, Book 69.

21. Clarkson, *History*, Vol. II, pp. 509–63; Porter, *Abolition*, p. 135; Lipscomb, 'William Pitt', pp. 483–6.

22. Clarkson, *History*, Vol. II, pp. 565–8.

23. Wilberforce, *Life*, Vol. III, pp. 273–4.

24. William Wilberforce, *Letter on the Abolition of the Slave Trade; Addressed to the Freeholders and Other Inhabitants of Yorkshire* (1807), p. 2.

25. Yorkshire elections for 1806 and 1807 based on 'The Great Yorkshire Election', author's unpublished study.

26. *Life of Allen*, Vol. I, p. 82.

27. The advertisements may have been placed by the London Committee but its records do not show it.

28. Clarkson, *History*, Vol. II, p. 570; Anstey, *Atlantic Slave Trade*, pp. 393–5, 395–6, 398–400; Wilberforce, *Life*, Vol. III, pp. 291–2, 293–4; Davis, *Problem of Slavery*, p. 446; Porter, *Abolition*, p.137.

29. Anstey, *Atlantic Slave Trade*, p. 396; Porter, *Abolition*, p. 138; Wilberforce, *Life*, Vol. III, p. 295.

30. Wilberforce, *Life*, Vol. III, p. 296; Clarkson, *History*, Vol. II, pp. 572–5; Plymley Diary, Book 30; Yvette Wilberforce, *William Wilberforce* (1967), introduction by C. E. Wrangham.

31. T. Clarkson to J. Corbett, Plymley Diary, Book 70; T. Clarkson to J. Wadkin, 24 February 1807, Thomas Clarkson Papers, St John's College Library, Cambridge University; T. Clarkson to T. Richardson, 24 February 1807, author's collection; T. Clarkson to D. Alexander, 24 February 1807, Boston Public Library, Mss Acc 490. For the significance of the passage when the slave trade was still fully viable, Seymour Drescher, 'Capitalism and Abolition: Values and Forces in Britain, 1783–1814', in Roger Anstey and P. E. H. Hair (eds), *Liverpool, the African Slave Trade, and Abolition* (Bristol, 1976), pp. 167–95.

32. Committee Minute Book, 24 February 1807.
33. Clarkson, *History*, Vol. II, pp. 579–80.
34. Morley (ed.), *Henry Crabb Robinson*, Vol. I, pp. 113–14.
35. T. Clarkson to J. Taylor, 26 January 1807, Clarkson Papers, St John's College.
36. 'The Great Yorkshire Election'; see note 25 above.
37. T. Clarkson to J. Wadkin, 1 May 1807, Anti-Slavery Papers, Rhodes House Library, Oxford, Mss Brit. Emp. S18, C107/156.
38. Peter F. Dixon, 'Politics of Emancipation: the Movement for the Abolition of Slavery in the British West Indies 1807–33', DPhil thesis, Oxford University (1971), p. 117.

10 The Problems of Victory

1. Thomas Clarkson, *History of the Rise, Progress and Accomplishment of the Abolition of the Slave-Trade* (1808), Vol. I, pp. 32, 268–9; T. Clarkson to W. Roscoe, 26 July 1807, William Roscoe Papers, City of Liverpool Record Office; Earl Leslie Griggs, *Thomas Clarkson the Friend of Slaves* (1936), p. 96; M. Lamb to C. Clarkson, 23 December 1806 in E. V. Lucas (ed.), *Letters of Charles Lamb* (1935), Vol. II, pp. 32–4; T. Clarkson to R. W. Fox, 30 May 1808, Huntington Library, San Marino, California, HM 35526; 'Prospectus 30 June 1814 [1807]', Huntington Library, HM 35528. Clarkson sent out two prospectuses, one for a Quaker audience and a second, revised, for 'the World'.
2. The three outcast Cabinet members were Windham, Lord Sidmouth and the Earl Fitzwilliam. The Earl, an uneasy supporter of abolition in 1806, was absent on the day of the vote in the Lords.
3. T. Clarkson to H. Taylor, 31 May 1808, Clarkson Letters, Wordsworth Library, Grasmere.
4. 'Prospectus 30 June 1814 [1807]'; Seymour Drescher, *Capitalism and Slavery: British Mobilization in Comparative Perspective* (1986), p. 1; Roger Anstey, *Atlantic Slave Trade and British Abolition 1760–1810* (1975), pp. 157–8.
5. David Brion Davis, *Problem of Slavery in the Age of Revolution 1770–1823* (Ithaca, NY, 1975), p. 447; D. Wordsworth to C. Clarkson, 30 August [1807] in Mary Moorman (ed.), *Letters of William and Dorothy Wordsworth, Middle Years, Part I* (Oxford, 1969), pp. 160–61; Griggs, *Thomas Clarkson*, p. 95. The abridged edition cited was published at Augusta, Maine in 1830. R. R. Gurley's introduction quotes.
6. S. T. Coleridge to R. Southey [February 1808], in Earl Leslie Griggs, *Unpublished Letters of Samuel Taylor Coleridge* (1932), Vol. I, p. 395. Coleridge, from a sickbed, disposed of 25 copies: S. T. Coleridge to unknown [8 May 1808], Manuscript Department, William R. Perkins Library, Duke University, Durham, NC.

7. C. Clarkson to H. C. Robinson, May 1808, Henry Crabb Robinson Letters, Dr Williams's Library; [Thomas Allsop], *Letters, Conversations and Recollections of Samuel Taylor Coleridge* (1836), Vol. II, pp. 112–13; S. T. Coleridge to [J. G. Lockhart], [1828], in Griggs, *Unpublished Letters*, Vol. II, pp. 407–9. Coleridge reviewed the *History* to 'prevent Thomas Clarkson's feelings from being turmoiled by any unhandsome treatment'. He told Jeffrey it should not be judged solely as a literary composition: Griggs, *Thomas Clarkson*, pp. 96–7.

8. Coleridge's review appeared in the *Edinburgh Review* (July 1808), pp. 355–79. The offending insertions about Wilberforce began 'At the head of this list unquestionably stands the name of Mr Wilberforce.... He it was who first brought the evil to light.... Mr Wilberforce indubitably has been the great captain of the abolitionists, and without his courage and skill, and unwearied perseverance, their cause must long since have been lost and abandoned', (p. 362). S. T. Coleridge to [J. G. Lockhart]; S. T. Coleridge to T. J. Street, 19 September [1809], in Griggs, *Unpublished Letters*, Vol. II, p. 4; A. S. Byatt, *Wordsworth and Coleridge in Their Time* (1970), pp. 206–7.

9. [Allsop], *Letters*, p. 113.

10. W. Wilberforce to T. Clarkson, 20 May 1808, Rare Books and Manuscripts Department, Boston Public Library, Ms Eng 183(9) and copy in Henry Crabb Robinson Letters, Dr Williams's Library. Wilberforce enclosed a sonnet by William Hayley to Clarkson, which Wilberforce called a '*just tribute* from a veteran poet in whom your publication has kindled a generous flame'. It started, 'Thou just historian of those toils complete/ That terminate a nation's guilt and shame/ In virtue's blaze of philanthropic fame/ Hail! generous Clarkson!' Robert Isaac Wilberforce and Samuel Wilberforce, *Life of William Wilberforce*, 2nd edn (1839), Vol. I, p. 141n; H. C. Robinson to C. Clarkson, 7 May 1808, Henry Crabb Robinson Letters. The poem is printed in Griggs, *Thomas Clarkson*, p. 98.

11. T. Clarkson to W. Wilberforce, 20 November 1814, Wilberforce Papers, Wrangham Collection when consulted, now Bodleian Library, Oxford University; W. Wilberforce to E. H. Locker, 23 October 1820, Locker Papers, Huntington Library.

12. Stephen's writings before 1807 were more on slavery in the West Indies than the slave trade, which was Clarkson's subject. T. Clarkson to W. Wilberforce, 20 November 1814. In 1838 Clarkson was asked by the Central Negro Emancipation Committee to bring his *History* up to date and he made a start, catalogued as 'Account of Efforts, 1807–1824, to Abolish the foreign slave trade and slavery in the British colonies', *c.* 1839 [August 1838], Clarkson Papers, Huntington Library. It was done hastily and needed thorough review if ever used, Clarkson commented.
   'There is also too much of Egotism in it, for it was written only for our own Committee', he added. Lord Brougham thought it was unprintable and couldn't be used with a new edition of the *History*. Robinson, who had hoped it would form part of a life of Clarkson,

and Clarkson himself, agreed. It is useful, however, for its transcripts of various papers Clarkson wrote up to 1838. Henry Crabb Robinson Diary, 11, 14, 20 and 22 February 1839, Dr Williams's Library.

13. Prospectus for the African Institution in Clarkson, *History*, Vol. II, pp. 1–4. It lists Wilberforce as a vice-president and Clarkson as a director; Thomas Clarkson, 'Account of Efforts', ff. 1–2; *Life of William Allen* (1846), Vol. I, pp. 85–6. If it was true that Macaulay always framed the resolutions for the African Institution, then he was responsible for the snub to Clarkson in the vote of thanks which named Sharp, Wilberforce and the Duke of Gloucester: C. Clarkson to H. C. Robinson, 4 May 1839, Henry Crabb Robinson Letters.

14. *Life of Allen*, Vol. I, p. 112; Diary of Katherine Plymley, Corbett of Longnor Papers, Shropshire Record Office, Books 77, 82; T. Clarkson to W. Roscoe, 12 June 1809, and T. Clarkson to Z. Macaulay, August 1809, William Roscoe Papers, City of Liverpool Record Office; T. Clarkson to R. W. Fox, 16 August 1813, Huntington Library, HM 35527.

15. Helena Hall, *William Allen 1770–1843, Member of the Society of Friends* (Haywards Heath, 1953), p. 13; T. Clarkson to J. Beaumont, 24 January 1844, copy, Anti-Slavery Papers, Rhodes House Library, Oxford, Mss Brit. Emp. S18, C107; Martha Braithwaite (ed.), *Memorials of Christine Majolier Alsop* (1881), p. 69; 'James Grahame's Diary 1815–1824', *Journal of Friends Historical Society*, XXXVIII (1946), p. 51; *Life of Allen*, Vol. I, p. 7. Davis, *Problem of Slavery*, pp. 242–9 gives an excellent picture of Allen's significance.

16. *Life of Allen*, Vol. I, pp. 37–8.

17. John Ormerod Greenwood, *Quaker Encounters* (York, 1977), Vol. II, *Vines on the Mountains*, p. 92, quoting Braithwaite (ed.), *Memorials*.

18. Hall, *William Allen*, p. 30; *Life of Allen*, Vol. I, p. 123.

19. Principal sources for the unusual Paul Cuffe are Sheldon H. Harris, *Paul Cuffe. Black America and the African Return* (New York, 1972); Henry Noble Sherwood, 'Paul Cuffe', *Journal of Negro History* VIII (1923), 153–229; Cuffe Collection, Free Public Library, New Bedford, Mass. Lamont D. Thomas, *Rise to Be a People, a Biography of Paul Cuffe* (Urbana, Ill., 1986) discusses his pan-African plans and attitudes to race, pp. 118–19, 26–7. Also, for this section, James W. St. G. Walker, *Black Loyalists: Search for a Promised Land in Nova Scotia and Sierra Leone 1783–1870* (1986), p. 284; *Life of Allen*, Vol. I, pp. 114–15, 135–6; Wilberforce, *Life*, Vol. III, p. 501.

20. African Institution, *Sixth Report* (1812), pp. 26–8; Harris, *Paul Cuffe*, pp. 47, 50, 60, 62–3; Sheldon H. Harris, 'An American's Impressions of Sierra Leone in 1811', *Journal of Negro History*, XLVII (1962), pp. 39, 40, 41; 'Memoir of Captain Paul Cuffee', *Philanthropist*, II (1812), p. 41; Paul Cuffe, *Brief Account of the Settlement and Present Situation of the Colony of Sierra Leone* (New York, 1812), printed in Harris, *Paul Cuffe*, as Appendix B, p. 182.

21. W. Allen to H. Warren, 15 August 1813, William Allen Papers, Allen & Hanbury Ltd, African Correspondence, Vol. I; *Life of Allen*, Vol. I, pp. 186–7, 188, 224–5; J. Wise to W. Allen, 3 July 1814 and J. Kizell to

T. Clarkson, 30 May 1813, Allen Papers.

22. *Life of Allen*, Vol. I, pp. 139, 144, 155; W. Allen to J. Kizell, 30 April 1812, Allen Papers. The ship carrying the very first consignment, Indian cloth, sank, but the goods were insured.

23. T. Clarkson to J. Wise, 25 February 1819, Allen Papers; *Life of Allen*, Vol. I, p.338. Allen and Clarkson interceded with the government to settle the long-disputed land titles: T. Clarkson to Lord Bathurst, 22 June 1815, PRO, CO 267/41. Among other blows to the enterprise was the death of Cuffe, the inspiration of it, in 1817.

24. Harris, *Paul Cuffe*, pp. 175–8; T. Clarkson and W. Allen to P. Cuffe, 1 July 1812, Allen Papers.

25. T. Clarkson to W. Allen, 4 July 1813, Temp Mss 4/6/7, Library of the Religious Society of Friends.

26. For the Thompson period, Walker, *Black Loyalists*, pp. 259–74; W. Wilberforce to Lord Liverpool, 30 June 1810, PRO CO 267/27; John Pollock, *Wilberforce* (1977), pp. 226–7.

27. *Philanthropist*, III (1813), 301–25.

28. *Life of Allen*, Vol. I, p. 184.

29. Ibid., pp. 168, 172, 178, 180, 184, 185.

30. Ibid., pp. 178, 184–5.

31. W. Allen to J. Clarkson, 10 May 1815, Clarkson Papers, BM Add Ms 41 263; *Life of Allen*, Vol. I, p. 185.

32. African Institution, *Special Report of the Directors ... respecting the Allegations Contained in a Pamphlet entitled "A Letter to William Wilberforce Esq"* (1815).

33. Robert Thorpe, *Letter to William Wilberforce Esq ... Containing Remarks on the Reports of the Sierra Leone Company, and African Institution*, 3rd edn (1815), p. 68. Macaulay's answer was published as *Letter to His Royal Highness the Duke of Gloucester ... Occasioned by a Pamphlet ... by Dr Thorpe* (1815).

34. *Life of Allen*, Vol. I, p. 179; Davis, *Problem of Slavery*, p. 247. The quote is from Richard Reynolds.

35. Diary of William Wilberforce, 11 February and 2 March 1814, Wilberforce Museum, Hull, included in Wilberforce, *Life*, Vol. IV, pp. 152, 153 where the entry is garbled and the Clarksons disguised as the 'N— —s'.

36. *Life of Allen*, Vol. I, pp. 180, 223; W. Allen to Governor MacCarthy, 10 August 1815, Allen Papers.

37. *Philanthropist*, IV (1814), 97–116, 244–64; V (1815), 29–37.

38. Wilberforce, *Life*, Vol. IV, pp. 188–9; Robin Furneaux, *William Wilberforce* (1974), pp. 336–7; Pollock, *Wilberforce*, pp. 242–3.

39. T. Clarkson to C. Clarkson, n.d., endorsed 'Petitions – 1814', and same to same, 'Tuesday morning', Clarkson Papers, Huntington Library.

40. William Allen presented Clarkson's abridgement of evidence for 1789, 1790 and 1791 to the Emperor. T. Clarkson, 'Account of Efforts', pp. 4, 5; *Life of Allen*, Vol. I, pp. 193, 194–200; Wilberforce, *Life*, Vol. IV, pp. 190–91; Pollock, *Wilberforce*, pp. 244–5; T. Clarkson

to W. Wilberforce, 'Sunday evening' and 15 June 1814, Wilberforce Papers, Wrangham Collection; Griggs, *Thomas Clarkson*, p. 114; Plymley Diary, Book 104.

41. T. Clarkson to C. Clarkson, 21 June 1814, Clarkson Papers, Huntington.

42. Plymley Diary, Book 103; T. Clarkson to W. Wilberforce, 'Saturday morning' [1814], Wrangham Collection; Wilberforce, *Life*, Vol. IV, pp. 192–7. Wilberforce alone was responsible for the petition drive in 1814, his sons imply: 'it must be his care to call forth such a spirit in this country as should compel Ministers to take a higher tone' (p. 192); 'He had not called in vain. . . . More than 800 petitions, with near a million of signatures, soon covered the table' (p. 197). Clarkson's printed call for petitions, 30 June 1815, Huntington Library.

43. T. Clarkson to Z. Macaulay, 8 June 1823, Macaulay Papers, Huntington Library; T. Clarkson to C. Clarkson, 'Tuesday morning' [1814], quoted in Griggs, *Thomas Clarkson*, p. 115; *Life of Allen*, Vol. I, pp. 203, 204.

44. Wilberforce, *Life*, Vol. IV, p. 197; Furneaux, *Wilberforce*, p. 338; Pollock, *Wilberforce*, pp. 245–6; Howard Temperley, *British Antislavery 1833–1870* (1972), p. 8; James Walvin, 'Public Campaign in England Against Slavery, 1787–1834', in D. Eltis and James Walvin (eds), *Abolition of the Atlantic Slave Trade* (Madison, Wis., 1981), pp. 63–74; Plymley Diary, Book 104; Clarkson's letter on his Paris mission, 1814, Macaulay Papers, Huntington. Published figures on the 1814 petition signatures range from 250 000 to 1 000 000. Clarkson's figure – bound to be the most accurate – is 755 000: T. Clarkson to W. Wilberforce, [11 August] 1814, Wilberforce Papers, Wrangham Collection.

45. African Institution, *Eighth Report* (1814); Minutes of the Committee of the Society for Effecting the Abolition of the Slave Trade, 2 July 1814, BM Add Ms 21 256.

46. Griggs, *Thomas Clarkson*, pp. 115–16; W. Wilberforce to Z. Macaulay, 6 August [1814], Wilberforce Papers, Wrangham Collection. Said Wilberforce, 'I am shocked to hear that Clarkson has been proposing to go as a Delegate from the Afr Instn & that the D of Gloster &c seemed to favour his plan. Surely it would be of a most mischievous tendency for enabling Lord Castle[r] to allege if he fails that it was owing to our tampering with y[e] Business'. Stephen was much annoyed at Clarkson's initiative: J. Stephen to W. Wilberforce, 26 August 1814, Manuscript Department, William R. Perkins Library, Duke University. According to Clarkson, 'Account of Efforts', pp. 6–7, John Villiers MP, at a board meeting of the African Institution, read Clarkson's Address detailing the atrocities of the trade and suggested he talk to the Duke of Wellington, who was not versed on the subject, before he left for Paris (and later Vienna), and arranged the interview. Clarkson had an hour with Wellington and agreed to send him his abridgement of the evidence and *Essay on Impolicy*.

Macaulay also sent him papers to help him master the subject.

47. Clarkson's 'Account of Efforts'; Wilberforce, *Life*, Vol. IV, pp. 209–18.

48. Clarkson's Address was called 'A Summary of the Evidence Delivered before a Committee of the English House of Commons on the Subject of the Slave-Trade Addressed to the different Potentates of Christendom at this Particular Crisis'. Fifty copies were delivered to Vienna in the Duke of Wellington's diplomatic bag to be distributed by the papal delegate: T. Clarkson to Lord Grenville, [8 October] 1814, Clarkson Papers, Huntington.

49. T. Clarkson to W. Wilberforce, 10 August 1814, also 'Thursday' [11 August] and 15 August, all Wilberforce Papers, Wrangham Collection; W. Wilberforce to T. Clarkson, copy, 9 August 1814, Wilberforce Manuscripts, Bodleian Library, Oxford University, d 15/1 f 86; W. Wilberforce to T. Harrison, 18 August 1814, Wilberforce Papers, Duke University.

50. Comte de St Morys to T. Clarkson, 5 October 1814, Clarkson Papers, Moorland-Spingarn Research Center, Howard University, Washington, DC; T. Clarkson to W. Wilberforce, 'Thursday' [11 August] 1814, Wrangham Collection.

51. Thomas Sadler (ed.), *Diary Reminiscences and Correspondence of Henry Crabb Robinson* (1869), Vol. I, pp. 440–46; Henry Crabb Robinson, Paris Journal, 31 August to 11 September 1814, Dr Williams's Library; Plymley Diary, Book 104; C. Clarkson to S. Hutchinson, 14 January 1815, Clarkson Papers, BM Add Ms 41 267A.

52. Sadler (ed.), *Diary*, Vol. I, p. 447.

53. The first Clarkson Address was so badly translated the King laughed. The Abbé Grégoire sat up all night to do it over: 'Account of Efforts, p. 8; Griggs, *Thomas Clarkson*, pp. 116–17.

54. The day before Clarkson left England, Wilberforce had urged him to avoid his old abolitionist friends but Clarkson felt free to do so after talking with Wellington, according to W. Wordsworth to Lonsdale, 1 October [1814] in Mary Moorman and Alan G. Hill (eds), *Letters of William and Dorothy Wordsworth, Middle Years, Part II* (Oxford, 1970), p. 156. Wordsworth enclosed a copy of a letter from C. Clarkson in Paris.

55. T. Clarkson to Lord Grenville, [8 October 1814], and 'Account of Efforts', Clarkson Papers, Huntington Library. According to T. Clarkson to ?, n.d., Boston Public Library Mss Acc 493 (marked 1789 but which I believe to be 1814), he discovered the French abolitionists had 'not one Shilling' for propaganda and had to draw on the London Committee for £120 which Wilberforce and Henry Thornton had agreed to refund.

56. T. Clarkson to W. Wilberforce, 13 and 28 October 1814, Wilberforce Papers, Wrangham Collection. Clarkson's letters were sent to Wilberforce, Grenville, the Duke of Gloucester, Thornton, Macaulay and Stephen. The letter to Macaulay and an appreciative reply to Clarkson from Lord Grenville are in the Huntington Library, respectively MY 155 and H 33.

11   Of Friends and Family Matters

1.   S. J. Maling to C. Clarkson, 22 April 1806, Clarkson Papers, BM Add Ms 41 267B; R. P. Mander, 'Thomas Clarkson and His Anti-Slavery Campaign', *East Anglian Magazine* (December 1950), p. 221; Alec Clifton-Taylor, *Another Six English Towns* (1984), p. 103; Diary of Katherine Plymley, Corbett of Longnor Papers, Shropshire Record Office, Book 108; S. J. Maling to C. Clarkson, 7 September 1806, BM Add Ms 41 267B. The house is now two houses and the quiet square cut in half by a busy road and dominated by a brewery but what is left is pretty. A plaque high on the façade of the house reads 'Clarkson the promoter of the Emancipation Bill, 1833'. Catherine's sister married John Corsbie, a cousin, in 1812.

2.   D. Wordsworth to C. Clarkson, 27 June and July (n.d.) 1806), in Mary Moorman (ed.), *Letters of William and Dorothy Wordsworth, Middle Years, Part I* (Oxford, 1969), pp. 48–51.

3.   S. J. Maling to C. Clarkson, 7 September 1806, BM Add Ms 41 267B; D. Wordsworth to C. Clarkson, 17 February 1807, *Wordsworth Letters*, p. 136.

4.   D. Wordsworth to C. Clarkson, 10 May 1808, Clarkson Papers, Huntington Library, San Marino, California; Ernest de Selincourt, *Dorothy Wordsworth* (Oxford, 1964 reprint), p. 267.

5.   C. Clarkson to S. Hutchinson, 14 January 1815, BM Add Ms 41 267A.

6.   Plymley Diary, Book 3.

7.   C. Clarkson to H. C. Robinson, 1 and 6 December 1811, Henry Crabb Robinson Letters, Dr Williams's Library.

8.   R. W. Elliott, *Story of King Edward VI School Bury St Edmunds* (Bury St Edmunds, 1963), pp. 75, 91, 92, 481; *Biographical List of Boys Educated at King Edward VI Free Grammar School, Bury St Edmunds, from 1550 to 1900* (Bury St Edmunds, 1908), p. 75; C. Clarkson to H. C. Robinson, 1 and 6 December 1811.

9.   D. Wordsworth to C. Clarkson, 26 August 1809, *Wordsworth Letters*, p. 368.

10.   M. Lamb to C. Clarkson, 25 December 1805, in E. V. Lucas (ed.), *Letters of Charles Lamb* (1935), Vol. I, pp. 415–16; Edwin W. Marrs, Jr, (ed.), *Letters of Charles and Mary Anne Lamb* (Ithaca, NY, 1976), Vol. II, p. 193; same to same, 23 December 1806, Lucas (ed.), *Letters*, pp. 32–4; Marrs (ed.), *Letters*, pp. 252–5. Charles Lamb contributed paraphrases of the tragedies and his name alone appeared on the title page, but the *Tales* brought them 60 guineas: E. V. Lucas, *Life of Charles Lamb*, 5th edn (1921), Vol. I, pp. 332, 345–6.

11.   M. Lamb to C. Clarkson, [10] December 1808, Lucas (ed.), *Letters*, Vol. II, pp. 61–3; Marrs (ed.), *Letters*, Vol. 2, p. 289; Marrs (ed.), *Letters*, Vol. I, pp. 113–14; C. Lamb to C. Clarkson, [July, 1807], Marrs (ed.), *Letters*, Vol. II, p. 259.

12.   W. Wordsworth to T. Clarkson, [1816, n.d.], in Mary Moorman and Alan G. Hill (eds), *Letters of William and Dorothy Wordsworth, Middle Years, Part II* (Oxford, 1970), pp. 350–51.

13.   Indenture 27 March 1843, Suffolk Record Office, Bury St Edmunds,

HD 1107/1; *Guide to the Town, Abbey, and Antiquities of Bury St Edmunds* (Ipswich, 1821), p. 99; *Life of William Allen* (1846), Vol. I, pp. 94–5; David Brion Davis, *Problem of Slavery in the Age of Revolution 1770–1823* (Ithaca, NY, 1975), p. 248; Plymley Diary, Book 77.

14. William Canton, *History of the British and Foreign Bible Society* (1904), Vol. I, p. 67; T. Clarkson to S. Whitbread, 26 November 1811, Whitbread Collection, Bedford County Record Office.

15. *Life of Allen*, Vol. I, p. 92; Plymley Diary, Book 76; Elizabeth Isichei, *Victorian Quakers* (Oxford, 1970), p. 251; Mary Phillips, *Memoir of the Life of Richard Phillips* (1841), pp. 132–3; Earl Leslie Griggs, *Thomas Clarkson the Friend of Slaves* (1936), p. 159. The group was called the Society for the Diffusion of Information on Capital Punishments With a View to Diminish Their Frequency.

16. T. Clarkson to J. Wedgwood, 1 February 1821 and 4 March 1830, Wedgwood Manuscripts, Keele University Library; Clarkson circular letter, 6 March 1821, Clarkson Papers, William R. Perkins Library, Duke University, Durham NC. Sir Samuel Romilly spoke for penal code reform in Parliament. In one year (1822) more than 5000 persons were sentenced to death.

17. For detail on the Peace Society, Ellen Gibson Wilson, *John Clarkson and the African Adventure* (1980), pp. 159–70; *Life of Allen*, Vol. I, p. 191.

18. *Philanthropist*, V (1815), 219–21; Peace Society, *Address*, printed with its first tract, *Substance of a Pamphlet Entitled a Solemn Review of the Custom of War, Showing that War is One Effect of Popular Delusion, and Proposing a Remedy* (1817); Isichei, *Victorian Quakers*, pp. 220–21.

19. The rest of Clarkson's title was *Addressed to Those, Who Profess to have Regard for the Christian Name*, 2nd edn (1817). It was Tract No. 3 for the Peace Society.

20. *Christian Observer*, XVII (1818), pp. 22–6, 231–6.

21. Peace Society, *Ninth Report* (1825).

22. Thomas Clarkson, *Portraiture of Quakerism* (1806); Isichei, *Victorian Quakers*, p. 144.

23. Among those who have got the religious labelling wrong: Reginald Coupland, *British Anti-Slavery Movement* (1933), p. 204; Ernest Howse, *Saints in Politics* (1942), pp. 15, 20; 'Clarkson's Autobiography; the Slave Trade Eighty Years Ago', *Christian Observer*, LXVI (1866), p. 478, repeating a mistake first made when reviewing the Wilberforce, *Life*, p. 778 (1838). Thomas Clarkson, *Interviews with the Emperor Alexander I of Russia at Paris and Aix-la-Chapelle in 1815 and 1818* (Wisbech, 1930), p. 14; 'James Grahame's Diary 1815–1824', *Journal of Friends Historical Society*, XXXVIII (1946), 54. Other pictures allowed in a Quaker home were the diagram of the slave-ship, Penn's signing of the treaty of friendship with the Indians and the plan of Ackworth School. One other portrait in some homes was Bonaparte, who, according to James Grahame, was respected as a genius and a 'useful instrument in the hands of God for humbling the Pope'.

24. Plymley Diary, Books 29, 43; Ford K. Brown, *Fathers of the Victorians,*

the *Age of Wilberforce* (Cambridge, 1961), pp. 15–44; Asa Briggs, *Age of Improvement* (1959), pp. 66–7. Wilberforce's *Practical View of the Prevailing Religious Systems of Professed Christians in the Higher and Middle Classes in this Country, Contrasted with Real Christianity* (1797) was written to restore some religious fundamentalism.

25. T. Clarkson to J. Plymley, 27 August 1793, in Plymley Diary, Book 65; Clarkson, *Portraiture*, Vol. II, p. 12.

26. Biographical sketch preceding the third edn of his *Portraiture* (1869) probably by Robert Smeal, Glasgow publisher.

27. De Selincourt, *Dorothy Wordsworth*, p. 221; T. Clarkson to R. Southey, 21 September 1806, Huntington Library, HM 12301.

28. *Memoirs of the Private and Public Life of William Penn* (1813), and published in Philadelphia the same year. Griggs, *Thomas Clarkson*, pp. 99–101; William Hepworth Dixon, *William Penn, an Historical Biography* (1851), p. ix.

29. R. Southey to J. Murray, 9 July 1813, in Kenneth Curry (ed.), *New Letters to Robert Southey* (New York, 1965), Vol. II, p. 61.

30. *Edinburgh Review*, XXI (1813), 444–62, quoted by Griggs, *Thomas Clarkson*, pp. 100–101. Griggs says it was written by Jeffrey.

31. D. Wordsworth to C. Clarkson, 4 October [1813], in *Wordsworth Letters, Middle Years, Part II*, pp. 124–5.

32. T. Clarkson to W. Wilberforce, 3 February 1807, Wrangham Collection; Lord H. Petty to W. Smith, 12 February 1807, Duke University; John Pollock, *Wilberforce* (1977), p. 210. Wilberforce, who recommended Clarkson highly to Petty, wrote on Clarkson's letter 'impossible? besides wd injure abolition cause'.

33. Plymley Diary, Books 4, 7.

34. D. Wordsworth to C. Clarkson, 15 June 1809, *Wordsworth Letters, Middle Years, Part I*, p. 356; Plymley Diary, Book 104.

35. S. Hutchinson to M. Hutchinson, 29 June 1815, in Kathleen Coburn (ed.), *Letters of Sara Hutchinson* (1954), pp. 80–83; C. Clarkson to M. Wordsworth, 29 July 1815, Wordsworth Library, Grasmere; D. Wordsworth to C. Clarkson, 15 August [1815], *Wordsworth Letters, Middle Years, Part II*, pp. 244–8.

36. S. Hutchinson to M. Hutchinson, October 1808, in Coburn (ed.), *Letters*, p. 5; de Selincourt, *Dorothy Wordsworth*, p. 208.

37. C. Clarkson to S. Hutchinson, 13 May 1809, BM Add Ms 41 267A. Clarkson would not be in the same class with the forever-rambling Wordsworths but he showed Robert Southey a favourite walk over Kirkstone Pass (R. Southey to T. Clarkson, 29 May 1822 in Curry (ed.), *New Letters*, Vol. II, p. 236) and he could walk to Penrith and back to Pooley Bridge without fatigue (D. Wordsworth to C. Clarkson, 25 August 1821, in Alan G. Hill (ed.), *Letters of William and Dorothy Wordsworth, Late Years, Part I*, p. 72).

38. D. Wordsworth to C. Clarkson, 2 June 1810, in *Wordsworth Letters, Middle Years, Part I*, p. 412; D. Wordsworth to W. Wordsworth and S. Hutchinson, 14 August 1810, p. 426; de Selincourt, *Dorothy Wordsworth*, pp. 260–62; D. Wordsworth to Lady Beaumont, 14 August 1810, *Wordsworth Letters, Middle Years, Part I*, pp. 420–23; Robert

Gittings and Jo Manton, *Dorothy Wordsworth* (Oxford, 1985), pp. 182–4.

39. D. Wordsworth to Mrs Cookson, 29 August 1810, *Wordsworth Letters, Middle Years, Part I*, pp. 431–5.

40. D. Wordsworth to C. Clarkson, 23 February 1811, ibid., p. 462; Julia Smith Recollections, William Smith and Family Papers, Cambridge University Library.

41. Henry Crabb Robinson Diary, 12 October 1813, Dr Williams's Library; C. Clarkson to H. C. Robinson, 1 and 6 December 1811, Henry Crabb Robinson Letters, Dr Williams's Library; Edith J. Morley (ed.), *Henry Crabb Robinson on Books and their Writers* (1938), Vol. I, p. 47.

42. C. Clarkson to S. Hutchinson, 14 January 1815, BM Add Ms 41 267A.

43. Ibid.; D. Wordsworth to C. Clarkson, 11 November [1814], *Wordsworth Letters, Middle Years, Part II*, p. 166.

44. W. Wordsworth to C. Clarkson, [January 1815], *Wordsworth Letters, Middle Years, Part II*, p. 191. The whole letter (pp. 187–92) is in answer to criticisms by Patty Smith of *The Excursion*. W. and D. Wordsworth to C. Clarkson, [31 December 1814], *Wordsworth Letters, Middle Years, Part II*, pp. 181, 184; D. Wordsworth to C. Clarkson, 11 April [1815], ibid., pp. 299–31; *Philanthropist*, V (1815), 344, 357, 362 (whole, 342–63).

45. D. Wordsworth to C. Clarkson, 23 February [1811], *Wordsworth Letters, Middle Years, Part I*, pp. 462–7; S. Hutchinson to M. Monkhouse, 3 December 1811, in Coburn (ed.), *Letters*, p. 34; C. Clarkson to Mrs Wordsworth, 29 July 1815, Wordsworth Library, Grasmere.

46. De Selincourt, *Dorothy Wordsworth*, pp. 270–71, 275–7; C. Clarkson to H. C. Robinson, 28 December 1812, Henry Crabb Robinson Letters; Griggs, *Thomas Clarkson*, p. 105.

47. W. Wordsworth to C. Clarkson, 11 June 1812, *Wordsworth Letters, Middle Years, Part II*, p. 25; D. Wordsworth to C. Clarkson, 10 August [1812], ibid., p. 43.

48. Earl Leslie Griggs (ed.), *Unpublished Letters of Samuel Taylor Coleridge* (1932), Vol. II, pp. 349, 352–60.

49. C. Clarkson to H. C. Robinson, 28 March and April (n.d.) 1808, Henry Crabb Robinson Letters; S. T. Coleridge to H. C. Robinson, [3 May 1808], in Griggs (ed.), *Unpublished Letters*, Vol. I, pp. 415–16; Thomas Sadler (ed.), *Diary, Reminiscences and Correspondence of Henry Crabb Robinson* (1869), Vol. I, pp. 266–7. Robinson's letters to Catherine were published in 1849: Mrs Henry Coleridge (ed.), *Notes and Lectures on Shakespear*.

50. Barbara E. Rooke (ed.), *Collected Works of Samuel Taylor Coleridge, The Friend* (1969), Vol. I, pp. xxxvii–viii.

51. Clarkson's letters to Coleridge, Wordsworth Library, Grasmere, 6 December 1808 to 25 April 1809; Griggs, *Thomas Clarkson*, pp. 107–10.

52. De Selincourt, *Dorothy Wordsworth*, p. 245; D. Wordsworth to C. Clarkson, 8 December [1808], *Wordsworth Letters, Middle Years, Part I*, p. 282; same to same, 12 April 1810, ibid., p. 399; S. T. Coleridge to T. Smith, 22 June 1809, in Griggs (ed.), *Unpublished Letters*, Vol. II, p. 3;

William Knight, *Life of William Wordsworth* (1889), Vol. II, p. 184.

53. S. T. Coleridge to D. Stuart, [18 February 1809], in Griggs, *Unpublished Letters*, Vol. I, pp. 445–6. To Griggs, who studied both men, the correspondence provides insights into both the 'strange, unpractical poet' and the 'man of the world'. For all his genius, Coleridge was unsuccessful as a writer; his books went unsold and he relied on friends for support, while Clarkson, no match in literary talent, published three important works and made money on them: Griggs, *Thomas Clarkson*, p. 108.

54. T. Clarkson to S. T. Coleridge, 25 April 1809, Wordsworth Library; Griggs, *Thomas Clarkson*, p. 109.

55. Rooke (ed.), *Collected Works*, Vol. II, pp. 405–67; William A. Knight, *Memorials of Coleorton* (1887), Vol. II, p. 99, for S. T. Coleridge to Lady Beaumont, 21 January 1810.

56. S. T. Coleridge to Lady Beaumont, pp. 98–9, 105; A. S. Byatt, *Wordsworth and Coleridge in Their Time* (1970), pp. 213–14.

57. D. Wordsworth to C. Clarkson, 12 May [1811], *Wordsworth Letters, Middle Years, Part I*, pp. 485–91; de Selincourt, *Dorothy Wordsworth*, pp. 250ff., letters to C. Clarkson, May–December 1811; Byatt, *Wordsworth*, pp. 47–50.

58. C. Clarkson to H. C. Robinson, 15 May 1811, Henry Crabb Robinson Letters; same to same, 1 and 6 December 1811, ibid.

59. C. Clarkson to H. C. Robinson, [10 March 1813], ibid.; Edith J. Morley (ed.), *Correspondence of Henry Crabb Robinson with the Wordsworth Circle* (1927), Vol. I, p. 71; Knight, *Life of Wordsworth*, Vol. II, pp. 182–4.

60. C. Clarkson to H. C. Robinson, 23 March 1813, Henry Crabb Robinson Letters; Morley (ed.), *Correspondence*, Vol. I, pp. 73–6.

61. Griggs, *Thomas Clarkson*, p. 111; C. Clarkson to H. C. Robinson, 6 December 1811, 29 May 1812, [28 December] 1812, 25 November 1818, all Henry Crabb Robinson Letters.

62. Clarkson encouraged Hazlitt in his ambition to become a painter, as did several poets. His portraits of Lamb and Coleridge were said to be in Titian's manner, but he painted Wordsworth so dismally that he looked to Southey like a man at the gallows, 'deeply affected' but 'determined to die like a man' – Knight, *Life of Wordsworth*, Vol. II, p. 404. Clarkson brought him to Bury St Edmunds, where he also painted William Buck and Robinson's brother Thomas. The latter was so bad it was destroyed. Sadler (ed.), *Diary*, Vol. I, pp. 368 and n.; W. Hazlitt to T. Robinson, 11 July 1811, and C. Clarkson to H. C. Robinson, [21 July 1811], Henry Crabb Robinson Letters. The Hazlitt Clarkson was engraved by T. S. Engleheart and published in 1833.

12   Two Emperors

1. David Brion Davis, *Problem of Slavery in the Age of Revolution 1770–1823* (Ithaca, NY, 1975), pp. 67–8ff.; C. K. Webster, *Foreign Policy of Castlereagh 1815–1822* (1934), pp. 454ff.; Earl Leslie Griggs, *Thomas Clarkson the Friend of Slaves* (1936), p. 119; Lafayette to T.

Clarkson, 28 August 1815 in Melvin D. Kennedy, *Lafayette and Slavery from his Letters to Thomas Clarkson and Granville Sharp* (Easton, Pa., 1950), pp. 34–6.

2. C. Clarkson to S. Hutchinson, 14 January 1815, Clarkson Papers, BM Add Ms 41 267A. He was still studying French in 1821, according to D. Wordsworth to C. Clarkson, 27 March 1821, in Alan G. Hill (ed.), *Letters of William and Dorothy Wordsworth, Late Years, Part I* (Oxford, 1978), p. 52.

3. Webster, *Foreign Policy*, p. 89.

4. The Emperor's experiences with Quakers from *Life of William Allen* (1846), Vol. I, pp. 193–200, 204–5. An account of the visit to the Quaker family was circulated and copied into the Diary of Katherine Plymley, Corbett of Longnor Papers, Shropshire Record Office, Book 111.

5. Clarkson's 'Account of Efforts 1807–1824 to abolish the foreign slave trade and slavery in the British Colonies', [1838], p. 15, Clarkson Papers, Huntington Library, San Marino, California.

6. Clarkson's 1815 interview with Alexander, the first of two, was published in 1930 from a manuscript he prepared for friends to read. The published version includes a description of William Allen's audience: Thomas Clarkson, *Interviews with the Emperor Alexander I of Russia at Paris and Aix-la Chapelle in 1815 and 1818* (1930). It was published by the Slavery and Native Races Committee of the Society of Friends with a preface by Priscilla Peckover. The 1815 interview as described by Clarkson to Allen is also in *Life of Allen*, Vol. I, pp. 242–3 and in Clarkson's 'Account of Efforts'. Also see Griggs, *Thomas Clarkson*, pp. 119–20.

7. Events in Paris from T. Clarkson to C. Clarkson, 20 September 1815, Huntington Library.

8. Interview as in Note 6. Also Griggs, *Thomas Clarkson*, pp. 120–21. Three days later Alexander's treaty of 'Holy Alliance' was signed by Russia, Prussia and Austria. See Anthony Wood, *Nineteenth Century Britain 1815–1914*, 2nd edn (1982), p. 53.

9. For Haiti background, Earl Leslie Griggs and Clifford H. Prater (eds), *Henry Christophe and Thomas Clarkson, A Correspondence* (Berkeley, Calif., 1952); Hubert Cole, *Christophe: King of Haiti* (1967); Griggs, *Thomas Clarkson*, pp. 122–150.

10. Cole, *Christophe*, p. 252. Clarkson in 'Account of Efforts' says Henry first contacted him to send a subscription to the African Institution. Christophe would have been reassured by a connection with two prominent Englishmen for he was not secure. Pétion's neighbouring republic was hostile; the United States had cut off trade because of the southern-dominated Congress's repugnance to an 'independent nation of emancipated slaves'; Britain maintained commercial links but did not recognise Haiti's independence for fear of exposing its own colonies to the 'contagion of liberty'; in France, Henry was ridiculed. See William Goodell, *Slavery and Anti-Slavery: a History of the Great Struggle in Both Hemispheres* (New York, 1853), p. 268; Griggs and Prater, *Henry Christophe*, pp. 55, 61; Cole, *Christophe*,

p. 161; Griggs, *Thomas Clarkson*, pp. 125, 126.

11.   Robert Isaac Wilberforce and Samuel Wilberforce (eds), *Life of William Wilberforce*, 2nd edn (1839), Vol. IV, pp. 206, 356, 355, 354, 361; Vol. V, p. 108. The *Life* does not go deeply into Wilberforce's experience with Christophe and says nothing of Clarkson's collaboration. Robin Furneaux, *William Wilberforce* (1974), pp. 393–9; John Pollock, *Wilberforce* (1977), pp. 252–4. Robert Isaac Wilberforce and Samuel Wilberforce (eds), *Correspondence of William Wilberforce* (1840) prints 'Haytian Letters' in Vol. I, pp. 357–95, including one of 8 October 1818 from Wilberforce to King Henry.

12.   Griggs and Prater, *Henry Christophe*. It is also summarised with excerpts in Griggs, *Thomas Clarkson* and in Clarkson, 'Account of Efforts', pp. 27–109.

13.   Cole, *Christophe*, p. 230; *Life of Allen*, Vol. I, pp. 264, 268, 299–300, 301; Griggs and Prater, *Henry Christophe*, pp. 64, 66–7. There was a little friction between Wilberforce and Allen over the system to be sponsored. Wilberforce favoured the Church of England National School Society and managed to slip one of its teachers on to a ship for Haiti.

14.   Wilson seems to have been a tutor in the Biddell family, neighbours of the Clarksons at their new home at Playford Hall near Ipswich. Clarkson sent him an elaborate education plan. Griggs, *Thomas Clarkson*, p. 125; Griggs and Prater, *Henry Christophe*, pp. 66–7; T. Clarkson to Henry, 24 January 1820, Clarkson papers, BM Add Ms 41 266; T. Clarkson to W. Wilson, 6 September 1820; ibid.; T. Clarkson to W. Wilson, 8/9 September 1820, Clarkson Papers, St John's College Library, Cambridge University.

15.   T. Clarkson to Henry, 4 May 1816, BM Add Ms 41 266; Griggs, *Thomas Clarkson*, pp. 126–7.

16.   Cole, *Christophe*, p. 253; Griggs and Prater, *Henry Christophe*, p. 69.

17.   E. Lewis to T. Clarkson, 12 June 1816, Clarkson Papers, Huntington Library.

18.   [T. Clarkson to F. S. Key], 18 March 1817; F. S. Key to T. Clarkson, 3 November 1817; E. B. Caldwell to T. Clarkson, 10 November 1817, all Huntington Library.

19.   T. Clarkson to P. Sanders, 3 February 1819 and T. Clarkson to R. Vaux, 8 March 1819, Huntington Library.

20.   E. B. Caldwell to T. Clarkson, 10 November 1817; T. Clarkson to P. Sanders, 3 February 1819 and 'Account of Efforts', all Huntington Library; R. Vaux to T. Clarkson, 13 May 1819, Clarkson Papers, Moorland-Spingarn Research Center, Howard University, Washington, DC; Griggs, *Thomas Clarkson*, pp. 133–4. A list of places suitable for colonisation prepared by Clarkson is also in the Huntington archive. Although preferring that the freed blacks stay in the United States, Clarkson was not unfriendly to the idea of Africa and advised the American Colonization Society to send emissaries there to study the prospects. Samuel J. Mills and Ebenezer Burgess went and chose what became Liberia.

21.   T. Clarkson to [Alexander, January 1818] and 25 February 1818, drafts, BM Add Ms 41 266; Betty Fladeland, 'Abolitionist Pressures

and the Concert of Europe, 1814–1822', *Journal of Modern History*, XXXVIII (1966), 355-73; Griggs, *Thomas Clarkson*, pp. 153–4. Also a lucid account of the international congresses and the abolitionist issue in Reginald Coupland, *British Anti-Slavery Movement* (1933), pp. 372–5.

22. T. Clarkson to Lord Castlereagh, 30 September 1818, and 'Account of Efforts', both Huntington Library.

23. Wilberforce, *Life*, Vol. V, pp. 1–3. The quotation is from a letter to J. Stephen, p. 3. Furneaux, *Wilberforce*, errs in saying Wilberforce 'sent' Clarkson to Aix, p. 396.

24. T. Clarkson to W. Wilberforce, 14 August 1818, Wilberforce Papers, Wrangham Collection when consulted, now in Bodleian Library, Oxford University; T. Clarkson to C. Clarkson, 29 September 1818, BM Add Ms 41 267A; T. Clarkson to C. Clarkson, 3 October 1818, Huntington Library; Ellen Gibson Wilson, *John Clarkson and the African Adventure* (1980), pp. 168–70; Webster, *Foreign Policy*, pp. 131–2, 168, 454–6.

25. T. Clarkson to C. Clarkson, 29 September 1818.

26. T. Clarkson to C. Clarkson, 3 October 1818.

27. T. Clarkson to Lord Castlereagh, 5 October 1818, Huntington Library; Griggs, *Thomas Clarkson*, pp. 154–5.

28. *The Times*, 12, 16, 17 October 1818.

29. T. Clarkson to C. Clarkson, 7 October 1818, BM Add Ms 41 267A; Griggs, *Thomas Clarkson*, p. 155.

30. T. Clarkson to C. Clarkson, 7 October 1818; Griggs, *Thomas Clarkson*, pp. 155–6.

31. Account of interview based on T. Clarkson to C. Clarkson, 11 October 1818, Thomas Clarkson Collection, Trevor Arnett Library, Atlanta University; description of the 1818 interview in Clarkson Papers, Huntington Library; Thomas Clarkson, *Interviews with the Emperor*, pp. 18–32; Griggs, *Thomas Clarkson*, pp. 156–8.

32. Clarkson had sent the Emperor a prized letter from King Henry of 18 October 1816 to show the King's good character and intentions. Alexander in turn showed it to the King of Prussia and Emperor of Austria. According to Clarkson's note on the translation, their united opinion was that none of their own ministers could write a better letter. BM Add Ms 41 266. The Haiti letters in this volume of the Clarkson Papers are English drafts of Clarkson's letters and Henry's in French with translations.
     The Peace Society's Address is printed in the Appendix to its Third Annual Report (1819) along with one to the Prince Regent. Also see T. Clarkson to unknown, 3 November 1845, Clarkson Papers, Reference Department, Ipswich Borough Libraries; Webster, *Foreign Policy*, p. 89.

33. Clarkson's Address for Verona was published as *Cries of Africa, to the Inhabitants of Europe; or, a Survey of that Bloody Commerce Called the Slave-Trade* (?1823); Griggs, *Thomas Clarkson*, p. 158; Coupland, *Wilberforce*, p. 374.

34. *Life of Allen*, Vol. II, pp. 240, 243, 257–62, 264–6, 279, 284–7. Allen also

met the Emperor at St Petersburg where he went to promote schools, a journey Clarkson had explained to Alexander at Aix. British diplomats believed that the Emperor's sponsorship of anti-slave-trade efforts was designed to embarrass the colonial maritime powers at little cost to himself.

35. Plymley Diary, Book 117.
36. T. Clarkson to W. Wilberforce, 15 June 1819, Department of Rare Books, Olin Library, Cornell University, Ithaca, NY.
37. Instructions to Thomas Clarkson, 21 November 1819, BM Add Ms 41 266.
38. Griggs and Prater, *Henry Christophe*, pp. 71–3; Griggs, *Thomas Clarkson*, pp. 135–40.
39. 'Accounts of Efforts'; F. Turckheim to T. Clarkson, 21 February and 4 April 1820, Howard University; Griggs, *Thomas Clarkson*, pp. 140–41.
40. T. Clarkson to Henry, 10 July 1820, BM Add Ms 41 266; Griggs, *Thomas Clarkson*, pp. 141–2, 143.
41. G. Clarke to T. Clarkson, 4 November 1820; W. Wilson to T. Clarkson, 5 December 1820 and 30 January 1822, BM Add Ms 41 266. The teachers' accounts varied slightly. Wilson sent a bundle of papers found strewn on the floor of the pillaged palace. He said the Haitians had some grounds for complaint; though they owed their freedom and good order to Henry, he had become an autocrat and the first to break his own good laws. Griggs and Prater, *Henry Christophe*, pp. 73–6.
42. The Christophes had only their jewellery, which they sold, and £5700 remaining from the £6000 letter of credit Henry had sent Clarkson for his 'ambassadorship'. Plymley Diary, Book 130; Cole, *Christophe*, p. 275; Griggs, *Thomas Clarkson*, p. 144.
43. Griggs and Prater, *Henry Christophe*, pp. 78–9.
44. W. B. Pope (ed.), *Diary of Benjamin Robert Haydon* (Cambridge, Mass., 1960), Vol. V, p. 42; Griggs, *Thomas Clarkson*, p. 147.
45. T. Clarkson to Z. Macaulay, 31 January 1822; C. Clarkson to Z. Macaulay, 21 March 1823, both Macaulay Papers, Huntington Library; Griggs and Prater, *Henry Christophe*, pp. 38, 245.
46. T. Clarkson to Z. Macaulay, 19 November 1821, Macaulay Papers, Huntington; Griggs and Prater, *Henry Christophe*, pp. 237–40; Griggs, *Thomas Clarkson*, pp. 144–6.
47. T. Clarkson to Z. Macaulay, 8 April 1822, Macaulay Papers, Huntington Library. Clarkson kept meticulous accounts so when Sutherland gave him £150 for the guests' extra expenses, he returned the balance over the £103 he had reckoned up. This was for such things as extra laundry, hire of carriages and music and drawing lessons for the girls.
48. H. C. Robinson to D. Wordsworth, 6 July 1821, Henry Crabb Robinson Letters, Dr Williams's Library. Some of Clarkson's friends could scarcely credit Alexander's sincerity as described by Clarkson, but neither could they see why the Tsar of all the Russias should flatter an 'ordinary' man like Clarkson by saying what he did not believe. T. Robinson to Hab Robinson, 6 January 1819, Henry Crabb

Robinson Letters. Henry Robinson decided that Clarkson, at least, was a 'sincere believer in the Emperor's sincerity'. Thomas Sadler (ed.), *Diary, Reminiscences, and Correspondence of Henry Crabb Robinson* (1869), Vol. II, p. 118.

49. T. Clarkson to Z. Macaulay, 31 January 1822, Macaulay Papers, Huntington Library; Griggs and Prater, *Henry Christophe*, p. 245; T. Clarkson to Z. Macaulay, 19 November 1821, Huntington; W. Wilson to C. Clarkson, 12 November 1821, BM Add Ms 41 266.

50. Clarkson was anxious that Sutherland not be in full charge of the Christophes' affairs and urged that Wilberforce control their funds, acting as the '*Head* of our cause' and 'their Protector & Guardian'. T. Clarkson to Z. Macaulay, 18 December 1821, Macaulay Papers, Huntington Library.

51. W. Wilberforce to C. Clarkson, 11 March 1822, BM Add Ms 41 266; Furneaux, *Wilberforce*, pp. 398–9.

52. Pollock, *Wilberforce*, p. 254. Wilberforce's apparent reluctance to get involved with the Christophes does not square with his reputation for generosity, but Furneaux, *Wilberforce*, p. 51 calls attention to the death of a daughter in 1821.

53. *East Anglian Daily Times*, 11 February 1986, 'The First Flight from Haiti – to Rural Suffolk', on the occasion of Duvalier's flight to Europe.

54. Plymley Diary, Book 131.

55. D. Wordsworth to C. Clarkson, 24 October 1821, *Wordsworth Letters, Late Years, Part I*, pp. 87–91; Griggs, *Thomas Clarkson*, pp. 147–9.

56. The poem is printed in both sources in Note 55 but is not in Wordsworth's collected works. Mrs Wilberforce called her husband 'Wilby'.

57. D. Wordsworth to C. Clarkson, 16 January [1822], *Wordsworth Letters, Late Years, Part I*, p. 103; S. Hutchinson to M. Monkhouse, 22 February 1822 in Kathleen Coburn (ed.), *Letters of Sara Hutchinson from 1800 to 1835* (1954), pp. 238–9. Sara Hutchinson thought that Catherine probably would not show the poem to her husband.

58. Letters from the Christophes to C. Clarkson, 26 October 1822 and 13 September 1824, BM Add Ms 41 266; Griggs and Prater, *Henry Christophe*, pp. 247, 254.

59. M. F. Smith to C. Clarkson, 24 November 1840, BM Add Ms 41 266; C. Clarkson to W. Wilson, 4 March 1833, 14 February 1841 and 22 February 1842, St John's College Library. Sir Robert and Lady Inglis were guardians of Henry Thornton's children after both parents died in 1815. The Christophes lived for a time near Clapham and the Thornton daughters became their friends.

13 The Slaves Set Free

1. T. Clarkson to C. Clarkson, 3 October 1818, Clarkson Papers, Huntington Library, San Marino, California.

2. Correspondence between T. Clarkson, J. Cutting and A. Biddell, 19 May to 16 June 1815, Suffolk Record Office, Ipswich, HD 494;

Thomas Sadler (ed.), *Diary, Reminiscences, and Correspondence of Henry Crabb Robinson* (1869), Vol. II, pp. 15–16. Lord Bristol's seat was Ickworth just outside Bury St Edmunds. A Whig grandee, he owned more than 30 000 acres in four counties. He was a cultivated man, a fellow Johnian and known to Clarkson as least from 1810 when Clarkson brought his African treasure chest to dinner. *Journals of the Hon William Hervey ... from 1756 to 1814* (Bury St Edmunds, 1906), p. 489. Almost 20 years later Clarkson's rent was referred to as £360. S. Hutchinson to Mrs Hutchinson, [4 March 1834] in Kathleen Coburn (ed.), *Letters of Sara Hutchinson from 1800 to 1835* (1954), p. 406.

3. Herman Biddell Ms, 'Thomas Clarkson and Playford Hall, Reminiscences and Recollections...', Reference Department, Ipswich Borough Libraries; T. Clarkson to A. Biddell, 28 July [1815], Suffolk Record Office, Ipswich; Henry Crabb Robinson Diary, 4 April 1820, Dr Williams's Library.

4. Playford poem by Barton, *People's Journal*, II (1847), 220. He wrote other verses about Playford and at least two poems about Clarkson, 'The Starting Post, or Clarkson at Wade's Mill' and 'The Goal; or Clarkson in Old Age'. He lived at Woodbridge, 4 miles away, as did Clarkson's brother John and family. Barton, son of an original member of the Abolition Committee, is best known as a correspondent of Charles Lamb, to whom the Clarksons introduced him.

5. T. Clarkson to A. Biddell, 18 August 1815, Suffolk Record Office, Ipswich.

6. Maud Gross, Suffolk Moated Houses, Book II, bound Ms, Woodbridge Library; Benjamin Stanton, 'A Rambler in England from America', *New York American* (1840), copy in Wisbech and Fenland Museum with Clarkson Papers. Stanton was thrilled to find that parts of Clarkson's home dated to 1492 when America was discovered. W. A. Copinger, *Manors of Suffolk: Notes on their History and Devolution* (1905), Vol. III, pp. 86–92; Sadler (ed.), *Diary*, Vol. II, pp. 15–16.

7. Ibid., p. 1.

8. D. Wordsworth to C. Clarkson, 11 April 1815, in Mary Moorman and Alan G. Hill (eds), *Letters of William and Dorothy Wordsworth, Middle Years, Part II* (Oxford, 1970), p. 231; same to same, 16 October 1817, ibid., p. 400.

9. T. Clarkson to A. Biddell, 30 May and 3 June 1820, Suffolk Record Office, Ipswich; R. Southey to C. W. W. Wynn, 25 January 1823 in John Wood Warter, *Selections from the Letters of Robert Southey* (1856), Vol. III, p. 374; T. Clarkson to Lord Bristol, 14 June 1830, Suffolk Record Office, Bury St Edmunds, 941/56/51; Diary of Katherine Plymley, Corbett of Longnor Papers, Shropshire Record Office, Book 130; C. Clarkson to D. Wordsworth, [25 December 1825], Wordsworth Library, Grasmere; D. Wordsworth to C. Clarkson, 16 January 1822 in Alan G. Hill (ed.), *Letters of William and Dorothy Wordsworth, Later Years, Part I* (Oxford, 1978), pp. 103–4; C. Clarkson to H. C. Robinson, 25 December 1845, Henry Crabb Robinson

Letters, Dr Williams's Library; Biddell, 'Thomas Clarkson', p. 22.
10. S. Hutchinson to T. Monkhouse, [17 January] and 22 February [1818], in Coburn (ed.), *Letters*, pp. 116, 126.
11. S. Hutchinson to T. Monkhouse, 25 January [1818], in Coburn (ed.), *Letters*, p. 118.
12. Henry Crabb Robinson Diary, 6 April 1820 and 24 October 1824; D. Wordsworth to T. Monkhouse, 14 December 1820, *Wordsworth Letters, Middle Years, Part II*, p. 655; C. Clarkson to H. C. Robinson, 17 January 1824, Henry Crabb Robinson Letters; C. Clarkson to D. Wordsworth, [25 December 1825]; Biddell, 'Thomas Clarkson', p. 54; S. Hutchinson to Mrs Hutchinson, [1 April 1834], in Coburn (ed.), *Letters*, p. 410. Thomas Clarkson completed the occupation section of the 1841 census form as 'Independent'.
13. H. C. Robinson to D. Wordsworth, 6 July 1821, Henry Crabb Robinson Letters; Lafayette to T. Clarkson, 15 February and 16 September 1821 in Melvin D. Kennedy, *Lafayette and Slavery from His Letters to Thomas Clarkson and Granville Sharp* (Easton, Pa., 1950), pp. 37, 39; C. Clarkson to H. C. Robinson, [19 May 1821] and 17 January 1824, Henry Crabb Robinson Letters; D. Wordsworth to C. Clarkson, 31 May and 25 August 1821, *Wordsworth Letters, Later Years, Part I*, pp. 61, 72–3; T. Clarkson to R. Southey, 10 April 1824, Clarkson Papers, St John's College Library, Cambridge University.
14. S. Hutchinson to T. Monkhouse, 30 January and [28 February] 1818, in Coburn (ed.), *Letters*, pp. 120, 126–7; Henry Crabb Robinson Diary, 6 and 28 February, 16 March 1818; C. Clarkson to H. C. Robinson, 15 January 1818, Henry Crabb Robinson Letters. Clarkson enrolled Tom as a member of Middle Temple while he was still at university, according to T. Clarkson to S. Tillbrook, 29 October 1816, Thomas Clarkson folder, Wilberforce Papers, Wilberforce House, Hull.
15. C. Clarkson to D. Wordsworth, 16 March 1818, Wordsworth Library.
16. Henry Crabb Robinson Diary, 8 April 1818.
17. Ibid., 26 October 1816.
18. C. Clarkson to H. C. Robinson, 15 January 1818, 14 December 1819, 17 February 1820, all Henry Crabb Robinson Letters.
19. C. Clarkson to H. C. Robinson, 19 May 1821, ibid.
20. Henry Crabb Robinson Diary, 5 April 1825; T. Clarkson to R. Spence, 25 June 1825, HM 33541 and same to same, 14 April 1825, HM 33540, both Huntington Library, San Marino, California; T. Clarkson to T. Mounsey, 30 June 1826, Mss Portfolio 24, Library of the Religious Society of Friends.
21. Henry Crabb Robinson Diary, 22 June 1836; Lord Brougham to W. Wilberforce, December 1831, Wilberforce Papers, Wrangham Collection when consulted, now in Bodleian Library, Oxford University. Correspondence between Clarkson and Lord Brougham over a place for Tom, Brougham Papers, University College, 14 January 1834–2 April 1836 *passim*. Brougham's patronage extended to the offspring of Smith, Romilly and Macaulay, among others.
22. Ellen Gibson Wilson, *John Clarkson and the African Adventure* (1980),

p. 154; C. Clarkson to unknown, 9 February 1812, Clarkson Papers, BM Add Ms 41 267A; C. Clarkson to H. C. Robinson, 28 March 1826, Henry Crabb Robinson Letters; Henry Crabb Robinson Diary, 22 May 1829.

23.   D. Wordsworth to H. C. Robinson, 6 January 1827 in Edith J. Morley (ed.), *Correspondence of Henry Crabb Robinson with the Wordsworth Circle 1808–1866* (Oxford, 1927), Vol. I, p. 174.

24.   Wilson, *John Clarkson*, p. 173, 175–6. John Brassey Clarkson died 9 November 1824. Emma was buried 27 August 1825.

25.   Ibid., pp. 183, 184; C. Clarkson to H. C. Robinson, 5 August 1828, Henry Crabb Robinson Letters.

26.   C. Clarkson to D. Wordsworth, [30 July 1831], Wordsworth Library.

27.   D. Wordsworth to C. Clarkson, 27 March 1821 in *Wordsworth Letters, Later Years, Part I*, p. 51; Edith J. Morley (ed.), *Henry Crabb Robinson on Books and their Writers* (1938), Vol. I, p. 35; Requisition for a meeting of freeholders to support reform in Parliament, 1831, Suffolk Record Office, Bury St Edmunds, E 3/29; T. Clarkson to Lord Brougham, 18 August 1825, Brougham Papers, No. 36 224; *Suffolk Chronicle*, 3 February 1821.

28.   W. Wordsworth to Lord Lonsdale, 11 March 1818, *Wordsworth Letters, Middle Years, Part II*, pp. 437, 448–9n.

29.   W. Wordsworth to Lord Lonsdale, 18 February [1818] in ibid., p. 432.

30.   D. Wordsworth to C. Clarkson, 30 March [1818], ibid., pp. 453–6.

31.   S. Hutchinson to T. Monkhouse, 6 and 22 February and 13 April 1818, in Coburn (ed.), *Letters*, pp. 122, 125, 132.

32.   C. Clarkson to H. C. Robinson, 31 March 1821, in Morley (ed.), *Correspondence*, Vol. I, p. 101.

33.   Thomas Clarkson, *History of the Rise, Progress and Accomplishment of the Abolition of the African Slave-Trade* (1808), Vol. II, p. 586.

34.   William Goodell, *Slavery and Anti-Slavery: a History of the Great Struggle in Both Hemispheres* (New York, 1853), p. 354.

35.   Minute Book of the Committee on Slavery, 1823–1825, Anti-Slavery Papers, Rhodes House Library, Oxford, Mss Brit. Emp. S, E 2/1, for 31 January 1823; *Life of William Allen* (1846), Vol. II, p. 326. Allen said a majority on the organising committee were Friends. Clarkson was put on subcommittees for publications, home correspondence and finance.

36.   David Brion Davis, *Problem of Slavery in the Age of Revolution 1770–1823* (Ithaca, NY, 1975), p. 311, n. 43. Davis notes there was no American counterpart for the continuity of leadership in the British movement from the 1790s into the 1820s.

37.   Robert Isaac Wilberforce and Samuel Wilberforce (eds), *Life of William Wilberforce*, 2nd edn (1839), Vol. V, pp. 233–9; Sir George Stephen, *Antislavery Recollections: in a Series of Letters Addressed to Mrs Beecher Stowe* (1854), p. 78; Charles Buxton (ed.), *Memoirs of Sir Thomas Fowell Buxton*, new edn (1860), pp. 59, 62; Davis, *Problem of Slavery*, pp. 236–7.

38.   Thomas Clarkson, 'Account of Efforts 1807–1824 to Abolish the Foreign Slave Trade and Slavery in the British Colonies' [1838],

Clarkson Papers, Huntington Library, p. 110; *Life of Allen*, Vol. II, pp. 325–6. The Duke of Gloucester became president, Clarkson a vice-president.

39. Z. Macaulay to C. Clarkson, 14 March 1823, Clarkson Papers, BM Add Ms 41 267A; Earl Leslie Griggs, *Thomas Clarkson the Friend of Slaves* (1936), p. 162; Clarkson, 'Account of Efforts', pp. 113–14; T. Clarkson to Z. Macaulay, 30 March 1823, Macaulay Papers, Huntington Library.

40. *Thoughts* was published in instalments in the *Inquirer* in March 1823 and as a pamphlet, in two editions.

41. Goodell, *Slavery*, pp. 356–7; T. Clarkson to ?W. Wilberforce [1815], Clarkson Papers, Huntington Library; Davis, *Problem of Slavery*, p. 419 and n. 58. Granville Sharp had pioneered the position that slavery was illegal. T. Clarkson to T. F. Buxton, 4 March 1823, Clarkson Papers, Moorland-Spingarn Research Center, Howard University, Washington, DC. T. Clarkson to Z. Macaulay, 30 March 1823, and Speech used in forming the committee in 1823 and 1824, both Macaulay Papers, Huntington.

42. *Memoirs of Buxton*, p. 64; Roger Anstey, 'Religion and British Slave Emancipation', in D. Eltis and James Walvin (eds), *Abolition of the Atlantic Slave Trade* (Madison, Wis., 1981), p. 38; Howard Temperley, *British Antislavery 1833–1870* (1972), p. 11.

43. Z.Macaulay to C. Clarkson, 31 March 1823, BM Add Ms 41 267A.

44. T. Clarkson to Z. Macaulay, 13 April 1823, Macaulay Papers, Huntington Library.

45. T. Clarkson to Z. Macaulay, 19 May 1823, ibid.

46. K. Charlton, 'James Cropper and Liverpool's Contribution to the Anti-Slavery Movement', *Transactions of the Historic Society of Lancashire and Cheshire for 1971*, CXXIII (1972), pp. 57–61; David Brion Davis, *Slavery and Human Progress* (Oxford, 1984), pp. 180–83; Anstey, 'Religion', p. 37.

47. Clarkson, 'Account of Efforts', p. 112; T. Clarkson to Z. Macaulay, 8 June 1823, Macaulay Papers, Huntington Library, Minute Book of Committee on Slavery, 9 June 1823.

48. Ibid., 20 June 1824; *Life of Allen*, Vol. II, p. 383. The highlight of the meeting, Allen said, was an eloquent seconding speech by Macaulay's son, Thomas Babington, a young MP.

49. Clarkson, 'Account of Efforts', p. 113. A part of Clarkson's MS journal of the tour survives: Diary of Travels, 30 June 1823 to 26 February 1824 and 28 June 1824 to 11 November 1824, National Library of Wales, covering the western English counties and Wales. Clarkson found a division between the large trading towns, keen to agitate, and rural strongholds with a strong inclination to wait and see what government would do. High churchmen and high Tories would not do anything. He angrily termed mid-Wales *'half a century behind'* South Wales and a 'CENTURY behind' England.

50. Clarkson's Ms Diary of Travels, 21 August 1824.

51. Plymley Diary, Book 130; D. Wordsworth to C. Clarkson, 11/12 November 1823, *Wordsworth Letters, Later Years, Part I*, p. 229.

52. Clarkson, 'Account of Efforts', p. 116; T. Clarkson to W. Smith, 12 August 1824 and 18 July 1826, Clarkson Papers, William R. Perkins Library, Duke University, Durham, NC; Plymley Diary, Book 135; T. Clarkson to W. Stevens, 11 January 1826, Duke University. When the West Indian legislatures made clear they would do nothing to improve conditions, much less emancipate slaves, Clarkson turned again to the sugar boycott, urging that the English people abstain from West Indian sugar to show their abhorrence for slavery. T. Clarkson to Mrs Townsend, August 1825, extract of a letter, John Rylands University Library, Manchester, English Ms 741/20.

53. Griggs, *Thomas Clarkson*, pp. 164–5; Robin Furneaux, *William Wilberforce* (1974), p. 442; Reginald Coupland, *Wilberforce* (Oxford, 1923), p. 418.

54. About 250 of the petitions came from Suffolk under Clarkson's direction. Among other innovations, women were mobilised and in 1833 a monster petition signed by 187 000 of them was borne into the Commons by four MPs. There are many sources for this lively period, including William A. Green, *British Slave Emancipation: The Sugar Colonies and the Great Experiment 1830–1865* (Oxford, 1976), pp. 111–12; Davis, *Slavery and Human Progress*, pp. 186, 347, n. 131; Temperley, *British Antislavery*, pp. 12–13; Anstey, 'Religion', pp. 46, 47, 48; *Memoirs of Buxton*, p. 152. Also Anti-Slavery Society circular letter, 1 October 1830, Wedgwood Manuscripts, Keele University Library; T. Clarkson to R. Spence, 27 October, HM 33543, Huntington Library.

55. Green, *British Slave Emancipation*, pp. 114–18; Jack Gratus, *Great White Lie: Slavery, Emancipation and Changing Racial Attitudes* (1973), p. 214 calls it the 'last great slave sale'.

56. T. Clarkson to W. Smith, 1 September 1833, Duke University; quoted in Edith F. Hurwitz, *Politics and the Public Conscience* (1973), pp. 174–5.

57. T. F. Buxton to T. Clarkson, 20 August 1833, quoted in Frank J. Klingberg, *Anti-Slavery Movement in England* (New Haven, 1926), p. 301; T. Clarkson to T. F. Buxton, 25 September 1833, Clarkson Papers, Huntington Library.

14 The Wilberforce Affair

1. W. Wilberforce to T. Clarkson, 19 January 1833, Rare Books and Manuscripts, Boston Public Library, Ms Eng 183(75).

2. C. Clarkson to W. Smith, 18 August 1834, Clarkson Papers, William R. Perkins Library, Duke University, Durham, NC.

3. C. Clarkson to D. Wordsworth, [27 November 1833], Clarkson Letters, Wordsworth Library, Grasmere.

4. T. Clarkson to W. Smith, 1 September 1833, Duke University. Smith was to die in 1835 at 79 and Richard Phillips in 1836 at age 80. T. Clarkson to R. Southey, 10 April 1824, Clarkson Papers, St John's College Library, Cambridge University; T. Clarkson to Lord

Brougham, December 1835, Brougham Papers, University College, No. 36 228.

5. C. Clarkson to D. Wordsworth, [27 November 1833]; C. Clarkson to H. C. Robinson, 13 August 1832, Henry Crabb Robinson Letters, Dr Williams's Library.

6. C. Clarkson to D. Wordsworth, [30 July 1831], Wordsworth Library; H. C. Robinson Diary, 15 November 1832, Dr Williams's Library; H. C. Robinson to Mrs Finch, 4 December 1832, H. C. Robinson Letters.

7. It was called *Researches Anti-Diluvian, Patriarchal, and Historical, concerning the way in which men first acquired their knowledge of God . . .* (1836). S. Hutchinson to Mrs Hutchinson, [4 March], 1 April 1834, in Kathleen Coburn (ed.), *Letters of Sara Hutchinson from 1800 to 1835* (1954), p. 409.

8. S. Hutchinson to Mrs Hutchinson, [4 March 1834], in Coburn (ed.), *Letters*, p. 405.

9. D. Wordsworth to C. Clarkson, 19 December [1819], Mary Moorman and Alan G. Hill (eds), *Letters of William and Dorothy Wordsworth, Middle Years, Part II* (Oxford, 1970), p. 572; S. Hutchinson to Mrs Hutchinson, [1 April 1834], in Coburn (ed.), *Letters*, p. 408.

10. T. Clarkson to Lord Brougham, 1 June 1834, Brougham Papers, University College; S. Hutchinson to Mary, 27 May 1834, in Coburn (ed.), *Letters*, p. 415; C. Clarkson to H. C. Robinson, 10 May 1834, Henry Crabb Robinson Letters. Sara Hutchinson was in London at the same time to have a set of false teeth made. She reported Tyrell's charge for the cataract operation was 50 guineas plus a 'compliment' for subsequent attendance and Clarkson gave 75 guineas.

11. T. Clarkson to Earl of Bristol, 7 July 1834, Suffolk Record Office, Bury St Edmunds, 941/56/89.

12. T. Clarkson to R. Spence, 17 July 1836, Huntington Library, San Marino, California, HM 33544; T. Clarkson to Earl of Bristol, 2 August 1835, Suffolk Record Office, Bury St Edmunds, 941/56/29.

13. Ibid.; T. Clarkson to J. Grahame, 4 August 1836, Clarkson Papers, Moorland-Spingarn Research Center, Howard University, Washington, DC.

14. The *Essay on Baptism* was published in 1843. T. Clarkson to – – Clarkson, 5 May 1843, letter owned by St Paul's School; Thomas Sadler (ed.), *Diary, Reminiscences and Correspondence of Henry Crabb Robinson* (1869), Vol. III, p. 180.

15. W. Wordsworth to H. C. Robinson, 24 June 1835, in Alan G. Hill (ed.), *Letters of William and Dorothy Wordsworth, Later Years, Part III* (Oxford, 1982), p. 65; Edith J. Morley (ed.), *Correspondence of Henry Crabb Robinson with the Wordsworth Circle 1808–1866* (Oxford, 1927), Vol. I, p. 277; W. Wordsworth to C. Clarkson, 6 August 1835, *Wordsworth Letters, Later Years, Part III*, pp. 83–4; C. Clarkson to W. Wordsworth, 21 August 1835, Wordsworth Library.

16. Ernest de Selincourt, *Dorothy Wordsworth* (Oxford, 1933, reprint 1965), pp. 380–87; C. Clarkson to H. C. Robinson, 23 October 1833, in

Sadler (ed.), *Diary*, Vol. III, p. 35. Catherine also said Dorothy's letters contained the history of the Wordsworth family. 'I felt compelled to destroy some of them but many of them are too good to be hastily disposed of.'

17. *Gentleman's Magazine* (1837), pp. 443–4.
18. T. Clarkson to Lord Brougham, 12 March 1837, Brougham Papers, no. 36 232.
19. C. Clarkson to H. C. Robinson, 5 September 1837, Henry Crabb Robinson Letters.
20. Henry Crabb Robinson Diary, 9–16 March 1837. It would appear the woman companion was not killed.
21. T. Clarkson to R. Wilberforce, 27 August 1833 and same to same, n.d. (after August), both Wilberforce Papers, Wrangham Collection when consulted, now Bodleian Library, Oxford University. Clarkson saved relatively few papers, for unlike Wilberforce he had not arranged for a biography to be written. He did not keep, for example, the voluminous correspondence he engaged in while travelling for months in each of the early years. The Wilberforce brothers were 5 and 2 when the *History* was published. None of the letters Clarkson sent was used.

   For the Wilberforce controversy, see Earl Leslie Griggs, *Thomas Clarkson, the Friend of Slaves* (1936), pp. 169–81. Recent biographies of Wilberforce have skirted the issue as it did not, of course, involve Wilberforce, but both Robin Furneaux, *William Wilberforce* (1974), p. 442n and John Pollock, *Wilberforce* (1977), p. 55, are critical of the sons' behaviour. Among other sources, Sadler (ed.), *Diary*, Vol. III, pp. 152–3, 157–60; John Milton Baker, *Henry Crabb Robinson of Bury, Jena, The Times and Russell Square* (1937), pp. 225–35; Standish Meacham, *Lord Bishop, the Life of Samuel Wilberforce 1805–1873* (Cambridge, Mass., 1970), pp. 37–8 and n. 50; Edith J. Morley, *Life and Times of Henry Crabb Robinson* (1935), pp. 111–15.
22. T. Clarkson to S. Wilberforce, 22 May 1835, Wilberforce Manuscripts, Bodleian Library, c 7 f 104.
23. Z. Macaulay to R. Wilberforce, 8 October 1833, Wilberforce Manuscripts, Bodleian Library, d 14 f 67a. Clarkson's letters to Macaulay frequently refer in respectful, even flattering terms to Wilberforce, examples of Clarkson's complete lack of vanity. For instance, 18 September 1821 (Macaulay Papers, Huntington Library), where Clarkson responds to an inquiry whether his name should appear on a pamphlet he helped to write for circulation in France. Clarkson doubted he was as well-known abroad as many imagined. Wilberforce's name would be recognised as the 'Head of our Cause', and a man of highest moral character, but he had not written it. Macaulay was free to use Clarkson's name if it would be 'of *any use*'. Macaulay and other Evangelicals were hostile to the Clarksons in Sierra Leone matters, yet he and Clarkson were able to ignore their differences in the antislavery campaign.
24. J. Stephen to R. Wilberforce, 25 September 1833, Wrangham Collec-

tion. Stephen was now legal counsel in the Colonial Office. The DNB article on Clarkson notes Stephen's involvement in the controversy.

Clarkson's *History*, far from excluding any co-workers, was crammed to bursting with names, most of them totally unknown since. An interesting collection of autographs is based on it and held in the Library of the Religious Society of Friends, called the Thompson Clarkson Collection, three volumes of letters, portraits and biographical notices of persons mentioned in the *History*. It was formed by Thomas Thompson of Liverpool and indexed by his daughters. Thompson married a daughter of James Phillips, who supplied much of the material.

25. T. Clarkson to W. Wilberforce, 20 November 1814, Wrangham Collection; C. Clarkson to H. C. Robinson, 15 May 1835, Henry Crabb Robinson Letters; C. Clarkson to Wordsworths, [1834, wrongly labelled 1838], Wordsworth Library; W. Wordsworth to H. C. Robinson, 8 June [1840] in Alan G. Hill (ed.), *Letters of William and Dorothy Wordsworth, Later Years, Part IV* (Oxford, 1988), pp. 83–5; C. Clarkson to W. Smith, 18 August 1834, Duke University. Clarkson advertised his *History* as history and biography. He had been urged by friends to write his own experiences while in the Lakes but for unknown reasons did not begin until the battle was nearly over. The Clarksons read Stephen's *Crisis of the Sugar Colonies* while living at Eusemere and were impressed by it. Clarkson admitted the shortcomings of the *History* but denied it was factually inaccurate or misrepresented the story it told.

26. T. Gisborne to R. Wilberforce, 10 October 1833, Wrangham Collection.

27. 'Copy of my letter to Clarkson', 31 October 1833, Wrangham Collection.

28. A rough, much altered draft of a letter from R. Wilberforce to T. Clarkson, 26 July 1834, Wilberforce Manuscripts, Bodleian Library, c 7 f 73, quoted in C. Clarkson to W. Smith, 26 July 1834, Duke University.

29. C. Clarkson to Wordsworths, [1834, wrongly marked 1838], Wordsworth Library.

30. T. Clarkson to R. Wilberforce, 12 August 1834, Wilberforce Manuscripts, Bodleian Library, c 7 f 94. Clarkson had six copies of his reply printed to give to friends and one is attached to C. Clarkson to W. Smith, [9 September 1834], Duke University.

31. Draft letter to T. Clarkson, n.d., Wilberforce Manuscripts, Bodleian Library, c 7 f 98, quoted in full in C. Clarkson to W. Smith, [9 September 1834].

32. C. Clarkson to W. Smith, [9 September 1834].

33. Robert Isaac Wilberforce and Samuel Wilberforce (eds), *Life of William Wilberforce* (1838). The Wilberforces refused to use Clarkson's record of events as a source or any of his writings and brushed aside the corroborating testimony of persons such as Smith and Corbett who were close to events, although their letters were

requested by the Wilberforces (W. Smith to C. Clarkson, [August 1834], Duke University). The reason given was that they were simply writing a biography, not a history of abolition. Reading it aloud to Clarkson, Catherine found it 'amusing' to see the pains taken to keep Clarkson out, considering the documents they had to work with (C. Clarkson to H. C. Robinson, 2 August 1843, Henry Crabb Robinson Letters).

34. *Edinburgh Review*, LXVII (April 1838), 142–80; (October 1838), 188–90, a review of *Strictures* which corrected the claim that Clarkson undervalued Wilberforce and the statement that he was paid by the Committee, and endorsed Clarkson's place as first in the field. Stephen, however, repeated his allegation that Clarkson was paid ('a reasonable salary') by the Abolition Committee in his *Essays in Ecclesiastical Biography* (1849), Vol. II, p. 245. Clarkson is not named in the snide passage which makes light of Clarkson's work. Patronisingly, he suggests that Clarkson be given 'love and honour' and Wilberforce immortality. This continues down the years. Leslie Stephen in his DNB article on Wilberforce says the Committee 'employed Clarkson to collect evidence'.

35. H. C. Robinson Diary, 13 July 1839; T. Clarkson to A. Haldane, 21 May 1838, author's autograph collection. Wordsworth's sonnet, 'To Thomas Clarkson', was written in March 1807 but only printed in a collection of sonnets in 1838, enraging the Wilberforce children and their cousin Stephen. Thomas Noon Talfourd's *Letters of Charles Lamb with a Sketch of His Life* was published in 1837. Stephen disputed both. Wordsworth defended his statement that Clarkson 'first led forth that enterprise sublime' and said that if Clarkson did not reckon it worthwhile to maintain his claim, Wordsworth would provide the evidence. Morley, *Life and Times*, pp. 114–15. Wordsworth called the *Life* an example of 'idolatrous biography': W. Wordsworth to T. Powell, 9 June [1838], *Wordsworth Letters, Later Years, Part III*, p. 596.

36. Clarkson, *Strictures*, p. v; T. Clarkson to Lord Brougham, n.d., Brougham Papers, no. 1000. The full title is *Strictures on a Life of William Wilberforce by the Rev W. (sic) Wilberforce and the Rev. S. Wilberforce. With a Correspondence between Lord Brougham and Mr Clarkson; also a Supplement containing remarks on the Edinburgh Review of Mr Wilberforce's Life.*

37. C. Clarkson to H. C. Robinson, 6 November 1838, Henry Crabb Robinson Letters.

38. Henry Crabb Robinson Diary, 19 and 22 August and ff., recording comments by the *Sunday Times* (quoted), *Chronicle, Sun, Courier, Bury Post, Record, Globe, Patriot, Morning Herald* and even *The Age* which Robinson described as 'virulently Tory'. C. Clarkson to C. Hanbury, 29 August 1838, Temp Mss 416/17, Library of the Religious Society of Friends.

39. — — to W. Wordsworth, [30 September 1838], Wordsworth Library; Henry Crabb Robinson Diary, 13 November 1838 and 24 February 1839.

40. Ibid., 7 April 1839; C. Clarkson to H. C. Robinson, 9 October 1838, Henry Crabb Robinson Letters.

41. The Room portrait was exhibited at the Royal Academy 1839. Thomas Taylor, *Biographical Sketch of Thomas Clarkson, MA, with Occasional Brief Strictures on the Misrepresentations of Him Contained in the Life of William Wilberforce . . .* (1839). Taylor calls it a brief sketch of abolition's 'great originator'.

42. *The Times,* 29 November 1838; Henry Crabb Robinson Diary 28 and 29 November 1838; 24 February and 11 April 1839.

43. Ibid., 6 and 15 April 1839.

44. *Christian Observer* for September and December 1838, especially p. 775. On p. 777 the writer says Clarkson joined the Society of Friends, a mistake often repeated.

45. W. Wordsworth to H. C. Robinson, [*c.* 5 December 1838], *Wordsworth Letters, Later Years, Part III,* p. 642.

46. The remark is Patty Smith's to Robinson, Diary 12 November 1838.

47. Ibid., 15 March 1841; Morley (ed.), *Correspondence,* Vol. I, p. 590.

48. J. Stephen to S. Wilberforce, 24 August 1838, Wilberforce Manuscripts, Bodleian Library, d 46 f 21.

49. J. Stephen to S. Wilberforce, 26 September 1838, d 46 f 25; 24 and 29 December 1838, d 46 f 29, 33, all Wilberforce Manuscripts, Bodleian Library.

50. Robert Isaac Wilberforce and Samuel Wilberforce (eds), *Correspondence of William Wilberforce* (1840). S. Wilberforce to 'My dearest Robert', 24 September 1838, printed in A. R. Ashwell, *Life of the Right Reverend Samuel Wilberforce . . . with Selections from his Diaries and Correspondence* (1880), p. 136.

51. T. Clarkson to [S.] Wilberforce, 17 August 1840, Wilberforce Manuscripts, Bodleian Library, c 7 f 162.

52. Wilberforce, *Correspondence,* Preface, pp. v–xxvii, entirely devoted to a justification of the authors' treatment of Clarkson. Its contemptuous attack on Robinson precipitated his enthusiastic *Exposure of Misrepresentations Contained in the Preface to the Correspondence of William Wilberforce* (1840). Correspondence attempting to retrieve Clarkson's letters and the supposedly damaging documents described in Henry Crabb Robinson Diary, 13 April 1842; C. Clarkson to H. C. Robinson, 13 April 1843, and same to same, 18 May and 13 December 1844, Henry Crabb Robinson Letters; T. Clarkson to R. Wilberforce, [November 1844], copy in Henry Crabb Robinson Letters; Griggs, *Thomas Clarkson,* pp. 177–80. The letters from Wilberforce to John Clarkson were returned through Robinson and are in the Clarkson Papers at the British Museum.

53. The Sismondi quotation is in the Wilberforce, *Life,* Vol. IV, p. 215. R. Wilberforce to Lord Brougham, 3 July 1838, Brougham Papers, no. 29 063.

54. Henry Crabb Robinson Diary, 5 July 1838.

55. R. and S. Wilberforce to T. Clarkson, 15 November 1844, copy in Wilberforce Manuscripts, Bodleian Library, c 7 f 233, printed in Sadler (ed.), *Diary,* Vol. III, pp. 158–9. It is an open question whether

this acknowledgment of error in 'manner' and 'tone' constitutes an apology for Bishop Wilberforce stated in conversation that he had retracted nothing. Henry Crabb Robinson Diary, 25 June [1848]; H. C. Robinson to T. Robinson, 30 June [1838], marked 1834.

56.   T. Clarkson to R. Wilberforce, copy n.d. [November 1844], Henry Crabb Robinson Letters.

57.   S. and R. Wilberforce to C. Clarkson, 17 November 1846, Henry Crabb Robinson Letters. Copy in Clarkson Letters, Wordsworth Library; Sadler (ed.), *Diary*, Vol. III, p. 159.

58.   C. Clarkson to M. Wordsworth, 19 November 1846, Wordsworth Library.

59.   [Henry Crabb Robinson], review of Wilberforce *Life*, *Eclectic Review*, III (1838), 669–92; IV (1838), 80–99. Robinson said (p. 682) that Clarkson's book would be chiefly in the homes of Quakers by this time.

60.   'He will not rest till he had put his justification into form', said his troubled wife, 'For it is not his *fame* but his good name that is at stake'. C. Clarkson to W. Smith, 18 August 1834, Duke University; Fiona Spiers, 'William Wilberforce: 150 Years On', in Jack Hayward (ed.), *Out of Slavery: Abolition and After* (1985), p. 48.

15   The Father-Figure

1.   H. C. Wright to C. Clarkson, 25 October 1845, Clarkson Papers, Moorland-Spingarn Research Center, Howard University, Washington, DC. Certificates of honorary membership from the New York Society for ... the Manumission of Slaves, 28 August 1788, and Pennsylvania Society for Promoting the Abolition of Slavery, 10 May 1790, are in the Clarkson Papers, Huntington Library, San Marino, California. In 1832 Clarkson was elected an honorary member of the New England Anti-Slavery Society. Francis Jackson Garrison and Wendell Phillips, *William Lloyd Garrison 1805–1879, the Story of His Life* (New York, 1885), Vol. I, p. 283.

2.   Howard R. Temperley, 'British and American Abolitionists Compared' in Martin Duberman (ed.), *Antislavery Vanguard* (Princeton, 1965), pp. 343–61.

3.   William Goodell, *Slavery and Anti-Slavery: a History of the Great Struggle in Both Hemispheres* (New York, 1853), p. 342; David Brion Davis, *Slavery and Human Progress* (Oxford, 1986), p. 187; Aileen S. Kraditor, *Means and Ends in American Abolitionism: Garrison and His Critics on Strategy and Tactics, 1834–1850* (New York, 1967), p. 4; Betty Fladeland, *Abolitionists and Working-Class Problems in the Age of Industrialisation* (1984), p. 95; Garrison and Phillips, *William Lloyd Garrison*, Vol. I, p. 301n.

4.   W. Wilberforce to T. Clarkson, 10 October 1831, in Thomas Clarkson, *Strictures on a Life of William Wilberforce* (1838), pp. 90–91.

5.   Garrison and Phillips, *William Lloyd Garrison*, Vol. I, p. 301n., 328 quoting T. Clarkson to E. Cresson, 1 December 1831 and the *African Repository* for November 1832.

6. R. Vaux to T. Clarkson, 13 May 1819, Howard University.

7. Garrison and Phillips, *William Lloyd Garrison*, Vol. I, p. 329. *Proceedings at the Public Breakfast Held in Honour of William Lloyd Garrison . . . in . . . London . . . 1867* (1868), p. 37, Garrison's speech.

8. Garrison and Phillips, *William Lloyd Garrison*, Vol. III, p. 317. The name applied by George Thompson.

9. Kraditor, *Means and Ends*, pp. 3–4.

10. Dan Lacy, *The Abolitionists* (New York, 1978), p. 25.

11. Kraditor, *Means and Ends*, pp. 4, 5; Lacy, *Abolitionists*, p. 27. The pamphlet was *Thoughts on African Colonization* (1832).

12. Lacy, *Abolitionists*, p. 27; John L. Thomas, *The Liberator: William Lloyd Garrison* (Boston, 1963), pp. 86, 122.

13. Garrison and Phillips, *William Lloyd Garrison*, Vol. I, p. 329; Howard Temperley, *British Antislavery 1833–1870* (1972), pp. 20–21; Lacy, *Abolitionists*, p. 27. Garrison did not collect enough money to pay his expenses, as it happened. Thomas, *The Liberator*, p. 163, says Garrison borrowed $200 from his companion Nathaniel Paul.

14. Cropper was one of many younger British leaders attracted to Garrison, creating a division in the British movement. Garrison and Phillips, *William Lloyd Garrison*, Vol. I, pp. 354, 356. *Life of William Allen with Selections from His Correspondence* (1846), Vol. III, p. 154. Allen attended such a meeting but gives the date as 13 July.

15. James Cropper, *Letter Addressed to Thomas Clarkson Against the American Colonization Society* (Liverpool, 1832). David Brion Davis, 'James Cropper and the British Anti-Slavery Movement, 1823–1833' in *Journal of Negro History*, XLVI (1961), pp. 169–70; W. Wilberforce to T. Clarkson, 19 January 1833, Rare Books and Manuscripts Department, Boston Public Library Ms Eng 183 (35); W. Wilberforce to T. Clarkson, 18 March 1833, in Clarkson, *Strictures*, pp. 93–4.

16. Garrison and Phillips, *William Lloyd Garrison*, Vol. I, pp. 358–9.

17. Ibid., p. 361.

18. Ibid., pp. 361, 362–5; Davis, *Slavery*, p. 187; Thomas, *The Liberator*, pp. 163, 159.

19. C. Clarkson to H. C. Robinson, 23 and 31 October 1833, Henry Crabb Robinson Letters, Dr Williams's Library. Clarkson thought many of Garrison's charges were unsubstantiated and regretted deeply his violent language and the schism he was creating among British abolitionists. He highly approved of the ACS so long as the settlers went to Liberia freely, but believed it should be closely monitored: T. Clarkson to ?, 24 October 1833, Clarkson Papers, Huntington Library.

20. Davis, 'James Cropper', p. 170 and n. Clarkson's letter of 18 July 1840 was published in *The Liberator* in September 1840. Garrison and Phillips, *William Lloyd Garrison*, Vol. II, pp. 388, 416; Clare Taylor, *British and American Abolitionists, an Episode in Transatlantic Understanding* (Edinburgh, 1974), p. 116. The 1840 general convention resolved that the American Colonization Society settlement plan was inadequate to overthrow slavery and 'unworthy' of support.

21. Garrison and Phillips, *William Lloyd Garrison*, Vol. III, p. 364n.

22. Garrison became known in England as 'anti-government & anti-scripture'. C. Clarkson to J. B. Estlin, 19 May 1846, quoted in Taylor, *British and American Abolitionists*, p. 262.

23. Goodell, *Slavery and Anti-Slavery*, pp. 459, 460, 462–4; Temperley, *British Antislavery*, p. 208.

24. T. Clarkson to J. A. Collins, [c. June–July 1840], Clarkson Papers, BM Add Ms 41 267A, draft of notes f 223.

25. T. Clarkson to J. Sturge, 5 March 1841, in Henry Richard, *Memoirs of Joseph Sturge* (1864), p. 227.

26. Izhak Gross, 'Parliament and the Abolition of Negro Apprenticeship 1835–1838', *English Historical Review*, XCVI (1981), pp. 560–62; Temperley, *British Antislavery*, pp. 30–34. Bermuda and Antigua freed their slaves completely in 1834.

27. Fladeland, *Abolitionists*, pp. 49, 50–51, 52; Margaret A. Hirst, *Quakers in Peace and War: an Account of their Peace Principles and Practice* (1923), pp. 244, 254. Sturge married a daughter of James Cropper. He later became president of the Peace Society.

28. Gross, 'Parliament', pp. 564–5; Temperley, *British Antislavery*, pp. 32, 36, 37; Elizabeth Isichei, *Victorian Quakers* (Oxford, 1970), p. 228; *Life of Allen*, Vol. III, p. 282.

29. G. E. Bryant and G. P. Baker (eds), *Quaker Journal, Being the Diary and Reminiscences of William Lucas of Hitchin* (1934), Vol. I, p. 126; William A. Green, *British Slave Emancipation, the Sugar Colonies and the Great Experiment* (Oxford, 1976), p. 155.

30. *Life of Allen*, Vol. III, p. 278.

31. Sir George Stephen, *Antislavery Recollections: in a Series of Letters Addressed to Mrs Beecher Stowe* (1854), p. 86, discounted Clarkson's influence. T. F. Buxton to T. Clarkson, 16 November 1838, Howard University.

32. Clarkson's petition, f.150, BL Add Ms 41267A and copied in his 'Account of Efforts, 1807–1824', [1838], Clarkson Papers, Huntington Library.

33. Gross, 'Parliament', p. 567.

34. *Life of Allen*, Vol. III, p. 288.

35. Clarkson, 'Account of Efforts, pp. 120–28; Earl Leslie Griggs, *Thomas Clarkson the Friend of Slaves* (1936), pp. 192–3. Some 1838 Clarkson correspondence with Buxton and Brougham in Brougham Papers, University College, and Howard University.

36. H. C. Robinson to M. Wordsworth, 18 September 1844, in Edith J. Morley (ed.), *Correspondence of Henry Crabb Robinson with the Wordsworth Circle 1808–1866* (Oxford, 1927), Vol. II, p. 568. When Texas was annexed as a slave state in 1845 Clarkson was heartbroken. T. Clarkson to G. Smith, 3 April 1845, Gerrit Smith Papers, Syracuse University Library. Afterwards he seldom conversed on American subjects but wished the northern states had seceded after the annexation. C. Clarkson to J. B. Estlin, 2 June 1846, in Taylor, *British and American Abolitionists*, pp. 263–4. Appeals to President Sam Houston of the briefly independent Texas were signed by Clarkson for the British and Foreign Anti-Slavery Society. Heloise Abel and Frank J. Klingberg, *Side-Light on Anglo-American Relations, 1839–1858*

(Lancaster, Pa., 1927), pp. 12, 13, 17, 18–22.

37.   T. Clarkson to Mrs Smith, 11 March 1846, Howard University.

38.   J. Soul to T. Clarkson, 30 January 1844, Clarkson Papers, Huntington Library.

39.   Fladeland, *Abolitionists*, p. 50; Isichei, *Victorian Quakers*, p. 229, says 14 of the 27 committeemen were Friends. Temperley, *British Anti-slavery*, pp. 66–8.

40.   Temperley, *British Antislavery*, p. 78; T. Clarkson to J. Beaumont, 8 March 1841, Anti-Slavery Papers, Rhodes House Library, Oxford, Mss Brit. Emp. S18, C107, letters from Clarkson to the Society. Griggs, *Thomas Clarkson*, p. 193, counts 150 letters from Clarkson 1839–45.

41.   C. Clarkson to H. C. Robinson, 6 April 1843, Henry Crabb Robinson Letters.

42.   *Western Africa; its Condition, and Christianity the Means of its Recovery* (1844); T. Clarkson to D. J. East, 11 October 1844, Howard University.

43.   Thomas Clarkson, *Review of the Rev. Thomas B. Freeman's Journals of Visits to Ashanti &c with Remarks on the Present Situation of Africa, and Its Spiritual Prospects* (1845); T. Clarkson to Mrs Smith, [7 May 1843], Howard University.

44.   T. Clarkson to Earl of Bristol, 29 May 1846, Suffolk Record Office, Bury, 941/56/51.

45.   *Life of Allen*, Vol. III, p. 377, diary for 1 June 1840; R. N. Phillips to T. Clarkson, 1 June 1840, BM Add Ms 41 267A. Clarkson was made a vice-president of the Civilisation Society, chiefly organised by Buxton, but never attended its meetings. C. Clarkson to M. Clarkson, 13 July 1840, Add Ms 41 267A.

46.   The international convention was the idea of Joshua Leavitt, editor of the *New York Emancipator*, and enthusiastically agreed to by the British and Foreign Anti-Slavery Society with Sturge working hard on arrangements. Stephen Hobhouse, *Joseph Sturge: His Life and His Work* (1919), pp. 92–3. Also Temperley, *British Antislavery*, pp. 85, 86–7. The following year Clarkson signed an appeal for funds for the BFASS which spent £2000 on the affair. To Brougham's copy he added 'the most hateful thing to me is to interfere in money matters, even of this sort'. T. Clarkson to Lord Brougham, Brougham Papers, 21 December 1841, no. 507.

47.   'The World's Convention', John Greenleaf Whittier, *Poetical Works* (Boston, 1883), Vol. III, pp. 72–3.

48.   M. Clarkson to C. Clarkson, 12 June 1840, BM Add Ms 41 267A; H. Martineau to W. Ware, 21 June 1840, quoting Julia Smith, Ms Eng 244 (12), Boston Public Library; Minutes of 1840 convention, Anti-Slavery Papers, Rhodes House, Ms Brit. Emp. S18 E/2/18; *Quaker Journal*, Vol. I, p. 201; James Mott, *Three Months in Great Britain* (Philadelphia, 1841), p. 24.

49.   T. Clarkson to C. Hanbury, n.d. [1840], Temp Mss 4/6/6, Library of the Religious Society of Friends. Clarkson's son was never involved publicly in abolition. He had refused to be made a member of the

African Institution lest it be thought he was pushing himself forward on his father's reputation. He said, 'My Father has never received any worldly benefit from his Labours nor shall his Son', according to C. Clarkson to H. C. Robinson, 2 May 1838, Henry Crabb Robinson Letters.

50. *Speech of Thomas Clarkson Esq., as Originally Prepared by him in Writing and Intended to have been Delivered at the Opening of the General Anti-Slavery Convention* [1840].

51. F. B. Tolles (ed.), *Slavery and 'The Woman Question': Lucretia Mott's Diary of her Visit to Great Britain to Attend the World's Anti-Slavery Convention of 1840* (Haverford, Pa., 1952), p. 39; Garrison and Phillips, *William Lloyd Garrison*, Vol. II, p. 367.

52. *Speech of Thomas Clarkson Esq.*; 'Thomas Clarkson, the Advocate of the Extinction of Slavery by Means of India' in *Howitt's Journal of Literature and Popular Pogress*, 27 November 1847, Vol. II, pp. 338–9. Clarkson offered his name to a Manchester committee founded to investigate the East India Company, according to T. Clarkson to G. Thompson, 19 August 1840, in a cutting from an unknown periodical in Clarkson Papers, William R. Perkins Library, Duke University, Durham, NC. He told Joseph Pease of Darlington that villainy was too soft a word for the Company's record in India (T. Clarkson to J. Pease, 12 October 1842, Huntington Library, HM 35529) but he hoped the Company could be used to end abolition in America.

53. M. Clarkson to C. Clarkson, 12 June 1840, BM Add Ms 41 267A; *Description of Haydon's Picture of the Great Meeting of Delegates Held at the Freemason's Tavern June 1840 for the Abolition of Slavery and the Slave Trade Throughout the World*, n.d. [1841], copy in Add Ms 41 267A, f 240.

54. Among the honours paid Clarkson, a medal was struck with his head on one side and the kneeling slave emblem on the other, along with Clarkson's age and autograph. One of the medals is in the possession of Dr R. G. M. Keeling, a collateral descendant. A Philadelphia delegate gave Clarkson a copy of *History of Pennsylvania Hall* destroyed by a pro-slavery mob in 1838. The book is in the Clarkson Collection at the reference department, Ipswich Borough Libraries. Mary Grew Diary, Alma Lutz Collection, Radcliffe College, Cambridge, Mass.

55. Temperley, *British Antislavery*, pp. 87–90; Garrison and Phillips, *William Lloyd Garrison*, Vol. II, pp. 367–9; Mott, *Three Months*, pp. 14, 17, 18–9.

56. Taylor, *British and American Abolitionists*, p. 91; Garrison and Phillips, *William Lloyd Garrison*, Vol. II, p. 373; Kraditor, *Means and Ends*, pp. 66–7, n. 31; Donald R. Kennon, '"An Apple of Discord": the Woman Question at the World's Anti-Slavery Convention of 1840', *Slavery and Abolition*, V (1982), 244–66.

Influenced by Garrison, the Leeds Anti-Slavery Association was in 1853 the first in Britain to admit women. There were 12 on the first committee. They (as some Americans did) used the Wedgwood cameo with a female figure and the motto 'Am I Not a Woman and a

Sister'. Irene E. Goodyear, 'Wilson Armistead and the Leeds Anti-slavery Movement', Thoresby Society Publications, *Miscellany*, XVI (1975), 120.

57.   Mary Grew Diary, 15 June 1840; Tolles (ed.), *Slavery*, pp. 32–3; Mott, *Three Months*, p. 25.

58.   Tolles (ed.), *Slavery*, p. 33; M. Clarkson to C. Clarkson, [14 June 1840], BM Add Ms 41 267A, f 191.

59.   T. Clarkson to G. Smith, 28 February 1844, Gerrit Smith Papers, Syracuse University. Many requests turn up in Clarkson's correspondence, including H. C. Wright to T. Clarkson, 12 October 1845, Howard University, and T. Clarkson to A. P. Moor, 7 October 1844, Duke University.

60.   J. Sturge to T. Clarkson, 4 September 1846, Howard University; T. Clarkson to J. Sturge, [24 August 1846], Syracuse University. The very last letter Clarkson wrote was to Lord Russell, the Prime Minister, on behalf of mercantile seamen. He did not live to read the reply. *Gentleman's Magazine* (1846), 545.

61.   Correspondence of B. R. Haydon with the Clarksons in Clarkson Papers, BM Add Ms 41 267A from f 203; Tom Taylor (ed.), *Life of Benjamin Robert Haydon*, 2nd edn (1853), Vol. III, pp. 154ff. Here quoted from W. B. Pope (ed.), *Diary of Benjamin Robert Haydon* (Cambridge, Mass., 1960), Vol. IV, pp. 640–61, 650, 663; Vol. V, pp. 41–2.

62.   Pope (ed.), *Diary*, Vol. V, p. 46; also Taylor (ed.), *Life*, Vol. III, pp. 174–5; John Glyde, 'Materials for a History of Woodbridge', p. 91, Reference Department, Ipswich Borough Libraries; Griggs, *Thomas Clarkson*, p. 185.

63.   *Quaker Journal*, Vol. I, p. 241.

64.   C. Clarkson to M. Clarkson, May 1841, BM Add Ms 41 267A, f 252.

65.   Pope (ed.), *Diary*, Vol. V, p. 43; Temperley, *British Antislavery*, p. 194; Griggs, *Thomas Clarkson*, p. 182; E. H. Doyle to C. Clarkson, 2 November 1841, Clarkson Papers, Huntington Library. The *Letter* was published in 1841. It had a good circulation in the North and was smuggled into the South.

66.   T. Clarkson to Lady Bunbury, [1841], Duke University. She was the wife of Sir Henry, sometime MP for Bury St Edmunds.

67.   Quoted in John Purcell Fitz-Gerald, *Quiet Worker for Good, a Familiar Sketch of the late John Charlesworth* (1865), p. 96.

68.   *Not a Labourer Wanted for Jamaica; to which is added, an Account of the newly erected villages by the peasantry there . . . and the Consequences of re-opening a new slave trade . . .* (1842). T. Clarkson to Lord Brougham, 6 August 1842, Brougham Papers, no. 3727.

69.   *Grievances of our Mercantile Seamen, a National and Crying Evil* (1845). It was in two parts, the first recalling the plight of seamen in the slave trade and the second relating their present ill treatment on shipping arriving in London. T. Clarkson to J. Soul, 11 May 1846, author's collection; T. Clarkson to Mrs Smith, 8 August 1845, Howard University. The *Morning Chronicle* printed it, according to T. Clarkson to A. Haldane, 22 August 1845, author's collection.

70. Clarkson expressed alarm over the potential of the treaty to threaten the security of fugitive slaves in Canada to Lord Brougham (10 March 1843, Brougham Papers, no. 204) and Sir Charles Metcalfe, Canadian Governor-General (6 September and 7 December 1843, both printed in Abel and Klingberg, *Side-Light*, pp. 159–61, 162–3). Clarkson had met deputations from the Canadian settlements of fugitive slaves in England when they were seeking money for schools. Also Griggs, *Thomas Clarkson*, pp. 194–5; *Gentleman's Magazine* (1846), 545.

71. In 1841 Clarkson was asked to give information on the aftermath of emancipation to a French royal commission 'so that the report will not be the Production of frivolous, ignorant, prejudiced, and volatile Frenchmen', as he interpreted the request. Eternally hopeful, he was sure the commission's findings would lead to French emancipation, followed by that of Cuba, then the United States. T. Clarkson to Rev. E. Moor, [1841], Duke University. On the 1843 convention, Henry Crabb Robinson Diary, 25 May 1843 and H. C. Robinson to T. Robinson, 28 May 1843, Henry Crabb Robinson Letters.

72. Goodell, *Slavery*, p. 200; Temperley, *British Antislavery*, p. 196; T. Clarkson to Lord Brougham, 25 September 1841, Brougham Papers, no. 485.

73. T. Clarkson to unknown, 22 June 1846, Bodleian Library, Oxford University, Ms Eng Litt c144, f 42. The badly-written letter with its sloping lines is inscribed 'Quantum mutatis!'. J. Sturge to T. Clarkson, 26 March 1841, Howard University; T. Clarkson to L. Tappan, 10 January 1844, in Abel and Klingberg, *Side-Light*, pp. 164–5.

74. This *Letter*'s title continued *and have never sanctioned it by defending it, and to such, also, as have never visited the southern states* (1844). Clarkson thought this tract was 'as entertaining as it was instructive', T. Clarkson to G. Smith, 3 April 1845, Syracuse University.

75. C. Clarkson to H. C. Robinson, 24 March 1845, Henry Crabb Robinson Letters; L. Tappan to J. Scoble, 9 November 1844, in Abel and Klingberg, *Side-Light*, p. 195; L. Tappan to T. Clarkson, 28 February 1844, Howard University; T. Clarkson to G. Smith, 3 April 1845, Syracuse University. *Governor Hammond's Letters on Southern Slavery, Addressed to Thomas Clarkson, the English Abolitionist* (Charleston, SC, 1845); Davis, *Slavery*, pp. 233–4, 240–41.

76. Clarkson's 'Reply to the Assertions of the Clergy of the Southern States of America that Abraham was the founder of Slavery' may not have been published. 18pp. script [1845] in Antislavery Papers, Rhodes House.

77. *On the Ill-Treatment* (1844). His friends might think him too severe, Clarkson said to Gerrit Smith, transmitting the booklet. 'I really feel so much for the *future moral Welfare* of your Country that I believe Nothing but very strong and decisive Language will have any Effect'. T. Clarkson to G. Smith, 28 February 1844, Syracuse University. Fifty thousand copies were printed in the United States. T. Clarkson to S. Wilberforce, 25 October 1844, Wilberforce Manu-

scripts, Bodleian Library, c 7 f 229 and 24 March 1841, c 7 f 182; 29 March 1841, f 184.

78. T. Clarkson to S. Wilberforce, 24 and 29 March 1841.

79. C. Clarkson to H. C. Robinson, 6 and 13 April, 15 September 1843 and 28 July 1845; H. C. Robinson to T. Robinson, 28 May and 2 June 1843, all Henry Crabb Robinson Letters; Henry Crabb Robinson Diary, 26 and 28 May 1843; C. Clarkson to Mrs Clarkson, 4 April 1844, Correspondence and Researches of Mr and Mrs Augustus Clarkson, held by Mrs A. M. Wray.

80. Julia Smith Recollections, William Smith and Family Papers, Cambridge University Library. The third Thomas Clarkson went up to Trinity College, Cambridge, in 1850 and later read law before settling at Playford. He married a respectable but uneducated village girl, Sarah Ann Bloomfield, daughter of a market gardener, the year before Catherine died in 1856, but she was not told. According to village gossip, he drank and squandered his inheritance. He left Playford in the late 1860s and died in Jersey, leaving no children, in 1872: *The Times*, 14 December 1855; Julia Smith Recollections; Herman Biddell, 'Thomas Clarkson and Playford Hall', Reference Department, Ipswich Borough Libraries; M. Dickinson to Mrs S. Robinson, 23 February 1866, Mrs A. M. Wray.

81. C. Clarkson to H. C. Robinson, 13 and 30 December 1844, Henry Crabb Robinson Letters; C. Clarkson to 'My dear Friend', 10 March 1846, Suffolk Record Office, Ipswich, HD 494/194.

82. C. Clarkson to 'My dear Friend', 20 July 1846, Suffolk Record Office, Ipswich, HD 494/195. Haydon shot himself in 1846, Buxton died in 1845. *Life of Allen*, Vol. III, p. 421.

83. Taylor, *British and American Abolitionists*, p. 262, quoting C. Clarkson to M. W. Chapman, 1 May 1846.

84. W. L. Garrison to T. Clarkson, 19 August 1846, Clarkson Papers, Huntington Library; C. Clarkson to M. Wordsworth, 2 November 1846, Wordsworth Library, Grasmere; Taylor, *British and American Abolitionists*, p. 275 quoting C. Clarkson to M. W. Chapman, 2 August 1846; Temperley, *British Antislavery*, pp. 215–16. The League lasted only about a year, p. 219.

85. Garrison and Phillips, *William Lloyd Garrison*, Vol. III, pp. 168–9 and n. *Life and Times of Frederick Douglass from 1817 to 1882* (1882).

86. C. Clarkson to M. Wordsworth, 2 November and 28 December 1846, Wordsworth Library.

87. W. L. Garrison to C. Clarkson, 3 November 1846, Ms A. 1. 1, Vol. IV, p. 44, Boston Public Library; C. Clarkson to H. C. Robinson, [November 1846], Henry Crabb Robinson Letters. Her letter to the BFASS also reassured the Americans: W. Jay to C. Clarkson, 10 February 1847, Huntington Library.

88. C. Clarkson to M. Wordsworth, 28 December 1846, Wordsworth Library.

89. Griggs, *Thomas Clarkson*, p. 197, quoting Mrs Shewell, 'Death of Thomas Clarkson', *Ipswich Express*, 30 September 1846.

90. C. Clarkson to E. Shewell, 9 November 1846, Clarkson Papers,

Wisbech and Fenland Museum; C. Clarkson to M. Wordsworth, 28 December 1846.

91. William Ball of Rydal, copy in Gibson Manuscripts, Vol. I, f 17, Library of the Religious Society of Friends; Griggs, *Thomas Clarkson*, pp. 190–92 gives a selection of poems to Clarkson.

92. Funeral account taken from *Suffolk Chronicle*, 7 October 1846; *Illustrated London News*, 10 October 1846; *Gentleman's Magazine* (1846), 542–6; *People's Journal*, II (1847), 220–21, and a collection of unidentified cuttings at Reference Department, Ipswich Borough Libraries, Clarkson Papers.

93. Thomas Clarkson, *Portraiture of Quakerism* (1806), Vol. II, p. 35. The Quaker views on funeral processions, pp. 28–9.

94. H. C. Robinson to M. Wordsworth, 19 December 1846, Henry Crabb Robinson Letters; C. Clarkson to H. C. Robinson, [November 1846]. Clarkson's absence from the pantheon of abolitionists in the Abbey (Sharp, Wilberforce, Buxton, Macaulay) allows, for example, David Brion Davis to speak of 'Wilberforce and the other abolitionist heroes buried in Westminster Abbey' as if all were there. *New York Review of Books*, 31 March 1988, p. 43. Sharp's memorial was put up by the African Institution. Clarkson was on the committee for a monument to Macaulay, who died in 1838.

95. C. Clarkson to H. C. Robinson, 14 April 1847, Henry Crabb Robinson Letters. A. Airy (Mrs G. B. Pocock) to A. Clarkson, 24 and 28 March 1933, Mrs A. M. Wray; obituary of Airy, *East Anglian Daily Times*, 3 and 9 January 1892. The obelisk was built by subscription of 13 friends, among them Arthur Biddell, the Marquis of Bristol, Lord Brougham, Henry Crabb Robinson and Joseph Sturge. It is inscribed 'Thomas Clarkson, Friend of Slaves'.

96. Richard Whitmore, *Victorian and Edwardian Hertfordshire from Old Photographs* (1976), Plate 126. An earlier plan for a marker was dropped, perhaps out of doubts such as Charles Lamb expressed to Mrs Basil Montagu, 'I should be sorry that any respect should be going on towards [Clarkson] and I be left out of the conspiracy. Otherwise I frankly own that to pillarize a man's good feelings in his lifetime is not to my taste. . . . The vanities of life . . . are subjects for trophies; not the silent thoughts arising in a good man's mind in lonely places.' C. Lamb to Mrs Montagu, n.d. [summer 1827], in E. V. Lucas (ed.), *Letters of Charles Lamb* (1935 edn), Vol. III, p. 102.

97. Harriet Beecher Stowe, *Sunny Memories of Foreign Lands* (1854), pp. 290–91.

Index

The frequent references to Britain, England and London are not indexed.